Personal Problems
of
The High School Girl

Personal Problems
of
The High School Girl

BY

Frances S. Miller

HEAD OF THE HOME ECONOMICS DEPARTMENT
LAKEWOOD HIGH SCHOOL, LAKEWOOD, OHIO

AND

Helen H. Laitem

LAKEWOOD HIGH SCHOOL
LAKEWOOD, OHIO

SECOND EDITION

New York: JOHN WILEY & SONS, Inc.
London: CHAPMAN & HALL, Limited

THIS BOOK HAS BEEN MANUFACTURED IN
ACCORDANCE WITH THE RECOMMENDATIONS
OF THE WAR PRODUCTION BOARD IN THE
INTEREST OF THE CONSERVATION OF PAPER
AND OTHER IMPORTANT WAR MATERIALS.

PRINTED IN THE UNITED STATES OF AMERICA

PREFACE

There are many high school girls who, because of the numerous requirements of their various curricula, do not have time to study all the courses offered in the home economics curriculum; these girls, nevertheless, are interested in knowing how to select food and clothing for health and good looks, to care for their clothing, to handle their money to the best advantage, to behave in different social situations, and to understand human relationships. All these things they are anxious to know so that they may live more completely.

It was in response to their need that the course, general home economics for girls, was organized at Lakewood High School some years ago. From an outline of this course, formulated by the teacher and pupils, the book *Personal Problems of the High School Girl* has been developed. The present edition is an enlargement and revision of the first one, which was published in 1935 at the Lakewood High School print shop. The material has been used in mimeographed form in the classes of the authors for the past five years. During this period of experimentation only the subject matter and methods of approach which most successfully meet the needs and interests of the students have been retained.

The material is presented in a personal, informal way which experience indicates is interesting to young people. Emphasis is placed on the girl's immediate problems, with the assumption that young people will be able to solve their future problems if they learn how to cope successfully with their present ones.

Since an individual's success in life depends to a great extent upon her ability to get along peaceably with her fellow beings, an effort has been made to present the importance of and the method for understanding human nature and making satisfactory adjustments to one's family, friends, school, and, later, work. It is through such understandings and realizations that a healthy mental life is maintained, and a foundation for a democratic home life is laid.

v

This important phase of education is presented in the sections entitled Understanding Ourselves, Personal and Family Relationships, and Understanding and Caring for Children.

Physical factors such as good health and attractive appearance resulting from correct dress and good grooming, knowledge of the rules governing social contacts, and the ability to use money and leisure time wisely are helpful in making necessary psychological adjustments in life. Methods of acquiring these aids are presented in the sections Using Money Wisely, The High School Girl and Her Clothes, The Health of the High School Girl, Personal Care, Leisure-Time Activities, The Social Life of the High School Girl, and Planning for the Future.

This book may be used either as a textbook in courses in home economics or as a source of material for club work or homeroom guidance programs. Although it is written especially for girls, much of the material can be used in boys' classes in home economics.

Since the units are independent of each other, they may be studied in any order. The references at the end of each unit may be used to broaden the pupils' understanding of the subject matter. There are questions to help pupils recall the points discussed and class activities to provide application of the principles presented.

The authors wish to express their appreciation to the people who have helped make this book possible: to the pupils for their helpful cooperation in building the course; to Mr. John C. Mitchell, former principal of Lakewood High School, Dr. Lawrence E. Vredevoe, principal of Lakewood High School, Mr. George A. Bowman, former superintendent of Lakewood Schools, and Mr. Paul A. Rehmus, superintendent of Lakewood Schools, for freedom to develop the course and use the material in their classes; to the commercial department of Lakewood High School, especially Miss Grace Powell, who so kindly mimeographed copies of the manuscript for use in their classes; to the librarians of Lakewood High School, the Lakewood Public Library, and the Cleveland Public Library for their help in finding source material; to Miss Margaret Carfrey, who drew the sketches; to Mrs. Edith Infield and Mrs. Ethel Lechner, for their careful work in preparing the manuscript; and to the various people, companies, and colleges who lent pictures and other materials acknowledged in the pages of this book.

F. S. M.

H. H. L.

May, 1945

CONTENTS

SECTION V.   THE HIGH SCHOOL GIRL
AND HER CLOTHES

SECTION VI.   THE HEALTH OF THE HIGH
SCHOOL GIRL

SECTION VII.   PERSONAL CARE

SECTION VIII.   LEISURE-TIME ACTIVITIES

SECTION IX. THE SOCIAL LIFE OF THE
HIGH SCHOOL GIRL

SECTION X. PLANNING FOR THE
FUTURE

A wholesome personality depends upon a balance of mental, emotional, and spiritual qualities.

SECTION I

UNDERSTANDING OURSELVES

UNIT ONE. WHAT IS PERSONALITY?

When Mrs. Brown, who has charge of the employment bureau in a large high school, recommended Mary for a certain position, because she has, in addition to the basic requirements for the job, a pleasing personality, and John for another job, because he has a forceful personality, just what qualities do these two young people have? What qualities would their employers have a right to expect?

PLEASING PERSONALITY

Mary's employer would expect that she would make a good appearance, that she would be neat in her dress and well groomed, that she would have the habit of being courteous, and that she would have a pleasing voice.

When Mrs. Brown said that John has a forceful personality, she meant that he has, in addition to the qualities of a pleasing personality, the ability to direct his own behavior and that of the people with whom he comes in contact. When John enters a room, those present will be impressed by him. They will unconsciously notice him, and when he speaks they will give him their attention. Furthermore, it will be easy for John to influence other people's behavior. He is a natural leader. Others will have confidence in him and will be easily influenced to do his bidding.

Both Mary and John have what we call social stimulus. People react favorably to them. Some other people seem to lack all power to stimulate any social response. They are often spoken of inaccurately as lacking personality. They may have a poor personality or a weak personality, but they do have a personality.

The mental hygienist thinks of personality in a broader sense. To him personality does not include merely a person's social

1

traits; it is a sum total of all his traits. The mental hygienist includes mental, emotional, and spiritual qualities, such as intelligence, knowledge, ideas, beliefs, and attitudes. To him the term wholesome personality is more important than pleasing or forceful personality.

WHOLESOME PERSONALITY

Why does the mental hygienist consider a wholesome personality more important and more desirable than a pleasing or forceful personality? The reason is that a wholesome personality means a healthy personality. Probably the outstanding characteristic of a person possessing a wholesome personality is her ability to fuse her emotional, physical, and mental qualities together to form a unified whole. Such a person knows what is important and what is unimportant in developing her plan of life. She will not be torn between one course and another in making a decision.

More than one girl has allowed her plan for a good school record to be spoiled because she was unable to keep a balance in her emotional, physical, and mental development. Mary was such a pupil. She was attractive with a pleasing manner, and came into senior high school with a high scholarship record and the respect and admiration of her fellow-students. She was well on her way to becoming a wholesome, well-rounded personality when she became involved socially to such an extent that she didn't have time to keep up with her regular school work. By the time she reached the first semester of her senior year her grades had dropped below average and she was becoming restless and worried-looking. When questioned by one of her teachers as to why she wasn't keeping up her former standard of work, she replied, " Well, what can a girl do when a group of friends barge in? She can't tell them to go home." On further questioning Mary revealed that she was working Monday afternoon and evening, meeting with one social group on Tuesday evening and another on Wednesday, and dating Friday and Saturday evenings. Is it any wonder she wasn't able to keep up her school work? As time went on, Mary became more restless and unhappy. She lost her self-assurance and natural gaiety. She was no longer able to concentrate on her work.

How far Mary might have gone on the road to failure we can't tell. Fortunately for her, an older friend was able to convince her that she was developing an unwholesome attitude toward work and was wasting her mental powers. Before she graduated she decided to go on to college. This decision gave her a purpose. She was anxious to have her grades show up well for college entrance and to re-establish good work habits. She let her friends know that she must study at definite times. She was interested too in getting proper rest and food so that she would keep physically fit. She was convinced that, in order to realize her ambition to succeed in college, she must be able to control and coordinate her whole self, her physical, mental, and emotional powers. She must be able to direct herself according to her ideals; her mind and body must work together.

When Mary graduated from high school she was well on the way to establishing habits that would insure mental health. She had learned to focus her mental and physical energies on the task in hand, and was able to react as a unit to a situation. She appeared to realize the value of play as well as work, but she had learned not to neglect one for the other. The person who has a wholesome personality will not only be able to react as a unit but will also be sincere, honest, unselfish, and open-minded. A criminal may be able to react as a whole to a situation, but he does not have a wholesome personality. To have such a personality, one must have desirable qualities of character in addition to a unified personality.

VALUE OF STUDYING PERSONALITY

We have pointed out above that wholesome personality is an indication of mental health. We all realize that mental health is essential to both happiness and success, and that the person who lacks mental health is unable to shoulder his responsibilities in life. He is a dependent. Somebody else must take care of him. The degree of his dependency will be determined by the extent of his inability to concentrate. If, through the study of our personalities, we are able to realize the importance of mental health and to gain some knowledge of how to keep ourselves mentally healthy, our time and effort will have been well employed.

STUDY-GUIDE QUESTIONS

1. Name the characteristics of a pleasing personality, a forceful personality, and a wholesome personality.
2. Why is a wholesome personality desirable?

ACTIVITY

Select from among your acquaintances a person who you consider has a pleasing personality. How do his or her characteristics compare with those given in your text? Do the same for a forceful personality and a wholesome personality.

UNIT TWO. IS MY PERSONALITY DETERMINED FOR ME?

If you have ever gone to a county fair, a carnival, or a large amusement park, you probably have seen a fortune-telling tent. The seeress claimed, no doubt, that by reading the lines of your palm, feeling the lumps on your head, gazing into a crystal, or utilizing some other method she could analyze your personality and give advice concerning your future.

It would be too bad for a serious-minded person to put faith in any such method of planning a life career or of deciding on an important course of action. Science has taught us that our personality traits are neither a matter of mystery nor determined by the shape of our head or the lines of our hands. There are many influences affecting personality. Some of the most important are our physiological make-up, our inheritance, the way in which we satisfy our basic needs, and our environment.

PHYSIOLOGICAL MAKE-UP AND PERSONALITY

Probably the most evident influence upon our personality is the physiological. You know how uncomfortable you feel when you have eaten something which disagrees with you or when you have not had a good night's rest, and how cross and irritable young brother or sister becomes when hungry. Have you ever known a person suffering from either an overactive or underactive thyroid gland? If so, you found him either abnormally active and excitable or unusually inactive and quiet. From these examples and many others that you yourself may name, we can readily see that our behavior is influenced by our physical condition. However, there are many people who are able to control and dominate a frail body to the degree that they develop good personalities and do the work of normal people. The writers Elizabeth Barrett Browning, Robert Louis Stevenson, and Clarence Day were invalids for some years.

Our physical appearance is also a factor in our behavior tenden-

5

cies. Probably appearance is a greater factor in determining our personality traits than we realize. Undoubtedly, the person with a pleasing physique has an advantage over the less fortunate person who has uneven features and is either over- or undersized. However, physical handicaps may have favorable as well as unfavorable influences on personality development. Many a girl has compensated for her homely features by diligent effort to acquire a charming manner and a witty tongue. Brilliant professional and business executives have achieved success in spite of physical defects. Demosthenes became a great orator despite a natural tendency to stutter, and Beethoven remained a great composer of music even after he was unable to hear his own compositions.

INHERITANCE AND PERSONALITY

It is not so easy to see the relation between inheritance and personality as it is between physical make-up and personality. It is true that in so far as physical make-up is due to inheritance, the connection is evident. On the other hand, when it comes to determining whether Johnny is lazy, unfriendly, and dull because he has grown up in the environment created by his parents or because he has inherited such traits and qualities from his parents, we are not sure of the answer.

Generally, it is considered that our mental traits are inherited. What we are capable of doing is determined by our endowed traits, but what we become depends upon how these traits are developed. You may have the native qualities that would produce a great singer, but unless you have some training in the rudiments of the art and a desire and determination to perfect your natural endowment, you will probably not become an opera star.

THE SATISFACTION OF BASIC NEEDS AND PERSONALITY

In a similar manner, the kind of person we become — whether we are agreeable, even-tempered, self-confident, and courageous or irritable, discourteous, and fearful — will depend upon the way in which we respond to the inner stresses caused by our basic needs. Modern psychologists agree that human nature is what it is because of these common basic needs, which are classified somewhat differently by various authorities. The list given by Thorpe and Holliday follows:

1. The need to maintain and further our physical well-being by satisfying the stresses set up by hunger, thirst, excessive heat or cold, physical pain, fatigue, and the like.
2. The need for personal recognition, self-expression, realization of personal ambitions, and of being regarded as individuals of worth.
3. The need to nurture and care for other members of society by offering them recognition, sympathy, and generous service.*

The person who allows the need for physical well-being to dominate his behavior may become so obsessed with the desire for the things that money can buy that he loses sight of his need for doing something for other people. Another person may so enjoy recognition and honor that he will use any means to achieve them. Even the need to do for others may become a vice instead of a virtue if it is practiced to the point that the individual exhausts himself in a mad frenzy of doing for others. Therefore the kind of person we become depends, to a large extent, upon how we respond to or satisfy these basic needs which are natural to all of us. When our satisfactions of these needs are well balanced, we become useful members of society.

If the self-centered person could but realize that his intense desire for self-recognition could be relieved by helping somebody less fortunate than himself, he would, no doubt, make an effort to be more unselfish. There is nothing that does more to give a person a feeling of worth-whileness than to do something for others.

ENVIRONMENT AND PERSONALITY

Webster defines environment as " the surrounding conditions, influences, or forces." It will help in our discussion to think of environment as both physical and human. Such things as our dwelling, including the furnishings, lighting, and heating; our neighborhood, either with green lawns and trees or barren, narrow streets; and our community, whether it be the great expanse of the outdoors or the busy city, may be thought of as our physical en-

* Louis P. Thorpe and Jay N. Holliday, *Personality and Life*. Longmans, Green & Company, 1941.

vironment. The members of our family, our friends, and our nation may be considered our human environment.

It is not hard to see that the child brought up in the squalid environment of the slums, with dark, crowded rooms lacking beauty and cleanliness, and narrow, cluttered streets for a playground, does not have the same opportunity to develop a wholesome personality as the child who grows up in more desirable surroundings or environment. Usually, the slum child's mother is either away from home, working, or absorbed with caring for a large family, so that the youngster entertains himself as best he can. Often his only source of inspiration is either a drunken father or a neighborhood boy or girl who has " got on in the world " by questionable means. Although all children born into undesirable surroundings are not delinquents, financially secure parents are usually better able than slum-dwelling parents to direct the development of their children.

However great the influence of our physical environment may be in molding our personalities, that of our human environment is greater. It is generally believed that children who grow up without the companionship of a loving family do not develop mentally to their capacity. Many famous people have given credit to their parents, teachers, or some other person who has either believed in them and encouraged them, or who has actually directed their training. Lincoln's stepmother is said to have encouraged his desire for reading and study in a period when it was not the fashion for poor people to spend their time in other than physical labor.

The ideals of one's family and nation may be considered a part of his human environment. The majority of people who are graduated from college have parents who have planned for their education and have helped to set up college graduation as a goal for their children. In a democracy the good citizen's behavior is influenced by the ideals of liberty and justice for all. Sometimes these ideals are ignored by selfish individuals, but a democratic government is so set up that the intelligent citizens who are not too lazy and selfish to concern themselves with the welfare of others may achieve equal opportunities and rights for all.

Which environment is more likely to produce good citizens? Courtesy, Federal
Public Housing Authority.

In summary, our personalities are influenced by our physical make-up, our inheritance, the way in which we satisfy our basic needs, and our environment. All these influences, excepting inheritance, which is probably the least important, are factors which we can, to a great extent, control. Therefore our personalities are not determined for us, but are largely a product of our own making. The important factor in personality development is not so much what happens to us as it is our response to situations.

STUDY-GUIDE QUESTIONS

1. Give examples showing how our physiological make-up influences our personalities.
2. Show how one's personality may be influenced by his ancestors.
3. What are the basic needs of humanity? Give examples showing how each of these needs has influenced the actions of an acquaintance. Why is it necessary for us to satisfy all our needs? Give examples showing how a person may become either altruistic or selfish through the response which he makes to these fundamental needs.
4. Explain the meaning of the following terms: environment, physical environment, human environment. Give examples showing how physical environment may affect one's personality. Why is human environment a more important factor in molding a personality?

UNIT THREE. HOW CAN I MAINTAIN A WHOLESOME PERSONALITY?

The following are some rules which will help you to maintain a wholesome personality:

1. Face reality.

The greater the extent to which we recognize the truth in any situation, the easier it is for us to deal with it. The father who decides that his son should become a minister without first considering the boy's natural abilities and personal ambitions is not facing the facts in the situation. Neither is the boy who decides to become an engineer although he is unwilling or unable to master the mathematics required for such a vocation. We all must accept our limitations and make the most of our natural endowments.

Many high school pupils would be happier if they recognized the real reason why they do not make satisfactory marks in a subject and did something about it, rather than blaming the teacher or their own inability to do the work. Usually a pupil who doesn't do well in a subject either hasn't sufficient background and experience for it, isn't working consistently, or doesn't know how to study.

There is a tendency among some pupils to side-step issues instead of facing them. When a pupil feigns illness and stays at home on the day when there is a difficult test scheduled, he is side-stepping a hardship. Every time he does such a thing, he is decreasing his power to meet reality. Every time a pupil goes to class in spite of difficulties to be encountered, every time he attends a social function of which he is afraid, and every time he overcomes his timidity for public speaking by giving a class report, he grows in the power to overcome difficulties. By meeting these everyday obligations he forms the habit of overcoming difficulties and thereby grows in the power to meet reality.

There is another situation where some people fail to accept

11

reality. The person who has a physical handicap must accept it and make adjustments to it. Sometimes it is possible to overcome a physical defect by correcting it. An example which is often cited is the case of crippled young Glenn Cunningham, who, by exercise, so developed his muscles that he ran the fastest mile on record. Other times it is necessary to develop some other ability or asset to the point where it compensates for the deficiency. The girl who covers her large ears with her beautiful hair is making compensation for the ears. Sometimes homely boys and girls are stimulated to perfect themselves in some intellectual or social ability, such as debating or piano playing.

2. Keep your body in the best possible physical condition.

Good health is important, because, as was pointed out in Unit 2, our physical well-being influences our personality development. The ability to relax completely in sleep is especially important to mental health. Because physical health is treated rather fully in Section VI of this book, we shall not discuss here the ways and means of maintaining good health.

3. Put first things first.

The girl who is unable to decide whether she should stay at home and study, go to the movies, or work on her hobby hasn't matured to the point where she has a sense of values. Such a person will always be in a state of confusion because she doesn't realize that some things are more important than others. She doesn't know that a successful life is directed and unified by ideals and plans for the future. The girl who has decided to go into nursing after she graduates from high school and realizes that she must keep her work up to standard in order to carry out her plan will know whether she needs to spend the evening studying.

Again, the mother who realizes that the most important part of her work is caring for her baby will not hesitate to postpone washing the dishes or performing any other household task until the baby has been given his regular feeding or his bath. Such a woman has a sense of values.

Thus it is in all of our daily activities — we must develop a sense of values if we are to live a unified, integrated life.

4. Forget self.

The self-centered individual has anything but a wholesome personality. He is so concerned about making himself comfortable that he loses sight of his other basic needs. Usually, a selfish person thinks so much about himself that he evaluates everything in

One way to forget oneself is by doing something for others. Courtesy, Bradford Junior College, Bradford, Massachusetts.

reference to self. The cause back of sensitiveness and self-consciousness is usually selfishness. When we are concerned in seeing that other people are happy and comfortable, we forget about ourselves. We do not have time to worry about the impression we are making on someone else.

Every person who wants to maintain a well-balanced, integrated personality should become interested in some worth-while cause or work to which he can consciously give his best self. He must select something in which he has faith and the ability to do successfully, or at least in which he can develop his native powers. We speak of a person finding himself when he has identified his mind and heart with an interest greater than himself. When this happens, he will be so busy pursuing his chosen work that he will not have time to think of self.

Just an ordinary job which a person pursues to earn a living does not usually suffice to give him this unselfish attitude. Most jobs, especially those concerned with mechanical skills, will need to be supplemented by affiliation with social groups, churches, or charitable organizations in order that the individual may find real satisfaction in doing for others or for a cause.

5. *Pay attention to the task in hand.*

Give your undivided attention to whatever you are doing. Learn to think about the thing you are doing. This is a very important law of mental health. We must not only pay attention to the immediate task, but also we must school ourselves to live in the present. The person who is constantly thinking about how much better it would have been had he done something different, or if circumstances had just been different, loses his power to do efficient work; that is, his personality becomes disintegrated.

In like manner, we must guard against living in the future and planning what we shall do at some later time instead of doing the task at hand. We grow in power to do by doing. If we give our undivided attention to the present situation, we shall be better able to take care of the problems of the future when they come. For example, how much do you think you would achieve if, when you sat down to prepare your history lesson, you kept thinking about how poorly you have been doing in class and how much better you hoped to do in the future, instead of actually making preparation for the next day? How long could you maintain such a line of procedure and keep yourself in fit mental condition to do your work? In other words, how long would you maintain an integrated, wholesome personality?

6. Realize the importance of the task you are doing.

Unless you recognize the value of the work you are doing, it will be almost impossible for you to put your best effort into it and to give it your attention. The person who dawdles is establishing habits of inattention. Such a person will soon lose the power to concentrate. In other words, he will lose the power to respond as a unit to a situation. When a person reaches this stage of disintegration, he is on the road to failure.

As far as school work is concerned, every pupil who is interested in his own mental health and mental growth should make it a point to realize the relationship of each subject he is taking to his present and future plans for happiness and success.

7. Depend upon your own judgment as far as your present experience warrants.

The high school girl who is gradually taking the responsibility for the care and selection of her own clothes is learning to make decisions. The girl who can carry out an assignment without detailed instruction from her teacher is exercising her own judgment. You should welcome every opportunity to help plan your own problems or assignments and the method of carrying them out, rather than depending upon your teacher for detailed methods of procedure.

8. Watch the mental attitudes that you are developing.

By studying Unit 4 you will find out which attitudes are desirable to cultivate, which ones to avoid, and which ones to control.

STUDY-GUIDE QUESTIONS

1. State briefly the eight rules given in your text for maintaining a wholesome personality.
2. Why should we form the habit of facing reality? Cite instances in which a person shows a tendency not to face facts.
3. Illustrate with an incident the meaning of the term a sense of values.
4. Show the relationship between selfishness and self-consciousness. What are some possible means of forgetting yourself?
5. Look in a dictionary for the definition of the word disintegrated. Apply this meaning to personality.

6. Why is it imperative that we pay attention to the task in hand? Do you agree with your text in the statement, " We must guard against living in the future "? Explain your viewpoint.
7. What is the relationship between a realization of the importance of the task you are doing and your personality?
8. Why should not a high school girl depend entirely upon her own judgment in making decisions which affect her alone?

UNIT FOUR. OUR MENTAL ATTITUDES

By attitudes we mean the habits of behavior that determine our actions. The child who has been made the center of attention at home over a period of time will get into the habit of having his every wish granted and will develop the attitude of selfishness. In living a healthful mental life, certain attitudes are desirable, others are definitely undesirable, and still others may be helpful if they are kept under control.

HEALTHFUL ATTITUDES

POISE

Each of us has for friends people who are calm and composed at all times, who seem to know just what to do and say to meet any demand. If they are temporarily unable to meet a situation, they remain calm and undisturbed until they can think of the right response. When called on for a recitation, such a pupil either gives a correct recitation immediately or hesitates a few seconds until he is able to collect his thoughts on the subject. If he does not understand the question, he asks for a restatement of it. Why is this pupil able to act in this manner? The reason is that he is prepared and has confidence in himself because of his preparation. When a person is able to respond to a situation in a calm, self-assured manner, we say he has poise. The best way for a person to acquire poise is to prepare himself to meet the situation which he is called upon to face. Then, gradually, as he is able to cope successfully with a situation, he gains confidence in himself and acquires the poise which comes with self-assurance.

PERSISTENCE

That person who is able to stay with a disagreeable task until it is finished has persistence. If one does not cultivate the habit of overcoming obstacles to success, he will become discouraged easily and not be able to accomplish worth-while things.

17

Do you suppose José Iturbi and Alec Templeton became famous artists by sitting down at the piano and playing just easy selections or enjoyable compositions when they felt in the mood? Of course not; you know that back of their ability to make a piano " come alive " are hours and hours of practicing to master the intricacies of the proper use of their fingers as well as their instrument. Hours of practicing scales and difficult exercises may not be especially enjoyable, but they are necessary to develop the ability to play with confidence, power, and beauty.

So it is in your school life. If you work just the easy algebra problems, and think, when you come to a hard one, that there is no use trying, because you can't solve it, or if you ask someone else to do it for you, you are not going to develop the habit of persistence. Obstacles that can be overcome by repeated efforts should be a challenge to you.

This habit of persistence may be formed as all habits are formed, that is, by making a start in small matters and using every opportunity to grow in the power of working at a task until it is accomplished.

COOPERATION

The person who is able to forget himself to the point where he can put aside his personal interests for those of the group has learned to cooperate. In his family he is willing to do his share of the work to keep the home running; in school he not only uses his abilities in the classroom to make the recitation periods interesting and helpful to all members of the class, but he also gives freely of his time to extracurricular activities; in his social group he thinks of helping to make it possible for his friends to enjoy themselves. In other words, he is able to cooperate with others in work and play. He has learned to subordinate his own personal wishes to those of the group.

Someone may say, " Well, and what has he gained? He would be able to get farther ahead if he spent his time doing his own work." It may be true that he could acquire more knowledge from books, but one of the most important things to learn in life is the ability to work and play with people, to get along peaceably with one's fellows.

Again, if a person wants to acquire this attitude of cooperation, he must do it through cooperating. He must begin in a small way and gradually gain in power. The ability to cooperate with

Through the production of a play, these young people are learning to work together. Photograph by Russell R. Benson. Courtesy, News Bureau, Denison University, Granville, Ohio.

others comes with maturity. The very young child is too self-centered to think in terms of a group, but as he matures he becomes interested in other people and has an understanding of his relations to them.

SYMPATHETIC UNDERSTANDING

If we are going to enjoy people, we must have a sympathetic understanding of them. Unless we understand others, we are not at ease with them, because we are afraid of them.

By realizing that people are fundamentally alike in that they have the same feelings and many of the same problems, we shall gain an understanding of others. On the other hand, we need to realize that, although people are fundamentally alike, they differ greatly in their reactions, because of the variety of environments and ideals which play such an important part in forming personality. We need to try to imagine how we would behave under the circumstances in which we find our friends. Would we be critical of Jane's manners if we realized that she lives with an aged grandmother who can't speak English and doesn't know our customs? No, we would understand that she has not had an opportunity to learn the things which have become second nature to us. We would excuse her actions and try to help her become acquainted with our customs.

Unhealthful Attitudes

REGRESSION

When a child refuses to take part in the activities which are going on around him, when he seems to live within himself, his elders should make an effort to correct his habits and get him interested in the life about him. The danger of such a practice lies in the fact that he ceases to make an effort to adjust to his present environment. Thus, through lack of use, his power to react normally to everyday living ceases to function. For example, suppose that after Evelyn has learned to be a good swimmer, she develops ear trouble which makes it necessary for her to stay out of the water. If she is of the regressive type, she may, instead of going into tennis and learning to enjoy it, gain her satisfaction from thinking over the good times she had swimming. The point is that, if Evelyn learns to play tennis, she will be developing her body and enjoying the satisfaction which comes from active participation in a game with others; whereas if she thinks only of past achievements, her muscles will become flabby and she will lose a certain alertness of mind which comes with activity.

There are many cases not so pronounced where children are failing to gain pleasure from being active members of a group. Often the child who is considered good, because he is quiet, needs someone to help him learn to work and play with others. The longer the habit of withdrawal is allowed to continue, the harder it will be to change it. However, it can be broken. There is, for example, the story of how a young mother, who allowed her life to become narrowed because of her home duties, suddenly awoke to the fact that she was living too much alone for her own good. It took a great deal of courage and will power for her to re-establish herself in a group of congenial people. She achieved her goal by joining the local chapter of the college club and attending their regular meetings until she gradually became acquainted with the members and found some useful work to do in the organization. She tells of how she had to force herself to attend afternoon teas when she didn't know even one person who would be there. Thus, when one finds himself becoming a daydreamer or a wall-flower living apart, he must make an effort to overcome the situation.

SUSPICION

We are suspicious of people when we mistrust them. There are times when we should mistrust people, but we should not be suspicious of everyone. We should learn to understand people, to realize that they do not all have the same ideals that we have, and that we should not expect them to behave as we do under all circumstances. Then, too, we must remember that other people have the same emotional reactions which we ourselves have, and that if we are honest and can be trusted, in all probability other people can also be trusted.

Alice was a high school girl who seemed to mistrust both her teacher and her fellow pupils. She had the feeling that her teacher was trying to catch her when she wasn't prepared and that the other pupils were working against her. It took time to get Alice to see that the teacher wanted her to succeed and was trying to cooperate with her in developing her abilities.

The person who allows the habit of being suspicious of others to grow on him is making a mistake. He will soon get to the point where he loses confidence in mankind. A healthier attitude to cultivate is to have faith in others until they, by their actions, give reason to be mistrusted.

BLAME

How many times during the day do we find fault with some-thing that a member of our family has done? In so doing, we are blaming him for having made a mistake. This habit may even reach the point where we blame another for our own mistakes. Did you ever blame someone near by when you hurt yourself through some careless act, such as striking your fingers when you were driving a nail or cracking a nut? Such an accusation is a childish trick. It is a carry-over of the early stage of development when the child's interest is centered on himself.

The habit of blaming others is a waste of energy. It brings only hatred and heartaches, and creates a disagreeable atmosphere. We should watch ourselves to keep from reverting to this attitude of childhood.

If we are interested in creating a feeling of good fellowship, instead of blaming the other person, we shall attempt to find out the reason for the mistake and try to avoid a repetition of the same error.

JEALOUSY

Jealousy is probably the most common of all the unhealthful attitudes. Who has not been jealous when a fellow-student has gloated over a high mark, or who has not seen evidences of jealousy in another when he has related some of his triumphs?

Why do we act in this way? The reason is that we haven't outgrown the selfishness of early childhood. We have not learned to appreciate the abilities of others, to realize the relation of our own and other people's performances. Jealousy is a symptom of lack of self-confidence. We are afraid either that we won't be able to retain someone else's affection or that we cannot match another's achievement.

How can we overcome jealousy? From the cause of jealousy given above, the cure seems evident. We must grow up. We must reach the point where we are interested in the other person's success. This will not be hard if we have an appreciation and understanding of our relationship to other people. We should realize that there is room at the top for more than one person, that every individual has many qualities of personality, and that we cannot excel in all things. If we choose one or two lines of activity and pursue them to the best of our ability, we shall develop confidence in ourselves. Self-confidence helps greatly in overcoming jealousy. It is easy for the person who knows that he is superior in some respect to rejoice over the achievements of another. Again, if we are sure of another's affection, we do not fear losing it.

ATTITUDES TO CONTROL

RATIONALIZATION

Have you ever done something on the impulse of the moment and then racked your brain for some good reason for your action? Have you ever bought a new dress just because it was pretty, and later, when your mother asked you why you bought it, you concocted any number of plausible reasons — for instance, because you were going to a party next week, and the old dress was too short, or faded, or otherwise unsatisfactory? Whenever we do a thing impulsively and justify our action afterwards, we are rationalizing.

This method of justifying our acts may be allowable on occasions when it saves ourselves and others from embarrassing situations. However, we need to analyze our actions and be honest with ourselves. By allowing the habit of rationalization to grow, we may become first-class hypocrites, deceiving not only others, but ourselves as well.

Another common function of rationalization is to justify our emotional upsets. When John flies into a rage and says things for which he is sorry afterwards, he may excuse himself by saying that he did it because he wasn't well. It is true that when we are ill we are more easily upset, but we should have ourselves under control at all times. In this case John would be better off if he would face the situation and say, " I made a mistake. Next time I will try to control myself."

One's intelligence should be used to guide and control one's acts, not to find excuses and reasons for them after they are done. The right way to buy a dress, for example, is to determine one's needs before going to shop and the amount of money one has to spend. In this way intelligence is used to direct one's action, and not to make excuses for it.

FEAR

Who is not afraid of something or somebody? Fear comes into the world with us and takes on many forms as we go through life. Psychologists tell us that a newborn baby is afraid only of a loud noise and lack of support. The many other fears which beset mankind are acquired or learned fears. If each member of the class were to list all the things of which he is afraid, we should probably have a list something like the following: various people and animals, storms, the dark, diseases, etc. Fear takes many forms. In its less violent form it may be anxiety or caution.

Fear is desirable in so far as it causes people to be cautious enough to protect themselves against danger. Beyond this, fear itself is dangerous. The person who is afraid is unable to succeed. The child who is afraid of his teacher or is overanxious about succeeding in school is very likely to do poor work. Again, the child who is afraid of the water has great difficulty in learning to swim.

The person who has the greatest dread of a disease is frequently the most seriously affected by it. It is really very foolish and childish for people to allow fear to keep them from using their abilities to the best advantage.

You may say, " Such statements are easy to make, but overcoming a fear isn't so easy." Usually, if one will become acquainted with the person or thing of which he is afraid, he will overcome his fear. If a pupil is afraid of his teacher, he should make an effort to know her, should try to analyze her methods and to see why she does the things she does. Intimate acquaintance with the object feared will do much to banish this attitude.

ILLNESS

Is there anyone who has not at some time in his experience enjoyed being ill, liked being made the center of attention? Children and egocentric people often enjoy the experience to the extent that they pretend illness in order to get the things they want. A headache may be an excuse for staying home from school on test day or avoiding some other disagreeable duty.

The person who allows this habit to develop is making a grave mistake. He is not only losing an opportunity for developing the ability to meet situations and overcome difficulties, but he is depriving himself of many pleasures which go along with health. The person who is sought out is not the one who must always be encouraged and pampered, but the happy, joyous person who can contribute something toward the pleasure of the group.

DAYDREAMING

When daydreaming, we are living for the time being in an imaginary world, free from the responsibilities of reality. In childhood, this escape is natural and desirable. It helps the child to escape from the adjustments which are beyond his ability to make; but as he matures, it is desirable that the images which occupy his dreaming moments be related to reality.

The young child imagines situations of all sorts to meet his wishes — a stick becomes a horse; a chair, a carriage; or a cotton suit, a rich velvet costume. As the child grows older and copes successfully with the problems of living, makes friends, succeeds in school life, and develops confidence in his own abilities, he gains satisfaction from taking an active part in life about him rather than from living in a make-believe world. His daydreams will become an incentive to push on and accomplish things rather than an escape from reality. Probably every normal child dreams about the time when he will be graduated from school. If he merely dreams about graduation and does not work toward that goal by preparing each day's assignments to the best of his ability, it is unlikely that he will ever be graduated.

INFERIORITY COMPLEX

The normal person feels inferior to other people in some respects and superior in others. Either feeling, if allowed to dominate an individual's actions, tends to produce an undesirable personality. The person with the inferior feeling is unhappy, and the superior-feeling person makes others unhappy. If one has a physical or mental defect, or if his social background is inadequate, he is likely to feel inferior.

It is impossible for one to succeed when he lacks confidence in his own ability. An inferior feeling may be overcome by analyzing oneself to discover one's special talents and developing them. Every individual has some talent which, when developed, will bring satisfaction to himself. Also, in the process of this analysis he may find that some of his defects may easily be overcome.

It sometimes helps in gaining self-confidence to realize that everyone else has some deficiencies. No one is perfect.

STUDY-GUIDE QUESTIONS

1. List the healthful attitudes which your text gives.
2. What underlies poise? How can we acquire poise? From among your acquaintances select one who you consider has poise. Give reasons for your opinion.
3. Show how persistence is valuable in helping one to succeed.
4. Show how the ability to cooperate is a characteristic of maturity.
5. Why is sympathetic understanding essential for social adjustment? Do you know a person who you consider has a sympathetic understanding of people?
6. What is regression? Why is it an undesirable attitude? How can it be overcome?
7. What are the causes of suspicion? What are the results of a suspicious attitude? How can this attitude be corrected?
8. Why do we sometimes blame another person for our mistakes? What is a good substitute for the habit of blaming others?
9. What causes jealousy? How may we overcome jealousy?
10. What are the unlearned fears of mankind? How may fears be acquired? How do fears affect our behavior? To what extent are fears useful to us? How may foolish fears be overcome?
11. Explain how illness is used as a defense. How does it satisfy the egoist? Why are such people usually uninteresting? Have you ever developed an illness on test day? What is the cure for this type of illness?
12. How is daydreaming a means of compensation? In adult life what should be substituted for daydreaming? What is the result of failing to make this substitution?
13. What is an inferiority complex? Is it common only to the defective or handicapped? Of what value is it to a normal person? How can it be harmful? How can an inferiority complex be overcome?
14. Define rationalization. From your own experience give an example of rationalization. Why is it unwise to encourage young children to give reasons for their conduct? How can we free ourselves from the habit of rationalization?

ACTIVITIES

1. Although Robert, aged six, has an opportunity to play with other children, he prefers his own society. He will play by the hour alone in the sand

pile, but when the neighbor's children come, he just stands and looks on at the others. Robert's mother says that he gives her so little trouble and is so good when he is alone she thinks it is best to let him do as he pleases. Is she right? Give a reason for your answer.

2. Jimmy, aged eight, is suspicious of his playmates. He refuses to let Albert play with his toys for fear he will deliberately break them. If his teacher makes a suggestion for improving his method of work, he thinks she doesn't like him. Why should we want to change Jimmy's attitude? What can be done to change it?

3. Grace and Mary, both high school pupils, were playing tennis. In trying to return the ball with a backward motion, Grace sprained her wrist. She became angry with Mary and told her the accident was her fault, that she should have served the ball differently. What is wrong with Grace? How might she overcome the fault?

4. Mildred and Sarah were good friends and members of the senior class at high school. They both entered an essay contest. Mildred received first place, and Sarah second. After the awards were announced, Sarah snubbed Mildred and told people that the reason Mildred got first place was that she knew the judges. This statement was false. Why did Sarah act as she did? Can you make any explanation of her conduct?

5. Betty, aged fifteen years, is overconscientious about her work. She always does more than is assigned, but when test time comes, she is invariably absent because of illness and must be given a special test. When a project is called for, she always asks for a few days' extra time, because she hasn't been well. Explain Betty's conduct. How might she correct the fault?

6. Since Anna's parents do not speak English, she has had difficulty in learning to speak the language. Because of this handicap, she has become discouraged. She feels that there isn't any use in her trying to compete with children who come from English-speaking homes. What can Anna do to overcome her feeling of inferiority?

7. Henry, at the age of twelve years, had gained quite a reputation for ice skating. Later, he was in an accident which left him a cripple, so that he was unable to skate again. Henry spent his leisure thinking of the many good times which he had experienced when he used to skate. He enjoyed talking about the time when he could skate so well, but made no effort to become interested in some other activity. Why should Henry be encouraged to become interested in another form of activity? Make suggestions of things which he might do.

8. When Ellen was asked by her teacher why she had not made preparation for her lesson, she said that she didn't have time to study, that she had to help her mother with the housework. The real reason was that Ellen had used her usual study period to visit with a friend. Do you think Ellen deliberately told a lie? Why should Ellen be careful to analyze situations and give the correct reasons for her actions?

9. Ann, a high school senior, has her gymnasium locker next to a freshman,

Sadie. Sadie, who is poor, likes pretty things. Ann saw Sadie take some money from another girl's locker. What should Ann do about it? If she reports it to the teacher, Sadie will probably deny having taken the money; if she speaks to Sadie, the younger girl will become angry. Would it be better to let the matter drift and allow Sadie's misdeeds to find her out?

10. Henry, aged eight, has formed the habit of sulking when his playmates cross his wishes. How can he overcome this habit?

UNIT FIVE. HOW CAN I LEARN TO CONTROL MYSELF?

Who does not admire the well-poised person who is able to meet his everyday problems with confidence? Such a pattern of behavior may be acquired by anyone who knows how to control himself.

CONTROL BY MEANS OF SUBSTITUTION

If you have had the responsibility for even a short time of caring for children, you know that the simplest way to manage them is to keep them interested in some healthful form of activity. This fact was demonstrated a short time ago by a resourceful father. When his children's play turned into an argument over who should ride the bicycle, he brought out a ball and bat and suggested a game. Soon the children were happily engaged in playing ball.

As children develop and grow into maturity, they gradually learn to control themselves by substituting some wholesome, desirable form of activity for an undesirable one. A certain young man found it necessary to give up smoking. Following the advice of his physician, every time he wanted to smoke, he ate an apple instead. Another young person found that he was spending more time at the movies than he should. He kept an interesting book at hand, and when the time came to go to the movies, he began reading. He found reading a profitable substitute. Such forms of self-control are healthful, and are to be recommended rather than control by repression.

If, when John becomes angry with his sister, instead of sulking or fighting, he mows the lawn; and later, when his anger has subsided, he calmly talks the situation over with her, no doubt their differences can be satisfactorily settled. By such a procedure John will learn to control his emotional reactions by substitution, and not by repression, as he would if he sulked. It would be better for John to tell his sister what he thinks than for him to repress his feelings. In the latter case, he is apt to become morose and resentful. As a general rule, it is better for people to react normally to their feelings than to repress them. When a feeling is expressed in action, the mind and the body are freed of pent-up emotion and are put in condition to react normally to other situations.

CONTROL BY MEANS OF SUBJECTIVE RESTRAINT

Why do you suppose some people always tell the truth and are honest in their dealings, whereas others seem to have no regard for truth? The honest person is not tempted to steal, no matter how great is his need, while the dishonest one takes money when he is sure no one else will know it, regardless of his need. If we could know the early training of the two, we should probably find that the environment of the honest person was such that he got more satisfaction from being honest than dishonest, and that the dishonest one secured more satisfaction from being dishonest than honest. If, from the very beginning, parents show approval when their child tells the truth and disapproval for untruth, he soon establishes the habit of being honest, and in later life he is not tempted to lie or to steal. He does not need fear of the courts to keep him honest. The restraint which keeps him honest comes from within. When a person controls his actions, not because he is afraid of punishment or because some physical barrier intervenes, but because he thinks it is the right thing to do, we say the restraint is subjective.

Another illustration might be taken from school life. The person who is tempted to take another's pocketbook, but restrains himself because of the presence of the teacher, is practicing objective restraint. If, on the other hand, he restrains himself because he remembers the commandment, " Thou shalt not steal," he is practicing subjective restraint.

CONTROL THROUGH IDEALS

Why did the Puritans come to a new country and endure the hardships of frontier life, when they might have lived in more comfort in their native country? Why do missionaries go to foreign countries and there undergo hardships? The reason in both cases is ideals. Ideals, all through the ages, have been the stimulus for advancement and achievement. In the life of the ordinary person, too, ideals are very helpful in giving confidence and courage to carry on. An ideal may take the form of a goal. Every ambitious person works toward some end. This goal may change from time to time. Before one realizes the satisfaction of having achieved the ideal set for himself, another has been set. When a pupil enters high school, his purpose in life is to earn his diploma. As he begins to feel sure of this accomplishment, he starts planning either for a job or for further study in college. Then, as he goes on, either in work or study, as one task nears completion, another takes shape in his imagination. There is always an ideal to be reached for the person who is achieving.

It is a good thing for us to keep our goal just a little ahead of our accomplishments as long as we keep it within our capabilities.

STUDY-GUIDE QUESTIONS

1. What are the best methods of self-control? What is repression? Why is repression harmful?
2. What is meant by subjective restraint? Of what value is it in developing such traits as honesty and truthfulness?
3. In what way do ideals influence our actions?
4. What part have ideals played in the progress of the world? Of what value can they be to you? When are they harmful?

UNIT SIX. DEVELOPMENT OF SELF IN VARIOUS STAGES OF LIFE

Have you ever seen a two-year-old boy scream and kick when some other child took a toy away from him? If so, you probably felt sorry for the child rather than angered by his action. You felt that he was justified in his tantrum. If, on the other hand, your little brother came up to the table where you were playing a card game with some of your friends and mussed up the cards, how would you act? In all probability you would use words as an outlet for your feelings.

Why is it, do you think, that you would not scream, kick, or cry as a little child does? I can hear you say, " Well, I am no longer a child." That is just the point — you are no longer a child; therefore you have put aside childish things. But would all your friends act as you did? Do you think there are some who might have screamed at their little brother or even might have shed a few tears? To go a step further and perhaps closer to your own experiences, how would you act if your mother refused you permission to attend a dance to which all your friends were invited? Would it be more difficult for you to control your temper in this case than in the other?

To carry our reasoning a little further, how do you think your minister would act if you interrupted his line of thought when he was preparing a sermon? Do you think he would be pleased? Probably not, but certainly he would not scream or cry. He would say, " I am very busy just now. Will you wait a few minutes?"

What is the difference between the way the child, you yourself, and the minister would react to an annoying situation? In the case of the child there was a violent outburst; in that of the minister, a controlled response. Your own reaction might be called intermediate.

Do all mature people show the same self-control as that indicated for your minister? Alas, such is not the case. We all know people who do not act their age, and whom we call childish. In order that we may understand why we do not all act our age, and, too, to know just how we should act at various ages, we shall discuss the natural characteristics of the various stages in our personality development.

EARLY CHILDHOOD

In early childhood, that is, up to the age of seven or eight, the child is interested primarily in himself. He loves those who do things for him. Thus a young child loves his mother, because she is the one who feeds him and makes him comfortable. He would give his affections to any other person who did these things for him. All through this period the child is self-centered. His actions are governed by his personal needs. He thinks about himself. He is not even concerned with trying to make others understand his thoughts and actions. He simply fills in with his imagination anything that is not real to him.

Unless the adults who control a child of this age understand how to allow him to express himself without making him a little lord in his own domain, they will produce a spoiled child with an inflated ego. Such a child will find it difficult to make adjustments in the next phase of his development. Adults must, on the other hand, be careful not to suppress all the natural self-confidence of a child. When a child is overcontrolled, he is likely to develop into a dependent, spineless person or to become very antagonistic. Some psychologists say that when a parent doesn't know what to do, it is better not to do anything.

The child that is made the center of the household learns at an early age different ways of controlling his environment. He finds that if he cries long enough, he can get almost anything he wants. Then, too, he learns that adults are anxious to have him eat certain foods and that he can gain the attention of the entire family by not eating. Under these conditions a child's natural ego is developed. He is aided in fixing habits of selfishness. We must expect a child of this age to be selfish, but we must not make selfishness a permanent characteristic of his personality. As a spoiled child grows older, he expects the same treatment from his associates as he receives from his parents.

People who have grown to adulthood but still fly into a rage or cry when their plans are interfered with, who live by flattery, and who act generally as if the world were made for them have developed no further than an eight-year-old child in their personality development.

LATER CHILDHOOD

As the child passes from early childhood to later childhood, from about eight to twelve years of age, he gradually becomes interested in people and things outside himself. However, during this period there are recurrences of his egocentric qualities. He has not yet learned to accept the consequences of his own actions. He can always find someone else or something else to blame for the results of his mistakes.

These traits are especially strong in the child who has been made the center of attraction during early childhood. He continues to demand attention. Let us take as an example young Harry Smith, aged eleven, who is the only child of devoted parents. When he plays with the children in the neighborhood, he is unhappy unless he can be the center of attention all the time. When another boy is at bat, Harry makes comments on how he should hit the ball. When he himself makes a mistake in playing, it is, according to him, because the bat is either too light or too short, or because one of the other players is standing too near him.

However, during this period from about eight years to twelve, the normal child is learning to think and to act less in terms of self and more in terms of others. He is progressing on the road to unselfishness.

ADOLESCENCE AND MATURITY

The years from about twelve years to approximately twenty, or the " teen " years, are spoken of as adolescence. The average person has reached maturity at twenty years of age. We cannot, however, stress too strongly the fact that age does not indicate maturity. Some people mature at a younger age, and others never mature mentally and emotionally.

Certainly it is during the years of adolescence that people develop most rapidly both physically and mentally. If we are to develop a wholesome personality, that is, to reach maturity in our attitudes and behavior, we should make some progress in this direction during these years. It is during these maturing years that an individual discovers himself — that he finds himself. During these years people make decisions that influence their entire lives. Usually they decide on their lifework and make at least partial preparation for it. The adjustments that they are required to make at this time are important factors in determining their character and personality.

We have mentioned the fact that maturity is not a matter of years, that some people never mature. You no doubt will find it interesting and profitable to consider for a few minutes the qualities of maturity. What are the earmarks of a mature person?

QUALITIES OF MATURITY

The mature person is no longer self-centered. He has found that there is something in life more important than himself. He has found himself and has discovered his own possibilities. He has evolved a philosophy of life that gives him a sense of values. He no longer blames others for his mistakes. He faces facts, recognizes his own mistakes, and makes compensations for them. He no longer relies upon others to make decisions for him and to give him self-confidence. He is self-reliant. If he has physical defects, he does not hide behind them but compensates for them.

You may well ask, " Should we high school students be expected to measure up to the mature person described?" Of course, you must remember that age is not an indication of maturity. Although it may be expecting too much to ask all high school students to reach maturity, there will be a few who will. If you are all aware of the desirability of reaching maturity and are progressing in that direction, you will be well along the road to mental health and happiness.

You will be interested in the following poem, " An ' If ' for Girls," by Elizabeth L. Otis, which gives characteristics of maturity for the high school girl.

An ' If ' for Girls

If you can dress to make yourself attractive,
Yet not make puffs and curls your chief delight;
If you can swim and row, be strong and active,
But of the gentler graces lose not sight;
If you can dance without a crave for dancing,
Play without giving play too strong a hold,
Enjoy the love of friends without romancing,
Care for the weak, the friendless, and the old;
If you can master French and Greek and Latin,
And not acquire a priggish mien;
If you can feel the touch of silk and satin
Without despising calico and jean;
If you can ply a saw and hammer,
Can do a man's work when the need occurs,
Can sing, when asked, without excuse or stammer,
Can rise above unfriendly snubs and slurs;
If you can make good bread as well as fudges,
Can sew with skill, and have an eye for dust;
If you can be a friend and hold no grudges,
A girl whom all will love because they must;
If sometime you should meet and love another
And make a home with faith and peace enshrined,
And you its soul — a loyal wife and mother,
You'll work out pretty nearly to my mind,
The plan that's been developed through the ages,
And win the best that life can have in store,
You'll be a model for the sages —
A woman whom the world will bow before.*

— Elizabeth L. Otis

STUDY-GUIDE QUESTIONS

1. Name the various stages of human development. At what ages do these occur?
2. Describe the usual behavior characteristics of early childhood; of later childhood.
3. Describe a mature person. Do people mature mentally and physically simultaneously?
4. What do we mean when we say a person has a philosophy of life?

* Courtesy of Marjorie B. Rice, *Poems of Worth*. The Buehler Printcraft Co., Cleveland, Ohio, 1921.

5. Analyze the poem, "An 'If' for Girls," listing the qualities of maturity mentioned therein. Of the qualities and skills listed in this poem, what do you consider the most difficult to achieve?

ACTIVITIES

1. Formulate a series of statements or principles for guidance in getting along peaceably and happily with one's family. When might these principles become a philosophy?
2. What would you say was the philosophy of Silas Marner? Of Abraham Lincoln?

BOOKS FOR FURTHER READING

Fedder, Ruth, *A Girl Grows Up*. McGraw-Hill Book Company, New York, 1939.

Fosdick, Harry Emerson, *On Being a Real Person*. Harper and Brothers, New York, 1943.

Marsh, Hattie, *Building Your Personality*. Prentice-Hall, New York, 1939.

Myers, Gary C., *Learning to be Likable*. School and College Station, Columbus, Ohio.

Shacter, Helen, *Understanding Ourselves*. McKnight and McKnight, Bloomington, Illinois, 1940.

Thorpe, Louis P., and Jay N. Holliday, *Personality and Life*. Longmans, Green & Company, New York, 1941.

Strong family unity is fostered by doing things together.

SECTION II
PERSONAL AND FAMILY RELATIONSHIPS

UNIT ONE. ADJUSTING TO SCHOOL LIFE

WHEN IS A STUDENT ADJUSTED TO SCHOOL LIFE?

The student who gets along peaceably with his teachers and fellow students, who takes an active part in the activities of the school, and who does his work in a creditable manner is adjusted to school life.

ADJUSTING TO SCHOOL LIFE THROUGH A REALIZATION OF THE PURPOSE OF EDUCATION

To introduce this idea of the value of a purpose, let us consider two girls — Mary and Betty — who were taking courses in clothing in a large high school.

Whenever Mary came into the classroom, she got her materials ready and was settled for work before the bell rang. Whether she was working on her workbook or on a garment, Mary always began her work on time and paid attention to it throughout the period. She consulted the teacher when she needed help and gave attention to any general discussion or instruction given. During one semester Mary made all the required garments for two semesters of work. One day the teacher asked her why she always paid such close attention to her work and why she was able to accomplish so much. Mary replied, " My mother will buy material for as many garments as I can make in class, but she will not buy all the ready-made clothes I would like to have."

As you see, Mary had a purpose in her work. She knew what she wanted to accomplish in her clothing class. It is true that hers was a selfish purpose, but it was a purpose, and she was conscious of it. There is no doubt that Mary worked better and faster because she had the conscious aim of making as many garments as possible during a limited time.

39

On the other hand, when Betty came into the classroom, she went to the mirror and fixed her hair; then she talked to her companions. She was never ready for work before the bell rang, and very seldom when the bell rang. She had some interest in making a garment that she might wear, but it was not sufficient to keep her regularly occupied. She was much more interested in talking with her neighbors than in doing her work. When her teacher asked her why she took the course, she replied, " Well, I had to take something, and my home-room teacher suggested this course. I am not really interested in school."

In the first case we have an example of the value of a felt purpose. Generally, pupils who feel a need in their own lives for the work they are doing get more value and satisfaction from doing their work than those who see no value in it.

What are the things which you expect to get out of your high school experiences? Why are you in school? These are questions which we shall discuss.

Someone may say, " I can answer the second question. We have to come to school whether we want to or not. We haven't any choice." Very well, let us start with this fact. Perhaps you wonder why the state not only furnishes buildings, equipment, teachers, and, in many cases, books for your education but also insists that you take advantage of these facilities. The state first enacted laws making attendance at school compulsory because many parents were having their children work at an early age. Only the well-to-do could afford to keep their children in school. After a while civic-minded people woke up to the fact that the children of the nation were being imposed upon, and that, if the future citizens were going to be able to carry on life in a democracy, they would have to have some training for such a life.

EDUCATION FOR CITIZENSHIP

In a democracy, where the government is entrusted to the people, it can be only as good as the masses are able to make it. In a dictatorship it is not so important that the citizens, who are not expected to make decisions, but who are expected to do only as they are told, become acquainted with national problems and learn how to solve them. In a democratic country such as ours, it is imperative that our future citizens be educated for intelligent citizenship. It is the ignorant person whose vote can be controlled by propaganda. We must know how to interpret what we read in newspapers and magazines, what we hear on the radio, and what the candidates for public offices tell us. In other words, we must be intelligent enough and interested enough in the affairs of our country to take time to understand its problems and their possible solutions, so that we can recognize propaganda when we meet it.

So, today, if all of us understood the problems of our government and were able to analyze the solutions proposed by our political leaders, we would not have millions living in unfit homes and millions of undernourished and poorly clothed children in this land of plenty, where such conditions exist despite the fact that there are enough food, enough building materials, and enough labor to provide necessities for all.

The United States has realized the need for an educated populace. The percentage of boys and girls attending high schools in the United States is greater than in any other country.

EDUCATION FOR A FULLER PERSONAL LIFE

The state realizes that in addition to its people being able to cast an intelligent ballot, they must also be able to take care of themselves and not be dependent upon the government. Therefore our public schools are planned to help educate our young people to be mentally and physically healthy, to be honest and straightforward, and to discover their own powers and abilities, so that upon leaving high school they can either enter a vocation or decide intelligently upon a course for further preparation for a vocation.

Although the state is concerned primarily in educating its young people to be honest, independent, intelligent citizens, it also gives these young people an opportunity to develop (a) a variety of interests which will provide many possibilities for their leisure-time activities; (b) self-assurance, which is necessary to their future success; (c) a philosophy that will give their life meaning and direction; and (d) the ability to work and play with people.

If more high school students realized the significance of their school life, they would not allow themselves to develop the attitude that school is a place to be endured, but instead would feel that school is a privilege and that their teachers are guides who are trying to help them to develop their best selves.

ADJUSTING TO SCHOOL LIFE THROUGH A WISE CHOICE OF CURRICULUM

It is impossible for a student to enjoy his school work and do it well unless he has some aptitude for it. There are some people who enjoy studying geometry and other mathematical subjects and others who can see no sense in them. It would be foolish for a girl who neither understands nor enjoys mathematics to select a curriculum that requires three or even two years of mathematics. When a student struggles with a subject in which she cannot succeed, she only loses her self-assurance and wastes her time. A person who is not mathematical may do very well in social sciences, language, creative writing, or subjects in other fields such as home economics or business.

However, sometimes interest will play a very strong part in a person's ability to do satisfactory work in certain subjects. When a girl wants to be a dietician, she will master the required chemistry although she has not previously shown any aptitude for the subject. Even though interest stimulates many people to do creditable work in subjects for which they have not previously shown ability, a student will be able to do best the thing in which he has natural ability as well as interest. Usually a person is interested in doing the thing he does well.

The problem of choosing a curriculum is sometimes very difficult. However, it is a matter that should be given serious consideration by the student, his parents, and his teachers. Of course, if a student knows he is going to college and that he will study to be a teacher of English or a journalist, his choice of curriculum will be a simple matter. If, on the other hand, he knows he cannot go to college but does not know what kind of job he should fit himself for, the question is more difficult.

There are books in which vocational experts analyze different jobs, giving the qualifications required for each and the possibilities for employment. Such books are valuable for students, teachers, and parents to read.

If, after enrolling in a curriculum in high school, a student finds that he does not enjoy the work and does very poorly in the required subjects, he should not hesitate to make a change to another curriculum in which he has more interest. If one is to adjust to his school life, he must pursue subjects in which he can succeed reasonably well.

ADJUSTING TO SCHOOL LIFE THROUGH UNDERSTANDING THE LEARNING PROCESS

One of the ways in which you become adjusted to school is by doing creditable work. The pupils who get the most pleasure and enjoyment from their school life are those who succeed in their work. If you have some understanding of how learning takes place, you will be able to do more efficient work.

If you have made several articles of wearing apparel, you probably can remember how, when you cut out the first one, you were afraid of spoiling your material and of getting the wrong pieces together. However, by the time you had finished your first garment, you felt you could do a better job next time. If your first sewing project had been a failure, you probably would have lost confidence in yourself and not have tried again.

The successes or failures which you had when making your first garment affected your attitude toward sewing and the way in which you approached your second problem. In your first experience you learned something about selecting suitable materials, choosing a desirable pattern, making alterations in the pattern to suit your needs, and following the chart and directions given in the pattern. Although you did not learn all there is to know about these different phases of dressmaking, you did learn enough so that when you decided to make your second garment you were better able to direct yourself and to make your own decisions.

While your second project was, no doubt, more difficult, you were more independent of your teacher in carrying it out. In addition to learning how to select the material and pattern and how to make a garment, you also acquired a definite attitude toward sewing. The speed with which you worked and the perfection of the finished product depended upon how keenly you felt a need for the garment, how much interest you had in learning how to select materials for it and to make it, how well you understood what you were going to do before you did it, and how much you learned from your previous experience in selecting material and making a garment.

In the preceding paragraphs a learning process has been described. Learning takes place best in the following way: first, the learner should feel an interest in the thing which he is about to learn and a need to master it; second, he should get a clear mental picture of what he is trying to learn and an understanding of the way he is going to proceed; third, he should go through with the planned procedure.

Let us apply these phases of the learning process in a more general way. Whenever you start a new course of study, it is very important that you have an understanding of the purpose of the course and how it will help you to attain your own goals or objectives in getting an education. Is it planned to help you better to understand society and its problems, to help you enrich your experiences, to help you discover your latent possibilities, to help you to maintain good health, or to aid you in some other way? When you can see the relationship between the subject matter you are studying and your own needs, you are in condition to get the most out of your work. You will then apply yourself to your work in such a way that it will mean something to you.

ADJUSTING TO SCHOOL LIFE THROUGH PARTICIPATION IN
SCHOOL ACTIVITIES

Why should a student take part in school activities? The reason is that we learn how to work and to play with people by actually working and playing with them. The girl who works on a committee to create an attitude of civic pride on the part of the student body or sells wieners at a football game or writes invitations for a class party is learning how to work with people. She will be more interested and better able to work as a member of the civic organizations of the community, such as the library board, the Y.W.C.A., and the League of Women Voters. In a democratic country such as ours, the most effective work for public improvement is carried on through such organizations rather than by individuals.

There is also a purely selfish reason why a student should take part in the activities of the school. Everybody wants to be well liked and to have friends. As we work and play with people, we gain a sympathetic understanding of them and realize that their problems and ours are the same. Sympathetic understanding is the foundation of our interest in people.

STUDY-GUIDE QUESTIONS

1. Of what value is it to a pupil to realize why he is in school and why he is taking a certain subject?
2. Explain why we have free schools in the United States of America.
3. What does the government expect that each of its young people will get from a high school education?
4. Which do you think is more important in determining a pupil's success in a school subject — interest in the subject or so-called natural ability for it?
5. Show how each one of the subjects which you are now taking relates to your future plans.
6. Show how a wise choice of curriculum helps you in adjusting to school life. What points should be taken into consideration when selecting a curriculum?
7. According to your textbook, how does learning take place? Compare this method with the way in which you study.
8. How does participation in school activities aid a pupil in adjusting to school life?

UNIT TWO.   ADJUSTING TO FAMILY LIFE

Whether we are pleasant and happy or sullen and grouchy will depend to a great extent upon whether we feel secure in our family's affection. If there is unhappiness in a family, the members will reflect this situation in their attitude toward people outside the home. Haven't you had a friend say something like this to you on a morning when you had quarreled with your brother before leaving home: " Why, what's the matter? You look so grumpy "?

The behavior pattern of our family life not only determines to a large extent how we treat our friends and acquaintances but it also establishes a pattern for our national life. People who have established habits and attitudes required for unselfish, democratic living in their homes are likely to follow the same pattern in their business and social life outside the home. Some people say that if our homes are run on a truly democratic basis, we need not be afraid of our democratic society decaying.

Another reason for our being interested in understanding how we can live harmoniously with our families is the fact that mental health demands an atmosphere of contentment and calm. Human nature can endure just so long in an atmosphere of nervous stress and strain. After the limit, which varies with individuals, has been reached, we literally go to pieces — we do not function as a unit. For these reasons we should expect the assistant homemakers of today, who are the future homemakers of tomorrow, to be interested in knowing how to create and maintain a happy, successful home life.

WHEN IS A HOME CONSIDERED HAPPY AND SUCCESSFUL?

When the members of the family get along peaceably and happily together without one or more of the members making undue sacrifices for the others, when each is able to develop his individual personality, and when all are able to make satisfactory adjustments

46

to life outside the home, we call the family life happy and successful.

Let us consider the home life of such a family. The Grays live on a small truck and chicken farm near a large city in the Middle West. The family consists of Mr. and Mrs. Gray; their sons Robert,

The assistant homemakers of today are the homemakers of the future. Courtesy, Good Housekeeping Institute.

fifteen, and Tom, twelve; and a daughter Eleanor, who is seventeen. When the children were quite small, Mr. Gray suffered an accident which left him a semi-invalid. He and Mrs. Gray have acted as partners at all times. They have acquired a family unity the equal of which is very hard to find. Each member of the family has assumed responsibility for some phase of running the farm. Eleanor manages the chickens and does much of the work involved in their care; Mr. Gray stays in the roadside stand, where the produce is sold to customers from the city; Robert specializes in the raising of vegetables; Tom assumes the responsibility for the fruit; and Mrs. Gray keeps the books, manages the house, and acts as assistant to anyone who needs her. Although each takes a special responsibility, the farm is operated as a unit. At one time the whole crew picks raspberries, and at another time they cultivate vegetables. Eleanor may gather beans for Robert while he cleans the chicken houses.

A strict account is kept of the amount and kinds of produce sold with the price received. The money is banked in Mrs. Gray's name, and she pays the bills. Each member of the family has a small allowance to cover the cost of clothing and personal needs.

The Grays have plans for taking care of the educational needs of the young people. Robert will take a college course in agriculture; Eleanor will prepare for teaching; and Tom thinks he wants to be an aviator. Eleanor plans to take part-time work at the university in the near-by city. Under this plan she will be able to assume most of her regular duties at home. She will begin her college work immediately after graduation from high school. Robert will work for two years on the farm after he is graduated from high school, with the expectation that Eleanor will by that time be able to teach and someone can be hired to take Robert's place on the farm. When Tom is ready for advanced training, either in aviation or in whatever other field his permanent choice may be, the family will help him. The boys are planning to work on the farm during the summer season.

As you see, the Grays must make sacrifices for one another and work hard; but you must not think that their life is nothing but work, for such is not the case. It is true that they do not indulge in expensive forms of recreation. They have a sense of values which has been achieved through necessity and the wise guidance of their parents. The family share many good times together, such as picnic suppers with invited guests. These suppers are cooked on an outdoor oven which the boys built in their backyard. The Grays also read together five nights a week for an hour after the work is finished. Their reading together has become quite an institution. Mr. Gray started the custom of reading nursery rhymes to the children in their early years; then, as they grew older, he enjoyed finding books that would entertain them. He still makes most of the choices for the family hour of reading; however, other members sometimes make selections.

The Grays take an active part in community affairs. They are regular attendants at the local church and the social activities of the school. The children enjoy meeting with the young people of the community at a near-by river for swimming in the summer and skating in the winter.

Mr. Gray has long been an ardent student of nature. He knows the habits of all the local birds and can identify most of the wild plants and trees in the neighborhood. The children have learned a great deal about nature from their father, but only the daughter has made any special study of it. Eleanor has been collecting wild flowers ever since she was five years old, when her father enlisted her help with his collection. Her ever-growing collection is a source of great pleasure to her. Tom reads everything he can find on airplanes and has a small collection of models which he has made. Robert plays a horn in the school band, an activity which takes a good deal of his spare time. He is also interested in stamps and has a fine collection of domestic issues.

VALUE OF A PHILOSOPHY UNDERSTOOD BY THE FAMILY

What may we consider the secret of the success of the Gray family? No doubt you agree that theirs is a successful family. Early in their married life Mr. and Mrs. Gray worked out a philosophy to guide them in the business of rearing a family. They believe that each individual member should be able to express his best self in his own way, that each individual has a special contribution to make to society, and that he alone can determine what this is to be and how best it can be made. In their opinion the greatest satisfaction comes to people through self-realization; consequently, individual rights should be recognized and personal originality encouraged.

Although the Grays have this strong belief in the importance of individual development, they think that such development can best be achieved through cooperating with others in a common purpose. They believe that the greatest satisfaction comes through striving for the attainment of a better society in which to live, that each life should be guided by ideals and principles that will enable each person to do his duty without being forced or bribed to do so, and that most people make their greatest contribution to society through their daily contacts with the members of their families and friends. Therefore, right habits governing daily life in the home are important.

The Grays have not only formulated a philosophy to guide them in managing their family, but they also have explained this philosophy to their children and have planned some ways of putting it into practice. The parents agree that if their children are to develop into unselfish individualists, they must have confidence in themselves and in their fellow beings, must feel secure in their world, and must learn how to work and to play with others.

LEARNING TO HAVE CONFIDENCE IN SELF

Mr. and Mrs. Gray believe that the best way to gain confidence in oneself is to succeed in whatever is undertaken and to plan, as far as possible, one's own activities. When the children were very small, they were allowed to choose, as far as their judgment would warrant, their form of entertainment. Mrs. Gray used to answer Robert's early demand, " Mother, what should I do now?" with " Well, now, what do you want to do? There is the sand pile, or how about the large square blocks?" As the children developed, their parents were careful to provide some toys that would challenge their ingenuity, their aim being to keep the children interested and stimulated in activities that were within their capacity to do successfully. The same method was used in the work assigned to them. The difficulty and the amount of work were kept in proportion to the ability of the child. In this way the children gained confidence in their powers to achieve; they developed the feeling of personal adequacy.

The attitude of the parents toward the children played no little part in developing this feeling of adequacy. The children knew they could depend upon their parents for recognition, approval, and help when they needed it. They also knew that their own opinions would be treated with consideration and respect. For these reasons, they found satisfaction in working out their problems, while at the same time they were achieving a feeling of self-confidence.

ACHIEVING A FEELING OF SECURITY

Because the Gray children can depend upon their parents for sympathetic understanding of their problems, they have learned to trust them and are building up a faith in other people. If parents are dependable, honest, and sympathetic with their children, it is natural for the youngsters to trust other people. This helps to give the children the feeling of security that comes from belonging to a successful family.

This feeling of security has been strengthened in the Gray family by the organization of team work in the family. Each member feels that his efforts are important to the life of the group, that what he does or does not do is vital to the others. This feeling of importance to a group helps greatly in making people feel secure.

LEARNING TO WORK AND TO PLAY TOGETHER

The description of the Gray family might lead you to believe that the Gray children are just naturally good, or that their situation is an ideal one in which to learn how to work and to play together. By nature, however, they are no better than other children, and although their environment is conducive to habits of cooperative living, all families which have similar surroundings have not acquired these habits. Why, then, have the Grays been able to work and to play together harmoniously?

Mr. and Mrs. Gray decided before they were married that they would try to achieve harmony in their home by discussing their differences and arriving at a course of action that seemed right after they had considered together the issues involved, each seeking for the truth and not trying to gain his own way. They disagree with the theory that people will make satisfactory adjustments in family relationships by taking turns in making decisions. Although we do obtain a certain satisfaction from doing something to please someone of whom we are fond, we should get greater satisfaction from doing something in which we have an interest or for which we feel a need.

By the time the Gray children began expressing their opinions, Mr. and Mrs. Gray had acquired the habit of giving careful consideration to their own differences and were able to take a sympathetic attitude toward their children's ideas. They always treated their children as individuals. This fact doesn't mean that they al-

Happy home life is achieved by playing together as well as by working together.
Courtesy, *Better Homes and Gardens.*

lowed immature minds to dominate important family issues. They did, however, welcome and consider the children's opinions. The final decision for a course of action in the Gray family is always made by the group in a democratic manner. It must be added, lest you misunderstand, that when Mr. and Mrs. Gray feel it necessary, they express a command; and it is obeyed by the children without question.

A typical incident from the life of the Grays may serve to exemplify their cooperative decision on a course of action. One January when Mrs. Gray balanced the books for the preceding year, she found that they had one hundred fifty dollars more than they had anticipated; so she raised the question, " What shall we do with the money?" Eleanor suggested that it be divided equally among the members of the family. Her share would be just enough to buy longed-for mounting equipment for her collection of wild flowers. Robert thought the money should be put aside toward a fund for the purchase of a new car. Tom said he would like to have it divided, so that he could use a part of his share to purchase some materials to make airplanes, although he still had some on hand that hadn't been used. Mr. Gray suggested that they enumerate some things that would bring satisfaction to the whole family. Someone mentioned an electric refrigerator; someone else, a new radio. Robert again said he thought a fund should be started for a new car, and Eleanor suggested a davenport. It was finally decided that for the present the refrigerator would bring the most satisfaction, since the old icebox could not be used another season, whereas the radio was still in fair condition. Mrs. Gray appeased Eleanor with the suggestion that they might make a slip cover for the davenport. Robert gave up his idea when he realized that the refrigerator would lessen the work for his mother as well as save the bother of bringing ice from town twice a week. When the decision was finally reached, everybody was satisfied, although Tom remarked, " Well, it seems strange to want a refrigerator when the ground is covered with snow." He hadn't reached the point where he could plan far ahead.

HOW PARENTS HELP YOU ACHIEVE MATURITY

Many boys and girls of high school age are looking forward to the time when they can be independent, when they will be on their own, when they can take their place in the world of adults. This is a normal feeling and is one of the important needs of your age — the urge to achieve independence. As is true of other fundamental needs, this inner urge for independence must be understood and guided. When you were small, you felt secure in the love and protection of your parents. They were strong and brave. You had very few responsibilities. Someone decided when you would eat, what you would eat, when you would sleep, what you would wear, with whom you would play, and how you would spend your free time. Gradually you have been assuming the responsibility for making many of these decisions.

There are still many issues relating to your personal and family life that you need help in deciding. Most young people need and want assistance in answering such questions as these: What time should I come home from an evening's outing? How should I choose my companions? Should I drink if the others do? Should I smoke? How should I spend my allowance? What should I prepare to do for a living? Should I go to college?

Fortunate indeed is the girl who has a parent or parents who understand her need for achieving independence and are wise enough to guide her. Such a parent or parents will give a daughter the benefit of insight born of experience and will help the girl to scrutinize each issue as it arises and to evaluate its pros and cons. From such conferences a young person will learn how to make decisions. The wise parent will insist that a girl abide by the consequences of her decisions. If she makes a mistake, then she must face the consequences. It is important that both the parent and the daughter realize that self-confidence, independence, and the ability to direct one's own life can come only through practice. At all times the girl should exercise her own judgment in as far as she is capable. The parent should be ready to help and to prevent any serious crises. This is, of course, impossible unless the girl is willing to accept the guidance offered and to seek help when she needs it.

If a girl finds that she is chafing under parental authority, she may well consider whether she has shown herself capable of self-direction. She will do well to study the following questions: Do I assume responsibility for my share of the family work without being told what to do and when to do it? Do I go to bed early enough to keep myself physically able to carry my personal and family responsibilities without sleeping half the morning away? Can I decide what dress to wear? Can I keep my clothes in repair? Can I get along with my schoolmates and teachers? Do I pattern my conduct after the ideals and standards agreed upon in my family, or do I follow entirely the pattern of my associates? Do I compensate for my own mistakes, or do I expect my parents to come to my rescue?

Conscientious parents are loath to relinquish authority over their children before they have shown signs of being able to substitute inner control for exterior control. Then, too, most parents have learned from experience that even adults are not free from authority. In a family, as in any other organization of people, each individual must think for himself in relation to others. He can be an individualist just so far as he does not interfere with the rights and privileges of the other members of the group.

HOW TO GAIN INDEPENDENCE IN SPITE OF PARENTS

Parents are human and sometimes make mistakes. These mistakes may be due to the personality make-up of the parents, over which they have had no jurisdiction. It may be that the children of a family have had advantages that have been denied their parents. Some parents, for example, are overprotective; others are domineering; and still others may be neglectful.

If you happen to belong to a family where the parents love their children wisely and understand them, your problem of adjusting yourself to your parents is very simple. Under such circumstances you need only to understand that in achieving independence, you should take as much responsibility for your own actions as you are capable of doing, but that you still need the guidance of your parents. If your parents happen to be domineering, overprotective, or neglectful, your problems are more difficult.

Let us consider together Georgia Anderson's case. Georgia's father grew up in a house where the father was a dictator who loved power for its own sake. For a child to question the opinion of the father was heresy. The mother and all the children took orders from the father. The family pattern of Mrs. Anderson's home was similar to Mr. Anderson's. Since both Mr. and Mrs. Anderson loved and respected their parents, they saw no reason for changing the pattern of their own home.

Mr. Anderson loves his family and provides amply for their physical comforts. He works hard, taking very few vacations himself, although he insists that the other members of the family go away for a change sometime during the summer. Until recently Mr. Anderson thought of himself as the undisputed master of his household. When the other members of the family wanted any money, they asked him for it; when they wanted to go somewhere, they asked his consent; and before they had company, his approval was solicited.

Georgia's older sister Ellen reached maturity without too many family upheavals. She is mild in her reactions and is satisfied to have someone else make decisions for her. Georgia is different. Apparently she inherited her father's strong will and dominative personality. She is very popular with the girls and boys of her acquaintance.

Georgia began her campaign for independence by asking her father for an allowance when she was in junior high school. Her father's reply was, " Why, daughter, don't you have all you need? You are too young to know how to manage money. In no time you would be coming back for more. No, daughter, you let your father take care of the finances of the family." Georgia felt discouraged. She talked over the situation with her home economics teacher, who advised her to keep account of the money she spent for several weeks and then to go back to her father with another appeal. This time she told her father that she had been studying budgeting in school and was convinced that an allowance would give her good practice in wise spending. She asked her father if he had read about Benjamin Franklin's paying too much for a whistle. This line of argument pleased Mr. Anderson, but he was uncertain about the amount Georgia should receive. When his daughter showed him her accounts for the past several weeks, they turned the trick. Georgia had won a victory. She was very careful to show herself worthy of the confidence entrusted in her. She offered to show her account book to her father, but he said, " No, all I ask is that you live within your allowance. It is yours to do with as you please. If you need help, I shall be glad to give you the benefit of my own experience."

When Georgia entered senior high school, she found it harder and harder to live up to the family rule of getting home at ten or eleven o'clock from all parties. In fact, she didn't always do it, but her father made her feel that she was disobedient when she didn't live up to the rule. Mrs. Anderson found that Georgia was becoming irritable and resentful toward her father's attitude about the hour she came home from parties. She talked to some of the other mothers of high school pupils on the subject and decided that her family should discuss the issue and come to some agreement that would relieve the family tension.

Georgia presented her side of the story — that the parties didn't start until late and after they were over the crowd stopped at the restaurant for something to eat, that she didn't want to seem different from the others. Mr. Anderson explained how concerned he was when his daughter stayed out late at night for fear of an automobile accident, since many young drivers are reckless. Furthermore, young people need a sufficient amount of sleep to insure good health, and the reputation of the family for decent conduct must be maintained. After much talk on both sides, it was agreed that they would do away with the traditional dead line and that each occasion would be considered an individual case. It was agreed that Georgia would not go out on dates or parties on school nights and that on Sunday night she would be in bed by ten o'clock. After this experience the Andersons found themselves more and more deciding their differences through a family discussion of the issue involved.

The case of the Anderson family shows how a high school girl may help to establish harmonious relations in a family. Just how each girl will meet the situation will depend upon the family and the girl. The policy of frank, open discussions of problems has been found by many families to be a very good method.

Occasionally a girl finds that her family is unable to agree on a method of settling family differences, thus making it impossible for her gradually to achieve independence of family authority. In such a case she will have to take the attitude of facing the facts and using her tact and ingenuity to work out the difficulties. When she is ironing out family problems, she will be growing in power to meet problems outside the home. It is selfish for parents to expect an only girl to give up all social contacts to keep them company, for a mother who has lost her husband to demand the entire affection of her sons, for the younger members of a family to allow an older brother or sister to sacrifice his life for them, or for an overfearful parent to keep his daughters so closely at home that they lose the power to adjust themselves to people.

STUDY-GUIDE QUESTIONS

1. Do you think the Grays overinfluenced their children? Give reasons for your answer.
2. What conditions helped the Grays build a strong family unity? Do you think it would be as easy for an urban family to achieve a strong family unity as it was for the Grays?
3. Cite some circumstances in family life when a parent should command and be obeyed.
4. What is your understanding of the term behavior pattern?
5. Do you agree with the conditions specified in your textbook for a happy, successful home? What are they? Do you think of any conditions that should be added to the list given?
6. List the beliefs of the Gray family which directed their actions and determined their family behavior pattern. Explain the meaning of the term unselfish individualists. What conditions did the Grays consider necessary to the development of unselfish individualists?
7. How did the Grays believe one could best gain self-confidence? Tell how they helped their children grow into self-confidence.
8. How did Mr. and Mrs. Gray give their children a feeling of security?
9. What things should the Gray children have learned from the refrigerator incident?
10. Explain what is meant by the *urge* to achieve independence. How can parents help their children acquire independence? How can young people prove that they are capable of directing their own course of action?
11. Give examples showing that even adults are not free from authority.
12. What is the difference between external and inner control?
13. Give examples showing how a parent may be overprotective, domineering, or neglectful.
14. How did Georgia convince her father to give her an allowance? Do you think her reasons were sound?
15. Why did Mr. Anderson think Georgia should be at home by eleven o'clock? Give Georgia's arguments for staying out later.
16. Under what family conditions is it difficult for young people to achieve independence?
17. To what extent should a family make sacrifices to provide training for a gifted child?

ACTIVITIES

1. With the help of your teacher and class members, make a list of family responsibilities which should be assumed by the father. Did Mr. Gray assume all the responsibilities on your list? Which ones did he leave for someone else? Do you think he could have assumed more responsibilities than are indicated in the description in your textbook?

2. Working with your teacher and classmates, list the family responsibilities which should be assumed by the mother. How does Mrs. Gray measure up to the standards you have set for the mother of a family? Could your list be applied to all families?

3. Make a list of books that you think your family would enjoy reading together.

4. Show how the Grays's plan of achieving harmony in their home through discussion is better than taking turns in making decisions.

5. Anna Smith's mother died when she was born, and for several weeks Anna wasn't expected to live. On Anna was lavished the affection and protection of a father filled with fear that he might lose his only child. Anna was not allowed to play outdoors in cold weather for fear she would take cold; she could not go into the water for fear she would drown; she could not roller skate for fear she would break a leg; she could not be away from home when Mr. Smith was there because he would be lonesome. When Anna reached junior high school, she was underweight, nervous, and afraid to enter into the activities of the school. What would you suggest should be done for Anna? How might her father be led to realize his mistake in his attitude toward his daughter?

6. Gretchen Van Horn is a high school senior. Her father has been very strict about Gretchen's social activities. He does not allow her to stay out after ten o'clock at night or to go out with girls and boys whom he does not know. Gretchen is finding that she is being left out of many parties to which she would enjoy going. She is becoming unhappy over the situation. One of her friends has advised her to defy her father and to go without his consent. What would you advise Gretchen to do? Is her father right in requiring her to be home at ten o'clock? At what hour should young people come home? Who should decide on the correct time for young people to get home at night? Is Gretchen's father right in demanding that she should associate only with people whom he knows? Who should choose the friends of young people?

7. In the Graham family there are two boys, Charles, ten, and George, eighteen, and one girl, Betty, who is sixteen. When the children were small, the Grahams employed two maids, but now, because of financial reverses, they have no hired help. Mrs. Graham has always encouraged her children to bring their friends home with them. There is always a crowd of boys and girls at the Grahams, and the children serve refreshments from whatever food they can find in the refrigerator. Mrs. Graham never knows if the food left from dinner will be available for next day's lunch. She may think she has enough leftover meat to make sandwiches, but often finds the plate bare when she looks for the roast. The children have never formed the habit of helping with the housework. Mrs. Graham usually irons in the evening, often as late as twelve o'clock. The boys have a clean shirt every day, and other members of the family keep equally clean. Make a plan of work for the Graham family, showing

how the children might help with the responsibility of housekeeping. Do you think housework will make boys "sissy"?

8. Talk with at least two mothers to ascertain how their pattern of family behavior has been determined. You might ask them whether they have modelled their family set-up after that of their parental home or have established their homes on different lines, because they disagreed with the methods of their parents.

9. Do you know of any families that agree upon family policies through group discussions? Study at least one family that maintains harmonious relationships and be prepared to explain the secret of their success.

UNIT THREE. FRIENDSHIP AND MARRIAGE

It was necessary for Betty Johnson to live away from home with her grandmother during her high school years. Betty had always talked freely with her mother and continued to do so by means of frequent letters to her. In turn, Mrs. Johnson tried to help Betty solve her problems through letters. Those dealing with Betty's relationship with girls and boys follow:

Number 1. *Getting Acquainted*

Dear Betty,

It is natural for you to want boys and girls to notice you and to like you. I, too, want you to know many boys and girls. It is through acquaintance with a number of different people that you will find out the type you want for friends.

You asked me how you can attract their attention and make them like you. That is a big order. Making friends is something that cannot be hurried. Please do not become impatient. You know we do not invite into our living room every stranger who knocks at our door, nor do we open our hearts to all the people we meet. We have many acquaintances, but few friends.

You will do well to adopt the attitude of watchful waiting. Please do not misunderstand me! I should not like you to act snobbish and as though you thought your new associates inferior to you. On the contrary, I hope you are friendly and courteous to everyone. All of them would not enjoy having you for a friend any more than you would find all of them congenial.

I can hear you say, " But, mother, I just want to know them well enough to have someone with whom I can do things and go places." I am sure of that, and I am going to make some practical suggestions.

Suppose you speak to your home-room teacher about the extra-curricular activities of the school. You have always enjoyed the work you have done in music. Perhaps you could join the chorus or Glee Club, and probably you could join a dramatic club. Find out about athletics in your school. Do the girls play badminton or basketball? Of course, you have affiliated with the church, and no doubt there will be church parties.

These are just a few suggestions. Your home-room teacher will be able to tell you more about the activities of your school. Be

Common interests are a basis for congenial companionship. Courtesy, Heidelberg College, Tiffin, Ohio.

careful not to join too many groups at one time. Usually common interest is a basis for congenial companionship. It is through working and playing with people that you will learn to know them.

Affectionately,

MOTHER

Number 2. *Choosing Our Companions*

Dear Betty,

So you have joined the Dramatic Society and the Friendship Club! I think you made a very wise selection, especially since you are getting some music in your class work. From your description of your social activities, I am sure you are meeting a number of interesting boys and girls. I am wondering if you realize the difference between popularity and friendship. It is easy to achieve a cheap kind of popularity if you are willing to pay the price. It takes courage to say no to a group of boys and girls of your own age with whom you want to be popular, especially when they say, " Oh, come on! Be a sport just once."

In this connection I am always reminded of one of my childhood acquaintances, Jane Martin. When Jane first came to spend the summer with her aunt, who was a neighbor of my family, she was a sweet, lovable, accomplished, pretty girl of sixteen. She played the piano and sang beautifully. All through that first summer she went around with the neighborhood boys and girls of her own age. Although she never seemed to make any decisions for herself, she was agreeable, and everybody liked her. We were sorry to have her go away when fall came and eagerly awaited her return the next season.

About the middle of the second summer Jane began to go with an older set in the town. The people of this set did not have a very good reputation. They frequented a near-by night club where drinking was common. At first I tried to get Jane to give up her newly acquired friends, but she found them more and more interesting. In answer to my protest about her drinking, she said, " Oh, well, if the rest can, I can. I don't really like to drink, but I want to be popular, and I am going to do what the others do."

Toward the end of the summer Jane was killed in an automobile accident. Her companion had been drinking and had lost control of his car on a sharp curve. Jane paid her life for a cheap popularity. She didn't have the courage of her own convictions. The right kind of people respect a girl who makes her own decisions, who is able to stand on her own feet.

It is always maturing for a girl to make as many decisions for herself as possible. However, a young person should realize that decisions are not wisely made without due consideration of the issues involved. Our companions and the way we spend our leisure are determined by the standards by which we live.

I believe that each of us should formulate in his own mind some reason for his life. Do you remember the talk the Reverend George gave to your Camp Fire group last summer? Do you remember that he told you that each person should think of his personality as a gift from our Creator and that what happens to it depends upon himself? We all have a duty to ourselves to be our best selves.

Our companions can do a great deal to help us to be our best selves. On the other hand, when a person influences, or tries to influence, us to neglect our work and our duty as we see it, he is helping to cultivate our weaknesses, not our strength.

In one of your letters you spoke of Marian's taking you several times to the corner drugstore and your spending some time there over your sodas. You realize that you must decide how much time you can afford to spend in idle visiting. Some is, of course, valuable. From your letter I get the impression that your grandmother wasn't so well pleased with your going.

Whenever we are in doubt about our conduct, as you seem to be in this case, I believe we should face the issue, analyze it, and then let our better judgment, our conscience, guide us. It might help you to ask yourself some questions such as the following: Did you go to the drugstore without your grandmother's consent? If she objected to your going, do you know why? Have you considered her reasons? Should you have been helping your grandmother by going on an errand? Did the group conduct themselves in a creditable manner, or were there conspicuous laughing and talking? Would you have been physically and mentally better off to have spent the time playing tennis, badminton, or some such game? Were your companions the kind you would be proud to introduce to your family?

Affectionately,

MOTHER

Number 3. *Boys Need Guidance in Dating*

Dear Betty,

The letter in which you wondered why the boys in your class so often stand on the sidelines at the school dances watching the girls dance together, rather than asking them to dance, and why the boys seem so friendly but do not ask for dates, came yesterday.

Betty, I think you are mistaken in assuming that the boys are rude or do not like the girls. Boys do not mature as early as girls, and therefore are not interested in dating as soon as girls are. However, the average boy of your age will enjoy the companionship of boys and girls together, and an occasional single date when he has had enough social contact with girls to know how to treat them.

I suggest that you girls arrange some group meetings with the boys. Why not ask your grandmother if you may have some of the boys and girls to a picnic supper to be cooked on the grill in the backyard? Then maybe Annabelle's mother will let her invite the group to play ping-pong in their recreation room. After a few entertainments of this kind, the boys will no doubt realize that they can have a good time with girls and will either ask their mothers to entertain for you or will take you to a movie. I feel sure that in a short time the boys will be seeking the girls' company, not only en masse but also singly.

Affectionately,

MOTHER

Number 4. *Strengthening Friendships*

Dear Betty,

Since I received your letter, in which you told of your disappointment in the way Elizabeth Banning, a person who evidently has the qualities which you admire and whom you would like to have for a friend, has been treating you, I have been wondering if you might not be somewhat at fault. Maybe it would help you to review some of the qualities and values of true friendship.

We do not really make friendships. They grow out of friendly acquaintances. We should cultivate the qualities in ourselves that we admire in others. Then, when we have made these qualities a part of our personalities, we shall attract persons of similar characteristics. You know the sayings, " Birds of a feather flock together " and " You are known by your friends."

I can hear you say, " But, mother, some of my best friends have qualities quite different from my own." That is often true. We do have for friends some people of different temperaments; some who are older; some younger; and others better or less educated than we. However, we do not have friends who are dishonest, insincere, and lacking in sympathy if we ourselves do not possess these qualities. There must be a spiritual similarity before we can have friendships.

I am assuming, Betty, that we have the same conception of friendship. We agree, I believe, that a friend is a person in whose company we can express our thoughts freely and know that they will be understood as we intended them and not misrepresented. We expect that our friends will be trustworthy, sympathetic, understanding, sincere, generous, and loyal, and that they will show respect for our individuality. When we are in our friends' company, we feel happy, contented, and inspired; we can be our true selves with our friends. Our friends help us to achieve better things than we can do alone. They encourage us, rejoice with us in our successes, and grieve with us in our sorrows. It is through working and playing with people who understand and love us that we satisfy our natural longing for human understanding. Our friendships increase our strength and minimize our weaknesses. Of course, you know a friendship must be a give-and-take arrangement. It cannot be one-sided. Each must give as well as receive.

Again I can hear you say, " But, mother, I don't know Elizabeth well enough to know whether she would mean to me all the things you are talking about. I simply admire her and should like to know her better, but she doesn't seem to want to know me better. Can't I do something to make her want to know me?"

I have been trying to say to you, Betty, that the best way to have friends that are really worth while is to live up to your own ideals and standards and to make contacts with people who have interests common with yours. From these acquaintances will evolve friendships.

Of course, you know too that exterior factors, such as personal appearance, manners, and mannerisms, are important when it

Spiritual kinship is necessary for friendships. Courtesy, Ohio Wesleyan University, Delaware, Ohio.

comes to making a favorable impression, which is a forerunner of friendship. To be able to attract people, we must keep ourselves neat and clean; our clothes must be fresh, our bodies clean, our nails manicured, our hair neatly arranged, and our shoes shined and in good condition. All these are important, because strangers judge us from our appearance. They cannot see into our souls and minds.

Our general pattern of behavior is also important in making people like us. We need to be courteous, unselfish, good listeners, and good conversationalists, and we should have many interests. To be really interesting to other people we must feel an interest in them and in life itself. The person who radiates good cheer and good health and has an interest in other people is always well liked.

Now, to speak specifically about Elizabeth, I suggest that you ask your grandmother if you may invite Elizabeth, with another friend or two, over for dinner and games some evening. In this way you will be opening up the avenue of approval to a possible friendship.

Affectionately,

MOTHER

Number 5. *Qualities of Friendship*

Dear Betty,

I was not surprised that you feel a little confused in trying to understand how trustworthiness, generosity, loyalty, sympathy, understanding, and sincerity apply to friendship. In my effort to give you a picture of true friendship, I failed to clarify all my statements. I am sorry.

No doubt, you understand what we mean by the words sympathy and understanding. I like to put the two words together to form the term sympathetic understanding, which means the ability to imagine yourself in another's place and to treat him as you would want to be treated under the circumstances. If you have a sympathetic understanding of a fellow pupil who makes an honest effort to present an interesting class report but fails because of timidity, you will compliment her on the time evidently spent in preparation. You will try to help her overcome her timidity by building up her self-confidence.

When a person is trustworthy, she is worthy of the trust you put in her. We do a lot of thinking out loud in the presence of our friends. It is through this free discussion that valuable thoughts are born. Unless we know that our partners in conversations can be depended upon to interpret our remarks as we mean them, we cannot talk freely in their presence. It is not necessary to say to a real friend, " Now, don't say anything about this." If she is a friend, she respects your confidence. Whenever you find that something which you have said to an acquaintance in confidence has been repeated and given a meaning other than that originally intended, you will know that your acquaintance has not lived up to the trust you have put in her. Unless she changes, she will not be able to qualify as a friend.

Generosity originates in an unselfish personality. The person who is able to forget self and find happiness in doing for others is generous. With a friend we want to share our prized possessions. When our friends come to our house, we get out our good dishes and silver because we want to share with them our best. There is no account-keeping between friends. Each enjoys sharing with the other. On the other hand, a friendship soon dies when one person is a parasite. Most people feel that, when there is no return to their overtures of friendship, the other person isn't really interested in being friendly. Consequently they spend their time with someone else who appreciates being with them.

To be sincere is to be honest, to be free from pretension and hypocrisy. We cannot hope to develop an affection and respect for people who pretend something they are not. Sometimes you will find boys and girls who cultivate a girl because they like to go to her parties or a boy because he is a free spender; that is, they choose their associates on the basis of what they can get from them, not because they like them. They are not sincere.

I am wondering if you are thinking, " Well, I do not want all my acquaintances for friends. I cannot see any harm in going to a girl's party even if she is not a real friend." Yes, you may go to her party, and you may entertain her without being real friends; that is, you may do so occasionally. You will not want to seek her company and spend a great deal of time with her, however, just because she entertains often and nicely. If you do not admire and respect the girl herself, you cannot do this and keep your own self-respect.

We are loyal to our friends when we remain true to them through times of sorrow as well as times of joy. We are tolerant of our friends' mistakes and even of their follies. When someone makes unkind remarks about them, we try to interpret our friends' best selves. We must never expect our friends to be perfect. They have faults, as we have.

However, we do not sacrifice our principles and self-respect to be loyal to a friend. If our friend tells an untruth, we do not shield her by telling another untruth. If our friend has proved herself unworthy of the trust put in her, we must allow her to suffer the consequences so that she can overcome this weakness. If a classmate cheats on a test, it is not an act of friendship to shield her by telling the teacher that she did not. It is better for the girl to realize that she cannot be dishonest and get away with it, that her friends do not approve of such actions. We must not forget that in all our relationships with other people we must be true to our best selves. We should put loyalty to honor above loyalty to friends. We should expect the President of the United States to show loyalty to his country before loyalty to personal friends. In the same way we expect our friends to put loyalty in guiding principles, to their country, and to their duty before loyalty to friends.

Affectionately,

Mother

Number 6. *The Value of Having More Than One Friend*

Dear Betty,

I think you have cause to be displeased with Sallie for wanting to monopolize your time. I also think you are right in not allowing her to do so. No one person can fulfill all the needs of another personality. Everyone has many sides to his personality and is able to enjoy many different people. One person may stimulate you to do some good deed, another to read a fine book, another to play a better game of tennis, another to be more sympathetic or unselfish, and still another to have more self-confidence. The more friends we have, the greater opportunity we have for developing our capacity for being a good friend. This is especially true for young people of high school age. This is the time when you should be learning to understand people. You should be learning

Our capacity for friendship is developed by having a number of friends. Courtesy, Heidelberg College, Tiffin, Ohio.

how to get along with all sorts of people, not with just one person.

I have always liked the following poem by Vlyn Johnson, and I believe you would enjoy reading it:

> I have a friend whose stillness rests me so
>   His heart must know
> How closely we together, silent, grow.
>
> I have a friend whose brilliancy inspires
>   And rarely tires
> When we two warm our spirits at his fires.
>
> I have a friend whose charity delights
>   In others' rights.
> We two sit talking often late of nights.

I have a friend whose discipline I need.
    We have agreed
That neither from this schooling shall be freed.

I have a friend whose calmness some mistake
    But we two make
Of suffering more than just its grief and ache.

I have so many friends — each one fulfills
    Just what God wills;
For he through them His best in me instills.

And so twice fortunate am I to find
    Friends great and kind,
Each one himself, yet part of God's own mind.

    Betty, I am afraid I have been selfish in thinking of you first in this instance. We must also consider Sallie. I hope you will be able to help her see the folly of wanting to confine herself to one person. Sometimes such an attitude is the result of a girl's not having someone in her own family to give her freely of an understanding love. She may be seeking an outlet for her pent-up affection, or perhaps she hasn't been able readily to make friends with a number of girls and boys. I believe it would be a good thing for you to talk frankly with Sallie and to give her some advice on how to get along with other people. You might suggest taking her on a double date sometime. Try to pick out a boy who would be congenial. Then get her to affiliate herself with some group at school, such as the Camp Fire Girls. This will give her an opportunity to become better acquainted with other girls, and a widened circle of friendships will help her to overcome her unnatural attachment for you.

Affectionately,

MOTHER

Number 7. *Dealing with an Uninteresting Proffered Friendship*

Dear Betty,

    Your problems are varied and many. This new friend, Don, is persistent. If he is really anxious to know you better, he is making a mistake by rushing you, but then he hasn't asked me for advice on how to get you to like him. You are the person who wants help, so I shall confine my remarks to your side of the problem.

The friendship of a sincere person is a rare gift. No matter how we feel about another person, we should avoid doing anything that will hurt him when he is offering his friendship. First impressions cannot be depended upon as a basis for friendship. There may be a fine, unselfish character concealed under a rough veneer. We all need to watch for evidences of character in our new acquaintances rather than to judge by more superficial qualities. Maybe this statement does not apply to Don, but I believe you said that he is a new boy in your school who has come in from another state. Of course, I don't know him. Maybe you are right in your judgment of him, but I want to help you judge people with an open mind.

Now for some practical suggestions. Can you introduce him to some other girls whom he might find attractive? Why not try inviting him and Louise Brady, the girl who entered your clothing class a few weeks ago, with some others to a buffet supper? You mentioned that Louise seemed to be having difficulty in getting acquainted. A common difficulty is often a means of drawing people together. After such an effort to help them, maybe someone else will include them in an outing, and gradually they will find congenial companions.

Affectionately,

MOTHER

Number 8. *Should I Pet?*

Dear Betty,

Betty, I believe you would be interested in the reaction of Grace Dunn, a young married friend of mine. She came in soon after I had received your letter asking about petting. She said she could well remember how she felt about her husband when she became engaged to him. She was so glad she had not indulged in petting with the young men whom she had dated before she met the right man.

I wish I could make every girl realize how much early control of her emotions helps in establishing happy relations in marriage. When young people really fall in love, they are fortunate indeed if they can come to their new relationship with a clean slate as far as petting is concerned. Then it is very gratifying to know that you have saved your more intimate expressions of affection for the person you love.

In answer to your question, " How about a good-night kiss?" you should know, Betty, that nature is concerned with the perpetuation of the race and for this reason has constructed our bodies so that this purpose can be accomplished easily. Certain areas of our bodies have direct nervous connection with the sex organs. The lips are one of these areas. A light good-night kiss or a gentle pressure of the hands may mean nothing more than an expression of sincere admiration. A prolonged kiss or continuous embracing, however, is dangerous practice for young people. Girls should realize that they can probably enjoy light petting without feeling a desire for the more intimate expression of love, but that boys are much more easily aroused sexually.

No matter how much you may wish to maintain your own self-respect and keep yourself free from cheapness in your relationship with boys, you cannot play with fire and not be burned. No normal boy or girl can indulge in petting without being aroused to go further.

I am sure I don't need to tell you that in any premarriage sex relationship the girl is the one who pays. Not only does society put a stigma on the girl for such conduct, but also she loses her own self-respect and that of the boy involved.

Girls usually set the pattern for their friendships with boys. The girl who wants to maintain a wholesome comradeship with boys should cultivate a variety of interests. Plan to do things with your boy friends. Take an interest in the athletics and all-school parties as well as in skating, playing tennis, badminton, and any other sports which are available. Then read some interesting books and magazines. You will find, I believe, that as long as you have interesting things to do and to talk about, petting will not become a problem.

Do not forget that some boys try petting because they think the girl expects it, and they do not want to seem immature in the girl's eyes. Such boys are pleased with a girl who, through her varied interests and high standards of conduct, is able to be a comrade without indulging in petting.

Honest, sincere boys recognize as well as girls do that the instinct of love has been given to them for the distinct purpose of founding a home and having a family. They should realize that it will be years before they will be seriously interested in falling

Keep your friendships with members of the opposite sex on the basis of comrades.
Courtesy, Good Housekeeping Institute.

in love, that petting is really a forerunner of marriage, that the gift of creation is one of the most powerful forces in our lives, and that unless the early manifestations of it are kept under control, they are powerless to restrain it. There are many young people who have not heeded these facts and have handicapped their future and the future of the girls they thought they loved by marrying at an early age. In this day of keen competition it is necessary that young people make as thorough preparation for their future life as possible. This means, of course, that they must keep their friendship with members of the opposite sex on the basis of comrades, not lovers.

Affectionately,
MOTHER

Number 9. *Going Steady*

Dear Betty,

The last I heard of Don a couple of months ago, you were wondering how you could get him interested in other people. Now you are wondering if you should go only with him.

When girls first start going with boys, they seem to gain confidence in their ability to attract and keep a boy friend if they go continually with one person for a few months at a time. However, after they have convinced themselves that they have the power to attract and hold friends of the opposite sex, most of them prefer not to spend all their dating time with one person. I believe you will find that it is more exciting and stimulating to go with different boys. It is true that you will have to be a little more alert and " on your toes " to keep things interesting for the boys who are not sure dates, but I believe you will find it more fun than the more lazy attitude which you and your " steady " are likely to develop when dating only one another. You lose the excitement that comes from surprises and the unexpected.

The girl who tends to limit her friendship to one person, be it girl or boy, is limiting her opportunities to enrich her personality. Each person we know calls forth something different in our own personalities. Usually the girl who has known a number of boys rather well will make a better job of choosing a husband than the girl who knows only a few. By becoming acquainted with different people, a girl is better able to judge the qualities of personality and character which will be most congenial to her in a life companion.

If you enjoy going with Don, it seems to me that you can see quite a lot of him without reserving all your dating time for him. You might just tell him that you enjoy being with him and that you enjoy going out with him occasionally (if, of course, this is your feeling) , but that you think it would be better for you both to have the experience of dating other boys and girls also.

Yes, I realize that there are boys and girls who say they like the idea of knowing they will always have someone with whom to go to the school dances, to the movies, and to parties and games. They don't have to worry about whether someone will take them or whether they will have to stay at home alone, but can devote their time to their studies. I have known such cases. Do you remember Mary Williams, who went with Jim Smith all during her high school years, and then he went away to college and fell in love with someone else and married her? Mary had a very hard time getting back into circulation again. Everybody had gotten into the habit of thinking of Jim and Mary as belonging together. Young people who go together steadily should not hesitate to break off whenever either begins to tire of the arrangement.

In some schools there seems to be a great deal of going steady. Usually these attachments are of short duration. When such is the case, no harm is done. When steady dating extends over a period of months with people of high school age, there is a strong tendency for either the couple to become bored with one another but to go on because they don't know how to stop or because they are afraid no one else will date them, or for them to spend too much time petting. In either event the girl and boy involved lose their self-respect rather than gain confidence in their ability to meet their dating problem successfully.

Girls of high school age are more mature emotionally than boys. It sometimes happens that girls still in high school become engaged to boys who have finished school. Usually high school boys are not seriously interested in falling in love. They are too busy preparing themselves to take their place in the world.

Affectionately,

MOTHER

Number 10. *Should I Smoke and Drink?*

Dear Betty,

In your last letter you spoke of Marian's insinuating that you are immature, because you didn't smoke when most of the others in the group did. It is gratifying to your mother that you have enough poise and courage to make your own decisions, regardless of what your companions do. I am also pleased to suggest some points for your coming talk to the Friendship Club on " Why I Do Not Smoke." I shall review for you some of the reasons I used to give you.

We should make our decisions in this matter, as we do on other important issues, by considering its pros and cons, and not by imitating someone else just to make ourselves popular or to be sociable. What are the pros? Smoking gives one something to do with one's hands. It bridges a pause in the conversation when ideas are lacking. It creates a chummy atmosphere.

What are the cons? It is expensive. Statistics show that in 1936 there were consumed in the United States sixty-five packages of cigarettes for every man, woman, and child. Since there are any number of people who do not smoke cigarettes, those who do must consume a goodly number. It is an unclean habit, producing stained teeth and fingers. It leaves a characteristic odor on the clothing and personal belongings of the smoker, and many people feel that this odor is unfeminine. Smoking is habit-forming. People who smoke find it very hard to stop; they tell us it is much easier not to form the habit than to break it. Authorities say that smoking is injurious to one's health, shortening life and producing various ill effects such as speeding up the heart, increasing blood pressure, and irritating the throat and bronchial tubes. If one wishes to smoke with the least danger of impairing his health, he would do well to observe the following suggestions given by Dr. James J. Waring: " (1) Do not smoke until past the age of twenty-one years. (2) Use cigarettes, not more than five daily. (3) Do not inhale or blow smoke through the nose. (4) Smoke only immediately after meals. (5) At least once a year stop smoking for a month or more. (6) Have a health examination periodically."* Do you know of any smokers who are able to live up to these suggestions?

While we are considering the issue of smoking, there is another I have been wanting to talk over with you, one which you have not had to face before this — the matter of drinking. You will find

* James J. Waring, " Hygiene for the Smoker." *Hygeia,* Vol. 3, p. 320, June, 1925.

people who will drink for the same reasons that they smoke — to be sociable, to substitute for stimulating conversation, or to do as the crowd does. Again, these are not valid reasons. One should consider all the facts involved when making an important decision such as this.

Drinking is, of course, much more serious than smoking. One can smoke and still keep his self-control. When people are under the influence of alcohol, they do and say things they would not ordinarily; their inhibitions are dulled; their better judgment is gone; and the nerve cells that help them to direct their emotions are deadened. You know that the first thing we ask when a driver has lost control of his car is, " Was he drinking?" More often than not, the answer is yes. In an article in the *Journal of the American Medical Association* for March, 1937, the following statement is made: " Tests made on twenty subjects by means of a motor-driving apparatus showed that $2\frac{1}{5}$ ounces of whiskey increased the rate of driving 6 per cent and driving errors 13 per cent."*

Probably greater harm comes to girls through the loss of emotional control which accompanies drinking. You remember Emma, who went to a night club with a stranger and found the next day that she was married. That one episode almost spoiled her whole life. It took several years for her to readjust herself after the marriage was annulled. You remember that she changed schools and spent most of her summers away from home. It was a harrowing experience for a young girl to have, all for the sake of what she called a good time.

Again, you are probably saying, " Mother, you always paint the blackest pictures." I admit that it is possible for some people to drink in moderation without apparent harm, but many people are unable to drink in moderation. Even if you yourself are able to " sip the cup but not drain it," your companions, the people who do it because you do, may not be able to keep their drinking under control.

This brings to my mind the case of Margaret and her husband, who began going about with a crowd who served cocktails. Mar-

* " Alcohol and Automobile Accidents." *Journal of the American Medical Association,* Vol. 108, p. 984, March, 1937.

garet was able to take one and stop, but her husband couldn't. As time went on, he drank more and more, until finally their marriage terminated in the divorce courts.

In this day when liquor dealers are doing so much to popularize drinking, each one of us must decide for himself whether or not he is going to swallow their bait. We have to ask ourselves, " Is it worth the price?"

Affectionately,

MOTHER

Number 11. *Choosing a Husband*

Dear Betty,

The introductory sentences of your recent letter have caused me to do a great deal of thinking. When a daughter writes, " Mother, I am falling in love with John Brown, one of the young men from grandfather's office. How can I know that John is the one and only for me?" naturally her mother is concerned and anxious to help her.

Whether you realize it or not, you have in your mind ideals and standards by which you have been evaluating your boy friends. You have known rather well a number of boys who, you have found for one reason or another, did not measure up to your ideals; in fact, they have helped you to form the ideals and standards by which you have been judging John. However, I think it would be a splendid idea for you at this time to consider carefully the standards by which you can evaluate your would-be husband. No doubt some, if not many, of the failures in marriage result from the fact that young people exercise their right to make their own choice without thinking the matter through. We Americans demand that our marriages be maintained on an honest basis with the husband and the wife true to one another. In order to live up to this requirement, it is necessary that a wise choice be made in the beginning. With the freedom to choose comes the responsibility for making a wise choice. Maybe it will help you to clarify your thinking if we first consider your expectations in marriage.

I know you are thinking, " What is mother talking about? I am concerned now only with whether I should allow myself to continue falling in love with John." Yes, I know that is your problem, but how can you know the answer unless you have some purposes and ideals to guide you in your reasoning? Of course, if you were the kind who just drifts with the tide without steering your own course, you would never have written asking for advice. You would just have accepted John and muddled through, hoping for the best.

What, then, do you want in your future life? No doubt you will say, " I want to be happy, to be always in love with my husband, and to have him in love with me. I want my husband to succeed in his work and to be able to provide the necessities of life for our family. I want to be able to do my share toward making our life together happy and profitable to us both. I want us to grow together, and not apart, as the years go by."

With these ideals in mind, you can now ask yourself, " Can John and I build such a home and companionship together?" The most important question is, " Are you and John happier when together than when apart and would you rather be together than with any one else?" Of course, only you and John can answer this question. Are you each anxious to make the other one happy? As long as either of you is not sure, if either of you continues to compare the other with another friend, you had better look elsewhere for a life companion.

If you find that you are attracted to each other physically but do not have common interests — that you do not like to do the same things, that you do not like his friends and family, nor does he like your friends and family — you will do well to discontinue seeing him. You would find that, a short time after you were married, John would be spending his leisure away from home with the people who enjoy the things which he likes to do, and you would be seeking people with tastes and ideals similar to your own. You would have only one thing in common, physical attraction, which is not enough for successful marriage.

How about John's philosophy of life? Do you have the same purposes and aims? If John's ideal of a home has always been to have an apartment in the heart of a large city where he can be near his business, the theaters, and a fashionable club, whereas your dream is a small white house set in the trees, with a large garden in the back; if you get a great deal of satisfaction from attending church regularly, whereas John prefers spending his Sundays reading and attending the movies; and if successful marriage to you means having children to love and care for, whereas John thinks rearing children is a thankless job and a waste of time, you would probably find more things to disagree about in life than to enjoy together.

How about John's health and his family tree? Although it is possible for a couple, one of whom is not in good health, to find great satisfaction in marriage (provided, of course, that there is financial security), as we know from the marriage of Elizabeth Barrett and Robert Browning, the odds are generally against such a union. Life, as you know, can be lived with greater ease and happiness by vitally healthy people than by those for whom it is a struggle.

Every young couple who contemplate becoming engaged should have a physical examination to determine if they are physically fit for marriage. Although the venereal diseases are disastrous to happy marriage, it is possible for a person so infected to be cured if he is treated in the early stages of the disease. Other physical defects may be cured through proper treatment. Ask your grandmother to take you to her physician for such an examination.

And now what does the family tree have to do with it? You know from your study of inheritance that when the same inherited weaknesses or traits occur on both sides of the family, the chances are double that these weaknesses will occur in the offspring. It is wise to study your respective family histories to find how the weaknesses compare. When a couple finds there is danger of the children being born handicapped, they should decide either to forego having children of their own or not to marry. Your grandmother will be able to give you the history of your ancestors.

While age differences are generally not considered a matter of great significance, authorities tend to favor a difference of not more than five years, with the man the older. Generally, the most successful marriages have been between couples over twenty-one years of age. Since John is working in your grandfather's office, I presume that he is somewhat older than you. Then, too, probably you would not be considering marriage for a couple of years at least. You are, of course, about a year older than most of the girls in your class.

I am sorry that I have not had the opportunity of meeting John and of talking face to face with you. So many things which I am writing could be more quickly said, and some things would not need to be said at all. I am thinking now of John's social background. Similar social standing and background help greatly in establishing a harmonious home. Do you remember the wealthy city girl who visited our neighbors, the Butlers, and fell in love with Jack Smith, the football star, and married him? She seemed to make an honest effort to live on his income and to get along with his people, but she finally went back to her father's for a visit and has never returned. It seems that she just could not adjust to the social standards of Jack's friends and family. This same thing has happened in many similar cases.

Difference in social rank seems to be a greater factor in adjustment than do differences in education. Most men, however, are happier when their superiority is not questioned. For this reason, unless the man is unusually successful in his business or profession, he is happier married to a woman with fewer educational opportunities than to one having more education than himself.

Personality and character traits are important factors in any human relationship. Generally, the person who is unselfish, sympathetic, cooperative, nervously stable, free from jealousy, willing to accept responsibility and in the habit of doing so, and who has many interests will, provided the other necessary qualities are present, be an agreeable life partner.

Are you surprised that I have not mentioned money? Most people do not consider money a determining factor in marriage. Some people are happy with it; some, miserable with it. Some are happy without it; some, miserable without it. However, the chances for happiness are better where there is economic security. It is rather difficult to keep your family happy when you are worried about what they are going to eat tomorrow or whether they will have a roof over their heads. Since similar social rank is an important factor in marriage, it is wise for a couple to make sure they will be able to manage their income so that they will be able to maintain the social rank which they consider necessary to their well-being.

You did not mention religion in reference to John. I hope, since you are a Protestant, that he is also. It probably would not make very much difference which of the Protestant churches he belongs to. No doubt you would be able to agree to worship in the same church. There is a wider gap, however, between the Catholic and the Protestant, and couples usually find it more difficult to maintain a happy church life together when their faiths are so different. So often in cases where a Catholic marries a Protestant, one or the other gives up his church affiliation and lives a life apart from the church.

Dr. Roy A. Burkhart in his book, *From Friendship to Marriage,* suggests that people who are more alike than different in personality traits are likely to be happy together. He maintains that a person who is extrovertive, submissive, self-confident, and sociable and has good emotional development will be happier with a person of similar traits than with one who is introvertive, dominant, self-conscious, and nonsocial and has strong neurotic trends.

In this lengthy letter, Betty, I have tried to set up some standards by which you can determine the kind of person you would like to marry. I hope that they will help you come to a wise decision of your present problem.

Affectionately,
MOTHER

Letter No. 12. *Expectations in Marriage*

Dear Betty,

Since writing to you about choosing a husband, I have been wondering if you fully realize the importance of marriage. So often young people become involved in the romance of marriage and forget the more serious side of such an alliance. For a normal, mentally and physically mature couple, marriage can be the most satisfying of life's experiences. However, you need only to look about you to realize that it can bring great sorrow and disappointment.

The attitude a couple has toward marriage is a determining factor in the outcome of their life together. Some young people say, " Oh, well, if we don't get along, we can get a divorce. We can try it out."

I hope that you will never entertain such a thought. Unless young people are serious in their intentions and purposes in establishing a home, they probably will not be willing to take the responsibilities necessary to make a success of their marriage. Establishing and maintaining a happy, successful home require the best that two individuals have to give, and unless they are willing to work at making their marriage a success, it never will be. The person who makes a successful doctor, teacher, or business-man does so because he is determined to be successful. He thinks success; he acts success; and he succeeds. So it is with marriage. Young people who set out to establish and maintain a happy home will no doubt succeed in doing so. The majority of marriages are successful. It is because the failures in marriage are so unusual that we hear so much about them.

Some other young people think of marriage as they have seen it pictured on the movie screen. It is all romance, which takes place between glamorous people in the moonlight. These couples are sadly disappointed and disillusioned to find their romantic lover a real person with faults and annoying peculiarities. Still others marry in the hope of reforming their partners. They soon find that people are not changed by the wedding ceremony. The bride and groom are still real people with a desire to be themselves, with all their little peculiarities and faults.

Partners in marriage must be tolerant of one another. Each must allow the other the privilege of being a real human being with personal liberties and faults that are a part of his personality. Adjusting to one's life companion requires patience, understanding, and a sense of humor. A couple who have grown up in a family with sisters and brothers near their own age and who have worked and played with friends of the opposite sex are usually better able to strike a balance between romance and reality and make satisfactory adjustments to each other than a couple who have not had these socializing experiences.

Betty, I wish I could give you a formula for happiness in marriage, but I am afraid no such thing exists. Each couple must work out their own salvation. However, all families follow very much the same pattern and encounter many of the same problems; therefore intelligent people can profit by the experiences of others. A family is never static; it is constantly changing. With the changes come new problems requiring new solutions. In the beginning, as a couple are adjusting to one another, they are also learning how to carry the responsibilities involved in homemaking.

The new bride in moderate circumstances must learn how to keep her house clean, to plan and prepare meals, to buy household supplies, clothing, and food, and to manage her income so that it will cover all the necessities and leave a proportionate amount for recreation and a rainy day. Along with these homemaking activities, she must also take some part in the life of her community.

Later there are children to care for and educate. Parents must not only allow their children to be independent, but also they themselves must be individuals. They must not dominate the child's life with their desires and ambitions, nor must they be a burden to their children. After the children are educated and married, the parents must adjust to being alone again. Often a mother has given so much of her energy to caring for her family that she has made no place for herself in the community activities, and she finds this last adjustment harder than the others. So you see, there is need for continuous adjusting. There is no formula, but for the couple who are congenial, have courage and faith, and love one another, there are compensations and worth-while satisfactions.

As you know, one of the primary purposes of the home is to nurture children. Some say this is the primary purpose of the home. It is in the home that the citizens of tomorrow learn the ideals and customs of our civilization. You have heard it said that the home is the backbone of the nation. This is very true. When a child is taught to be obedient and to respect the rules governing home life, he is being taught to be a good citizen. As children learn to get along with one another and to respect each other's rights, they are learning how to take their places in society. Along with this training, children are encouraged to be individuals. They learn to respect themselves and to realize their own powers. They learn to express their feelings and ambitions normally and naturally in their own family.

The home also functions as an economic unit in society. Through the family, property is owned and passed on from one generation to another. In primitive times goods were produced in the home as well as consumed there, but today the home has been freed from most of the production processes. In the primitive home yarn was spun; cloth was woven; garments and household linens were sewed; stockings, gloves, and socks were knitted; butter was churned; vegetables and fruits were raised and preserved; meat was raised, butchered, and cured; and bread was baked. The home was heated with wood-burning stoves, the fuel for which had to be hewed in the forest and then cut into proper lengths. All water used in the home was drawn from a well in the yard and carried in. Contrast this picture with the modern city home heated with gas controlled by a thermostat, with its modern bathroom and kitchen. All the food is purchased practically ready to cook, and most of the clothing is bought ready to wear. It is not difficult to understand why women of yesterday (and today in rural communities) played an important economic role in the family life. Their work was as remunerative as the men's. There was no question then about women working outside the home. The wife, as well as her spinster sisters, was needed to produce for the needs of the family. Under such circumstances, a wife was a necessity; a man could not get along alone.

Things are different today. Very often young people must postpone their marriage because the man does not earn a sufficient amount to support a family. In many cases, the most satisfactory solution to this situation is for the girl to continue working after marriage.

When the home was a unit of production, the members of the family depended upon one another, not only economically, but also socially. The members of the family earned their living by cooperating together, and furthermore they played together.

This dependence upon one another drew the family very close together. They stayed together from necessity, and there resulted a strong bond of affection.

With the decentralization of the home has come a weakening of the family bond. The present-day family must consciously plan to strengthen its unity by doing things together. One way this can be done is to insist that the family eat the majority of their evening meals together in some orderly manner. Each member of the family must be taught that he owes something to the group. Then, too, it is wise to plan on spending at least Sundays together. Some families let their friends know that Sunday is family day.

Not only does a home exist for the benefit of the offspring and society, but also for that of the two people who have founded it. If these people are mutually stimulating to each other, so that each lives a richer, more satisfying life and does his work in the world better because of their life together, then the home that they have created will have been worth while. Marriage, even without children, presents many opportunities for developing character in the two participants. Through each one's striving to make the other one happy, they develop sympathy, unselfishness, and loyalty. This fact is clearly shown in the tenderness and concern which old couples who have lived congenially together through a period of time show for one another.

In this letter, Betty, I have been trying to put before you a picture of what you may expect in marriage. I have told you that marriage may be the most satisfactory of life's experiences, but it will depend upon your attitude toward marriage, your ability to adjust to your husband's and children's personalities, your willingness to carry on the responsibilities of homemaking, and your understanding of the purposes of your work as a homemaker. Only you can decide if you want to undertake such responsibilities. I think you are capable of growing into the job if you are willing to give it your best self. I hope you will consider all possibilities before making your final decision.

Affectionately,

MOTHER

Number 13. *Being Engaged*

Dear Betty,

So you have considered carefully the qualities which you think your husband should have, compared John with the standard, and found that he more than meets all your requirements. And, too, you have decided that you are willing, with John's help, to take over the responsibilities of establishing and maintaining a home and family. I am very well pleased with your decision. May your future hold all that you and John hope for it!

Your problem now is, what are you going to do with the two long years before you can get married? I know the time seems long to you, but I assure you it is none too much for you and John to prepare for your long life together. Usually a shorter engagement period, preceded by a long acquaintance, is considered desirable. You and John have reversed this procedure. Since you are both sensible, well-controlled individuals, I believe you will be able to profit by this period of preparation for marriage. You are, no doubt, thinking, " What is there to do? I am ready now."

In one of your letters you spoke of feeling a little inferior intellectually to John. You said he referred to so many things in history and literature about which you did not know. I wonder whether it wouldn't be interesting for you and John to outline a course in reading, either in history or literature, for you. You could do the reading and then discuss it with John. You would also, no doubt, find some things to read together. Or, of course, you could go to night school a couple of nights a week and take a course in either history or literature. In this way, you would be building up between you an intellectual interest, which is a necessary part of successful marriage.

Of course, you will have many personal problems to discuss and to decide, such things as the following: Where are you going to live? Are you going to buy or rent a house? Or are you going to live in an apartment? How much money should one have before buying a house? How should the cost of a home be related to one's income? What proportionate amount of one's income should be spent for the various items of household expenses? Are you going to have children? If so, how many? What church are you going to attend? Should you work after marriage? In order to answer some of these questions to your own satisfaction, you may want to do some reading.

Usually it is wise for an engaged girl to spend some time learning the skills involved in homemaking. Of course, you have had some very good courses in homemaking in school, so that in your particular case you might better spend your time for other study. You will, no doubt, continue to do a great deal of your own sewing.

One of the important purposes of the engagement period is to furnish an opportunity for the engaged couple to become acquainted with one another. You don't really know a person well enough to be married to him until you have seen how he reacts to a great many different situations. Since your engagement is going to be rather long, you will, of course, be seeing a great deal of one another. You should plan to do a variety of things together and to keep up your contacts with your friends. Use this time to enrich your personalities and to strengthen your comradeship by learning to enjoy a number of things together. I have suggested reading. You may add sports, such as golfing and hiking, and the study of nature. You must have already done some work on photography, since you have always been interested in it.

I think you are sensible enough to know, without being told, that it would be unwise for you to spend evening after evening indulging in caresses and fondling one another. It is perfectly natural for people who are in love, as you and John are, to show their affection for one another through physical contact, but you know that a marriage founded on physical pleasures alone will not last beyond the honeymoon. One of your friends may say to you, " Your mother is old-fashioned. Many people use the engagement period to find out if they are sexually suited to one another." Yes, I know the line of argument such a person would use to allow herself to indulge in extreme intimacy before marriage. She would say that morally it is all right with the person to whom you are engaged and that the physical tension experienced by two people in love is harmful to the mental and physical health of the lovers. It has been found, however, that the worries and loss of self-respect caused by extreme intimacy outside marriage are much more detrimental to the well-being of an individual than is the practice of self-control. Any self-respecting person controls not only his sex instinct but also his instinct to fight when he is angered and his desire to overeat when he is hungry. The girl who allows her emotions or those of her lover to be aroused to the point where either is tempted to break their moral standards is jeopardizing not only her present, but also her future, happiness. The psychological factors involved in intimate sex expression are of such importance that there can be no lasting satisfaction to two people who indulge outside wedlock.

Let me advise you again to plan to use your engagement period to prepare for your life together by improving your personalities and enriching your intellectual interests. Include some sports in your plan of activities.

The engagement period is a very good time to become better acquainted not only with the person whom you are going to marry but also with his family. You can't really understand a person until you know his home background. Then, too, if you are well acquainted with your prospective husband, you will know what to expect in your children, for you know there are as many chances that they will look and act like his people as like your own. Also, you may gain an idea of what John will look like when he gets older by the way his parents look now. Both you and John should face your relationship with your families frankly. If you find that either side is inclined to dominate and dictate to the point that you are not allowed to make your own decisions, you will have to learn how tactfully to take your affairs into your own hands. After all, each couple should have the privilege and responsibility of managing their own affairs.

Affectionately,

MOTHER

STUDY-GUIDE QUESTIONS

Letter 1

1. What is the background for the letters given in this unit, " Friendship and Marriage"?

65062

2. What do you think of the advice which Mrs. Johnson gave Betty in regard to getting acquainted in a new school? Give reasons for your answer.

Letter 2

3. What is the distinction Mrs. Johnson makes between popularity and friendship? Do you agree with her point of view? If not, why not?
4. Explain the meaning of the expression our best selves.
5. To what extent should you depend upon your parents in choosing your friends?
6. How can we determine that a person is helping us to cultivate our weaknesses instead of our strength?
7. Do you think that Marian was wise in using the corner drugstore as a place for meeting her friends? How else could she find satisfaction in associating with boys and girls of her age?

Letter 3

8. Why are boys not interested in dating as soon as girls?
9. How can girls prove to boys that they can be interesting company?

Letter 4

10. What does the author mean when she says, "We do not really make friendships. They grow out of friendly acquaintances"?
11. According to your author, what is the necessary foundation of friendship?
12. List the qualities of a friend.
13. How should we feel in the presence of our friends?
14. How do our friends help us achieve better things than we can achieve alone?
15. What can we do to gain friends that are really worth while?
16. What is the relationship between favorable impressions and friendships? What are some of the things that we can do to attract people to us? What is meant by "our general pattern of behavior"? What is the key to making ourselves interesting to people?
17. How did Betty's mother suggest that she might cultivate Elizabeth Banning's friendship? Why would it be better for Betty to invite Elizabeth with other people rather than alone?

Letter 5

18. What do we mean when we say a person has sympathetic understanding? Give an example.
19. Explain in turn the meaning of trustworthy, generous, loyal, sympathetic, and sincere.
20. Why isn't it necessary to say to a friend, "Now don't say anything about this"?

21. When is a person said to be generous? How is account-keeping related to friendship?
22. Why shouldn't we continue to keep our contact with people whom we do not admire and respect?
23. Discuss the relationship between loyalty to guiding principles and loyalty to friends. Give examples.

Letter 6

24. Why should we have more than one friend? Why is this especially true of high school boys and girls?
25. Explain the meaning of each stanza of the poem by Vlyn Johnson.
26. Why do some people want to confine their affections to one person?
27. How may this tendency be overcome? How did Betty's mother suggest that she might help Sallie get over her " crush " on Betty?

Letter 7

28. How should we regard the friendship of a sincere person?
29. Can we depend upon first impressions in choosing our friends? How can we tell if a new acquaintance could become a desirable friend?
30. What do you think of Mrs. Johnson's suggestions for dealing with an uninteresting proffered friendship?

Letter 8

31. How may young people avoid petting?
32. Why should girls take the responsibility of avoiding petting?
33. Why do some boys try petting?
34. Explain what is meant by keeping a friendship on the basis of comrades, not lovers.
35. Do you think Betty's mother has given her sufficient reasons for not petting?

Letter 9

36. What are the reasons for not reserving all one's dating time for one person?
37. What are some of the usual reasons of high school people for going steady?

Letter 10

38. Give the arguments in favor of smoking; those against smoking.
39. Give the rules quoted in your textbook to be followed by smokers who wish to impair their health as little as possible through smoking.
40. What are the arguments in favor of drinking? Those against it?

Letter 11

41. What are the disadvantages of our American custom of allowing young people to make their own choices in marriages?

42. Where does a girl get the standards by which she evaluates her boy friends?
43. Name the nine points which Betty's mother suggested that she consider when deciding whether she and John would be happy together. Be able to discuss each point, giving the reasons why it is important and your own reaction.

Letter 12

44. How does one's attitude toward marriage affect his or her likelihood to succeed in this relationship?
45. How does the picture of marriage usually depicted on the movie screen compare with marriage in everyday life?
46. What are the responsibilities of a bride with a moderate income?
47. Why is it often difficult for a mother to adjust to being alone after her children have left home?
48. Why do some people consider the nurture of children to be the primary purpose of the home?
49. Show that the home is an economic unit.
50. Compare the primitive home with a modern city home. How has the decentralization of home life affected the relationship of the members of the family?
51. How can the present-day family plan to strengthen its unity?
52. What are the purposes of family life, as given in your textbook?
53. Should people who cannot have children get married? Give reasons for your answer.
54. What special attitudes and abilities will help a girl make a success of her marriage?
55. What is the proof that a home has been worth while?

Letter 13

56. Usually, which is more desirable — a short or a long engagement period?
57. Make a list of problems which an engaged couple need to discuss.
58. What did Betty's mother suggest that she and John do to prepare for their life together?
59. Why should an engaged couple not spend most of their time together caressing one another?
60. Why should engaged people become acquainted with their prospective in-laws?

PROBLEMS FOR DISCUSSION

The following have been selected from problems presented by students of Lakewood High School and answered in *The Lakewood High Times,* the school paper.

Getting Acquainted

1. I am in the 10B grade. While in junior high I was only interested in books and studying, and I got for myself the name of " bookish." People thought I was dull — and maybe they were right. I never put myself out to make friends. Now I am sorry and I am trying to remedy this situation, but others seem to take the same attitude as the pupils in junior high. How can I make friends and have a few dates as the other girls do? I don't want to be a ." bookworm " all my life.

2. When I see a service man smile, nod, or speak, should I return or ignore this gesture? Both a newspaper writer and a radio commentator have urged girls to help the boys in the armed forces have a good time when on leave, but some of my personal acquaintances say this is definitely flirting. What should I do?

3. There lives across the street a beautiful girl whom my brother would like to meet. He has asked me to get acquainted with her, but it's just as hard for me because I very seldom see her, although I've spoken to her mother a few times, which might help eventually. Night after night, when he comes home from work he says, " Gee, sis, I wish I could get acquainted with that beautiful girl across the street." Please give me advice so I can give it to my brother.

4. A group of sailors are staying across the street from us. They seem very nice and I would like to get acquainted with them. How can I do this?

5. I have a friend who is out of high school. He is interested in the out-of-doors and likes to roller skate. He cannot dance, but is willing to learn. His best pal is going steady with a girl who has a pretty sister. He met the sister and is interested in her, but he hasn't succeeded in making a date with her. The nights that she goes to night school are the ones that he usually goes out. He has his Sundays free, but the sister is more interested in other things. How can he get the sister interested in him?

Friendships

1. Another girl and I were very good friends until not very long ago she accused me of doing something which I didn't do. Now she won't speak to me. Do you think that I should apologize even if I didn't do it? I would appreciate any help you can give me.

2. My girl friend is very much interested in church work. The boy whom she likes is prejudiced against the church. What can she do to interest him in the social aspects of the church?

3. Bertha felt hurt because her friend Emilie did not invite her to a party to which she invited most of their mutual friends. Emilie had entertained Bertha at dinner a week before the party, so she said she did not feel obliged to invite her to this party. Do you agree with Emilie?

4. Sarah, a junior in high school, has formed a strong attachment for her

English teacher. Should she neglect her friends of her own age, so that she can further cultivate the friendship of the older person?

Going Steady

1. The fellow that I have been going with asked me to go steady with him. I want to but I belong to a club which meets every Friday evening. Both boys and girls are members of the club. After the meeting we usually go some place. This means that I am out with other fellows. When I asked my friend if I should drop the club, he said that it was up to me. Please tell me the right thing to do.

2. I am at the present time going steady with a boy out of school. He isn't interested in going to school athletic events and parties.
I enjoy these activities and have had several invitations from other boys to go to these parties. I would like to know if it would be all right to accept these invitations. I took these things into consideration when I decided to go steady, but at the time I discounted them. If I go steady must I exclude all other dates? Just what is expected of one who is going steady?

3. Do you think a girl in high school should go steady with a boy in college in another state?

4. I have been going steady with a boy from church for four months. Last week my father told me he didn't want me to go steady. My boy friend is nineteen and I am sixteen. We have told each other of our love, but not our parents. I enjoy going with him and we are well suited to each other. I don't want to go with other fellows, because I know they wouldn't measure up to this one. Should I just keep on going with this fellow?

5. Jim and Carolyn had been going fairly steady for several weeks. When Carolyn went with other boys, she tried to keep Jim from knowing about it. Was Carolyn right?

Engagements

1. I have a very good friend who has been going steady for several months. Her boy friend wants to give her a diamond engagement ring for her birthday, which will be in a few months. She is only 18 years old and does not know if she wants to accept the ring. He told her about it. She says she loves him enough to marry him, but not right away. If she doesn't accept the ring, he will think she isn't sincere. This, she says, is not true. What is she to do if he is the type that will not even try to understand her side of the story?

2. A friend has been going with a certain fellow for a long time. He belongs to the Catholic church and she is a Protestant. No one knows about this but her, him, and me. This is a problem she asked me to help her solve but I can't. His parents will not let her marry him if she is not of his religion. What is she to do? Should she tell her parents?

3. I am a senior this semester and hope to graduate this June. After graduation I want to work, but my boy friend wants me to marry him. What shall I do? I don't want to lose him, but I don't want to get married so soon because he may leave for the army shortly.

BOOKS FOR FURTHER READING

Allison, Anne C. E., *Friends with Life*. Harcourt, Brace and Company, New York, 1924.

Black, Hugh, *Friendship*. Fleming H. Revell Company, 1898.

Burkhart, Roy A., *From Friendship to Marriage*. Harper and Brothers, New York, 1937.

Conde, Bertha, *The Business of Being a Friend*. Houghton Mifflin Company, New York, 1916.

Cunningham, Bess V., *Family Behavior*. W. B. Saunders Company, Philadelphia, 1936.

Dennis, Lemo T., *Living Together in the Family*. The American Home Economics Association, Washington, D. C., 1934.

Groves, Ernest R., Edna L. Skinner, and Sadie J. Swenson, *The Family and Its Relationships*. J. B. Lippincott, Philadelphia, 1941.

King, Henry C., *The Laws of Friendship*. The Macmillan Company, New York, 1909.

Price, Hazel Huston, *Living with Others*. Little, Brown and Company, Boston, 1942.

Rockwood, Lemo Dennis, *Pictures in Family Life*. American Home Economics Association, Washington, D. C., 1936.

Weiman, Regina W., *Popularity*. Willett, Clark, and Company, 1936.

Wicks, Robert R., *One Generation and Another*. Charles Scribner's Sons, New York, 1939.

One of the primary purposes of the home is to nurture children.
Courtesy, H. Armstrong Roberts.

SECTION III

UNDERSTANDING AND CARING FOR CHILDREN

UNIT ONE.   WHY DO WE STUDY CHILDREN?

Every child is a potential citizen and the embryo of a new family. The destiny of our individual families and our nation will be determined by the children of today, for the habits that are formed in childhood will be carried into adult life. In nine cases out of ten an honest child becomes an honest adult; a dependable child, a dependable adult; a selfish child, a selfish adult. These character traits will be determined to a great extent by the treatment the child receives from the people around him. Acts which meet with approval will be repeated and will eventually make up his pattern of behavior, whereas those which meet with disapproval will gradually be forgotten and will drop out of his experiences. Therefore the child's behavior pattern will depend on the ideals and standards of his elders.

World War II has made us acutely conscious of the value of children. With so many of our present young adults giving their lives, we must have children in order that our civilization may survive. Whether the best or the worst of the present customs are carried on will depend on how we educate our children. By education we mean not only the child's school experiences but also the things he learns in his home before he goes to school. Psychologists tell us that the child learns more during the first five or six years of his life than during any other equal period of time.

It is important, then, that we have some understanding of child development, so that we may help the children with whom we come in contact to grow into desirable home and community members. As we gain an insight into the lives of children, we also achieve a better understanding of ourselves and our relationship to our family, and thereby we also become better family members and citizens.

Before we can be ready to help in directing the development of children, we should form some conception of our goal. You wouldn't think of cutting into a piece of dress material until you had before you, or in your mind's eye, a partial picture, at least, of the proposed garment, and you would also want to have some knowledge of how to construct the garment. If we are to help direct the development of a child or of children, we should have some idea of what we want our children to be like and should know something of how desirable habits and traits are acquired.

If each of us were to make a list of characteristics of our ideal person, they no doubt would differ somewhat; however, we should agree on certain fundamental qualities, such as health, happiness, friendliness, self-reliance, obedience, courage, and self-control.

STUDY-GUIDE QUESTIONS

1. What reasons are given in your textbook for studying children? Do you know of any other reasons why such a study might be valuable?
2. Do you agree with the list of fundamental qualities of an " ideal " person?

ACTIVITY

Make your own list of the qualities of an ideal person. The list may be divided under such headings as: Character, Mind, Social Traits, Health.

UNIT TWO. WHY DO CHILDREN REACT DIFFERENTLY TO THE SAME TREATMENT?

CHILDREN ARE INDIVIDUALS AT BIRTH

A mother remarked, " I don't understand why Mary and Betty are so different. They have the same parents, have grown up in the same environment, and have always been treated the same." Children of the same parents are not necessarily alike. They differ in emotional make-up as well as in mental ability and in appearance. One child may be slow to react to stimulations of all kinds. He is the type that is calm, complacent, usually happy, and easy to manage and get along with. Such a child can stand interference with his routine without being upset. If this calmness, which is usually a desirable trait, is exaggerated to the point of sluggishness, the parents of a child so constituted should see that he has enough variety of stimulation to help him develop to capacity. Another child may be so alert to all external stimulation that he is constantly active. He is never interested in resting. When he gets tired, he becomes more active, and his voice grows louder and more shrill. Such a child will need the influence of a calm mother who is able to train him in regular habits of everyday living that will furnish a balance for his super-exuberant personality. As you can readily see, these two types of children cannot be treated exactly alike. One may need stimulation, and the other a calming influence.

Then there is the child who, when he is disappointed, withdraws into himself, and the other type who tries to work off the depressed feeling which accompanies disappointment. The former may find pleasure in reading, writing, and thinking, whereas the latter will enjoy activities of all kinds and varied contacts with people. The psychologist speaks of these types as introverts and extroverts. Betty and her sister Mary are good examples of these two types. Their mother can tell without being told when either has had a bad day at school. Usually when the girls come home they seek out their mother for a bit of quiet conversation about the day's happenings. After a trying school day, Betty is unusually quiet and spends more time than usual reading, whereas Mary talks at great length about her troubles and then organizes some activity with the neighborhood children.

Most people are really a combination of the two types; that is, they possess characteristics of each. Such people are called ambiverts. Authorities agree that the ambivert is the most normal and healthy.

The child who has strong tendencies toward the introvert type may need help in learning to enjoy and to appreciate people. He is inclined to brood over failure to adjust in his play or in social life and may use daydreaming as a means of escape rather than make further attempts to work and to play with others successfully. Such a child should not be punished by closing him up in a room alone or by making him sit in a chair to think over the situation. However, he should be allowed the pleasure of quietly thinking things through for himself.

On the other hand, the child who is strongly inclined toward the extrovert type should be taught to enjoy a certain amount of solitude. He will, no doubt, need to be taught to enjoy reading and thinking things out for himself.

Children differ also in their motor coordinations. They do not all learn to walk at the same age, nor are they all equally graceful in dancing or skillful in playing tennis. We older people must be very patient and must allow children to develop according to their own rate. We must not expect the same performance from all, and we must not try to rush them into activities for which they are not prepared.

THE ENVIRONMENT OF EACH CHILD IS DIFFERENT

There are factors in a child's life that subtly influence his personality development. One is his position in the family. It is very hard for parents to treat all children alike. The oldest is sometimes favored because he is the first born, or he may be spoiled because his parents knew very little about children when he was born. The youngest may be bossed by everybody or spoiled by everybody because he is the " baby." Often the only boy in a family of girls grows up with an exaggerated idea of his sex.

Jim was the only boy and the third in a family of five children. Each girl was responsible for some household task, but Jim was not expected to make any contribution toward the work of the family. The girls helped keep the house clean, launder the clothes, prepare the food, and wash the dishes, while Jim listened to the radio, built airplanes, or read the paper. When only part of the family could go on a trip, Jim was always chosen as one to go; and when money was scarce, Jim's clothes were bought first. In other words, Jim was the favored child. It was assumed that Jim would go to college, although the girls went to work on leaving high school. The mother said, " The girls will get married; they don't need to go to college." Is it any wonder that Jim grew up with the idea that his sisters should cater to him instead of feeling a responsibility to protect and take care of them? Is it any wonder that he treated all women as intellectually inferior? It is very important that children have a sane attitude toward themselves. They should feel that they occupy an important place in the family and in their world, but they should realize too that other people are also important.

Sometimes we think of environment as our physical surroundings. We forget that our environment is made up also of the people with whom we associate. Our human environment is as important as our physical in influencing our personality development. This fact is evident when we think of how much easier it is to do the right thing when we know that our associates expect us to, and how we may be stimulated by interesting and interested companions to think and express ideas and thoughts which are entirely new to us. We respond to the expectations of our companions. Since parents naturally expect different things from their different children, in this respect each child's environment is different.

STUDY-GUIDE QUESTIONS

1. In what ways do children differ at birth?
2. Do you agree that the environment of each child in the family is different? What reasons in support of this view are given in your textbook?

UNIT THREE. HOW CAN WE HELP CHILDREN TO BE HEALTHY?

VALUE OF GOOD HEALTH

Statistics show that children who are underdeveloped physically do not do so well in school as those who are properly nourished and generally well cared for. There is a correlation between vital health and ease of learning. We know also that the child who doesn't eat and sleep right is more given to temper tantrums and is generally irritable.

Today we say people are healthy when they have enough energy and vitality to meet their everyday problems without undue fatigue and irritation. They should be happy in doing their work and in carrying out their regular routine of living and should also have enough reserve power to adjust to occasions when the strain is a little greater or sickness comes. Similarly, we expect a normal child to be able to live peaceably and happily through his regular daily routine without undue fretting and crying. He should be adjusted to a scheduled living which brings joy and peace.

PRENATAL INFLUENCES

It is important that a child come into the world equipped with a sound body. Every pregnant woman should put herself under the care of a physician as soon as she is aware of her condition. He will be able to advise her as to how she should take care of herself and will give her any medical attention needed as well as advice concerning her diet.

In many states today a couple must pass a physical examination before they can procure a license for marriage; but if this has not been done, it is doubly necessary to have a medical examination during early pregnancy. The harm done by syphilis may be prevented if discovered before pregnancy is far advanced. Healthy parents need have no fear of not producing healthy offspring.

Although other diseases are not usually inherited, the tendency

104

toward them may be, and the child who inherits the tendency toward a disease starts out with a handicap.

There has been controversy for years over the effect of inheritance upon the mental ability of the child. Some of the more

Scheduled living promotes happy, healthy childhood.
Courtesy, H. Armstrong Roberts.

recent research tends to place the emphasis upon environment rather than inheritance as a factor in the development of the child. This is very heartening to both parents and educators. For physical characteristics, such as the color of the eyes and shape of the face, we know that inheritance is chiefly or entirely responsible.

Some people are still afraid of " marking " their children by unpleasant sights and experiences during pregnancy. Science tells us that abnormalities and birthmarks result from either inheritance, as in the case of six fingers or toes, or some constriction which interferes with the proper development of the fetus, as in the case of red or white spots on the child's skin.

CHOOSING FOOD FOR CHILDREN

Nature provides the best food for the infant, which is, of course, his mother's milk. The child who is fortunate enough to have a mother able and willing to nurse her baby will have few food problems. However, due no doubt to our modern tempo of living, few mothers of today are able to produce enough milk for their babies. Even when a child is breast-fed, additional foods are included in his diet at an early age.

The diet for breast-fed and artificially fed babies alike should be prescribed by a physician. Usually during the first year the following foods are added to the child's diet: cod-liver oil, orange or tomato juice, strained cereals, some vegetables, egg yolk, and some fruits.

By the time the child has reached the age of three years, he will have learned to chew his food and will be eating almost all the vegetables which the family eats.

Children should not be given highly seasoned foods, tea, coffee, or other drinks which contain the stimulant caffeine. Care should be taken to see that easily digested foods are given to children. Avoid giving them fried foods and too much fat. Boiled or baked potatoes, rather than fried potatoes, should be served, and whole milk, rather than cream, used for their cereal. A thorough understanding of the importance of food to health may be acquired by a study of Unit 7 in Section VI of this book.

The following list of foods given in *The Road to Good Nutrition*, a bulletin prepared by the Children's Bureau, United States Department of Labor, may be used to advantage in planning dietaries for children:

Milk. One and one-half pints to one quart.
Fruit. Two or more servings. One should be citrus fruit or tomatoes or other good source of vitamin C.

Vegetables. Potatoes and at least one or two other vegetables (green or deep-yellow vegetables often).

Eggs. One egg.

Lean meat, fish, or other protein-rich food. One or two servings.

Whole-grain or enriched bread and butter or fortified margarine. At two or three meals.

Whole-grain, enriched, or restored cereal. At one or two meals.

Cod-liver oil. One to two teaspoonfuls a day to children between one and two years of age. Older children need cod-liver oil during cold or cloudy seasons; ask the doctor how much to give.

Additional foods, as needed, to satisfy the child's appetite and to provide energy. The amounts will vary with the age and size of the child. These additional foods should not take the place of the foods already listed in the plan.

If a child gets these foods every day in the amounts specified, the parents can be reasonably sure that his needs are being met.

The following food plan, taken from the booklet, " How To Feed Young Children In The Home " by Sweeny and Buck, shows how the foods which are needed daily may be included in the menu:

BREAKFAST	DINNER	SUPPER
Fruit	A main dish of eggs,	A vegetable, creamed,
Cooked cereal	cheese, meat, or fish	scalloped, or baked
and	Cooked vegetable	Sandwich
Whole-wheat toast	Raw green vegetable	or
Milk to drink	Bread and butter	Bread and butter
	Dessert	Cooked fruit
	Milk to drink	Milk to drink

ESTABLISHING GOOD FOOD HABITS

A child is benefited by the food that he eats, but not by the food that he leaves on his plate. To be healthy and happy, he must eat not only the right food, but enough food. Although there are many children who do not have good appetites for the right food, there is really very little reason why this should be the case.

It is important that children be trained from infancy to eat at regular intervals. When our stomachs become accustomed to having food at regular times, the digestive juices are secreted at these times, and we become hungry. Not only should there be regular times at which to eat, but food should not be taken at other than mealtimes. This does not mean that the young child should eat only three meals a day, but rather that he should eat his meals at the same time every day. He may eat three, four, or five times a day, depending upon his age.

Since Mr. Brown had very little time at home, the Brown family took advantage of the dinner hour for discussing their family problems. The children's report cards were discussed, the various household bills were presented for Mr. Brown's approval, and family policies and discipline measures for the children were reviewed and discussed. Jim, who was a vigorous, athletic boy, was able to enjoy his food in spite of the many family arguments, but Sally, who was sensitive to emotional stresses, often asked to be excused before the others had half finished their meal. Mrs. Brown couldn't understand why Sally didn't have an appetite for her food.

Mealtime should be a pleasant occasion. Food is more easily digested in calm, friendly surroundings than in a strained, noisy atmosphere. Even though all the meals of the family cannot be taken with as much leisure as might be desired, at least whatever conversation there is can be free from arguments and tension. All the members of the family should come to the table at the same time and be seated in an orderly manner. If the food is served and passed to each individual without asking him to make choices, if the elders eat all the food served to them, and if there is quiet and peace during the meal, the children will usually grow up with the idea of eating whatever is served to them and will be able to digest their food.

Young children should not be served large portions. When Jimmie, aged four, was presented with an adult serving of turkey, potatoes, and all the trimmings of a Christmas dinner, he looked at it a few minutes, then slipped out of his chair, saying, " 'scuse Jimmie, please." Try to give children just about what they can eat. Too much food tends to discourage them and takes away their appetites. A small cup or glass for milk, refilled several times from a small pitcher, is more tempting than a large glass of milk, which is difficult to handle. Nor should too great a variety of food be served at one meal. This practice is confusing to the young child and encourages him to make choices, a habit which should be discouraged.

New foods should be added gradually to the child's diet. By reason of the strained vegetables which young children are given, many children grow up liking a variety of vegetables without being conscious of the fact. We tend to like the food which we are used to. The wise mother introduces new foods so gradually and in such small quantities that the child doesn't realize he is eating anything different.

Children should be allowed to handle their own eating equipment as soon as they are able. Courtesy, *Consumer's Guide.*

As soon as the young child is able to handle his eating utensils with any degree of skill, he should be allowed to feed himself. Usually, he can do this when he is about one year old. He enjoys doing it, and he is more likely to enjoy his food than if someone else feeds him. Do not make a child the center of attention at meal-time. Allow him to take his natural place in the family circle. Take his eating as a natural, normal process. If he doesn't eat something which is served to him, do not show concern. He will make up for it at the next meal if he is not given something between times.

Remember that children learn many things through imitation. Food habits are not an exception. Little Johnnie will drink his milk much more readily if father drinks milk. Little sister will very likely not like beans if older sister refuses to eat them.

In eating, as in other things, it is much easier to train a child to have good habits than to correct him after he has formed poor ones. However, eating habits can be changed if we are persistent and patient in following the suggestions given above. A child may have to go without a few meals, but that will do him less harm than eating the wrong foods for the rest of his life. The child who is allowed to drink soda pop or eat candy or ice cream at any time he chooses will naturally not be hungry for vegetables and milk at mealtime. It will take concentrated effort to retrain a child with irregular eating habits to a regular schedule.

SLEEP AND CHILDREN

An infant sleeps from eighteen to twenty-two hours out of twenty-four. At three years, he sleeps about thirteen hours, and when he has reached the age of six, he sleeps about eleven hours. The younger child should use about two hours of his total sleeping time for a nap in or near the middle of the day. After the child is three and one-half years old, he may or may not nap during the day. At any rate, he should rest quietly on his bed from one-half to one hour with his outer clothes removed.

When children enter school, it is wise to have them rest quietly for a short time before the evening meal. The afternoon nap and the rest period tend to improve night sleep for children and help to keep them happy and more stable.

It is not necessary to stop the normal activities of the family so that a child may sleep. Children are not disturbed by ordinary noises. However, a child will sleep or rest better if he is put on his own bed in a room alone. The older child who rests, but does not sleep, needs to have only his outer clothing removed. The young child, however, should be put to bed in the same way as he is for night sleeping.

After a child is one and one-half years old, he should sleep alone. He should not share a room with an adult. As soon as the child grows out of his crib, he should be put in a full-length bed.

When two children share the same room, two single beds are better than one double bed. The mattress should be firm, and the covering lightweight in the amount suitable to the season or climate. Children should sleep without pillows. Sleeping garments should be comfortably large and suitable in weight to the season. The room should be well ventilated without a draft over the child. Two chairs with a blanket stretched across them, placed in front of an open window, make a very good screen.

Undue restless sleep in children may result from one of several causes. When such a condition exists, check to see that the child gets plenty of exercise in the sunshine, that his bowels are regular, that he isn't too tired at bedtime (omitting the daytime nap or rest period may cause overfatigue), that he isn't too excited by vigorous play just before going to bed, and that his mind is free from disturbing fears or worries.

ACQUIRING HABITS OF CLEANLINESS

We must remember that children cannot enjoy their play and benefit from it if they are constantly being reminded to stay out of the dirt and to keep their clothes clean. We expect a child to be benefited mentally, physically, and socially by play. This is possible only when he is dressed in clothing that is washable, durable, and comfortable, when he is given some freedom to choose and to direct his own activities, and when he knows that his play clothes are for play and that he is free to use them accordingly.

Wise parents do not worry about how dirty their children get, but they are careful to see that their faces and hands are washed before they eat and that they have a warm, cleansing bath once a day. The younger child, who goes to bed very soon after eating his supper, is usually given his bath just before his nap time. Sponging a child at bedtime in hot weather will make him more comfortable and less apt to be restless.

A child should gradually be taught to bathe himself. When he shows an interest in helping himself, allow him to do so. It takes more time to show him how to give himself a bath than to do the job for him, but the benefits are worth the effort. The child who does things for himself is happy and is learning to be independent. Children who have been taught are able to wash their hands at from three to four years of age and are able to take a bath at five or six.

Children should be taught not to dawdle in the bath. Have the child get his soap, washcloth, and towel, run the hot water (so as to heat the tub) and then the cold until the bath water is comfortably warm, get into the tub, and wet his entire body. He

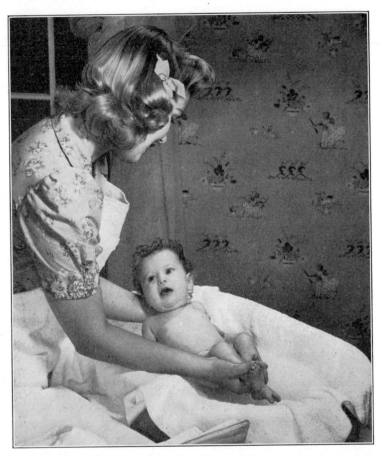

Care is necessary in bathing a baby. A towel placed in the pan gives the infant a feeling of security. Courtesy, *Better Homes and Gardens.*

should then stand up, lather himself, scrub his body thoroughly with the washcloth, sit down in the water, wash off all the soap, and, lastly, rinse himself with a warm spray gradually becoming cold. If the child does not react normally to cold water, use only a warm spray.

LEARNING DESIRABLE HABITS OF ELIMINATION

By the time children reach the age of eighteen months, they should usually have dry days; and at two to two and one-half years, they should usually go through the nights without wetting the bed. Notice that we have used the word *usually*. Don't be disappointed if there are mishaps. It is a difficult thing for a child to learn to eliminate only when he is on the toilet. To form this habit takes a long time. Be very patient! Compliment the child when he keeps dry, but do not expect him to be entirely reliable for four or five years. Mother must take the responsibility during the first few years.

Usually mothers start training their babies to use a small chamber for bowel movements soon after they are eight months old. They keep a record of the time of the bowel movement for several days previous to starting the training. It is wise to keep such a record, and then, following this schedule, to put the baby on the wide-rimmed vessel placed on one's lap a few minutes before the regular time for defecation. Do not hold the baby in this position for longer than ten minutes. If nothing happens, do not become discouraged. Repeat the procedure at the next regular time for defecation. In a short time, you will be rewarded for your efforts. Usually, by the time the child is one year old, he will be using the vessel for bowel movements.

Since the child urinates so often (at one year from twelve to sixteen times in twenty-four hours), and since the sensory experience is not very intense, it is more difficult to train him to urinate only when on the toilet. He may, however, be trained for this habit in the same way — by keeping a record of the times when he urinates and then placing him on the chamber or toilet a few minutes before you expect him to urinate.

After the child is able to sit alone comfortably, he may be trained to use a small toilet seat, which can be placed over a regular-sized toilet seat. As he becomes able to care for himself, small portable steps placed in front of the toilet will be helpful.

It is necessary that the child's clothes be made with large buttons

about one-half inch in diameter if he is to learn to help himself at
the toilet. He can usually acquire this ability by the time he is
four years old.

HEALTHFUL CLOTHING FOR CHILDREN

Clothing for children should be simple in design, lightweight,
and durable. It should be warm enough to keep the child's body
at its normal temperature. The season, climate, and the child's
activity determine how much clothing he should wear. A child
should not perspire too much when he is playing. Many mothers
who live in well-heated homes dress their children in the same
clothing for house wear in the winter as they do for cool days in
the summer. Snowsuits are used to cover their entire bodies
when they go outdoors. On warm summer days sunsuits enable
children to get the benefit of the ultraviolet rays of the sun.

In order that children may learn to undress and dress themselves, their clothing should be made so that they can easily
manipulate it. When possible, their clothes should be fastened
down the front with large buttons. The slide fastener is also suitable for children's clothes. Plackets should be long enough for
ease in taking off and putting on garments.

Children should be so dressed that they are unconscious of their
clothing. This will be the case if their garments are comfortable
and not too large nor too small, and if they are similar to those of
the other children in their group.

STUDY-GUIDE QUESTIONS

1. What physical factors affect the child's ability to learn easily?
2. How is a healthy person described in this section of your book? How
   does this description compare with that given in Section VI?
3. To what extent is a child's health affected by inheritance? His mental
   ability?
4. Why should a mother nurse her baby if she can?
5. What foods are usually added to the milk diet of a child during his
   first year? What foods should be avoided in children's diets?
6. What things can a family do to train a child in acquiring good food habits?
7. By referring to pp. 256–271 in Section VI of your textbook, state reasons
   why each of the foods included in the daily check list is important in a
   child's diet.

8. How many hours a day should an infant sleep? A three-year-old? A six-year-old? How much of the sleeping time of each age group should be used for daytime naps? Why are daytime naps desirable?

9. If a child is not sleeping well, what steps would you suggest to correct this condition?

10. Why shouldn't we expect children to remain immaculate when playing? At what age should we expect children to wash their hands and face? To take a bath?

11. Describe the procedure given in your text for taking a bath.

12. At about what age would you expect children to have dry days? Dry nights? To be entirely reliable in habits of elimination?

13. At about what age do mothers start training their children for bowel movements? Outline the method of training to be followed for both bowel movements and urination.

14. Why do mothers train their children to control their bowel movements before they teach them to control the emptying of the bladder? What are some aids that might be used in teaching children habits of elimination?

ACTIVITIES

1. Using the daily list and the food plan on pp. 106–107 of your textbook, plan a set of menus for a week for a child six years old.

2. Using magazines, daily papers, or catalogues from mail-order concerns, cut out pictures of suitable equipment for sleeping, eating, bathing, and training in bathroom habits for young children.

3. Either cut out or trace pictures of suitable clothing for a child three years old. Give reasons for your choice of pictures.

4. Ask a mother to give a demonstration in correct bathing of the baby.

5. If possible, observe a child either in his home or in a nursery school and write a report answering fully the following questions: Is the child happy? Does he live by a regular schedule for eating and sleeping? Can he control his eliminations? Are his clothes easy to manage?

UNIT FOUR. HOW CAN WE HELP CHILDREN MAKE DESIRABLE ADJUSTMENTS TO EVERYDAY LIVING?

A socially and emotionally adjusted person is happy, contented, independent, cooperative, unselfish, self-reliant, self-controlled, friendly, cheerful, and unafraid of harmless things. Such a person is free to develop his own personality. He has not been enslaved to his parents by bonds of dependence.

ACQUIRING INDEPENDENCE

Probably one of the hardest things parents, especially mothers, have to do is to allow their children to develop into independent, self-reliant personalities with the ability to make decisions and to control themselves. Often mothers say, " I hate to have my baby grow up." Such women are unknowingly harming their children and being very selfish.

Lessons in independence may be given very early in a child's life. The mother who teaches her child to amuse himself during his waking hours is teaching him to be self-reliant. Then, too, if he is allowed to explore the world about him and find out things for himself, he will gain in independence. He should be allowed from the very beginning to do as many things for himself as possible. Parents and older brothers and sisters should, of course, be willing and able to help enough to prevent him from becoming discouraged and should introduce new ideas when they will be stimulating. When the baby drops his rattle, let him reach for it himself; when you give him his bottle of milk, allow him to hold it himself as soon as he is able; when he begins to eat with a spoon, allow him to feed himself, even though in his first efforts he spills more food that he eats; when you put him to bed, allow him to do as much as he can toward undressing himself. A child learns to do by doing. In all these activities let the child do the thing his way; give him a chance to experiment and to find out things for himself.

Then, as the child grows older, allow him to help you do things. Even though it takes a little longer when he washes the dishes and they aren't done so well, let him do the job. The child will be acquiring self-reliance and learning to get satisfaction from accomplishment. He will also be learning to take some responsibility for the work of homemaking.

A child who does things is learning independence.   Courtesy, Brer Rabbit Molasses.

Even though you get satisfaction from doing things for a child, remember that, when you allow him to do for himself, you are helping him to develop into the kind of person who will be able to take his place in the world.

STEPS IN THE CHILD'S EMOTIONAL DEVELOPMENT

The very young baby shows an interest in the person who does things for him. Gradually he becomes interested in other people. A two-year-old enjoys playing near another child, but he won't really play with other children until he is about five years old.

Very young children enjoy playing near others of their own age, but do not actually play with them. Courtesy, British Information Service.

It is desirable that children have the opportunity to play with others of their own age. Only in this way are they able to learn to give and take, to lead some of the time and to follow some of the time. When a child is always the weakest and the least experienced in the group, he will grow to think of himself as inferior to others.

Jane was six years younger than her twin sisters. The twins were taught to protect and take care of their younger sister. They delighted in doing things for her. When Jane started to put on her rubbers, one of the twins did the job for her; when she started to build a house, she wasn't allowed to finish it alone. The twins were ready to help in every way. Fortunately Jane's older sister Betty took a course in child care at school. She began observing her sisters for a class project, and discovered how dependent Jane was becoming. She talked the situation over with her mother, who planned opportunities for Jane to spend some time each day with children her own age and explained to the twins that they were hindering instead of helping Jane by their constant attention. Under the new regime Jane gained in independence and self-confidence.

On the other hand, if a child is always the smartest and the most skilled, he will learn to think of himself as being superior to others. Neither attitude is desirable. A child should grow in respect for others' abilities as well as his own and should learn to respect the rights and property of others.

Most children go through the gang age at eight to ten years of age. This is a natural step in their development and should be so regarded. During this stage most of a child's social interest centers on the gang. He is loyal to his friends, and his conduct is governed by their standards. Such organizations as the Boy Scouts, the Camp Fire Girls, and other junior youth clubs provide excellent opportunity for the development of the natural cravings for group activities at this age. The foundations of many fine characters have been strengthened in these organizations.

At early adolescence, usually from twelve to fourteen years, young people tend to concentrate their affection and attention for a period of time on one person of their own sex. This is the age of hero worship. The hero may be a teacher, a leader of some group, or a character in literature or history. Since young people during this stage of their development are so easily influenced by others, it is easy to understand why parents are anxious to have their children associate with people of fine moral character during their formative years,   .

If these early foundations have been carefully laid, young people will be prepared for the next step of emotional life, that of making many friendships with girls and boys of their own age, which usually comes with later adolescence. They will have acquired standards and ideals by which to judge their new friends and patterns of behavior which will enable them to grow in the power of making friends. From these years of later adolescence, they will step naturally into the next step of their emotional development, that of choosing a life partner and founding a new family.

We have pictured for you the emotional development of a normal individual. Unless a child has understanding parents who are willing to free him from selfish parental love, however, he will not be able to travel smoothly through the various stages of his emotional life.

Every child at all ages should feel secure in the affection of his family. He should feel that his family care about his successes and failures and that they are ever ready to help him to succeed. Older sisters should show their love for younger brothers and sisters, not only by physical demonstration, but also by playing with them. Children should learn to love people for their spiritual and intellectual qualities as well as for their physical qualities.

On the other hand, if children are petted and coddled to excess, they will become very dependent. Such children will have difficulty in passing normally from one stage to another in emotional development.

DEVELOPING A WHOLESOME ATTITUDE TOWARD SEX

Writers on the subject of sex education seem to agree that the most important factor in this phase of education is the attitude of the child's parents toward sex. The child who grows up in a home where the parents love and respect one another, are able to maintain a harmonious relationship in the family, and treat the problems of sex in a matter-of-fact manner will stand a good chance of making satisfactory sex adjustments.

Although it is desirable to teach children to know the parts of the body by name and the function of each part, this knowledge is not an insurance against sex problems arising. Authorities appear to agree that whenever a child asks a question concerning where babies come from, the differences between girls and boys, and the like, it should be answered truthfully and just fully enough to satisfy the child's curiosity. It is advisable to find out what the child is thinking so that we may be able to answer the child wisely. The manner in which the first questions are discussed will determine whether the child will come with others as they arise.

Older people may help children regard members of the opposite sex as comrades rather than sweethearts by so regarding them in their own minds. Many an unconscious natural relationship with a playmate of the opposite sex has been spoiled for a self-conscious child by teasing from older people who should have had some absorbing interests of their own.

As the parent is teaching the child the physiology of his and his sister's body, the origin of babies, and the roles of the mother and the father in reproduction, he should also be instructing the child in the necessity for controlling many of our natural instincts and for considering the desires and rights of others.

LEARNING TO BE UNAFRAID OF HARMLESS THINGS

Psychologists tell us that children are afraid of two things at birth — a loud noise and lack of support. All other fears, such as being afraid of the dark, dogs, and policemen, are acquired.

Do you play as good a game of tennis when you are playing with someone of whom you are afraid? Most people find that they are very awkward and unable to hit the ball when they are overconcerned about how they are playing. This is almost always the case when fear is present. We lose our courage and self-confidence and are unable to cope successfully with the situation. Fear makes cowards of us all.

Children who are constantly afraid develop an inferior attitude toward meeting the problems of everyday living. Sometimes such a child becomes timid and shrinks from taking responsibilities. Instead he may try to hide his feeling of insecurity by bragging and boasting. In either case, he is developing undesirable character traits. A child should be taught to be cautious, but not afraid. He should be taught that it is sensible to learn to swim before going into deep water and learn something about riding before getting on a spirited horse. He should be taught to realize that there is danger when a person is not acquainted with a situation or does not have the skill required to cope successfully with it.

He should also learn through experience that, when he acts in such a way as to offend his companions, he will be ostracized by them; that when he spends his money today, he will not have it tomorrow; and that when he overeats, he will be sick. In other words, he should learn intellectual fear, which keeps adults from going hungry, prevents them from losing their self-control, and helps them in many cases forestall disaster by means of precaution.

Johnny may be afraid of the dark because sister Anne is afraid of it, or he may be afraid of a storm because his mother shows fear when a storm comes. Children learn a great many things through imitation, and, of course, all kinds of fears may be acquired in this way.

Sometimes children learn to be afraid of strangers because they have suffered some unpleasantness at the hands of a stranger. Such was the case with Susan, who, after spending the afternoon with a woman who was strange to her, showed great fear of all women except her mother, her grandmother (who wore glasses), and other women wearing glasses. Evidently Susan associated glasses with her grandmother, and since she was very fond of her grandmother, she was not afraid of any woman who wore glasses. After this fear had persisted for several weeks, Susan's family moved into a new neighborhood. Susan was very much interested in all the activities connected with moving, and her mother hoped she would forget her recent fear. However, when Susan first saw the new neighbor, Mrs. Brown, whose backyard joined theirs, she cried and ran to her mother. Susan would allow Mr. Brown to pick her up and she would sit on his lap; but when Mrs. Brown came near, she would become very much upset and would cry. Susan was not only afraid of Mrs. Brown; she would cry whenever her mother had a woman guest, when the cleaning woman came, or when she met a woman on the street.

Finally, the situation became very embarrassing to both Mrs. Brown and Susan's mother. Mrs. Brown decided to make a special effort to win the child's affection. She was careful not to go too near the child, but would make some friendly remark about the pretty dress Susan was wearing, would talk about Susan's dog, of which the child was very fond, or perhaps would offer her a pretty flower. Very, very gradually the child became more tolerant of her new neighbor, and finally, after some weeks, she became very fond of Mrs. Brown. With her affection for Mrs. Brown came a friendly attitude toward strangers, and today Susan has completely forgotten her old terror of them.

Do you see what Mrs. Brown did to help Susan overcome fear? She got Susan to associate her with pleasant things, things which Susan liked. Remember, too, that Mrs. Brown was very patient. Under no circumstances did she force the situation. She let Susan gradually become acquainted with her, always under favorable conditions. This is a very good method to use when helping a child to overcome an acquired fear.

Some parents are unwise enough to threaten children with, " If you aren't good, the policeman will come and get you " or " If you do that again, I will call the doctor to see you." Is it any wonder such children develop fears of people whom they should be taught to trust?

As in the case of Susan, a fear may be transferred from one person, thing, or situation to another which is similar. A small child who lived on a farm had been frightened by a hen which tried to peck him. After that he would say " bite " when he saw a feather in the yard. Sometimes children who are afraid of cats will express fear of a fur coat.

Fear may also be acquired by associating a person or thing with an accident which has frightened a child. A student relates the story of a young friend who was burned by a cup of coffee which was accidentally overturned by his aunt. As a result, the child refused to have anything to do with his aunt. It was a long time before she was able to win back his trust and affection.

CONTROLLING ANGER

Anger is one of the primary emotions. A newborn baby shows anger by crying when his arms are held close to his sides. In early childhood he resists in various ways any interference with his activities, and, as he grows older, he resents interference with his plans and thoughts.

Our aim in training children should be to teach them to control their anger, but not to suppress it altogether. If a person allows himself to throw a fit every time something goes wrong, he will soon be a nervous wreck without friends. There is, however, such a thing as righteous indignation. We should expect a decent boy to be aroused to action when a bully picks a fight with younger children or when thoughtless boys are cruel to animals. Honorable people will not stand by and see the innocent and weak persecuted.

Uncontrolled anger in children manifests itself in a violent display of rage, which we call a temper tantrum. The child who is allowed to form the habit of flying into a rage whenever his activities are thwarted will come to grief sooner or later. He is developing into a selfish, unstable person who will have a hard time making satisfactory social adjustments. Temper tantrums may be caused by overexcitement, overstimulation, lack of sleep, physical illness, or by giving in to a child's demands after he has protested for a sufficient length of time.

The treatment for temper tantrums is the removal of the cause. First, look to the child's health habits. Does he sleep as much as he should? Does he go to bed when he should? Is he being taken to exciting movies, or is he playing with children who annoy him or overstimulate him? Is his appetite good? Is his environment free from stress and strain? Next, consider the methods of disciplining the child. Are his parents consistent in their discipline; that is, do they say no only when necessary and then abide by their decision, or do they say no to something today and yes to the same thing tomorrow? Do they first say no, and then, if the child persists, give in to his demands? If his health habits are normal and the discipline methods sound, the child should have a medical examination to determine whether there is a physical reason for his tantrums.

If the case is one of mismanagement, the parents will have to change their methods of discipline. Some of the following suggestions may be helpful. Be careful not to interfere with the harmless activities of the child. Allow him as much freedom as he is able to use wisely. When you must refuse a request or ask him to do something in a different way, be pleasant but firm. Speak to him quietly, and wait calmly a few minutes for him to carry out your request. If he throws a tantrum, ignore him; under no circumstances appease him by giving him what he should not have. Usually all one has to do to cure a child of unsocial acts is to isolate him from the group. You may tell him that he is not wanted in the group when he is screaming but that he may return when he has finished.

Extreme cases may need severe treatment. One student tells how her father cured her of always protesting when the family went out together. Once, when she was about five or six years old and was dressed in a crisp summer dress, she threw a tantrum, as was her habit, because she was going to be taken downtown. Her father suddenly picked her up and dipped her in a tub of cold water which was standing near by. She says she never protested again.

Prevention is better than cure in the case of temper tantrums, as it is in all others. One mother relates how, when her young child came in from play one day, tired and overexcited, and on some pretext threw himself on the floor, screaming and kicking, she calmly picked him up in her arms and, holding him firmly, rocked him gently until he became quiet. She then gave him a glass of warm milk and put him to bed. After that, she said, she was careful to see that the children did not play together after they became tired, and that her child had regular meals. He never repeated the temper tantrum.

There is one point which we should remember in dealing with children. They should be given a normal amount of attention and affection and should be rewarded with approval for doing the right thing. With a small child, just a smile or a nod is sufficient. However, although approval and praise justly earned are provocative of good behavior habits, they should not be overused. Unearned praise tends to promote laziness.

As in all habit formation, the examples set by the older members of the family are important. Children tend to copy the behavior pattern of the members of the household. It is useless to tell a child to control his temper if you yourself are unable to control yours.

BECOMING OBEDIENT TO THE RIGHT AUTHORITY

Every good citizen is obedient to the laws of his community, state, and nation. Healthy people are obedient to the laws of health; religious people, to the laws of God. The good citizen, the healthy person, and religious person obey these various laws because they respect and have faith in the authority which has made them, and because they realize that the road to security and happiness is by way of these laws.

Our purpose in guiding children to be obedient should be to teach them to obey authority which is founded on justice and sound principles, not just to obey anybody and everybody who commands. This can best be done by having the members of the family, who represent authority to the child, show him that they are just and honest, that they can be trusted, and that they are worthy of respect.

Good parents will be guided by a philosophy of life in which they both believe and which they have agreed to use as a basis upon which to operate the home. They will cooperate with one another and will not discuss problems of discipline before the children. They will make few rules, but these will be based upon reason. They will see that these rules are observed by all members of the family. They will be consistent in their discipline.

The members of a home which is run on schedule, where meals are served on time, where baths and naps are taken regularly, and where there is a regular bedtime are learning to live according to law and order. In such a home many possible conflicts never occur. Children learn early to do the right thing as a matter of course. In such a household there is no argument about Johnny's taking a nap or Betty's drinking her milk.

We should plan as much as possible with children, pointing out to them the reasons for doing things in a prescribed way. However, a very young child must be taught to obey an order without question if he is to be kept from harm.

When commands are given to young children, care should be taken to use language that they understand and to speak slowly and distinctly, so that they will not be confused. Be sure that you have a child's attention before giving your command.

The most effective punishment is the natural consequence of an act rather than the infliction of physical or mental pain, though there are times when physical pain is desirable. When a child spills milk on the floor, he should be made to clean it up instead of being scolded. If he throws mud on the porch, he should be required to wash it off. This is an effective method for training a child to be careful.

We must remember that by teaching children obedience to the right authority, we are teaching them to discipline themselves and to become self-controlled. Only discipline from within is worth while in developing character.

IMAGINATION AND LYING

You are all familiar with the small child who will tell you today that he is a policeman, tomorrow that he is a truck driver, and the next day that he is a doctor. By this imaginary play the child dramatizes many incidents which he has seen and experienced.

Imitating adults is a part of childhood.   Courtesy, H. Armstrong Roberts.

Living through these experiences gives them real meaning for him and helps him to become familiar with his world. To what extent these dramatized incidents are enriched with details will depend upon the child's experiences. The richer the child's experiences, the richer will be the products of his imagination. It is natural for a child to imagine things. In fact, it is said that he is not aware that the products of his imagination are not real until he is about five years old.

Older people who work with children should enter into this make-believe world. It affords an opportunity for them to become acquainted with the child and also to help him use his natural ability to gain an understanding of nature and the world about him. The life history of the butterfly and the ants will be enjoyed in the same way as the fanciful stories of the child's own creation.

Imagination is valuable in other ways also. It is through imagination that inventions, literature, and art treasures have been created. Imagination is valuable to ordinary members of society as well as to geniuses. It helps a seamstress gain a clear picture of what she is trying to do; it helps a student understand the teacher's assignment; and it helps all of us recall and live over some past experience. Through imagination our lives are enriched and made more interesting. We should do all we can to help children develop their imagination.

Although the child's imagination should be encouraged, he must be taught the difference between fact and fancy. He must grow up with a sense of right and wrong. He must be taught to respect the truth and to tell the truth. A child's attitude toward the truth is largely determined by that of his parents. The father who keeps Johnny out of school to take him on a trip and then writes as an excuse to his teacher that Johnny was ill is making it very easy for Johnny to lie. As is true in all character training, example is better than precept.

Besides setting an example in telling the truth, parents must teach children to recognize the truth. It is easy to understand why the child whose only knowledge of a bear has been acquired from stories will call a large dog a bear. If such a mistake is made, it should be treated as a mistake. It can easily be corrected by showing the child pictures or by taking him for a trip to the zoo. On the other hand, in make-believe play a child may speak of a dog as a bear in the same way that he calls a stick a horse. In this case the older person should let the child know that he is aware of the difference. He may say, " Yes, the dog makes a good make-believe bear, doesn't he?" It would be a mistake to accuse the child of telling a lie. A lie is an untruth told with the intent of deceiving.

If, when the child grows old enough to know the difference

between truth and fancy, he still says things that are untrue, it is well to find out the reason for his so doing. When children are punished unjustly or severely they will tell a lie to protect themselves or others, and sometimes they will misrepresent the truth to attract attention to themselves. Parents and older people handling children should see that all punishment is reasonable and just. Unless the child feels sorry for having done the thing for which he is being punished, the punishment is not effective. The sympathetic, understanding adult will see that the child has a fair share of attention and that he feels secure in the affection of his family.

During the gang age, when loyalty to a group runs high, children may be likely to tell the truth to their friends but to think it is all right to tell an untruth to those not in the gang. Usually, with the right example set at home, as their friendships are widened their attitude toward truth changes. At all times, conditions should be such that children do not gain satisfaction from lying. If they are allowed to achieve things by untruths, they will learn to lie whenever it appears to their advantage to do so.

STUDY-GUIDE QUESTIONS

1. When is a person socially and emotionally adjusted?
2. How can a mother help her child become self-reliant?
3. Why should children play with other children their own age?
4. Describe the various steps or stages in a child's emotional development.
5. Why should a child have a normal amount of affection? What harm may result from a child's being petted and coddled to excess?
6. How can older people help children acquire a wholesome attitude toward sex?
7. Of what things are children afraid at birth?
8. What are the harmful effects of fear? What is meant by intellectual fear? Of what value is it?
9. Name the ways in which children may acquire fear of harmless things. How can they overcome these fears?
10. Tell how Susan acquired fear of strange women and how she was helped to overcome it.
11. Why do we speak of anger as a primary emotion?
12. Is a person ever justified in becoming angry? How can this emotion be used to benefit society? To harm society?
13. What causes temper tantrums in children? How can we prevent children

from forming the tantrum habit? How can the habit be corrected after it is formed?

14. What is meant by being obedient to the right authority?
15. Show how parents can guide their children to be obedient to the right authority.
16. How does living by a schedule help children learn to obey willingly?
17. Should a parent always explain the reason to a child when he requests him to do something?
18. Why should children be obedient to the right authority?
19. Why should we help children develop their imagination?
20. How is imagination related to lying? At what age should children know the difference between imagination and reality? How can we help children to know the difference between fact and fancy?
21. What can a parent do to help a child form the habit of telling the truth?
22. How do children of the gang age sometimes regard truth? How can they be guided to overcome this erroneous idea?

UNIT FIVE. HOW DO PLAY AND PLAY MATERIALS AID IN CHILD DEVELOPMENT?

Play is an important factor in the physical development of children. An infant may strengthen his eye muscles by following the movements of a brightly colored object suspended from his crib; the seven-month-old may develop his arms and shoulders by reaching for his rattle; the nine- to eighteen-month-old may gain in the power of locomotion by chasing a ball about the home; and the older child may grow in grace and skill by skating, dancing, and playing such games as tennis and badminton.

As children gain power and strength through learning to make their bodies do their bidding, they should be provided with play materials that stimulate them to further achievements. Care must be taken, however, not to confuse young children by providing too many toys or toys that are too complicated. Too many toys may cause a child to be irritable and unstable. Nancy was concerned about the way her younger sister Louise flitted from one activity to another. Louise would play a very few minutes with her doll, then would start working a jigsaw puzzle only to discard it for a picture book. Soon after Nancy noticed this condition of restlessness in her little sister, her mother began to complain about Louise's restless sleeping. One day when a neighbor who had had considerable experience with children was calling on the family, Nancy mentioned the problem to her and asked her for advice in the matter. After watching Louise for a while, the neighbor advised that Louise's play equipment be stored away and only a few pieces brought out at a time. In a very short time Louise was spending more time on one activity and was sleeping better.

Through play children develop not only physically but also mentally and socially. If you have ever watched a group of boys building a tree house from whatever materials they could find in a pile of old lumber, you will remember how they changed their original ideas to fit the material at hand. In making adjustments in play, children have experiences in developing their ingenuity, resourcefulness, self-discipline, imagination, concentration, and cooperation.

Play is a means of developing ingenuity, resourcefulness, imagination, and concentration. Courtesy, H. Armstrong Roberts.

These same qualities may be developed in any project which children plan and carry through. The younger child playing in the sand or with his blocks is exercising the same qualities as the older children building their tree house.

Older people help young children grow mentally and socially through play if they allow them to carry through their planned projects uninterrupted. In a well-organized household there are regular times in the day when children have work to do and other times when they play. The mother should, of course, know what they are doing and be ready to offer suggestions when it is advisable to change their type of play; but when they are carrying on some worth-while project, they should not be interrupted to run errands or perform other trivial tasks.

There are many opportunities for children to grow socially through play. When a child refuses to cooperate with the group, he soon finds that he is not welcome. After standing on the side lines for a while, an unwanted child will usually make an effort to regain the good will of the group. Through play, especially in their own age group, children learn to lead sometimes and to follow on other occasions. At all times, they learn to respect other people's rights and property. They learn at a very early age to take turns in using pieces of play apparatus.

When selecting toys for small children, be careful to choose something that the child may enjoy without injuring himself. Toys should be free from sharp edges, colored with nonpoisonous paints or dyes, too large to be put into ears or swallowed, and easily cleaned and durable. It is well to remember that children of all ages like to do things, not just look on. Therefore playthings which may be used in various ways, rather than mechanical toys, should be selected.

It is not necessary to buy everything which the child uses for play material. When he is young, empty spools which have had the labels removed and have been scrubbed are often used. These may be strung on a strong cord or used separately very much as blocks are used. Tin cans that have been opened with a can opener which leaves a smooth rim around the top may be painted with nonpoisonous paint and made up in nests. Then, as children begin to investigate and manipulate things, they make toys out of clothespins, chairs, boxes, blankets, cooking vessels, and many other articles.

The first toy that a child is able to enjoy is one of the brightly colored objects which, when fastened to his crib, he follows with his eyes. When he is three or four months old, he will enjoy reaching for a brightly colored rattle and celluloid toys in his bath. He will also enjoy having a hard rubber ring or a spoon to put in his mouth. About this time or a little later he will begin to enjoy soft toys, a string of large wooden beads, spools strung on a strong cord, or a few blocks with rounded corners. These toys will help him develop his power to grasp and hold objects. When he begins to play on the floor, he will enjoy a ball that he can chase around.

The child from one to three is interested in finding out about the world around him. His interests seem to be more in handling things than in making things. Dolls will be carried by their legs and arms; blocks will be taken from place to place and stacked up just to be torn down again. The child likes to take things apart and try to put them together again. It is at this age that he enjoys taking mother's pots and pans out of the cupboard. He also enjoys nests of cans, boxes, or blocks, and other toys that can be taken apart.

One child two years old enjoyed a wooden toy boat mounted on small wooden wheels. The boat had detachable smokestacks and could be pulled by a string with a large colored bead at the end. Another small girl played often with a toy in the shape of a shoe which had a number of little wooden figures representing the old lady and her many children. The figures were just the right size to go through the little door. When children from three to five years of age play in the sand pile, they spend the time filling a small bucket with sand and then emptying it again. They have not yet learned to build towns, roads, tunnels, and the like as older children do. When children of this age play with molding clay, they pat it and roll it, but they do not shape it into objects as older children do.

The child aged three to six is interested in building and making things. He uses blocks to build churches; he strings beads; he molds his clay into shapes. Gradually he learns to draw pictures with many correct details. He does a great deal of climbing during this period if he has suitable equipment.

Children do not all use the same type of toys an equal amount at the same ages or, for that matter, at any age. Some are more interested in one type than another. However, a wise mother will study her child's development and provide material that will stimulate his lagging habits or abilities.

Some playthings, such as balls, kiddie cars, skates, and tricycles, are especially helpful in developing strength and skill. Others are beneficial in stimulating the imagination and artistic tendencies. Crayons, molding clay, paints, drawing paper, pencils, soap for carving, needlecraft activities, construction sets, and similar play materials would be included in this group. Other materials,

Imagination may be developed through play.   Courtesy, H. Armstrong Roberts.

such as dolls, toy housekeeping equipment, toy machinery, and industrial equipment, as well as all kinds of costumes, are used in dramatic play. Games such as anagrams and authors are helpful in enriching a child's knowledge.

STUDY-GUIDE QUESTIONS

1. Show how children may grow physically, mentally, and emotionally through play.
2. Why should children be allowed to carry on a self-planned, worth-while project uninterrupted?
3. What general characteristics should toys for children have?

4. Name some homemade toys; some materials found in every household that may be used as play materials.
5. Name some toys that are especially suited to children under one year old; to children from one to three years old; to children from three to six years old.
6. List some toys especially suitable for developing strength and skill; for stimulating the imagination and artistic tendencies; for promoting dramatic play; for increasing knowledge.

ACTIVITIES

1. Make either a stuffed animal or some other kind of toy for young children.
2. Compile an illustrated list of play materials suited to each of the following age groups: under one year; from one to three years; from three to six years.
3. Compile an illustrated list of play materials for each of the following purposes:
   a. developing strength and skill.
   b. stimulating the imagination and artistic tendencies.
   c. promoting dramatic play.
   d. increasing knowledge.

BOOKS AND PAMPHLETS FOR FURTHER READING

Books

Arlitt, Ada Hart, *The Child from One to Twelve*. Whittlesey House, McGraw-Hill Book Company, New York, 1931.
Bacmeister, Rhoda W., *Caring for the Run-About Child*. E. P. Dutton & Company, New York, 1937.
Faegre, Marion L., and John E. Anderson, *Child Care and Training*. The University of Minnesota Press, Minneapolis, 1940.
Goodspeed, Helen C., and Emma Johnson, *Care and Guidance of Children*. J. B. Lippincott Company, Chicago, 1938.
Kawin, Ethel, *The Wise Choice of Toys*. The University of Chicago Press, Chicago, 1934.
Meek, L. H., *Your Child's Development and Guidance Told in Pictures*. J. B. Lippincott Company, 1940.
Strain, Frances Bruce, *Being Born*. D. Appleton-Century Company, Chicago, 1936.

Pamphlets

Sweeney and Buck, " How to Feed Your Children in the Home." The Merrill-Palmer School, Detroit, 1937.
United States Department of Labor, Children's Bureau Publications, " Infant Care," " The Child from One to Six," " Child Management," " Are You

Training Your Child to be Happy?" " Well Nourished Children." Superintendent of Documents, Washington, D. C.

United States Department of Agriculture Publications, Farmers' Bulletin
No. 1674, " Food for Children."

Child Study Association of America, " Sex Education — Facts and Attitudes."
New York.

A budget enables a family to realize some of their dreams.
Courtesy, *Better Homes and Gardens*.

SECTION IV

USING MONEY WISELY

UNIT ONE. FAMILY SPENDING

THE BROWNS ARE IN TROUBLE

Mr. Brown was worried. The bank had called him and inquired about the repayment of a small loan which he had taken out several years ago. It would seem that he should have repaid that three hundred dollars long before this. He always intended to do something about it but never seemed to be able to scrape together even twenty-five dollars to pay on it. As he thought back to those lean years when they had had sickness and unexpected hospital bills which necessitated the loan, he realized that, although his income had increased considerably since that time, the demands of his family had increased at a much greater rate. As the children grew older, it cost more to clothe and feed them, and their ability to think up expensive things to do was unlimited. At the present time, fifteen-year-old Phyllis was planning on going to camp with a group of her friends, and Mr. Brown just did not know how he was going to finance the two weeks at camp, to say nothing of the necessary clothing, equipment, and bus fare.

Then there was Dick. In two more years he would be going to college, with all the extra expense entailed. Dick had chosen a large eastern university, apparently without considering the cost. At the present time, he had a summer job which took care of his spending money, but Mr. Brown realized that both he and Dick should be planning for the future and making some provision for the financial burden which the college years would impose.

Young Jane was, at present, no great problem. Her music lessons were expensive but she had done very well with her violin, and since she appeared to have real talent, it seemed too bad not to let her continue. However, Mr. Brown knew that this year, when she entered junior high school, new desires and tastes would be developed. The time was not far off when clothes would be of prime importance, and Jane would be asking for more money for recreation of various kinds.

Meanwhile, mother had been called upon to make more and more sacrifices. She was having less and less paid help at home. As the girls grew older, mother thought they could help with the cleaning, ironing, and other household tasks. They had agreed to do so, but mother found that they were usually busy with their own good times when she needed them most, and consequently she found herself having less and less time for rest and recreation. Father noticed that she always looked tired and had lost all interest in her personal appearance. She didn't get a permanent wave regularly any more, because there never seemed to be enough money. By the time she got the girls what they felt they needed, there never seemed to be any money left for new clothes for her, so she just made her old things do. Since she was always busy and tired and never had anything new and pretty to wear, she soon got into the habit of staying at home. This worried Mr. Brown, as he realized that this was not good for his wife. She had always been an attractive woman who was interested in people and in doing things, and he felt that she was growing nervous and depressed over their situation.

As Mr. Brown thought the situation over, he saw that something would have to be done at once. The bank officials felt that prosperous years, with increased incomes, are the time to pay off debts, and Mr. Brown knew that this was sound reasoning. Thinking that possibly the Browns's difficulties came from not planning their expenditures ahead of time, they had given Mr. Brown some material on budgeting and had offered to help the Browns work out their financial plan.

That night, Mr. Brown talked the situation over with his wife. He told her about his experience with the bank and showed her the budget information which they had given him. Mrs. Brown felt chagrined about the bank loan and knew that her husband had been embarrassed by this episode. As she studied the budget material with her husband, she became very much interested in financial planning. She could see that it was just as necessary to have a plan for using money as it was to have a plan for building a house, taking a trip, or carrying out any other project in which you had a well-defined goal which you wanted to reach.

Mrs. Brown also realized that it was just as important to be able to spend money wisely as it was to be able to earn it. She felt, however, that it would be utterly impossible to have any plan succeed and to have everyone happy unless the wholehearted cooperation of the entire family was secured. She believed their children were typical young people who loved their parents and would not purposely worry them or put undue strain upon them. She knew that Dick, Phyllis, and Jane had little idea of the value of money and that they did not realize how difficult their individual demands made it for the family to accomplish desirable ends with their income. However, their mother felt that they would be willing to cooperate and make personal sacrifices and might even have ideas for economies if they were called in to help make the plan for using the income. She said the children were old enough to be confided in and that it was unfair for the parents to bear all the financial strain and to make all the decisions as to how the income should be used. Training in the use of money would be of great value to the children now and would give them some understanding of what it means to establish and maintain a home and a family. It would also encourage them to think of the family as a whole and would make them willing to sacrifice personal desires for family benefits.

THE BROWNS CALL A FAMILY COUNCIL

Mr. Brown thought his wife's reasons for a family council were sound. Therefore the children were asked to set aside the next evening, and as soon as dinner was over, the family gathered in the living room. Father explained to the children that they had met to discuss their financial situation. He said the time had come when it was no longer possible to satisfy all the wants and needs of the family with their present income. Since choices would have to be made, he believed that the only fair and just method was to have the entire family decide how the income was to be used. He explained that these matters were purely personal and must not be discussed outside the family circle. In making plans of any kind, he suggested, situations would arise where they would not all agree. In such cases, someone would have to be in authority and make the final decision, and the others abide by this decision.

The children agreed that their father and mother were the proper ones to have such authority, since they were experienced, mature people. They were willing to abide by any decisions made by their parents or to be overruled by them in case of a disagreement.

THE BROWNS CONSIDER THE BUDGET SYSTEM

As Mr. Brown explained the financial situation of the family to the children and showed his concern over their present demands and future needs, the children gradually became aware of the need for family understanding and planning. They began to realize how selfish each of them was in his personal demands and what a strain they had been placing on their parents. They were not sure, however, just what a budget was, and they were afraid it would put many restrictions on them and take all the fun out of doing things.

Mr. Brown explained that a budget cannot limit a person's expenditures, since the amount of his income does that. After all, it is fairly obvious that one cannot spend more money than he earns, if he wants to stay out of jail. A budget is merely a plan to guide one in using his income to the best advantage. Usually, the plan is made for a year or more at one time; records are kept; and the plan is revised as the need arises. Certain advantages of such a plan to the Browns were evident. First, Mr. Brown would be able to repay his bank loan. Through systematic planning, he would have money for large expenditures, such as life insurance and taxes when they came due. This arrangement would save him many hours of worry and would lessen the strain on the family purse in months when these obligations had to be met. In other words, it would tend to equalize matters. Then, too, planning would make possible future goals, such as college, as well as assure each member of the family the greatest possible satisfaction from the Browns's income.

STUDY-GUIDE QUESTIONS

1. What was the basis of the Browns's financial troubles?
2. How would you characterize the Brown children?
3. What are the disadvantages of parents' making excessive financial sacrifices for their children?
4. What is a budget?
5. What are the advantages of having the entire family plan the budget?
6. Does a budget restrict one's spending?
7. For how long a period of time is a budget usually made?
8. What are the advantages of a budget?

ACTIVITIES

1. Describe the method of handling family finances which is used in your home.
2. List the advantages and disadvantages of this method.
3. Describe how this method could be improved.

UNIT TWO. INCOME

THE MONEY INCOME

In planning future spending, Mr. Brown thought that perhaps they had better start by considering their income. Obviously, the father's salary was the chief income of the family, but, as Mr. Brown explained, any money earned by members of the family was also a part of the family income. This was an entirely new idea to Dick, who had always considered money which he earned as his personal property to spend exactly as he pleased. When he thought of the family as a unit working together to accomplish certain ends, however, and when he realized that his father considered the salary which he earned as family property, Dick began to look upon his earnings in a different way.

THE MOTHER'S CONTRIBUTION

Then, too, Mr. Brown told the children, they must not think of their mother as not contributing to the family income because she did not earn money outside the home. He asked them to consider the actual physical labor which she gave in keeping the house orderly, their clothes clean and mended, and the family well fed. They had some idea of the value of mother's work when they estimated how much it would cost to hire someone to do all these things. And then, as father pointed out, no one could possibly be paid to do all the little thoughtful things that mother did daily for them which made their home a pleasant, happy, smoothly running one. Mother's ability to manage well was also a priceless contribution to the family income. One reason they were able to give Jane such expensive music lessons was that mother knew how to keep food costs down to a minimum and, at the same time, have adequate meals. During the last few years mother had studied nutrition and meal planning, and she took a good deal of care to prepare appetizing dishes from low-cost foods. This careful planning served another end. It reduced their doctor bills to a minimum by keeping the family in good health.

144

EXTENDING THE INCOME

Mr. Brown also pointed out that the various services rendered
by the family members helped to extend the income. For example,

Through wise buying, food costs may be kept down.
Courtesy, Good Housekeeping Institute.

when Dick cut the grass and trimmed the hedge, he really added to
the family income. By caring for the yard, he made available for

the use of the family the amount of money which his father would
have to pay a hired man. When Phyllis and Jane did the ironing,
they released for family use the amount of money which their
mother would pay a laundress for this task. In planning the use
of the family income, mother thought they should not overlook
the importance of considering such ways to extend the family
income. Phyllis and Jane immediately volunteered to take over
certain household tasks and to do them regularly, so that mother
would not have to remind them of their responsibilities. Phyllis
said she knew Mrs. Kramer wanted a high school girl to look
after her two children in the afternoon and two evenings a week.
Phyllis felt sure Mrs. Kramer would hire her, and by going to work
at once, she could earn enough money for her camp expenses.
At the same time she would have her mornings free for her
responsibilities at home and would have five evenings a week for
good times, which she thought should be more than enough.
Mother suggested that if they made some of the clothes Phyllis
needed for camp, such as shorts and slacks, they could outfit her
more economically. Phyllis thought she might do this with her
mother's help.

Dick volunteered to take care of the yard, to keep the car clean,
and to keep the basement in order. In this way he would release
his father for the many small repair jobs around the house which,
for lack of time, father usually hired someone else to do. Dick
began to see how selfish he had been to spend his entire earnings
for fun and how necessary it was for him to help plan and save
for his college years. He said he knew of a job he could get three
evenings a week, and he thought he ought to be earning as much
as he could during the summer vacation.

Jane felt left out of the family circle when it came to earning
money, but mother assured her that she could be a great help
right at home. Besides, she added, three or four of the neighbors
often wanted someone to run errands, and maybe Jane could use
her bicycle and accommodate them for a small fee. Jane soon
found that she could earn the equivalent of her weekly allowance
by taking books back to the library, picking up yarn to be knitted
for the Red Cross, delivering garden bouquets, and bringing
grocery articles to forgetful housewives. Jane also discovered that

she could earn her lunch by working in the school cafeteria, and she planned to extend the family income in this way when she returned to school in the fall.

SOCIAL INCOME

Father also reminded the family that there were certain public services which helped to extend their income indirectly, such as libraries, parks, and museums. When the family found it possible to borrow a book at no cost from the library rather than buying it, the family income was extended. Also, when the family went to a public park for a swim and a picnic supper instead of attending a movie, their purse profited.

STUDY-GUIDE QUESTIONS

1. What does money income include?
2. In what ways does a homemaker add to the income?
3. In what ways did the Brown children extend the income of the family?
4. What is meant by social income?

ACTIVITIES

1. List some of the things your mother does for you to which it would be impossible to attach a money value.
2. Describe the ways that a girl in your community can extend the family income.
3. What services in your community can be considered social income?

UNIT THREE. THE BUDGET

In setting up a plan or budget, certain general divisions are used which include the necessities and some of the luxuries that the family desires. The Browns next familiarized themselves with this way of dividing the income and determined what proportion of the income should be used for each division and just what each division should include.

SHELTER

Shelter, or housing, is one of the necessities which every family must have. Mr. Brown explained that in selecting the house in which they lived he and his wife had considered several items, such as the location in respect to his business and to schools. One reason they had chosen this particular suburb was that the schools had very high standards and were well thought of throughout the state. They believed that their home should be conveniently located for Mr. Brown, so that he would not have to spend too much time traveling to and from his work, and that the school buildings should be easily accessible for the children. Then they considered the house from the standpoint of health and ascertained that it was well ventilated and light, had sufficient room to allow the family to carry on its various activities without undue crowding, and had a yard for outdoor activities. They considered also the type of people who would be their neighbors, for they realized that the social contacts of the children, as well as many of their own, would be made among these people. The cost of the house was also important, as most economists advise spending not more than one week's income for rent, and not more than two and one-half times a yearly income of $3000, such as the Brown's, to buy a house.

Phyllis could not understand why they need set aside any of their income for shelter, since the Browns owned their own home. Father explained, however, that even though they did not pay rent, they must set aside a certain amount of money each month for the interest on the mortgage, taxes, insurance, and repairs on the house.

FOOD

Food was an item which even Jane understood as a necessity. They did not all understand, however, that the amount of money which was set aside for food must cover not only the flour, butter, and eggs that mother used in preparing meals, but also all the meals eaten outside the home, such as lunches at school and the hot dogs bought at football games. Suddenly, it became quite clear that if, like Jane, they all earned their lunches at school, there would be about $3 more a week to spend for entertaining or for some other purpose that they all agreed upon. The Browns also realized that, when they all cooperated in eating the foods that mother prepared and did not demand elaborate dishes or out-of-season foods, it was possible to keep food costs down without endangering health. They also understood why mother vetoed Dick's suggestion that he could get along on a bottle of milk at noon and why she said that would be poor economy. Most economists allow one-fourth to one-third of an income like the Browns's for food. The actual amount used depends on what importance the family attaches to food, how skillfully the mother buys and prepares the food, and how well the family cooperates with her in eating whatever she prepares.

CLOTHING

Clothing is a division of the budget in which all the Browns were interested. Dick's and Phyllis' demands had increased rapidly within the last few years. Their father and mother recognized that it is natural for young people to want to dress and look like their companions. They also knew that being well dressed tends to make a person well poised and to give him self-respect. At the same time these parents realized that if they sacrificed their own appearances to indulge the tastes of their son and daughter, Dick and Phyllis would soon become selfish and unreasonable. Everyone should have his share. This meant that Dick would not spend more for clothing than his father, and Phyllis' clothing expenditures would not greatly exceed her mother's. Since Jane was younger, she need spend still less for clothes. The following scale* indicates to some extent what proportion each member should have of the clothing allowance on incomes from below $900 to over $2500:

Husband	1.0
Wife	0.9
Boy 15 years and over	1.0
Girl 15 years and over	1.2
Boy 12 to 15	0.6
Girl 12 to 15	0.7
Boy 8 to 12	0.5
Girl 8 to 12	0.5
Child 4 to 8	0.5
Child under 4	0.3

To estimate the amount of money each member of the Brown family should spend on clothing, Mr. Brown applied this scale to the family as follows:

Mr. Brown	1.0
Mrs. Brown	0.9
Dick	1.0
Phyllis	1.2
Jane	0.7
Total	4.8

To estimate the value of 1.0 in terms of dollars, Mr. Brown divided the family's clothing allowance by 4.8. The result gave him the amount of money that he and Dick could spend for clothes. He estimated the clothing allowances for his wife, Phyllis, and Jane by multiplying this figure by 0.9, 1.2, and 0.7 respectively.

Economists allow approximately 15 per cent of the moderate income for clothing, which includes initial cost and any expense involved in maintaining the wardrobe. Since it is difficult to spread clothing expenditures evenly throughout each month of the year, it is necessary to set aside a given amount of money each month to avoid too great a strain on the income in fall and spring,

* May L. Cowles, " Variations in Demand for Clothing at Various Income Levels." Doctoral thesis, University of Chicago, 1929.

when seasonal expenditures are greatest, or when it is necessary to buy expensive garments which involve a larger outlay and which are purchased only occasionally. Phyllis, Dick, and Jane could see the necessity of planning the purchase of winter and spring coats, so that not everyone in the family would need a coat at the same time. Mrs. Brown explained that she usually planned to buy Dick and Phyllis winter coats every two years in alternate Septembers. Frequently, Jane could wear Phyllis' coat if it was dyed and altered by the local tailor. She and Mr. Brown planned to have new coats every three years and usually bought them at the January sales on alternate years, although frequently they didn't get them because there wasn't enough money.

The Browns decided that there was plenty of room for improvement in this system. They could see the advantage of longtime planning and of setting aside some money each month for future needs. They understood how one or two selfish, unreasonable people in a family could upset even the best planning possible. As Mrs. Brown said, end-of-the-season sales could be a distinct advantage if they represented real savings. The period of service the buyer expected to get from a garment should bear a direct relation to the price he paid. Phyllis realized now why her mother had objected to her paying a certain sum for an evening dress which she had worn only a few times but was willing to pay three times that amount for the wool suit which Phyllis had worn almost daily to school and expected to use another year. When their mother explained that they could save nearly one-half the cost of garments by making them at home, the girls were anxious to help their mother sew. Mrs. Brown explained that sometimes a garment you made at home costs as much as one that is bought but wears twice as long, which means a saving of 50 per cent.

OPERATING EXPENSES

Operating expense was explained as all the expenditures it takes to maintain a house, such as those for heat, light, water, soap, and other household supplies, telephone, hired household help, and replacement of house furnishings. Usually from 10 to 15 per cent is set aside for this division of the budget, depending on how careful the family members are to turn out unnecessary lights, to shut off the radio when no one is listening, to turn off faucets and replace washers in them so that they do not drip, and to avoid wasting soap, leaving the cap off the tooth paste, and doing the many other little things which represent a large amount of waste if disregarded. Care in the use of household equipment and house furnishings means less money spent for repairs and replacement. Here, again, the Browns decided that everyone could help by observing care in these matters. Then, too, if everyone picked up after himself and kept his own room and things in order, mother would have less to do and more time for rest, recreation, and such activities as sewing, which would extend the income.

SAVINGS

Savings mean more than money in the bank. Mr. Brown explained that various types of savings are desirable for several reasons. Of course, some cash savings are desirable for emergencies. For example, if Mr. Brown had had a substantial savings account, it would have been unnecessary to borrow the $300 from the bank; therefore he was especially anxious to build up a savings account as well as to pay off the loan. He explained, however, that the family was not without assets. Their home was about half paid for, and he carried a substantial life insurance policy. These were both forms of savings. The amount of savings depends on the health, management, and cooperation of the individual family.

ADVANCEMENT

The advancement division of the budget is concerned with the cultural part of family life. Education, travel, recreation, magazines, charity and church contributions, club dues, and doctor and dentist fees are all items in this division. This part of the budget should be as generous as possible, but since it is never large enough to satisfy all the tastes and wants of the various family members, the Browns realized that in determining how this money should be spent they would have to compare values and balance choices carefully if they were to have the greatest satisfaction possible for their money. As they talked their financial plans over, they could all see that for the next few years education would require a large amount of this division of the income if the three younger members of the family were to have the opportunity to go to college.

STANDARD BUDGETS

At this point in the family discussion, one of the children asked, " Father, how do you know we should spend 15 per cent of our income for clothes?" Mr. Brown replied that he didn't know that that percentage would be exactly correct for their family, but that it was the percentage worked out by specialists in family management. He then showed the children the standard budgets which the bank had given him. The standard budgets for a family of five on various income levels* were as follows:

Monthly income		$175	$250	$300	$350
Federal income tax		3.80	15.60	23.60	31.60
Savings	12½%	21.40	29.30	34.55	39.80
Food	25	42.80	58.60	69.10	79.60
Shelter	25	42.80	58.60	69.10	79.60
Operating expenses	10	17.12	23.44	27.64	31.84
Clothing	15	25.68	35.16	41.46	47.76
Advancement	12½	21.40	29.30	34.55	39.80
		175.00	250.00	300.00	350.00

As the Browns looked these standard budgets over, they could clearly see the relation of the various parts of the financial plan to the income. It was also plain that it was the size of the income that limited spending. As the income decreases, there is a smaller percentage available for advancement, savings, and clothing, because a larger percentage must be used for food.

Since no two families have the same standards and goals toward which they are working, Mr. Brown explained that the same budget would not fit all families of the same size and income. Standard budgets are merely suggestive and can be used as guideposts to point the way, but they must be altered and adapted to fit the needs and desires of each family and then must be constantly revised as the family's income and desires change. Then, too, as

* Percentages from " Consider Your Pocketbook," by Ethel Laney of *The Cleveland Plain Dealer.*

the family grows more experienced in planning, they will probably become more skillful in buying and in caring for the things they purchase. Skill in these two respects is a great aid in making the most of one's income.

STUDY-GUIDE QUESTIONS

1. What are the usual divisions of a family budget?
2. If the family own their own home, what expenses would be included under shelter in the budget?
3. In selecting a home for a family, what should be considered besides the cost of the house or the rent?
4. What must the amount of money set aside for food cover?
5. Why shouldn't everyone in the Brown family have the same amount of money for clothes?
6. What expenses are involved in maintaining a wardrobe?
7. Why is it best to plan clothing purchases over a period from one to three years?
8. How can clothing expenditures be kept down?
9. What does operating expense include?
10. In what ways can you help to keep the operating expense in your home within your budget?
11. What various forms of savings are possible?
12. Why should people have some cash savings?
13. What is included in the advancement division of a budget?
14. Why is this division often a source of difficulty in financial planning?
15. Of what value are standard budgets?
16. Why is it impractical for a family to take a standard budget and follow it exactly?

UNIT FOUR. THE BROWNS'S BUDGET

Mrs. Brown suggested that perhaps they could formulate a tentative budget that would fit their family. They began by putting down the absolutely necessary expenditures. Although they had never kept any actual records of how they spent their money, they had cancelled checks and receipted bills for most of their purchases. In addition to these necessary expenses, father said they would have to decide just what they wanted to accomplish. Each family member was allowed to list all the things he would like to have. Some of father's ambitions were to pay off the $300 loan and to have a new overcoat. Mother wanted the davenport reupholstered, a permanent wave, and a new afternoon dress. Dick's immediate desires included a canoe and camping trip, some new clothes, and, of course, money for college in the near future. Phyllis' camp expenses were her immediate goal, and she would need a permanent by fall as well as new things for school. As the Browns looked over their lists, they saw how many things they hoped for, and how foresighted they would all have to be if they were to achieve their goals.

Father began by deducting the federal income tax from the income. Then, he set aside $10 per month to pay off on the loan, as everyone agreed this item was a " must." Mrs. Brown brought up the subject of war bonds next, and the family agreed that they should purchase at least one $18.75 bond each month. Each of the children resolved to put 10 per cent of his earnings in war stamps.

Next the family listed their costs for shelter and found that the taxes, interest on the mortgage, insurance, and repairs came to about 18 per cent of their income. Mr. Brown explained that he was allowing $120 per year for repairs, and although that figure seemed a bit low, he thought he could keep within it by doing much of the work himself.

From past experience mother knew about what it cost to feed the family. She thought that, with careful management and the wholehearted cooperation of all, they could manage on $55 per month, including father's lunches downtown and some entertaining, if the children earned their lunches.

In the matter of clothing, they all felt that their methods had been so haphazard in the past that probably the best thing to do would be to take 15 per cent of their income and divide it according to the table on p. 150. Then Dick volunteered to let father have his share of the clothing allowance for the coming year and to use part of his earnings for clothes. Everyone approved, since father had done without things for so long that his wardrobe needed replenishing.

To estimate operating expenses, the Browns had their receipts for water, light, gas, and fuel for the past year. Mother had to calculate about how much she would need for soap, cleaning agents, and the like. Any outside help was eliminated for the present, as Phyllis and Jane promised to take over certain household tasks and to do them on schedule.

For savings, the Browns listed the amount which they paid on the house, exclusive of the interest, life insurance payments, and the amount set aside for war bonds. In addition, they all thought they should set aside some cash savings, but father didn't see how this was possible at the present time. Furthermore, he said, any additional savings they could make should, as a patriotic duty, be put into war bonds until they were investing at least 10 per cent of their income.

The planning of the funds for advancement was a bit more difficult. There seemed to be so many items that had to be covered, and the ideas of the family were varied. Allowance had to be made for dental care, hospital insurance, doctor's bills, Jane's music lessons, church dues, club dues, charity, magazines, books, all forms of paid recreation, and personal allowances for father and mother. The children agreed to earn their allowances.

When the Browns's budget was finally completed it looked about like the one shown on p. 157.

Monthly income		$250.00
Federal income tax	$15.60	
Debt payment	10.00	
Net income		224.40
Shelter		$40.40
Interest on mortgage	16.60	
Taxes	9.30	
Insurance	4.50	
Repair and upkeep	10.00	
Food		55.00
Clothing		33.70
Father	7.02	
Mother	6.31	
Dick	7.02	
Phyllis	8.43	
Jane	4.92	
Operating expense		18.75
Electricity	2.50	
Gas	2.00	
Fuel	10.00	
Water	.75	
Soaps, etc.	3.50	
Savings		46.75
Life insurance	8.00	
Payments on home	20.00	
War bonds	18.75	
Advancement		28.80
Dentist	1.75	
Doctor	4.00	
Hospital insurance	2.55	
Church	1.00	
Charity	1.00	
Magazines, books, and newspapers	3.00	
Personal allowances		16.50
Mother	3.50	
Father	5.00	
Music lessons	4.00	
Future education fund	4.00	

NEED OF RECORDS

It seemed to the children that all possible expenses had been provided for, but mother warned them that many unexpected expenses would arise and that, although they had worked their financial plan out very carefully, it was probably far from perfect. However, at least it was a start. The family agreed to meet once a month to compare their actual accomplishments with the goals they had set. At this time all complaints would be discussed, and the financial plan would be revised and changed to meet more satisfactorily the family's needs and wishes. Meanwhile, it would be necessary for everyone to keep a record of his earnings and expenditures so that the family could see where they had made mistakes in the past and where improvement was possible. Since Phyllis had had some bookkeeping in high school, she volunteered to keep the accounts for the family spending, and each individual agreed to keep a record of his earnings and the way he used this money.

STUDY-GUIDE QUESTIONS

1. In making a budget, what is the advantage of having each family member list the things he wants?
2. What is the first step in actually making a budget?
3. Why must a budget be constantly revised and changed?
4. Why must records of expenditures be kept?
5. What is the purpose of having a family conference every month?
6. Upon what does the success of a family budget depend?

ACTIVITIES

1. Plan a budget for your own family or an imaginary family in your community. In making your plan
   a. List the members of the family and give their ages and tastes.
   b. Describe the financial status of the family. What are the assets and the liabilities? What is the income?
   c. State the goals that the family hopes to achieve.
   d. Set up a budget for the family. Show that this budget will help the family to achieve the desired goals.

UNIT FIVE.   AN INDIVIDUAL'S BUDGET

In making a budget for an individual, it is necessary to follow approximately the same procedure as for a family. When Phyllis saw that planned family finance was bringing satisfaction to the various members, she decided it would be well for her to plan her personal spending.

A girl may add to her income by taking care of children.
Courtesy, *Consumer's Guide.*

SETTING UP GOALS

She began by deciding what she wanted to achieve. First, she wanted to have $25 for her camp expenses by the last week in August. This amount would take care of her transportation as well

159

as a week at camp. She also wanted new shorts, a new housecoat, and a pair of play shoes before going to camp. When she came back, she would need a new permanent and money for school supplies and fees, and she would want very much to have a new skirt and some new blouses. In addition, she felt that she should have some money for movies, ice cream, and the like during the summer. She had promised to put 10 per cent of her earnings in war stamps.

THE INCOME

Phyllis found she could make about $6 each week during the summer by caring for her neighbors' children afternoons and two evenings. This work did not involve any transportation expense or any special clothing, so that her earnings were clear profit. She figured that in the eleven weeks of summer she could make $66. Therefore her problem was to plan the use of this money so that she would accomplish her aims. Her budget looked like this:

Income			$66.00
War stamps		$ 6.60	
Camp expenses		25.00	
Permanent		5.00	
School fees and supplies		3.00	
Clothing			
3 pairs of shorts (made at home)	$1.75		
housecoat (made at home)	2.15		
1 blouse (made at home)	2.00		
skirt	5.00	10.90	
Church ($.20 per week)		2.20	
Cosmetics		1.55	
Recreation ($.50 per week)		5.50	
Savings for future clothing		6.25	
		$66.00	$66.00

Phyllis felt that, if she followed this plan and controlled her impulses to spend money foolishly, she would have some of the things she wanted by the end of the summer. She felt that she should restrict her spending for fun to $.50 a week, since she was going to spend $25 for her own pleasure later in the summer. Then, too, she was anxious to build up a fund for future clothing purchases, as she knew her earning power would not be so great during the school months, and she was anxious to help with her own expenses.

ACTIVITIES

1. Keep an expense account for the next month, listing your expenditures under the following headings: food, clothing, savings, educational expense, church and charity, recreation, personal grooming.
2. At the end of the month, criticize your use of money.
3. Make a plan for the use of your money for the following month.

BOOKS FOR FURTHER READING

Andrews, Benjamin, *Economics of the Household.* The Macmillan Company, New York, 1935.

Donham, Agnes, *Spending the Family Income,* revised. Little, Brown and Company, Boston, 1941.

Friend, Mata R., *Earning and Spending the Family Income,* revised. D. Appleton-Century Company, Chicago, 1935.

Groves, Ernest R., Edna L. Skinner, and Sadie J. Swenson, *The Family and Its Relationships,* revised. J. B. Lippincott Company, Philadelphia, 1941.

Hamblen, Stewart B., and G. Frank Zimmerman, *Wise Spending.* Harper Brothers, New York, 1941.

Herrick, Allan, *You Don't Have to be Rich.* D. Appleton-Century Company, Chicago, 1940.

Nickell, Paulena, and Jean M. Dorsey, *Management in Family Living.* John Wiley and Sons, New York, 1942.

Being well dressed gives a feeling of assurance and poise.
Courtesy, Simplicity Pattern Company.

SECTION V

THE HIGH SCHOOL GIRL AND HER CLOTHES

UNIT ONE. CHOOSING BECOMING CLOTHES

CLOTHING AND PERSONALITY

Every girl wants to look attractive. We know good health, perfect grooming, and good posture underlie attractiveness, but we also recognize the fact that clothes play a part in our appearance. If we are well dressed, that is, if our clothes are becoming and are suited to the occasion for which they are worn, then we appear at our best.

When we are well dressed, we not only look better but also we actually feel better. The assurance and poise that come from knowing that we look our best enable us to forget our clothes and to concentrate on our work, the conversation of our companions, or whatever else requires our attention. Then, too, we must remember that in meeting strangers, our appearance makes the first impression upon them. If the impression is unfavorable, it may mean that the stranger will never be anything more than a name. In this way we may lose the opportunity of adding a congenial comrade to our group of friends or may immediately put ourselves at a disadvantage in applying for a job or in making a business contact.

If we are to look our best we must not only be able to select our clothes well, but also we must be able to purchase them on a given amount of money and to care for them after we have them. Most people do not have an unlimited amount of money to spend for any of the essentials of life, and many really do not have enough for the bare necessities. If we plan our clothing purchases carefully and buy with an eye to values in relation to the price asked, we shall be able to appear attractive within the limits of our budget. Then, too, caring for clothing properly promotes a well-groomed appearance and ensures better service from our garments. The time invested in taking care of our clothing gives double return by helping us to appear attractive and by making our clothes last longer, thus stretching our clothing dollars.

CLOTHING EXPRESSES IDEAS

Has it ever occurred to you that clothing expresses ideas? Study the clothing shown in some well-known picture and see if this is not true. Take, for example, " The Age of Innocence," by Joshua Reynolds. The soft, delicate texture of the dress and its light color, as well as the simple, unsophisticated style of the garment, all help to convey the ideal of youth, sweetness, and innocence that the artist has portrayed.

Now look at the picture of Whistler's mother. The long, dark-colored dress of fairly heavy material gives an impression of the dignity, calm, and somberness of old age, and the delicateness of the bonnet and collar emphasizes the old woman's fragility.

The movies and the stage present ideas through the use of certain types of clothing. Think over some plays or pictures that you have seen, and you will see that this is true. When a character appears in a picture for the first time, the producer cannot stop to give you a description of his mental and moral traits. Through dress and manner, therefore, he tells you something about the individual's personality. For instance, when a woman comes on the screen dressed in a very severe tailored suit, a blouse with a high, tight collar, and a mannish hat set straight on her head, you feel at once that here is a stern, unbending individual who will stick to her principles regardless of circumstances and will probably bring complications into the lives of the hero and heroine.

Since we have seen that clothing expresses ideas, in choosing our clothes we must decide what we want our clothes to express. Does this mean that all our clothes will have to express the same idea? Certainly not; it is possible to express self-assurance and efficiency at one time and gaiety and frivolity at another. Of course, we must be consistent in selecting our various articles of clothing. If we have chosen a dress that has a very businesslike air, we want to be sure that our hat and shoes are in the same mode. A fussy, frivolous hat would spoil the story that we are trying to tell others through our appearance.

Some girls seem to think that, because nature has made them rather plain looking, their clothes must emphasize this plainness

Sir Joshua Reynolds' " The Age of Innocence."
Courtesy, University Prints.

by being very severe. You have all seen examples of this in the girl who wears her straight hair in a boyish bob and chooses plain, mannish-type clothes that accent her angularly built body and

Whistler's "Mother."   Courtesy, University Prints.

make her seem half boy. It is true that this girl probably would look, as well as feel, ridiculous in fluffy, ruffled clothes. These are not for her. However, a modified hair dress and tailored clothes in less heavy materials made in a manner to soften her angles would make her plainness less noticeable and would emphasize her wholesome, healthy vigorousness without making her seem any less feminine. In any case, we must decide what we want to express to others through our dress and then choose our clothes with that idea in mind. Most of us cannot express these ideas as dramatically as movie stars do, for our lives are not like those portrayed by the movies. Each of us may choose, however, whether she will be poorly or distinctively dressed.

TYPES OF LINES

The type of line — straight or curved — which is dominant helps determine the idea expressed by the costume. Straight lines express force and integrity. When unbroken, they convey an impression of poise, dignity, vigor, and severity. Curved lines suggest grace, joyousness, flexibility, and activity.

This does not mean that a costume can have only one type of line. As you look through fashion magazines you will notice that most garments have more than one type. But have you noticed that in those garments which express ideas in a distinctive manner one type of line predominates? Many dresses have a majority of straight lines giving an impression of poise, dignity, and vigor, with some curved lines used in details to soften the whole effect and make it less severe without disturbing the general idea.

THE FIGURE

In selecting becoming clothes, the figure is the most important consideration, since it is usually noticed first. As you observe others, your first impression is created by the silhouette or outline of the figure. The build of the person is much more noticeable at first than are the details of the costume. The ideal figure is of medium height and is slender but rounded. Actually, the weight of the figure is not so important as its proportions. A person who is slender looks taller than a person of the same height who is stout.

Many of us believe that our figures are far from ideal. We think that we are too short or too tall, too stout or too thin, or that our shoulders are too narrow and sloping or our hips too broad. Height-weight tables tell us whether we are over- or under-weight. If we are uncertain about our figure defects, we can compare our measurements with those of some person who is recognized as the ideal, such as the current " Miss America," or we can compare our proportions with those of a standard figure. In judging proportions, the length of the head from crown to chin is the basic measure and all others should be in correct relation to it. Standard proportions* of a woman's figure are as follows:

Height	7½ heads. (The height of the average high school girl is 6¾ heads.)
Shoulder	1½ heads wide measured in a straight line from one shoulder to the other ⅓ head down from chin.
Bust Line	1 head down from chin.
Waist Line	⅔ head below bust line or just at bend of elbow.
Hips	Same width as shoulder. Widest part should be even with the wrist or 3¾ heads from crown.
Knees	5⁹⁄₁₆ heads from crown.
Ankles	7 heads from crown.

LINE AND THE FIGURE

Most of us are likely to feel that in selecting clothes the short, stout girl has all the problems. We envy the tall, thin person, who seems to be able to wear almost any type of garment. However, she too has problems. The short, stout person generally needs to select clothes which will suggest height and minimize her width. The tall, thin girl, on the other hand, must be careful not to emphasize her height lest she appear scrawny and angular.

In using dress to modify the proportions of the figure, we rely upon the lines used, such as the seamlines, hemline, waistline, neckline, pleats, and trimming, because the eye unconsciously follows these lines. To be becoming, these lines must be in harmony with those of the body, must make the body seem of good proportions, and must make the wearer's defects less noticeable by calling attention to her good points.

In general, horizontal lines lead the eye around the figure, thus creating an illusion of width. Vertical lines carry the eye up and down, thus making the figure seem taller and more slender. In using these lines, there are a few points to keep in mind. Al-

* *Practical Home Economics,* December, 1929.

though horizontal lines widen the figure, when they are curved or pointed, they are less widening. If they are used in a series that is evenly spaced, they tend to make the eye travel up and down. Horizontal and vertical lines may be made more conspicu-

In these historic costumes note that horizontal effects give width, whereas vertical lines give height.

ous by using contrasting colors or decorative effects, such as stitching, braid, bindings, ruffling, and the like. If vertical lines are used to divide the figure into even spaces, the eye is carried across the figure. When vertical lines are used to divide the figure into spaces that are pleasing in proportion, however, then the eye is carried up and down. Vertical lines may be emphasized as suggested previously.

THE FACE, THE CENTER OF INTEREST

A line, as we have learned, is used to direct the eye to the important part of an object. Obviously the face is usually the dominant part of our personal design. It is the most distinctive part of our appearance; it distinguishes us from others and is indicative of our personality. Therefore, the face, since it is an expression of the personality, should be made the center of interest in the dress design.

The large white collar calls attention to the face of the wearer or emphasizes it.
Courtesy, University Prints.

The face may be made the center of interest in a number of ways. Contrasting color or light and dark colors near the face, a flower near the face, a line of buttons which lead the eye to the face, bright embroidery around a neckline, and necklaces and scarves in contrasting colors all serve to emphasize the face.

NECKLINES

The neckline is so closely associated with the face that, along with the hairdress and the hat, it affects the appearance of the face more than the other items of our costume. For some time artists considered the oval-shaped face as the ideal. Any variations were considered defects. Many people still hold to this idea and select necklines which will make the face appear as nearly oval as possible.

Most of our faces are variations from the oval, the most common being the long-thin, the round, and the square-shaped faces. Obviously, any neckline is becoming to the oval-shaped face. If people whose faces deviate markedly from the oval wish to make their faces appear more nearly oval, there are certain principles which can be followed. Any neckline which repeats the shape of the face or which is in sharp contrast to it emphasizes that shape. For instance, a round neckline or one with a sharp V just at the base of the neck will make a round face appear more round, since the one repeats the shape of the face and the other is in sharp contrast to it. When transitional lines, that is, lines that neither repeat the shape of the face nor are in sharp contrast with it are used, however, the shape is modified and softened. A long-oval or a very deep V neckline, for example, will make a round face seem less round.

On the other hand, many people feel that perfection of features is not always the goal to be desired and that it is just as ridiculous to say that everyone's face should be oval as it would be to say that everyone must have blue eyes and blond hair to be good looking. Most variations from the oval are not so extreme that the contour of the face should determine the neckline to be worn. Rather, the neckline should be such that it helps to express the personality of the wearer but at the same time does not overemphasize any marked defects. For example, a person who has a slightly square face may feel that this squareness is an asset in expressing a strong, forceful, vigorous personality. If so, she should in no way attempt to make her face appear less square. At the same time, if her face is very square, she will not want to emphasize this quality to the extent that she seems pugilistic.

COLOR AND IDEAS

Color is another medium through which we express our ideas and personality. The symbolic significance of color has come down to us from ancient times. We associate purple with royalty and power, white with innocence and purity, black with mourning, and blue with sincerity and tranquility. In determining how color is used to express ideas, let us consider again the pictures which we analyzed previously. In " The Age of Innocence " the delicate color of the dress helps to convey the idea of youthfulness and gentleness. No bold, bright, strong color is used here. In Whistler's " Mother " the black of the dress conveys an impression of the dignity and calm of old age.

COLOR AND PERSONALITY

Colors which are becoming and which express our personality not only give pleasure to those who see us but actually give us poise and a sense of well-being. Of course, we all have emotional associations with various colors which are based on past experiences and which determine to some extent our use of color. Then, too, we must take care that, in our effort to express ideas through dress, we do not allow color to dominate our personality. It should provide the background so that the individual is the center of interest. Personalities that are quiet, gentle, and retiring may be eclipsed by strong, vivid colors, whereas forceful, vivacious, energetic personalities can wear bright, bold colors.

QUALITIES OF COLOR

There are certain qualities which color has and certain terms which are used in connection with it which we must know if we are to use it successfully. The primary colors — those from which all others are made — are red, yellow, and blue. The secondary colors, which are made by combining two primaries, are orange, green, and violet. The intermediate colors are achieved by combining a primary and a secondary color. For example, when orange and yellow are mixed together, we have an intermediate color, yellow-orange.

Black, white, and gray have not been mentioned. They are really not colors at all but are neutrals.

Color also has the quality of warmth or coolness. Red, orange, yellow, and red-violet are considered warm, since they are associated with the colors of the sun and fire. Blue, green, and blue-violet are considered cool colors, since they are associated with the colors of water, moonlight, and grass. Warm colors tend to stimulate and excite us, whereas cool colors are restful and make us feel calm. In planning a color scheme, we generally determine whether we want a cool scheme or a warm one. This does not mean that cool or warm colors will be used exclusively, but rather that the mass of color will be warm or cool with smaller areas of the other type.

Color also has the quality of advancing or receding. Warm colors, which seem to advance or to come to meet you, make the figure appear larger than cool colors, which recede.

VALUE

By the value of a color we mean the lightness or darkness of it. Light values are fresh, youthful, and delicate in feeling. Dark values give an impression of dignity, mystery, and sedateness. Light values attract attention more quickly than dark ones and hence make the figure seem larger.

If your body tends to be frail and your coloring is delicate, light values will be more becoming. Dark values may appear too heavy on you and will take away color from your face, making you look pale and tired.

Contrasts between dark and light often make a costume more interesting. Light collars are frequently used on dark dresses to draw attention to the face and to bring out its color. Dark collars, on the other hand, are sometimes very strikingly used on light dresses to draw attention to the face and to add interest.

INTENSITY

Intensity is the brightness or dullness of a color. Very intense color attracts our eye readily, but we soon tire of it. Because intense color attracts us, an object so colored seems larger than it is. Imagine a girl in a very bright green dress. If this girl entered the room, you would see her immediately. Because of the intense color of her dress she would stand out very sharply against the background of the room. Then imagine this same girl dressed in a soft, dull gray-green which blends with the background of the room. Can you see that the second dress is much less conspicuous and would therefore tend to make the wearer look smaller than the first one?

COLOR COMBINATIONS

Nature has used color combinations not only by combining the green of the stem and leaves with the color of the flower but often by making the flower itself a combination of colors. In combining colors, there are rules to guide us. If we arrange the colors on a circle before we begin combining them, we shall find it easier to apply the rules.

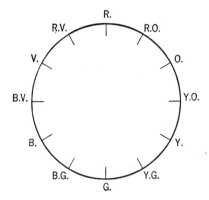

You will observe that, in arranging the colors on a circle, the secondary colors always lie between the two primaries from which they are formed, and the intermediate colors between the primary and secondary colors of which they are composed. These colors can be combined in different ways to create various color harmonies.

The *self-tone* color harmony consists of different values and intensities of one color. A combination of dark blue, medium blue, and light blue used in a coat, dress, hat, and accessories is an example of this type of color scheme. Touches of white, black, or gray may be used with this, as with any other scheme, to add interest.

The *analogous* color scheme has more possibilities and is more interesting than the self-tone harmony. In this type of combination, colors which lie next to each other on the color circle are combined. Those colors which lie between the primaries and have one color in common make the most pleasing schemes. For example, a satisfactory analogous color harmony is yellow, yellow-green, and green. In this case yellow is found in all three colors, and the colors lie between the primaries yellow and blue. If this scheme is made across the primary colors, it is much more difficult to handle and the effect is not likely to be pleasing. For example, it is difficult to combine red-violet, red, and red-orange in a pleasing effect, and yet these colors lie next to each other on the color circle.

In using analogous colors, it is important to have decided differences in the values and intensities of the various colors. Otherwise, it will appear that the colors were meant to be matched but that the matching was unsuccessful.

The *complementary* color harmony is made by combining colors which lie opposite each other on the color circle. Nature uses this color combination in the red and green of holly and the poinsettia. In its greatest intensities, this is a very startling color scheme and is often used in advertising because it attracts attention. However, in dress we do not care to resemble a billboard or a poster; therefore we should take care to have the large mass of color rather subdued, with smaller areas of the complement in more intense color for accent.

The *double complementary* color harmony is made by combining two adjacent colors and their complements. One color should be dominant and should be used in the largest amount and the lowest intensity. The color which is used in the smallest amount may be used in the highest intensity.

The *split complementary* harmony combines a primary or an intermediate with the two colors on either side of its complement. A combination of yellow with red-violet and blue-violet is an example of this harmony. As you can see from the color circle, violet is the complement of yellow. The colors on either side of violet are red-violet and blue-violet, that is, the two components of violet. This color scheme cannot be made by starting with the secondary colors orange, green, or violet. The complements of these three colors are primaries. Since primary colors are elements, they cannot be split into component parts.

With *triad* color schemes, rich, interesting combinations are possible if they are skillfully handled. They are made by placing an equilateral triangle on the color circle or by selecting a color, counting four beyond it on the color circle, and then counting four beyond the second color. The triad made from the three primary colors is the most difficult, as these colors have nothing in common.

You will notice that in discussing the various color harmonies, the statement has appeared frequently that the larger the area the duller the color should be, whereas smaller areas may use more intense colors. This rule is especially true for street and business wear but is not always observed for sport and evening clothes. Sport clothes have the brilliance of the outdoors for a background; consequently, intense colors, providing they are suitable for the personality of the wearer, do not seem too conspicuous. For evening wear, the background provided by bright lights, gay surroundings, and the brilliant colors of other gowns makes possible the use of more intense color.

COLOR AND THE COMPLEXION

We often hear people say, " I can't wear green; it isn't a bit becoming to me." Whether a color is becoming depends upon our personal coloring, that is, whether we are blonde, brunette, or red-haired. Let us analyze each of these types.

The typical blonde has pale yellow or golden hair, blue or gray eyes, and a delicate, pink complexion with blue in the shadows. A variation of the blonde is the Irish type, who has the same coloring in skin and eyes, but whose hair is blue-black. In general, we say the coloring of these people is cool.

The typical brunette has dark-brown hair, brown eyes, and yellow-orange skin tones with tinges of red-orange. The red-haired type has red-orange hair, brown, blue, or gray eyes, and creamy skin with red-orange tones. These two types have decidedly warm personal coloring.

The intermediate group, which is probably the largest, may have various combinations of hair, skin, and eye coloring. Neither warmth nor coolness predominates in their personal coloring.

In deciding what colors are most becoming to each type, the personality of the individual must always be considered. Then, too, the skin and hair must have greater consideration than the eyes, since they occupy much larger areas and are evident to others long before the eye coloring can be discerned. Colors related to the personal coloring of the individual are generally more pleasing than contrasting colors. Therefore, cool colors are best for cool types and warm colors for warm types. The intermediate type can probably wear almost any color if the values and intensities are right.

In selecting becoming colors, if we are able to try on the various colors in different values and intensities, we can see just which ones are best for us. Then, too, the following principles will help us.

Complementary colors intensify each other. If we wish to emphasize the pink coloring in our skin, we may wear green. If, however, we have a very red face, we should avoid wearing green.

Repetition of a color tends to emphasize it. Sometimes this emphasis is desirable and sometimes not. Tan will make a sallow skin look more sallow, since it repeats the skin tones. On the other hand, it may be advantageous to emphasize the color of the eyes by repeating it in the costume. Of course, it is foolish to wear a blue dress to make the eyes seem more blue if this color is unbecoming to the skin of the wearer.

Since the cool coloring of blondes is rather delicate, very intense color is not often becoming, as it may make them look dull and faded. However, there is very little contrast in the coloring of these people, and although light values are becoming, the effect may be monotonous. Accents of dark or bright color, such as a collar, flowers, or beads, help to provide variety and interest.

Light colors tend to darken the skin of the brunette. This effect may or may not be desirable. Present-day standards of beauty do not require that everyone have a pink and white complexion. Brunettes are a distinct type, and their dark skins merely serve to emphasize their particular kind of beauty. The goal that we strive for now in our personal appearance is to express our personality and make the most of our individuality. If the warm-type person is better able to express her personality by wearing colors and values which contrast with her skin, even though they make it look darker, she should by all means seek this contrast. If, on the other hand, light values merely make her skin look muddy and dirty, then surely she makes herself less attractive by wearing them.

In choosing colors, the red-haired girl must decide whether she wants to emphasize or to subdue the color of her hair. Colors which blend with her hair coloring, such as dark brown, will tend to subdue it, whereas greens and blue-greens, being complements of her hair tones, tend to emphasize the color of the hair.

COLOR AND THE WARDROBE

In selecting our clothes from the standpoint of color, we must consider not only the color combinations used in each garment and the becomingness of the color to the individual but also the color of each garment in relation to the other articles of clothing in the wardrobe with which it must be worn. Generally, in planning the wardrobe, it is best to select first those garments which will be worn for several seasons and which must be worn with several different garments. Coats are a good starting point in planning our wardrobes, since most of us have to wear a coat for more than one season and do not have a different coat for each dress. After selecting a coat, we can build our wardrobes around its color.

In planning your wardrobe in color units such as have been described, it is possible to plan just two units for a year, one for winter and one for summer. Each unit has a predominating color which can be used in various values and intensities. Variety and contrasts are achieved by combining different garments and through the use of different accessories. When the clothing allowance is very liberal, as many units can be planned as seem desirable and can be afforded. Each unit, of course, has a predominating color, and the various units may be related to each other or may be entirely independent.

STUDY-GUIDE QUESTIONS

1. What are the advantages of being attractive?
2. What factors underlie attractiveness?
3. What do we mean when we say a person is well dressed?
4. What are the advantages of being well dressed?
5. What should we know in order that we may be well dressed?
6. How is clothing used to express ideas in the pictures " The Age of Innocence " and Whistler's " Mother "?
7. What ideas are expressed by the following: (*a*) a nurse's uniform; (*b*) a policeman's uniform; (*c*) riding clothes; (*d*) a nun's habit?

8. Must our clothing always express the same ideas?

9. Define line.

10. What types of lines are found in clothing?

11. What does each of these types express?

12. Why should the figure be the first point of consideration when selecting becoming clothes?

13. What is meant by the silhouette?

14. Does the present-day silhouette modify the figure in any way?

15. What construction lines of a costume help in modifying the proportions of the figure?

16. What type of line is usually used to increase the width of the figure? To increase height?

17. Why should the face usually be made the center of interest of a dress design?

18. What devices may be used to make the face the center of interest?

19. What should we expect a costume to do for our personalities? Suggest ways in which this purpose may be achieved.

20. Why is the neckline important in dress design?

21. What shape of neckline would you choose to emphasize the natural shape of a face? To modify its shape?

22. What is the argument used against attempting to make all faces appear oval?

23. Give examples of the symbolic meaning of color. Do you know how these meanings became associated with these colors?

24. Show how the colors used in " The Age of Innocence" and Whistler's " Mother" express ideas.

25. What quality in color should be avoided by the quiet, gentle, and retiring personality? By the forceful, vivacious, energetic personality?

26. Name the warm colors; the cool colors.

27. Why do advancing colors make the figure appear larger, and receding colors make the figure appear smaller?

28. What qualities do light colors give to dress? Dark colors?

29. What is meant by intensity in relation to color?

30. How may value be used in dress to draw attention to the face?

31. Name the primary colors. How are they related to the other colors on the color wheel?

32. Name the secondary colors. How are they related to the other colors on the color wheel?

33. What is meant by intermediate colors? Give examples.

34. How may black, white, and gray be fitted into the world of color?

35. Name the six color harmonies given in your text. Tell how each is made.

36. Describe a typical blond, a typical brunette, and a typical red-haired type. What is the coloring of girls grouped under the intermediate type?

37. Why does green emphasize the pink coloring of the wearer?

38. Why should blondes be careful not to wear intense colors?

39. When is it desirable to repeat one's natural coloring in dress? Why?
40. How may a brunette make her skin look darker?

ACTIVITIES

1. Write a paragraph about the most attractive person you have ever known. State what made this person attractive.

2. Describe a character in a movie or play whose clothing expressed an idea. Explain what was done to express this idea.

3. From fashion magazines cut and mount an illustration of a costume which expresses self-assurance and efficiency and another that expresses gaiety and frivolity. Write a few statements about each illustration to show how the effect has been achieved.

4. From a fashion magazine cut and mount an illustration of a costume in which straight lines are dominant and one in which curved lines are dominant. Do these costumes use more than one type of line? What idea is expressed in each illustration?

5. From a fashion magazine cut and mount an illustration of a costume that makes the figure appear wider and one that makes the figure appear taller by the construction lines used. Indicate the lines that do this.

6. From a fashion magazine cut and mount several illustrations in which the face has been made the center of interest through different devices. Indicate in each case the method used.

7. Select people in your class with different shaped faces. Try various necklines on these individuals, and observe the effect on the shape of the face.

8. From a fashion magazine select a costume in color that would be suitable for a gentle, retiring person and one for a forceful, vivacious, energetic person. Write a few statements explaining why these color schemes would not be interchangeable for these individuals.

9. Mount samples of colored paper or cloth to illustrate (a) the primary colors; (b) the secondary colors; (c) advancing colors; (d) receding colors; (e) warm colors; (f) cool colors; (g) a light and a dark value of the same color; (h) a bright and a dull intensity of the same color.

10. Make a color wheel, using colored paper, water color, or crayon. Label each color.

11. Mount pictures of six costumes, each of which illustrates a different one of the color harmonies described in your textbook.

12. Classify the members of your group as to personal coloring.

13. Select a typical blonde, brunette, redhead, and intermediate type from your group. Try various colors in different values and intensities on these individuals, and observe the effect on their personal coloring.

14. Plan a wardrobe for yourself from the standpoint of color, choosing a key color for a coat and planning other garments around it.

UNIT TWO. SUITABLE CLOTHING

We should feel very conspicuous if we wore a bathing suit to school, yet we feel entirely happy on the beach in one. Garments may be beautiful in themselves, but we cannot feel poised or comfortable in them unless they are suited to the place and time in which we are wearing them.

Appropriate clothing does not necessarily mean expensive clothing. It means clothing that is suited to our activities and environment and is considered correct by the people who set our standards. Our environment determines to some extent our activities, which in turn determine the type of clothing we need. If you have no place to ski in your community, you certainly will not include a skisuit and shoes in your wardrobe. Climate too affects our choice of clothing. If you live in a warm region, fur-trimmed, woolen clothing will not be a necessity, as it is in cold, northern localities.

Inappropriate dress not only makes you feel conspicuous and ill at ease but also may actually cause you to fail to achieve a desired goal. When you apply for a job, inappropriate dress may mean that you do not get it. Employers say that 75 per cent of their opinion of you is based on your personal appearance. Again, the wrong type of clothing may mean that a club or social group will not be willing to consider you for membership, since they must base their opinion on your appearance before they really know you.

Most of us cannot afford a complete outfit for every occasion. However, we can always be appropriately dressed and still remain within our budgets if we analyze our needs carefully and then choose garments which are suitable for more than one occasion and which will harmonize with the same accessories and coat. In making our choices, it is well to remember that well-dressed people are never conspicuous. When there is any question in our minds as to the correct thing to wear, we should always choose the simpler garment. We are less conspicuous when we are underdressed for an occasion than when we are overdressed. The types of clothing which most of us find necessary are clothes for home, school, street, work, church, and social occasions.

This jumper can be made suitable for different occasions by varying the type of blouse worn with it.   Courtesy, Simplicity Pattern Company.

CLOTHES FOR HOME

The clothes which we wear to work around our homes should be comfortable, simple, easily laundered, trim, and attractive. Low-heeled oxfords that give the foot some support and at the same time are adapted to active physical exercise are best. Some people seem to think that their personal appearance around their home does not matter and that old party dresses and bedroom slippers are the proper things to wear. Their unsuitability is certainly obvious.

School clothes should be sturdy, comfortable, easy to care for, and attractive.
Courtesy, Simplicity Pattern Company.

In selecting lounging clothes, the type you buy will be determined by the amount of money you have to spend on this sort of clothing and the way in which you live. A tailored robe of durable material that can be washed will give greater service and cost far less to keep in good condition than a fluffy negligee in pastel colors. Since lounging clothes are worn only within one's own home, the colors can be as garish and the style as individual as you wish.

SCHOOL CLOTHES

Since most of your time is spent in school, classroom clothes are important. School clothes should be sturdy, as they must take continuous wear. If you are to work with the greatest efficiency and concentrate on your studies, your clothes should be light in weight and comfortable and should allow you to move freely. They should be of materials that hold their shape fairly well, do not wrinkle easily, and can be laundered. These qualities will keep the time spent in the care of your clothing at a minimum. Clothes that can be laundered are less expensive to keep in good condition than those which must be dry cleaned and are much more likely to be kept fresh and free from odors. All this does not mean that school clothes cannot be attractive. They should be good-looking and smart in a simple way, so that you will have the feeling of self-assurance which comes from being correctly dressed. Skirts worn with sweaters or blouses and extra jackets which can be worn with different dresses provide for changes with little extra expense. With school clothes a low-heeled sport shoe is most suitable as well as most comfortable and efficient.

CLOTHES FOR STREET AND CHURCH

Usually the clothes we wear for school are equally suitable for street and church wear. Their most important characteristics are that they are not fussy; they are generally rather conservative in color and design. This is especially true if you live in a large city, where stores and large buildings comprise a background against which light, bright colors are apt to be conspicuous.

SPORTS CLOTHES

Probably the outstanding qualities of active sports clothes, that is, those in which we really engage in activities, is comfort and freedom. To play our best game of tennis or basketball, to swim or ride horseback with enjoyment, we must be perfectly comfortable and must not feel hampered by our clothes.

Each type of physical activity has its own particular costume.

We have tennis dresses, riding habits, bathing suits, skating out-fits, skisuits, and many other specialized sports garments, each with its own particular type of shoes, headdress, and equipment. In these garments colors can be bright and gay, for they are generally worn outdoors, where we have the sky, grass, and trees as a background. Materials should be strong and durable, there should be no frills or ruffles, and jewelry should be limited to a simple watch or pin. Then, too, we should take care to be consistent in our sports clothes and to wear them in the proper places. High-heeled shoes with slacks are as absurd as snowshoes on the beach, and shorts, ankle socks, and halters scarcely have a place on city streets.

PARTY CLOTHES

Clothes for social occasions have beauty rather than durability as their keynote. Materials do not need to be so durable and therefore can be more luxurious. Colors are lighter and brighter. Hats may be larger, shoes more elaborate in cut and material with higher heels, and jewelry more striking. For afternoon, semisport clothes are appropriate. Clothes which are suitable for street and church wear can be worn, perhaps with more elaborate accessories.

For informal evening wear sleeves may be long or short, dresses may be floor length, and sandal-type shoes of fabric, fine gloves, and fabric bags are suitable. A formal evening dress is usually cut low in the neck, is sleeveless and floor length, and is worn without a hat.

CLOTHES FOR WORK

Business clothes should look as though the wearer meant busi-ness. They will vary according to the type of work which is done. In applying for a job, you must remember that first impressions are extremely important and that your appearance counts about 75 per cent in getting the job. To most employers a careless, un-suitably dressed girl conveys the idea that she will be careless and will use little judgment in her work. This statement does not mean that only beautiful girls will be employed. Few people have deformities or disfigured features, and, barring these handi-caps, anyone can be attractive if she will take the time to be well groomed and the thought and care to select appropriate clothes. Your general appearance should indicate that you are capable of handling the job for which you are being interviewed.

When applying for a job, your coat, suit, or dress should be conservative in color and cut. Skirt lengths should be fashionable but not extreme, and hems should be even. The neckline of your dress or blouse should not, be too low. Accessories such as light collars must be immaculate and in good repair. Your hat should be smart but not bizarre and your shoes suitable for business and clean, with straight heels. You should wear a girdle and brassière if your figure needs restraint to make you look neat and trim. Any jewelry worn should be suitable in type and inconspicuous. Your skin should be clean and clear, your hair clean and simply dressed, your nails conservative in length and well cared for, your hands free from stains, your teeth clean, and your eyebrows not plucked too thin. Fingernail polish and make-up should be conservatively used and should be suited to your natural coloring and to daytime wear.

The basis of a well-groomed appearance is cleanliness. A body kept clean by a daily bath is a good foundation on which to work. Underclothing and stockings may be washed out each night to keep them fresh and dainty. If dresses are worn alternately, there will be ample opportunity for airing them, which helps to keep them fresh. Clothes that cannot be laundered should be dry cleaned frequently. Deodorants are an invaluable aid in keeping free from perspiration odors. They are especially necessary during the period of job-hunting, when nervous tension causes most people to perspire excessively. Perfume of course has no place in your job. Marked odors are often obnoxious to others even though they may be pleasing to you. Too often perfume is used in an attempt to conceal body odors when a bath would be much more effective.

Since you are often asked to remove your coat during an interview, your coat lining must be neat and clean. If the lining is ripped or worn, be sure to mend it before starting to look for a job. Sometimes it is necessary to open your purse. An orderly purse with a clean, neat lining creates a favorable impression.

After you have a job, the type of work you do will determine the kind of clothes worn. Such jobs as those of the nurse, waitress, and cook require a standardized uniform which signifies cleanliness, efficiency, and comfort. They are made of inexpensive, durable materials that can be easily laundered. They should at all times look neat and be immaculately clean.

The office worker, clerk, teacher, social worker, and probably others will wear very much the same type of costume they wore in applying for their jobs. The amount of leeway in this respect will depend on the location of the work and the type of job. Those of you who work in a large city where it is necessary to ride busses, streetcars, or subways to work will naturally dress more conservatively than those of you who work in a small town where it is possible to walk to your job. Positions with banks, insurance companies, and schools are apt to require a more conservative type of dress than those with advertising agencies, fashion establishments, or theatrical organizations. Regardless of where you are located or what kind of work you do, you can bring dignity to your job and can gain the respect of others by means of your appearance as well as by your manner and through work that is well done.

ACCESSORIES

As far as accessories are concerned, let us see what general suggestions we may follow. Jewelry should be considered part of the decoration of our dress and should not be worn unless it harmonizes with the design and color of the dress.

Shoes should be appropriate, not only in cut but also in material, to the occasion for which they are worn. In general we may say that sturdy leathers, such as calf, buckskin, and elk, and materials such as linen are suitable for school and sports wear. Kid and suède are appropriate for church and afternoon wear, and the more perishable satin, crepe, and metallic materials may be worn for afternoon and evening.

Why is the cut of the shoe important? Why do physical education classes emphasize the importance of good feet? When our feet begin to ache, we are cross and irritable and are not inclined to be very active.

There are two bony arches in each foot. The longitudinal arch extends from the heel forward to the ball of the foot. Here we find the transverse arch, which extends across the foot just at the base of the toes. These arches are supported not by the heel of the shoe but by the muscles of the foot. The longitudinal arch gives spring and grace to our step. The transverse arch makes it possible to grip the earth with our toes and push off to the next step. When we wear high-heeled shoes, all our weight is thrown on our toes, and as a result our walk is very stiff and awkward. Eventually the arches of the feet will fall, not only because they are thrown out

A good school shoe.   Courtesy, *Consumer's Guide.*

of shape by high heels, but also because the muscles which support these bony strucures cannot function and hence receive no exercise to keep them strong. The result is flat feet. Have you ever seen a duck walk? Then you have some idea of how a person with flat feet appears.

In addition to a low, broad heel, our shoes should have a straight line on the inside of the foot and a toe sufficiently rounded to allow our toes plenty of room. A shoe that is too pointed not only crowds and distorts the toes, but also pushes the big toe of the foot inward, causing the joint of that toe to become enlarged.

In buying shoes we can be sure they are long enough for the feet if the tip of the largest toe is at least one-half inch from the end of the shoe. Surely in this day everyone knows of the harmful effects of too short shoes, and the era of the fashionably small foot vanished with hoop skirts and with the coming of sports for women.

It is also just as important that our hose be sufficiently long for our feet, not only for reasons of durability, but also for comfort. In selecting hose, service weight for school, business, and sports wear, and chiffon for afternoon and evening are appropriate.

Gloves, like shoes, should harmonize with the entire costume. Here, again, the materials from which the gloves are made determine to some extent where they will be worn. We have knitted wool, fabric, and suède gloves for sports wear. For street, church, and travel we have gloves of kid, chamois, doeskin, and silk. Gloves for evening are kid, silk, velvet, or suède fabric.

In the matter of purses, we have an even wider range of fabrics, from coarsely woven homespuns for sports wear through the many leathers such as seal, alligator, snake, calf, and ostrich for business, to an endless variety of materials for afternoon and evening. Fitness to purpose and harmony of color and design with the costume determine just what we shall choose from this endless array.

STUDY-GUIDE QUESTIONS

1. State several rules to follow in choosing a suitable wardrobe.
2. What points would you keep in mind when selecting clothing for (a) housework; (b) lounging; (c) school; (d) street and church; (e) sport; (f) parties; (g) business.
3. Describe the bony structure of the foot.
4. What causes flat feet?
5. What factors should we consider in buying shoes?
6. What factors would you consider in buying gloves and purses?

ACTIVITIES

1. Interview any businessmen that you know to find what they criticize in their employees' dress, make-up, and grooming.
2. Report any work experiences you have had where there were special requirements in regard to dress and personal appearance. Was there any reason for these special requirements?

UNIT THREE. BUYING CLOTHES

That the volume of buying is enormous is evinced by the fact that in 1942 more than fifty-six billion dollars were spent by consumers in more than one million retail stores throughout this country. Of these dollars, how many do you suppose brought real happiness to the spender, how many were wasted on useless articles, and how many were spent for articles of such poor quality that the pleasure which should have been derived from them turned to disappointment?

Each one of us in the course of a lifetime buys hundreds of thousands of articles in an effort to satisfy our needs and desires. The extent to which these needs and desires are satisfied is determined by how wisely we buy. The government and large business firms have specialists to do their buying and even maintain laboratories to check the quality of products before they buy. Under such a system needs are carefully analyzed to determine what type of product is required, a survey is made of the various types available, and these types are tested and compared for quality and price. All possible information is gathered so that avoidable errors in buying can be eliminated and wise choices made.

Agencies such as the government, hotels, and railroads, whose purchases run into millions of dollars, buy by specification; that is, they specify exactly the qualities the product must have. For instance, in buying sheets the government specifies the thread count or the number of threads per inch in warp and filling, the weight, tensile strength, weave, and size, and the requirement that they be torn rather than cut.

The average consumer cannot specify her needs in the same way that these agencies do, as she buys on a small scale, but she will do well in buying to approximate the government specifications as closely as possible as a measure of quality.

CONSUMER PROBLEMS

The average consumer not only lacks the aid of a private laboratory and the knowledge of a specialist but she is also beset by other difficulties. She is surrounded by a wealth of articles attractively displayed; advertising brings thousands more to her attention; prices of articles of the same type vary widely; and information about the article she wishes to buy seems vague and difficult to obtain. Everything is very confusing.

The modern shopper must choose from a wide variety of styles and types.
Courtesy, *Consumer's Guide.*

For example, if a girl goes to buy a pair of stockings, she will find many different brands offered for sale and a wide variety of prices even in the same brand. All these stockings will serve the purpose of covering her legs. How can she know which to buy and what price to pay? If the purchaser pays too little, she is afraid the stockings will not give service, and yet some of the most expensive ones are not the most durable either. If she asks the clerk about the difference in price, she will probably be told that the more expensive hose are of better quality. This is an indefinite statement which means little or nothing in terms of wear. If she pays $1.50 for the stockings, when hose priced at $1.00 would give just as good service and look as well, she has wasted $.50. On the other hand, if she buys $.59 stockings which will not survive one wearing, she has thrown away the entire purchase price.

When you consider that a modern department store carries about five hundred thousand articles in stock, which they display attractively and advertise widely to make each seem desirable, you can see that a sound basis for selecting goods, as well as a supply of sales resistance, is essential to a wise use of money.

UNWISE CHOOSING

If you were to ask a group of girls what brand of stockings they were wearing and why they had chosen that brand, you probably would get a variety of answers. Some would have bought a particular brand because it was cheap; some, because the brand chosen was expensive and therefore should be good; some, because the brand was advertised over the radio or because an advertisement in a magazine said it would give their legs allure; some, because a friend said that the brand was good; and some, because the clerk said that the brand was their best-seller. None of these so-called reasons is an intelligent one; that is, none is based on the qualities of the stockings which best meet the needs of the individual.

WISE CHOOSING

If we are to spend our money to the best advantage, we must analyze our needs and desires and determine just what we want most. The majority of us have a limited amount of money to spend, and the same dollar cannot be spent in two different places. Shall we spend it for a bottle of much-desired but unnecessary perfume, or shall we save it toward a new bag to carry with our new afternoon dress? Which course will give the greater satisfaction? The perfume will provide a few moments of pleasure but will soon be gone. The new bag will help to give us the poise which comes from knowing that we are well dressed down to the last detail of our costume and will last for several seasons. Money that is well spent brings us real lasting satisfaction. This fact does not mean that we should never spend our money for things which bring us only temporary pleasure, but that we should first analyze our needs and desires and be sure that we are getting what we want for our money.

Of course, wise spending involves making a plan so that we may set for ourselves goals which will give us the greatest satisfaction possible. It is wise to plan clothing expenditures at least a year ahead. First, take an inventory of the garments and accessories you have on hand that are wearable, then decide just what you need to purchase. If you plan your wardrobe in color units around staple garments as was suggested in Unit 1, you will find that the results will be more satisfying than if you have no particular system. Those garments are most expensive which do not harmonize with the rest of the wardrobe, which go out of style quickly, which wear out before they have given a reasonable amount of service, which require considerable time and money to keep in good condition, or which are so unsuitable that they are discarded soon after being purchased.

After your clothing plan has been made and necessary garments and accessories have been determined, the selection of each article is the next problem. We must consider each garment from the standpoint of type, style, care required, and price in relation to what we expect the garment to do. Immediately we feel a need for all the information and help that we can get in making our decisions.

AIDS IN BUYING

Advertising is an aid in buying because it acquaints the consumer with the new products which are constantly coming on the market and gives him information about the price and uses of the product, as well as tells him where it can be purchased. Good advertising is truthful and gives us facts on which we can make intelligent choices. However, we must realize that the purpose of advertising is to sell the product, and in order to do so the advertiser often appeals to our pride or our emotions rather than to our reason. Advertisements that advise the reader to use certain products because Mrs. Wealthy does scarcely appeal to reason. Advertisements of this type seldom give any facts about the product. Theirs is an emotional appeal which may reach the consumer by radio, billboards, magazines, newspapers, salesmen, or the mail and which tends to create a demand for the product. Even advertising which is not necessarily untruthful may be misleading. We must be careful to evaluate the article by examination and to investigate for ourselves rather than to accept the statements of the advertisement, which may be exaggerated. We must also analyze our needs carefully to be sure that they are genuine needs and not mere desires created by advertising.

Considerable help in buying can be obtained from printed material. Books have been written that will help us in buying many of the articles we use daily. Manufacturers, retail stores, finance companies, and certain departments of the government publish booklets giving consumer information on various articles. Many of these are free, can be purchased for a small sum, or can be secured from the public library.

There are private agencies which help the consumer, such as the American Medical Association, whose seal assures you of the purity and wholesomeness of the product on which it appears. Guarantees are useful in that they indicate that someone will assume some responsibility. However, a guarantee is useless unless it is written, is dated, and names the guarantor. In addition the guarantee should specify the period for which the article is guaranteed, the exact adjustment that will be made in case the product proves unsatisfactory, and just what is guaranteed. A label which says " Guaranteed fast color " does not say what the color is fast to. A better label would specify, " Color guaranteed fast to sunlight, to washing, and to perspiration."

Various testing services are also available to consumers. Many stores have laboratories where experts investigate the qualities of articles before placing them in stock and where they can make tests on goods which customers have found unsatisfactory. These laboratories can usually be a source of information for the consumer.

Some magazines have testing laboratories. A manufacturer may send in his product to be tested, and if it is approved, its advertising is accepted by the magazine. With such a business arrangement the standards by which the product is judged are apt to be low, and no explanation of why a product is accepted or rejected is ever given the consumer. Such organizations as Consumers' Research and Consumers Union also give some assistance to buyers. They are reputed to be nonprofit organizations receiving no money from manufacturers and supported solely by the fees of members. They rate the various commodities which they examine and give reasons for their rating. Naturally they cannot test all the articles that are offered for sale, they cannot keep pace with the many changes in these articles that are constantly taking place, and they cannot test brands which are peculiar to one locality.

Brand names and trade names make shopping easier, as it is simpler to ask for an article by a specific name. However, the consumer should realize that the manufacturer often makes several different grades or qualities under one brand name and also that the same product may be sold in several different stores under different brand names. Nationally advertised brands may be purchased in most cities throughout the country, but brand names and trade marks are not necessarily a sign of quality.

In buying specific articles of clothing there are some fundamental facts that will help us. If we learn to observe certain factors in buying, we will be more likely to make satisfactory purchases. Since practically everything we wear is made of some kind of textile, we will consider textiles first.

BUYING TEXTILES

The textiles used for clothing are cotton, linen, wool, silk, Aralac, rayon, and nylon. Materials for draperies and tablecloths are being made from Fiberglas, but at present this fiber is not being used for clothing. A brief survey of some of the characteristics of each fiber should help us decide which material is best suited for each garment that we buy. After analyzing our clothing needs, a knowledge of textiles will help us to buy a sun-fast cotton tennis dress without being sidetracked by a linen or silk dress which may be more attractive when new but which we know is unsuited to our purpose. The chart on p. 196 will give you some information about the characteristics of the various textile fibers.

Science is constantly working on new fibers that can be used in our everyday living. We have mentioned Vinyon, which is made from synthetic resins, and the fibers made from glass. Fibers have been made from soybeans, and a wool-like fiber called Aralac is being made from casein. Aralac is warm, and is generally used in combination with wool fibers.

The quality of the wool fiber depends on the breed, climate, and health of the sheep. Courtesy, *Consumer's Guide.*

MAKING FIBERS INTO YARN

In making yarns, several fibers are twisted together to make a single yarn. The more twists there are to an inch, the harder and firmer the yarn will be. These tightly twisted yarns make stronger materials than do loosely twisted ones. Fine yarns are used to make fine materials, and coarser yarns are used for coarser fabrics and homespun effects. Different colored yarns may be twisted together to give tweed and mixed effects. Novelty fabrics may be made by using different sized yarns to form ribs in the fabrics, as in dimity; or sometimes the crosswise yarns heavier than those running lengthwise are used, as in poplin; or knots may be left at intervals on the yarn, which gives a rough, knobby texture to material, as in ratine. Usually fabrics made of evenly sized yarns give better wear than those in which the yarns are uneven in size.

	Cotton	Linen	Rayon	Silk	Wool	Nylon
	Fairly strong.	Strong.	Weak when wet.	Strong.	Very strong.	Strongest fiber.
	Easily laundered, can be boiled.	Easily washed, should not be boiled.	Should be carefully laundered; should not be boiled.	Can be washed; should not be boiled.	Must be washed carefully; is apt to shrink. Cannot be boiled.	Easily laundered.
	Fairly good conductor of heat; makes cool clothing.	Very good conductor of heat, is cool but heavy.	Good conductor of heat.	Poor conductor of heat; warm but light in weight.	Poor conductor of heat; makes very warm garments.	
	Inelastic, wrinkles easily.	Inelastic, wrinkles easily.	Inelastic, wrinkles easily.	Very elastic, holds shape well.	Very elastic, does not wrinkle easily. Holds its shape well.	Most elastic.
	Can be made in colors that are fast to sun and washing.	Can be purchased in colors fast to sun and washing.	Takes dye well.	Holds dye readily; is not apt to fade.	Holds dye well; is not apt to fade.	Takes dye readily.
	Can be made to look like other fibers.	Is sometimes combined with cotton.	Is made to look like other fibers.	Is sometimes weighted with metallic salts to make it seem heavier than it is. Pure dye is not weighted.	Is sometimes combined with cotton and rayon.	
	Naturally dull in appearance.	Naturally lustrous.	Naturally lustrous.	Very lustrous.	Dull in appearance.	

WEAVES USED IN MAKING MATERIALS

After the yarns are made they are woven into cloth. A closely woven fabric is usually firmer and more durable and shrinks less and holds its shape better than a loosely woven one. The closeness of the weave is expressed as thread count. The thread count of material is the number of warp (lengthwise) and filling (crosswise) yarns to one square inch of fabric. A fabric that has 80 warps

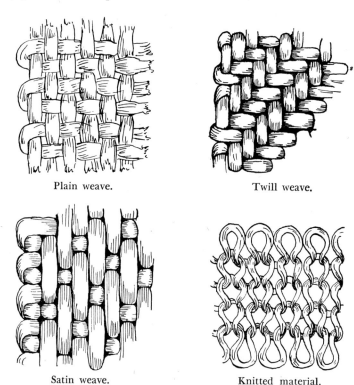

Plain weave.   Twill weave.

Satin weave.   Knitted material.

and 80 fillings is said to have a count of 80 square. If there are 80 warps and 72 fillings, the thread count is said to be 80 by 72. Materials with high count are closely woven, whereas those with low count are loosely woven. Approximately the same number of warp and filling yarns to the square inch makes a well-balanced, durable fabric.

In weaving, threads may be combined in various ways to give different qualities and thus make materials of different types.

The simplest weave is made by taking one set of threads over and under every other one of the second set. This is called the plain weave. Because of its simplicity it is cheapest, and, if made of tightly twisted yarns woven close together, forms a very strong material.

The diagonal lines that you see in serge are made by passing the crosswise threads over groups of lengthwise threads in such a way as to form these diagonal lines. This is called the twill weave and gives a very strong material.

The smooth surface of sateen is made by the sateen weave. The crosswise thread passes under a large number (as many as twelve) lengthwise threads and passes over one. As a result long, loose threads or floats are left on the surface of the cloth which reflect light and give a smooth, lustrous appearance to the material. The material may be firm, but the loose threads are easily pulled, making a less serviceable fabric. When the warp threads are left as floats instead of the filling threads, the weave is called satin.

Velvets, Turkish toweling, and some rugs are made with a pile weave. In this weave an extra set of lengthwise threads is looped over wires in the process of weaving. For velvet, these loops are cut; for Turkish toweling, they are left uncut. We can see why velvet dresses are unsuitable for school when we know that this pile crushes and must be brushed frequently to keep it free from dust.

Patterned materials, such as damask and brocade, are woven on special looms called Jacquard looms. As the design must be carefully worked out to the smallest detail and the Jacquard loom is an intricate piece of machinery, we can see why materials made by this weave are more expensive than those made by the plain weave.

Materials such as jersey are not woven at all, but are knitted. Knitting is looping a thread in itself. Knitted materials are more elastic than woven ones, but should not be so elastic that they will stretch out of shape. In addition, knitted fabrics are more porous and therefore warmer and more easily cleaned than woven materials. You can see then why knitted fabrics are suitable for sports clothes, hose, and underwear.

In selecting a fabric, the type of weave must be taken into consideration. If durability, economy, and ease in caring for the fabric are of greatest importance, the plain or twill weave is the wisest choice. If, however, beauty and interest in design are the first considerations, the satin, pile, or Jacquard weave is the most desirable.

FINISHES FOR FABRICS

After the cloth has been woven it may be finished in many different ways. Color may be applied to cloth in three ways. The yarns may be dyed before weaving, the cloth may be woven and then dyed, or color may be printed on after weaving. The colors of many materials are guaranteed fast to sun and washing and are so labeled. In case there is no label to this effect, the buyer should inquire whether the store guarantees the color.

Sizing material with starch and weighting with metallic salts are done for the purpose of making the material seem more closely woven and heavier than it really is. After washing or cleaning, the material appears loosely woven and sleazy, and the garment usually shrinks. Sizing can sometimes be detected by rubbing the material between the fingers. If a white, powdery substance appears, the material has been sized.

Cotton materials may be calendered, that is, given a temporary luster by passing them between hot rollers. This luster will disappear when the fabric is laundered. On the other hand, mercerization, which is a process of treating cotton with a chemical, will give a permanent luster and actually increase the strength as well as the beauty of the fabric.

Crease-resistant qualities are sometimes given to cotton, linen, and rayon fabrics by treating them with synthetic resins. The labels " Tebilized " and " Vitalized " mean that the material has been so treated. Weaves that give a springy quality to fabrics make them less likely to hold wrinkles. Zelan is a process which has been developed to keep fabrics fresh and to make them resistant to spotting with liquids and to perspiration. Since it makes the fabric resistant to moisture, it also helps to keep it from wrinkling, as the absorption of moisture is one cause of wrinkling.

Materials are napped by scratching up the ends of the fibers and loose yarns from woven fabrics. Materials such as outing flannel are finished in this way. If the material is firm and closely woven, this process is not harmful. However, if the material is sleazy and is loosely woven, the nap may merely cover up the loose weave and may actually weaken the yarns so that they do not wear well.

Sanforized materials have been put through a process which ensures no further shrinkage. Labels such as " Pre-shrunk " or " Shrunk," however, do not guarantee that there will be no further shrinkage. Since some materials shrink several times, you can see how meaningless such labels are. The Sanforized label, on the other hand, guarantees that there will be no further shrinkage and also assures the consumer that the color is fast to washing, since only materials with this quality can be Sanforized. Drisol is the name of a British process which makes wool unshrinkable.

Materials may be treated with waxes, resins, and chemicals to give varying degrees of resistance to moisture. These various processes have different labels, as well as providing different degrees of ability to repel moisture.

In buying garments we are interested in the material from the standpoint of serviceability, shrinkage, and color fastness. Consequently, as we examine garments which we are considering buying, there are definite things to observe about the fabrics used in them besides attractiveness. If consumers could satisfactorily answer the following questions about fabrics, they might be able to get better values for their dollars. Is the material made from the fiber best suited to the purpose for which we will use it? Will the fiber in the material render the service we expect? Does the yarn seem tightly twisted? Does the weave appear close and firm? Is the material sized or weighted? Is the color guaranteed fast to sun, washing, and perspiration? Is the garment guaranteed not to shrink after washing or cleaning? Is the finish temporary or permanent? Which finish suits our needs best? Which are we paying for? Will the material be expensive to care for, from the standpoint of time and money?

JUDGING THE FIT OF A GARMENT

After considering the materials a garment is made from, our next consideration may be its fit. What are the points to be observed in judging the fit of a garment? First, the general divisions of the dress should be correct. The normal shoulder seam lies about one-fourth inch back of the top of the shoulder in a straight line from the base of the neck to the top of the sleeve, and should not swing toward either the back or the front. Similarly, the underarm seam should follow a plumb line from the armhole to the hem. There should be sufficient width across the bust so that the figure does not look pinched and sufficient width across the back so that the arms can move freely without causing discomfort or pulling any seams.

The dress, unless cut low in the back, should fit up across the base of the neck, as should the collar, and should not pull away from the neck. The neckline should lie smooth all around the neck. If it tends to pull away at the sides, the dress may be too narrow across the shoulders.

The waistline is determined somewhat by the decree of fashion, but whether it is high, normal, or at the hipline, it should not " ride up " in front. A very slight drop in front is usually a better line.

Sufficient width in the hips and skirt is necessary to keep the garment from clinging to the figure below the hipline, and to allow ease in sitting.

The length of the dress is usually easily adjusted, but occasionally a garment cannot be altered in length without spoiling the proportions of the dress or without making a great many alterations. If set-in sleeves are used, the line of the armscye should be noted very carefully. This line should be straight in the back and round over the top of the arm. The measurement around the top of the sleeve should be greater than the measurement around the armscye in order to avoid puckering the armscye of the dress. The sleeve should be ample in width and length when the arm is bent, and should not wrinkle across the upper arm when the arm is in a relaxed position at the side. In trying on garments, look at yourself critically from all angles and in the brightest light available.

BUYING READY-MADE COATS

Since a coat requires a considerable investment in money, usually is worn several seasons, and often is the garment around which the rest of our wardrobe is planned, it is well to spend some time in planning this purchase and to exercise care in selecting it.

First you must consider the type of coat you are going to purchase. If you can have only one coat, it is better to select one that is neither decidedly dressy or too definitely a sport coat. A dressy coat is likely to be made of soft material that is not very durable, and a sport coat is not suitable nor does it look well for social occasions. Therefore a coat of conservative cut which is designed for general wear is a better buy for a person who has a moderate clothing allowance.

In the selection of a coat the following points will help you to judge quality:

a. Is the material all wool? Pure wool will be warmer, will hold its color and shape better, and will wrinkle less than wool and cotton.
b. Is the material firm and closely woven? Soft, stretchy materials are apt to sag out of shape.
c. Is the lining material firmly woven, and is the lining full enough to prevent puckering of the outside of the coat?
d. Is the coat interlined? If so, a wool interlining should be warm and light in weight without being bulky.
e. Are the seams stitched with strong matching thread in small stitches rather than long, loose ones?
f. Is the lower edge of the coat finished so that it is smooth and durable?
g. Does the coat have enough lap to be warm and to give a good appearance when you are seated?
h. Do the fastenings hold the coat properly closed?
i. Is there ample room in the coat for sitting and walking?

BUYING READY-MADE DRESSES

In selecting a ready-made dress suitability is the keynote of your thinking. Is the dress appropriate to the purpose for which you intend to use it? Does it answer your needs? If it is a dress for school that you need, you must not be persuaded to spend your money for a skating outfit just because it is cute. Such an outfit neither fulfills your needs nor is appropriate for school. Is the material suited to the style of the dress and to the purpose for which you intend to use it? A filmy chiffon may be most beguiling, but it will not be durable enough for school wear nor suitable for the semisports clothes you like for everyday use. Is the price consistent with the amount of wear you expect to get from the garment? If you are purchasing a party dress which you expect to wear only a few times on occasions when it will not be subjected to stress and strain, you will not be justified in spending a large amount of money. However, if you are selecting a tailored wool dress which will receive hard wear nearly every day for more than one season, then it will be wise to buy a dress of as good quality as you can afford.

The following qualities are characteristic of a well-made dress:

a. The parts of the dress are cut accurately and on the proper grain of material.
b. Ample material has been allowed for reaching, bending, walking, and sitting.
c. Ample material has been laid under pleats and allowed for hem.
d. Seam allowances are large enough to allow for alterations.
e. Seams in loosely woven fabrics have been bound or stitched to prevent fraying.
f. Stitching has been done in strong thread which matches the fabric in color. Short stitches have been used.
g. Trimmings are of the same quality as the dress fabric.
h. Pockets have been reinforced at the corners.
i. Closings are smooth and inconspicuous.

BUYING UNDERGARMENTS

Although most of us probably give very little thought to selecting undergarments, they are most important to a good appearance, as they are the foundation for our outer clothing. In addition they are essential to our health and comfort, for they protect the body from sudden changes in temperature and absorb the secretions from the body, thus helping to keep our outer clothing clean. If undergarments are well designed and properly fitted, they will not retard the circulation or keep the body from moving freely.

The following points are worth noticing in buying undergarments:

a. Materials: soft, porous, easy to launder. If material is knitted, it should be run proof.
b. Colors: usually pastel.
c. Trimmings: simple, durable.

d. Seams: flat, double stitched.
e. Reinforcements at places of greatest wear.
f. Design: conforming to figure, with ample room for sitting and walking.
g. Straps: adjustable, firmly fastened to garment.

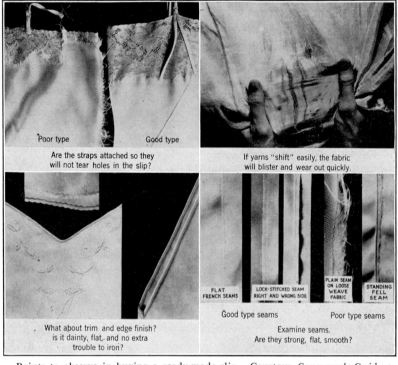

Points to observe in buying a ready-made slip.   Courtesy, *Consumer's Guide.*

BUYING GLOVES

In purchasing gloves you will find a wide variety of materials, colors, lengths, sizes, and types of construction, as well as prices, from which to choose. If you are to buy wisely it will be well before you go shopping to know something about the various kinds of gloves, the type that best suits your needs, and the approximate price you can afford to pay.

In deciding on what type of glove you should purchase, you must consider the material of which the glove is made. Knitted gloves of wool or string and gloves of fabric and the heavy, sturdy leathers, such as capeskin and pigskin, are suitable for sports and street wear. Gloves of finer leathers, such as kid and doeskin, are suitable for more dressy occasions.

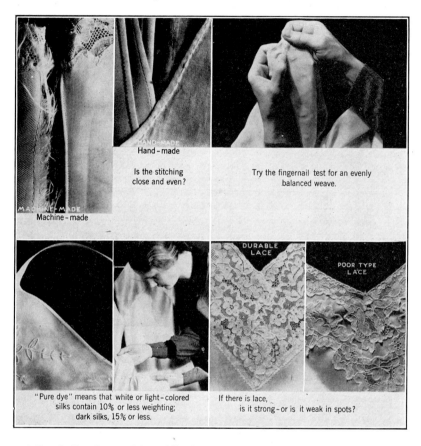

Hand-made

Is the stitching close and even?

Try the fingernail test for an evenly balanced weave.

Machine-made

"Pure dye" means that white or light-colored silks contain 10% or less weighting; dark silks, 15% or less.

If there is lace, is it strong - or is it weak in spots?

The following table will give you some idea of the sources of the various leathers and their characteristics:

LEATHER	SOURCE	CHARACTERISTICS
Buckskin	deer	velvety in finish, durable, soft, warm
Capeskin	sheep	smooth, heavy, durable
Kid	young goats and lambs	fine, thin, pliable
Suède	sheep	soft, velvety, supple
Doeskin	sheep	supple, soft of nap, strong
Mocha	North African sheep	soft, very durable
Pigskin	wild hog of Mexico and South America	coarse-grained, tough, durable, flexible

Gloves may be cut by one of three methods. Table-cut gloves are the finest. They are cut one at a time to accurate measurements and are often marked with the emblem of the " Glover's Guild," a pair of crossed scissors. This emblem is used only on table-cut gloves. Pattern-cut gloves are cut from a pattern requiring much less skilled cutters. The fit of the gloves depends on how carefully the pattern was laid on and cut. Block-cutting is used for inexpensive gloves. Many pairs are cut at one time from a pile of leather by using a die. These gloves will not fit so well, as you can see that little care is taken in cutting them.

Seams in gloves are made in various ways, depending on the effect desired and the price of the glove. The " pique " seam is the most expensive type, as it is the most difficult to make. The edges of the leather are lapped over each other to form a flat seam with one raw edge exposed but constituting a neat, elastic, and durable finish. These seams are used only in the best grade of gloves. The inseam is made by sewing the two right sides of the material together with a lock stitch and then turning the glove right side out. The outseam is just the reverse of the inseam. The wrong sides of the material are sewn together, leaving the seams on the right side of the glove. This is a strong seam, especially suited to gloves for sports wear. The overseam is made by placing the two wrong sides of the material together and then sewing over and over on the right side of the glove. The threads are exposed to wear and the seam is narrow, so that this finish is more suited to dress gloves.

Fabric gloves are made from cotton, wool, silk, and rayon. Generally the cloth for fabric gloves is knitted to make a more elastic and better-fitting product. These fabrics come in different pattern effects, and cotton fabrics are sometimes given a soft finish resembling suède.

In buying gloves, length as well as size must be considered. The length of gloves is expressed in terms of buttons, each button representing one inch measured from the base of the thumb to the top edge of the glove. In considering size, be sure to have your hand measured each time you buy and to have the right glove fitted, as manufacturers' sizes vary. A glove that is to be used for driving, riding, or any active sport should be looser than one that is being used for dress wear. The measurement is usually taken around the palm and over the knuckles. Leather gloves can be purchased in quarter sizes from 5¾ to 8½. Fabric gloves can usually be purchased in half sizes from 5½ to 8½. Knitted sports gloves are usually sold as small, medium, and large.

In putting on gloves, especially when they are new, work them on the fingers carefully. Pulling and straining at the gloves may stretch them out of shape and may break the stitching. In removing them, turn them back halfway over the hand and then remove them finger by finger. Carefully pull the gloves back into their original shape after each wearing. Do not wash gloves unless they are labeled " Washable."

BUYING STOCKINGS

Stockings take a large slice out of each person's clothing allowance. Since we do not get the thrill out of new hosiery that we do out of a new hat or a new dress, we are all anxious to know how to get better wear out of our stockings, so that we shall have more money for some of the more exciting items in our wardrobe.

Stockings may be made from silk, nylon, cotton, wool, rayon, and cotton lisle. Silk and nylon make the most beautiful hose, because they are smooth and can be made very sheer. Nylon resists wear from abrasion, and, although it snags, the threads do not break readily. However, when they are broken, runs form quickly. Wool makes our warmest stockings, which are used for active sportswear and outdoor work in cold climates. Cotton makes a durable stocking, but since it does not always hold its shape and color and is not so flattering as nylon or rayon, it is not a popular material for full-length hose. Cotton hose sometimes bear the label " Combed yarn." This is an indication of good quality, as combed yarns are finer, stronger, and smoother than carded yarns. Cotton lisle is generally made of good-quality, long-fibered cotton, which is tightly twisted. The yarn is usually singed to remove the fuzz and to make it appear smooth. It may or may not be mercerized. Rayon is not so satisfactory as silk or nylon for stockings. It tends to lose its shape, becomes baggy under tension, and stretches and loses strength when wet, thus becoming less durable. If rayon yarn is highly twisted, the stockings will hold their shape better and be more durable. Reinforcing the foot and top with cotton also increases their wearing qualities.

Stockings may be knitted in tubular form or in a flat piece which is seamed together. This latter type of construction is called full-fashioned. Tubular knit hose are knit around and around, with the size of the stitches decreased at the ankle. You can realize that there is very little shape either to the foot or the leg of a stocking made this way, and consequently they fit very poorly. Since they are knit in a tube, there is no need for a seam down the back, but many manufacturers put an imitation seam in the back of these stockings to make them look like full-fashioned hose. Nylon hose can be satisfactorily made in this way, as they are always steamed into shape and will keep that shape as long as the hose lasts.

Full-fashioned hose are knit from the top down in a flat seam. As the stocking approaches the ankle, stitches are dropped to decrease the size. Where the stitches are dropped, a small mark called a fashion mark is left. The number of fashion marks varies with the quality of the stocking. Generally, the more marks the better the shape of the hose, provided that the marks are not spaced too closely together, an indication that the stocking is narrowed too abruptly. A full-fashioned stocking, which is better fitting than a tubular-knit stocking but is more expensive to make, can be distinguished by the fact that it has a real seam, which goes down the back of the leg and through the sole of the foot to the tip of the toe, where it meets a short cross seam. In a full-fashioned stocking the fashion marks are real. They can be distinguished from imitation fashion marks by the direction of the ribs, or wales, in the knitting. In a tubular-knit stocking, where the fashion marks are imitation, all the ribs of the stocking run vertically. In full-fashioned hose, the ribs which lie between the center-back seam and the fashion marks run vertically, but those on the opposite sides of the fashion marks run into the marks in a diagonal direction.

In addition to tubular-knit and full-fashioned hose, fashioned seamless stockings are also made. In this method the stocking is knit from the toe to the hem, and extra stitches are added as they are needed to shape the stocking. This method of construction can be recognized by the fact that the stitches meet in a V-shape at the back of the leg. Although no seam is necessary, a false one is sometimes added. Since this stocking has no seam in the foot, it is more comfortable than one with a seamed foot. It cannot be made in fine gauges, however, and therefore is generally found in the coarser cotton and wool hose.

Lace and mesh hose are sometimes made by cutting the stockings from fabric and seaming them together. Although this method of construction is not common, it is possible and is occasionally used.

In selecting stockings, it is necessary to know the purpose for which they are to be used and then to buy hose of the proper fiber, gauge, and thread count. The size of the yarn used in making silk stockings is spoken of as the thread count. Hose may be purchased in from one to twelve threads. Each yarn used in making stockings consists of several filaments, which have been taken from the silk worm's cocoon. Several of these filaments are twisted together to make a single yarn for a one-thread stocking. To make a two-thread stocking, two of these yarns are twisted together. Of course, the heavier the yarn, the more durable will be the stocking. Stockings of four-thread count or less are made for appearance and not for durability. One- and two-thread hose are sometimes designated as sheer chiffon; three- and four-thread, as chiffon; five- and six-thread, as semiservice weight; seven-, eight-, and nine-thread, as service weight; and ten-, eleven-, and twelve-thread, as heavy service weight. The gauge, which means the number of stitches in every inch and one-half across the stocking, may range from thirty-nine to sixty. The higher the gauge number, the firmer the stocking and the more closely it has been knit. As a result it is less likely to snag. Obviously a very heavy yarn cannot be knit on very fine needles; therefore you would not expect to find a ten-thread stocking in a high-gauge number.

Literally, thread count applies only to silk hose. The weight of nylon and rayon yarns is expressed in deniers. Nylon may be made from fifteen to thirty in denier, and rayon from fifty to one hundred fifty. The lower number indicates the finer yarn. In a high-twist rayon yarn, fifty denier is similar to a three- to four-thread silk; seventy-five denier, to a four- to five-thread silk; and one hundred denier to a five- to six-thread silk.

Cotton is sold by the weight and ply of the yarn. The size of cotton yarn is expressed in the number of yards of yarn it takes to weigh one pound. The coarser yarns require fifteen yards, and the finest one hundred and sixty. By ply is meant the number of yarns used to make one thread. Single-ply is the finest, and four-ply the coarsest. If a cotton stocking is designated as 120/2, two threads of size 120 were twisted together to make the yarn.

In judging quality in hose, the following points are worth noting:

a. Are the tops of the stockings elastic? Do they stretch to eleven and one-half or twelve inches and go back to shape?
b. Is the instep elastic? For a smooth fit it should not stretch too much.
c. Is the welt or top of the stocking double and made of heavier material?
d. Is there a run-stop below the welt?
e. Are the feet reinforced across the toe, along the sides, and well up the heel?
f. Is the seam firmly sewed? Fewer than twelve stitches to the inch are unsatisfactory.
g. Are the stockings the correct size? The foot should measure one-half inch longer than your foot does when you are standing.
h. Are the stockings long enough in the leg? Your measure should be taken from the bottom of your hose supporter to the floor while you are standing.

STUDY-GUIDE QUESTIONS

1. Why is it important that we study the problems involved in buying?
2. How do such agencies as the government and hotels ensure getting their money's worth when shopping?
3. What are some of the common problems of the buyer or consumer?
4. What things should a buyer do before starting on a shopping expedition?
5. Outline the steps given in your text for planning clothing expenditures.
6. Name some aids to buying.
7. Name the textiles used for clothing. Give the characteristics of each.
8. Describe the process used in making fibers into yarn. Explain how tweed, dimity, and poplin are made.
9. Name the five weaves mentioned in your text. Explain how each is made.
10. If you were choosing a material for hard wear, what weaves would you consider? If you were interested in a fabric for its beauty and design, which weaves would you choose?
11. Why are knitted fabrics suitable for sports clothes, hose, and underwear?

12. What are the advantages of a closely woven fabric?
13. What is meant by the thread count of material?
14. What is meant by finishes for fabrics?
15. Why is material sometimes sized? How is this done?
16. Explain the terms calendering and mercerizing. Compare these two finishes.
17. If you were to see the labels " Tebilized," " Vitalized," and " Sanforized " on materials, what would you expect of each of them in use?
18. How has outing flannel been treated to give it a soft, woolly effect? How can you judge the wearing qualities of outing flannel?
19. How may a piece of material be treated to make it resistant to moisture?
20. When buying garments, how can you determine whether the material is serviceable? Whether it will not shrink? Whether it is color fast?
21. Describe the location of the following lines in a well-fitted dress: the shoulder seam, the underarm seam, the hemline, the waistline, and the line of the armscye. How can you prevent a skirt from clinging in to the figure?
22. When selecting a coat, how would you judge the following points: (a) style; (b) material; (c) lining; (d) interlining; (e) workmanship; (f) seams; (g) fastenings.
23. What points should one look for when selecting a ready-made dress?
24. Why are undergarments important items to consider when buying a wardrobe? What qualities should undergarments have?
25. Why are silks and rayons popular fabrics for undergarments? What are some points to notice when purchasing undergarments made of knitted materials? Describe a seam in a well-made undergarment.
26. What fibers are used for stockings?
27. Give the advantages and disadvantages of each type of hose.
28. In what ways may stockings be made?
29. How would you recognize a full-fashioned stocking?
30. What are the advantages of a full-fashioned stocking?
31. Are tubular-knit hose ever satisfactory?
32. What is meant by thread count?
33. What is meant by denier?
34. What is meant by gauge?
35. List some indications of good quality in stockings.
36. How do you know what size stockings to buy?

ACTIVITIES

1. From your own experience write an account of how poor buying practices failed to bring satisfaction.
2. Find an advertisement which you think is really informative and tell what you learned from it.

3. Find an advertisement which is not informative. Upon what is its appeal based? Is the advertisement misleading?

4. If there is a store in your community that has a testing laboratory, visit it and report what you learned about testing articles.

5. Examine any available exhibits of textile fibers and also textiles, noting the characteristic appearance and feel of the various textiles.

6. Study the chart of textile fibers on p. 196 and determine which one or ones would be best for a winter coat, shorts for use at a summer camp, a dress for a formal party, and a pleated skirt. Give reasons for your choices.

UNIT FOUR. CARING FOR CLOTHES

Surely no one will think Jane is well groomed if she has dirty fingernails. Neither can she be considered well dressed when her clothes need brushing and pressing and when she uses pins in place of snaps. Our clothes are kept in order, just as our teeth, hair, and nails are, by daily care. If we make this care of clothing a daily habit, it becomes as much a part of our routine as cleaning our teeth or combing our hair.

Perhaps a peek into Jane's closet will tell us why her clothes always look so untidy. Well, there seem to be plenty of empty hangers in the closet, but the clothes are mostly hanging on hooks, if they haven't slipped off onto the floor. There is an afternoon dress that can't slip off, because the hook has poked a hole right through the dress. Perhaps Jane thinks hangers are used only by dry cleaners to return clothes.

Her hats are tossed in a pile on the shelf, and her shoes are in a jumble on the floor where they must be walked over in order to get into and out of the closet. We see dresses with buttons hanging by a thread and dresses with spots and rips, along with slips which have broken straps, all hung away without any attention being given to repairs. With such a closet as this, is it any wonder Jane appears at school, untidy and disheveled looking, and " never has a thing to wear "?

THE CLOTHES CLOSET

Proper equipment and adequate space for keeping our clothes are essential if we are to take proper care of them. A chest of drawers or a dresser is necessary for articles which are best folded and stored in drawers to keep them fresh. A well-arranged and well-equipped clothes closet is desirable for garments which must be hung up or which must be stored on racks, in boxes, and on shelves. A well-arranged closet generally has a pole on which hangers can be placed and still be accessible. Some shelves which are within easy reaching distance and which will not become inaccessible when garments are hung in the closet are invaluable. Hangers, a shoe rack or a shoe bag, shoe trees, hat stands or hatboxes, and garment bags are all part of a well-equipped clothes closet.

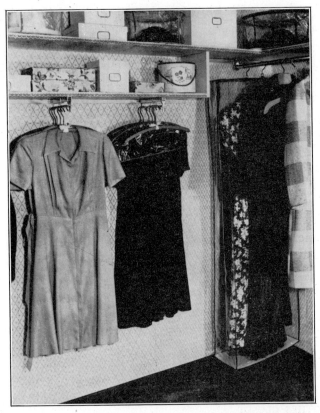

A well-equipped and well-arranged closet is a help in keeping clothes in good condition. Courtesy, *The Ladies' Home Journal,* Curtis Publishing Company.

ARRANGING THE CLOTHES CLOSET

When proper equipment has been obtained, the next problem is to arrange our wearing apparel in such a way that garments will not be handled unnecessarily. We should arrange our clothing so that the garments which are most often used are hung in the most convenient positions, and those which are used only occasionally are hung in garment bags in the least accessible part of the closet.

Skirts are best hung from the belt. One method is to use skirt hangers or the spring-type clothespin on the straight rod of a wire hanger. Instead, a safety pin may be fastened near each end of the skirt belt, and these in turn fastened to a wire clothes hanger. Folding a skirt and laying it over the rod of a clothes hanger is not a desirable method, as a horizontal crease is formed on the skirt by the rod.

When hats are placed on hat stands, they keep their shape much longer than when they are laid on the closet shelf. A Cellophane cover can be placed over each hat to keep it from collecting dust. Hats which are worn only occasionally may be stored in hatboxes. If you use this method, it will be necessary to stuff some tissue paper into the crown of the hat and to pack some around the hat to keep it in shape.

Shoe racks or shoe bags will keep your shoes off the closet floor, will keep the shoes from being scuffed and stepped on, and will make it easier to keep the floor of the closet clean and free from dust.

DAILY CARE

Choosing suitable clothing for each activity will help keep all our garments in good condition. Sports should be carried on in clothing suited to the particular activity. When we exercise violently in street or school clothes, they are likely to become dusty, dirty, and perspired, as well as torn from the stress and strain put upon them. Helping to get dinner in a wool or silk dress is unwise, as cooking processes involve heat and we are inclined to perspire. Our clothing will not only absorb perspiration but also will take on cooking odors, as well as spots and stains from splashing and spilling foods.

After taking off our street and school clothes, it is a good plan to brush them thoroughly and to hang them where they can air for a while before putting them in the clothes closet. Dusty clothes have the same unkempt appearance as a dusty room. When we see how much grime and dust our hands and face collect in a day, the need for daily brushing of our clothes should be unquestioned. For brushing heavy coats and dresses, a whisk broom is most effective. For finer materials, a clothesbrush with fine bristles is best. Use a light stroke, lifting the brush at the end of each stroke to pick up lint.

Putting garments on hangers as soon as they are taken off helps to keep them in shape and saves many hours of pressing. Hanging a garment on a hook may cause it to lose its shape, and the hook may poke a hole in it.

If coats or dresses have become wet, they should be taken off as soon as possible, shaken thoroughly, put on a hanger, and hung to dry where they will not come in contact with other garments. Fur should not be brushed while wet, but it should be shaken and hung to dry slowly away from any source of heat.

SHOES

Just as a hanger helps to retain the shape of a garment, so shoe trees help to keep shoes in shape. Keeping the shoe trees in a convenient place and making it a rule never to take off a pair of shoes without putting shoes trees in them will establish a good habit. Heels must be kept straight, too, if shoes are to stay in shape. Nothing gives such a worn-out, run-down impression as run-over heels and shoes that are out of shape.

In cleaning shoes, methods vary according to the materials used in the shoe. Patent leathers are best wiped off and then rubbed with Vaseline or a shoe cream that contains oil, as this method keeps them soft and prevents cracking. Suède shoes can be cleaned with a wire brush and rubbed with a powder, which helps restore the color. White linen shoes may be scrubbed with soap and water, and then gone over with a preparation for whitening them. Light-colored kid should be cleaned with a neutral dressing which removes dirt. Dark kid is usually cleaned with a preparation the same color as the shoe.

Shoes, like garments, should be aired frequently. They will give better service if two pairs are worn alternately instead of the same pair being worn every day.

When shoes are wet, they should be taken off and wiped free of mud; the toes should be stuffed with paper, and the shoes dried slowly. They should not be placed on a register or close to the heat to dry. When they are dry, they should be polished, and shoe trees should be put in them.

STOCKINGS

If we want our stockings to wear well, we should put them on properly. Using both hands, take hold of the stocking top. Roll up the leg of the stocking, and continue rolling until you reach the toe. Place your toe in the toe of the stocking, and, with one hand

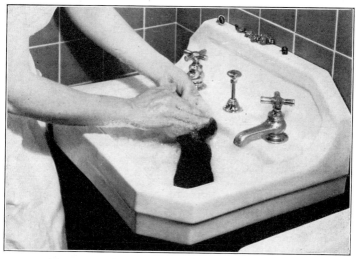

To remove stubborn spots, lay the stocking on the hand and gently work in a few dry flakes. Courtesy, Lux Educational Bureau.

at each side, bring the foot of the stocking along your foot and the stocking on up the leg, unrolling it as you go. In this way, the seam of the stocking can be kept directly down the center back of the leg, and there is the least possible strain on the hose. Manufacturers recommend that we wash our stockings whenever we take them off to prolong their life. Perspiration tends to weaken the fibers in stockings; therefore it is inadvisable to let stockings that have been worn lie about without washing.

To wash stockings, make suds in lukewarm water. Since heat and friction weaken the fabric, squeeze the stockings through the soapsuds and avoid rubbing or wringing them. Rinse them in clear water of the same temperature until they are free of soap. Press the water out of them, or squeeze them between the folds of a bath towel to remove excess moisture. Hang them over a smooth rod away from the heat to dry. Do not iron them. Rayon stockings should be allowed to hang from thirty-six to forty-eight hours until thoroughly dry if they are to wear well.

Darning stockings becomes drudgery if holes are allowed to grow large. Reinforcing thin places with running stitches will prevent stockings from wearing through into holes for a considerable time. Thin places usually appear first at toes and heels. When a hole has been worn in a stocking, it must be filled with stitches which resemble solid material and replace the fabric which

To dry stockings more quickly, knead out moisture with a Turkish towel. Courtesy, Lux Educational Bureau.

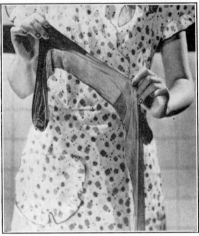

Gently ease stockings into shape; dry away from heat. Dry rayon stockings thoroughly (36-48 hours).

has been worn away. Runs may be repaired by a professional at a nominal charge. If the stocking is good in every other respect, this charge is well worth paying. When mending a run at home, it is best to draw the edges together with small stitches on the right side of the hose. Be sure to catch the dropped stitch at the end of the run, so that the run cannot go any further.

GLOVES

Putting on leather gloves carefully the first three or four times will pay dividends in durability and fit. Gloves should be worked onto dry, cool hands slowly and evenly with the seams straight. They should be worked down the fingers first, and then the thumb should be inserted. In taking gloves off, they should be drawn off over the hand until the second joint is reached, and then slipped off the fingers. They should be smoothed back into their original shape while they are still warm.

Most leather gloves have to be dry cleaned, but some doeskin, chamois, and pigskin gloves can be washed successfully. However, washing should not be attempted unless the gloves are stamped " Washable." The washing directions which come with either fabric or leather gloves should be followed carefully. After washing, excess moisture can be removed by kneading the gloves in a bath towel. Blowing into the gloves helps to restore their shape. Glove stretchers are an aid in shaping gloves, but if they are not available, the fingers may be pulled out and the gloves laid flat on a towel to dry. Care should be taken not to stretch rayon gloves while they are wet.

Use a cupping motion in washing underwear; gently squeeze rich suds through and through the garment. Courtesy, Lux Educational Bureau.

WASHING UNDERCLOTHING

Garments which are worn next to the skin, such as panties, brassières, and girdles, absorb the waste products given off by the skin. We feel cleaner and less likely to offend others with body odor if we put on fresh undergarments each day. However, if we change our undergarments daily, a burden is imposed upon the person who does the family laundry, and it is necessary to have a

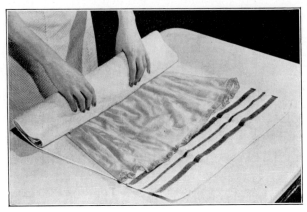

For quick drying remove excess moisture with a Turkish towel. Never leave garment rolled up damp.   Courtesy, Lux Educational Bureau.

very generous supply of undergarments. Most of these garments are made from silk or rayon fabrics which wear better if they are washed immediately after wearing than if they are allowed to

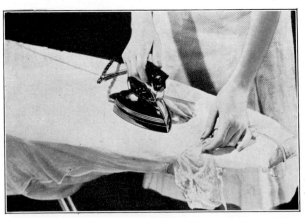

Use a cool iron. Press bias-cut garments slantwise, parallel to the threads of the material.   Courtesy, Lux Educational Bureau.

lie around for several days with perspiration in them. Thus it seems better for several reasons to wash our undergarments each night.

Since any rayon fiber loses strength when wet, we must not

strain rayon when washing it by rubbing, wringing, twisting, or stretching it. Heat also may damage rayon; therefore we should wash with mild soap flakes and lukewarm water. If you do not have soap flakes, make suds with cake soap before putting the garment into the water. Cake soap will not harm rayon, but the friction created by rubbing the soap on the garment will. Squeeze the suds through the garment; do not rub the garment on a board or between the hands. If shoulder straps or other parts have become very soiled, use a soft, fine brush to get them clean. Rinse the garment thoroughly in water of the same temperature. Generally, three rinses are sufficient to remove all the soap. Squeeze the water out carefully without twisting the fabric; then roll the garment in a bath towel and knead out the remaining moisture. Satin and crepes of either silk or rayon should be ironed at once on the wrong side with a warm iron. Knitted garments of synthetic fibers, such as are used in panties, slips, nightgowns, and pajamas, should be gently pulled into shape and then hung over the line or on a hanger to dry. Pinning these garments on the line while they are wet puts pressure on them which may start runs or cause holes to appear at the points of strain.

WEEKLY CARE

It is a good plan to go over all the clothes in the clothes closet once a week. Garments that need cleaning should be sent to the cleaner or put aside to be cleaned at home. All garments should be gone over; and holes repaired, tears mended, and missing snaps and buttons replaced.

REMOVING SPOTS

After you have made necessary repairs on your clothing, look over your garments for spots or stains. Any spots or stains are best removed at once, but this procedure is not always possible. Furthermore, spots may sometimes go unnoticed until we make a weekly inspection of our clothes.

In addition to treating the stain promptly, another general rule that we must follow in removing stains is to be sure the remover is suited to the material. To do this, we must be able to recognize cotton, linen, silk, wool, rayon, and other synthetic fabrics. Cotton and linens are injured by acids and strong alkalies. Weak alkalies are safe if the fabric is rinsed thoroughly. Bleaches also injure these fabrics if they are left on for more than a minute or two. Wool and silk are injured by alkalies and strong acids. Mild acids, except nitric acid, are safe to use on these fabrics. Bleaches which contain chlorine destroy silk and wool. Rayons are injured by strong acids and alkalies, but mild forms of these chemicals are safe if the fabric is rinsed thoroughly. Alcohol, chloroform, and acetone should not be used on acetate rayons. Nylon and Vinyon are unharmed by acids and alkalies and can be treated with bleach without being injured. Chloroform and acetone should not be used on Vinyon, as the fabric is dissolved by these substances. Since nylon and Vinyon do not absorb moisture readily, many common stains can easily be rinsed off these fabrics.

Not only must the remover be suited to the material, but it must also be suited to the stain. Always try to determine what the stain is before attempting to remove it. Substances which may remove one stain may act upon another in such a way as to set it and make impossible its removal from the material. If a stain is not greasy, try first to remove it with cold water. Hot water tends to set stains and makes them more difficult to remove. Before using water on a garment, test a sample of the material in some hidden place, such as the hem or a seam, to see if water spots it. If the fabric is not spotted, place the stain face down on several thicknesses of clean cloth. Sponge the stain with a soft, clean cloth dampened with cold water. In sponging, work with a light motion from the outside toward the center of the stain. To prevent a ring from forming, dry the fabric rapidly by patting it with a dry cloth.

If the stain is greasy, use some kind of grease solvent, such as carbon tetrachloride. Sponge the stain with the solvent in the same way that you sponged with cold water. Although gasoline and naphtha are grease solvents, they are not recommended for home use, as they catch fire easily and have been known to burst into flame from the friction of rubbing the garment. Carbon tetrachloride is safe to use, since it is non-inflammable.

In using bleaches, care must be taken, as most bleaches will take out the color and weaken the material as well as remove the stain. Sodium perborate is a safe bleach for all types of materials, provided that it is left on the fabric only a short time and the fabric is thoroughly rinsed in water.

The following chart for removing common stains may prove helpful:

Stain	Method of Removal from Washable Fabrics	Method of Removal from Unwashable Fabrics
Blood	Sponge with cold water or soak in ammonia water, using 1 tablespoonful of ammonia to two quarts of water.	
Chewing gum	Soften gum with egg white and wash garment.	Soak gum in carbon tetrachloride.
Chocolate	Wash with warm, soapy water and sponge remaining stains with hydrogen peroxide.	Remove grease with carbon tetrachloride. Dry and then sponge with warm water, dust with pepsin powder, let stand for one-half hour, and sponge with water.
Fingernail polish	Use polish remover except on Vinyon and acetate rayons. Moisten stains on these fabrics with carbon tetrachloride, put on drop of banana oil, brush lightly with clean cloth.	Same procedure as for washable fabrics.
Fruit	For cotton and linen, stretch stain over a bowl. Pour boiling water on stain from height of three to four feet. Bleach remaining stains with lemon juice and sunshine.	For wool and silk, sponge with cool water and work glycerine into stain; after several hours put a few drops of vinegar on stain and rinse thoroughly.
Grease	Wash in warm, soapy water.	Sponge with carbon tetrachloride.
Ink	Use soap and warm water on washable ink, or apply glycerine to fresh ink, rub lightly, and rinse.	
Lipstick	Rub Vaseline or glycerine into stain, wash with soap and water.	Rub Vaseline or lard into stain; sponge with carbon tetrachloride.
Paint	Remove with soapy water. If dry, soften with lard first.	
Perspiration	Moisten fresh stains with water; hold stain over open ammonia bottle. Sponge old stains with vinegar.	Same procedure as for washable fabrics.

WASHING SWEATERS

You will not need to wash your sweaters each week; but since they present a special problem in washing and cannot be taken care of with the family laundry, it is a good plan to wash any soiled sweaters at the time set aside for your weekly clothing care.

Before washing a sweater, measure and record the length of the sweater, the width of the shoulders, and the length of the sleeves. Instead, if you prefer, you may lay the sweater on a large sheet of paper, thumbtack it in place, and then draw around it with a pencil.

Using lukewarm water, prepare suds of mild soap. Squeeze the sweater through the soapsuds until it seems to be clean. Rinse in several waters of the same temperature until no trace of soap shows in the water. Squeeze the water out of the sweater, but do not wring or twist the garment. Roll the sweater in a bath towel, and knead to remove as much moisture as possible. Then place the sweater flat and stretch it to its original measurements or to the outline which you drew on paper. If possible, thumbtack it in this position and leave it until dry.

PRESSING CLOTHES

When all repairs have been made on clothing and all spots removed, if no further cleaning is necessary, it is a good plan to press our clothes at this time. Cotton and linen materials are usually dampened and then pressed on the right side if a glossy surface is desired and on the wrong side if a dull surface is desired. Washable silks and rayons should be pressed with a warm iron while damp, except pongee, which should be pressed dry. Other silks and rayons should be pressed with a warm iron on the wrong side. Wool garments require careful pressing to avoid damaging the fabric. You may work on either the right or wrong side of the material. In working on the right side, place a dry wool cloth over the right side of the garment. Place a damp cotton pressing cloth over the wool cloth and cover with a dry cotton cloth. Use a hot iron and press, but without the rubbing motion that is used in ironing. Lift the pressing cloth now and then to allow the steam to escape. Stop pressing while the material is still steaming. Hang the garment on a suitable hanger to finish drying.

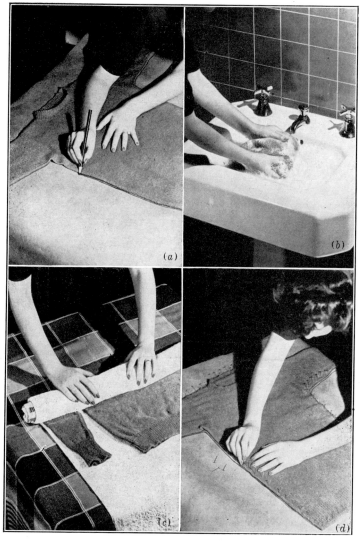

a. Draw outline around knitted garment to use as a pattern when restoring to original size.

b. Squeeze suds through with cupping motion. Support garment with hands to avoid sagging.

c. Remove excess moisture by kneading garment in a Turkish towel. Unroll it immediately.

d. Pat garment into shape, fitting outline previously drawn. Hold it in place with rustproof pins.

Courtesy, Lux Educational Bureau.

SEASONAL CARE

At the end-of the summer and winter it is advisable to store garments worn for the past season. In this way, we keep our garments clean and ready for use, have additional space in our clothes closet, and avoid destruction by moths.

Prevent moth damage by storing clean clothes in tightly sealed packages.
Courtesy, *Consumer's Guide.*

Before wool garments are stored for the summer, they should first be mended, all buttons put on, and any tears or holes repaired. They should then be thoroughly dry cleaned. If the garment does not seem soiled enough to warrant dry cleaning, it should be sunned and brushed very thoroughly before putting away. Moths usually seek the spotted and soiled places on a garment. The moth you see flying about in the spring is not the one that eats your wool clothing, but it is the beginning of trouble. This moth flies about until it finds a wool garment, preferably a soiled one, in a dark place in which to lay its eggs. Under collars, pleats, or pocket flaps, in seams, and folds are choice locations. These eggs, if undisturbed, hatch, and the resulting worms feed on the wool garment. Dry cleaning or washing a garment destroys any eggs or worms present but does not make the material resistant to moths. Brushing destroys the eggs, which are soft.

Storing moth-free clothes in tightly closed containers and sealing them with gummed tape, so that no moths can enter, is usually pretty good insurance against moth damage. Adding enough naphthalene, gum camphor, or paradichlorobenzene will further help to keep clothing moth free. The fumes given off by these substances stop the larvae from feeding, and in time, if strong enough, the concentrated fumes will kill them. Most cedar-lined closets and bags will not protect clothing against moths unless the garments are free from moths when placed in them and all openings are sealed tight. Most moth sprays are effective only if they hit the moth, and they must be applied thoroughly and repeatedly if they are to be of any value. Containers to hang in closets are useless unless the closet is sealed shut, as the concentration of fumes is never great enough to be effective.

Cotton, linen, silk, and rayon garments should be mended, put in order, and washed or cleaned before storing. They should then be placed in garment bags or boxes and stored away. Moths confine themselves to a diet of wool and similar animal fibers; therefore there is no need for preventive measures in the case of cotton, linen, rayon, or silk.

STUDY-GUIDE QUESTIONS

1. What are the advantages of having a plan for taking care of your clothes?
2. What equipment is necessary to keep your clothes in good order?
3. What equipment have you found especially helpful in keeping your clothes in good order?
4. What should you do daily to keep your clothes in good condition?
5. How can you prolong the life of your shoes?
6. How can you prolong the life of your stockings?
7. Describe the correct way to wash stockings.
8. Describe how to put on a pair of new leather gloves and how to remove them.
9. How can you determine whether gloves are washable?

10. How should gloves be washed?
11. In washing undergarments, how should cake soap be used?
12. Why should rayon garments be hung over the line rather than pinned on it?
13. When should garments be patched?
14. How would you press a cotton dress?
15. How would you treat a rayon-satin slip that has just been washed?
16. How would you press a wool skirt?
17. Why should clothes be stored at the end of a season?
18. How should wool garments be stored?
19. Of what value are cedar closets, moth sprays, and garment bags in preventing moth damage?
20. What chemicals are of value in preventing moth damage, and how should they be used?
21. How should cotton, linen, and rayon things be stored?
22. What weekly care should you give your clothing?

ACTIVITIES

1. Select various members of your class who are capable and willing to demonstrate washing stockings, gloves, undergarments, and a sweater for the class.
2. Select a member of the class to demonstrate putting on leather gloves and removing them correctly for the class.
3. Ask some students from a clothing class to demonstrate darning a stocking, mending a tear, sewing on a button, and sewing on snaps.
4. Select a class member to demonstrate removing common stains from various materials.
5. Select a member of your class to demonstrate the correct way to iron a cotton blouse, press a cotton dress, iron a slip, and press a wool skirt.

BOOKS FOR FURTHER READING

Ahern, Eleanor, *The Way We Wash Our Clothes.* M. Barrows and Company, New York, 1941.

Baxter, Laura, and Alpha Latzke, *Modern Clothing.* J. B. Lippincott Company, Philadelphia, 1938.

Brindze, Ruth, *Stretching Your Dollar in Wartime.* The Vanguard Press, New York, 1942.

Byers, Margaretta, *Designing Women.* Simon and Schuster, New York, 1938.

Dana, Margaret, *Behind the Label.* Little, Brown, and Company, Boston, 1941.

Goldstein, Harriet, and Vetta Goldstein, *Art in Everyday Life,* third edition. The Macmillan Company, New York, 1940.

Household Finance Corporation, " Better Buymanship Bulletins, Gloves, Shoes, Hosiery, Fabrics." Household Finance Corporation, Chicago.

Kennedy, Ada, and Cora Vaughn, *Consumer Economics.* Manual Arts Press, Peoria, 1939.

MacGibbon, Elizabeth G., *Fitting Yourself for Business.* McGraw-Hill Book Company, New York, 1941.

Marsh, H. M., *Building Your Personality.* Prentice-Hall, New York, 1939.

Ryan, Mildred G., *Your Clothes and Personality,* revised. D. Appleton-Century Company, Chicago, 1942.

Stratton, Dorothy C., and Helen B. Schleman, *Your Best Foot Forward.* Whittlesey House, McGraw-Hill Book Company, New York, 1940.

Trilling, Mabel B., E. Kingman Eberhart, and Florence W. Nichols, *When You Buy.* J. B. Lippincott Company, Philadelphia, 1938.

Trilling, Mabel B., and Florence Williams, *Art in Home and Clothing.* J. B. Lippincott Company, Philadelphia, 1936.

Weiss, E. B., and Maurice Merney, *The Shopping Guide.* Whittlesey House, McGraw-Hill Book Company, New York, 1939.

Wingate, Isabel B., *Textile Fabrics and Their Selection.* Prentice-Hall, New York, 1936.

Vigorous health gives a feeling of self-confidence and faith in the future.
Courtesy, *Look Magazine*.

SECTION VI

THE HEALTH OF THE HIGH SCHOOL GIRL

UNIT ONE.   QUALITIES OF A HEALTHY PERSON

What is your average in health? Your average in your school work may be very high, you may stand in the upper brackets in tennis, swimming, or social dancing, but have you ever scored yourself in health? If not, here is your opportunity. Study the health score card below. Score yourself according to the points given and find your total points. How do you compare' with the total given on the score card?

HEALTH SCORE CARD*

SIGNS OF HEALTH	PERFECT SCORE	YOUR SCORE
1. Can you work and play without being more than naturally tired mentally or physically at bedtime?	40	
2. Are you rested when you get up in the morning?	40	
3. Is your appetite good for wholesome food?	30	
4. Are you free from persistent trivial worry?	30	
5. Do you enjoy mingling with other people?	30	
6. Have you confidence in yourself?	30	
7. Is your weight within 10 per cent below or 15 per cent above the average for your height and years?	40	
8. Does your posture indicate health and efficiency?	30	
9. Are your arches normal and are you free from pain in your feet and legs?	20	
10. Are your muscles resilient?	20	
11. Is your vision either normal or corrected by glasses?	20	
12. Can you hear ordinary conversation at sixteen feet?	20	
13. Is your skin clear; your color, good?	20	
14. Is your hair glossy, but free from excessive oil (not brittle and dry)?	20	
15. Are your teeth either sound or filled?	20	
16. Are you free from constantly recurring infection, including colds?	30	
17. Are you free from constant or recurring pain?	30	

Score 470

* Parent and Health Education Association, Cleveland, Ohio

No doubt you have always felt that you were a very healthy person. Do you still think that this is true? Perhaps you have not had the correct idea of what is meant by good health.

MEANING OF HEALTH

Mary Lou is a girl who assumes she has good health because she is seldom sick in bed. Yet she has a succession of colds each winter and frequently complains of headaches. She is not often absent from school, but there are many days when she feels so listless and dull that she cannot keep her mind on the work of the class, and she does little more than occupy a seat in the room. At the end of the school day she is too tired and restless to enter into any kind of activity or to concentrate on preparing her assignments for the next day and consequently seeks diversion by listening to the radio or going to the movies. Certainly there are definite indications of poor health about Mary Lou, and you would hardly say she leads a vigorous, full life.

According to the modern viewpoint, good health has a much broader meaning than you may have realized. It includes both physical and mental fitness. When all parts of our bodies are working properly, so that we have the energy and endurance to carry on our activities successfully, and when we have a feeling of happy, wholesome well-being, we may say that we are truly enjoying good health.

VALUE OF HEALTH

You may be thinking that you manage to get along even though you are not 100 per cent healthy. Perhaps you would get along even better, have more ups and fewer downs, if you improved your health. It is true that there have been a few people who have achieved success in spite of the handicap of poor health; however, they are the exceptions rather than the rule. Good health is an aid to success in whatever you choose to do. The greatest physical and mental efficiency is impossible without it.

Then, too, from the standpoint of appearance, good health is an asset. Surely no one would debate the fact that a well-developed, wholesome, healthy girl is more attractive than a puny, sickly one. Good health gives her mental poise, and she attracts people to her not only because of her appearance, but also because of her disposition. Because she is mentally in good health, she enjoys having people around her, gets along with them easily, and is ready to enter into all kinds of activities with them. There is no doubt that she gets more fun out of life than her puny, sickly sister who always has an ache or a pain, is easily irritated, and tires so readily that she cannot enjoy any activity, mental or physical, that requires sustained effort.

Looking at good health from an economic point of view, you will find that illness is an expensive luxury, whereas good health is a wise investment from which you will receive dividends as long as you take care of your capital. Doctor bills, special diets, medicine, and sickroom equipment make inroads on the family budget. Large business concerns realize that illness is expensive, because it lowers the efficiency of their workmen. They provide safety education and safety devices to prevent accidents. They usually employ a doctor to look after their employees. They often organize baseball teams, bowling teams, and the like to provide recreation and exercise.

Some communities which recognize that illness is expensive, go to considerable expense and trouble to safeguard the health of their citizens. City garbage collections, sewage disposal, pure water supply, and quarantine of contagious disease are only a few of the ways in which the health of a community is looked after through government agencies.

But do individuals generally put forth any effort to safeguard and care for their own health? Some people evidently feel that health is something they can do very little about. They feel that they were born either well or ill, and that it is up to the doctor to keep them in good health. If the number of quacks that are able to make a living and if the various useless and even harmful remedies that are on sale are any indication, some people apparently think that health can be purchased.

However, there are a goodly number of people who realize that health is each individual's responsibility and that it can be maintained and improved only by spending time on the care of the body. Plenty of sunshine and fresh air, wholesome exercise and recreation, good posture habits, sufficient rest and sleep, cleanliness, proper clothing, and the right kinds and amounts of food all help to improve our health and keep us in a state of physical well-being.

STUDY-GUIDE QUESTIONS

1. Name the seventeen signs of good health given in your textbook.
2. When can we say we have good health?
3. State three or four reasons why good health is worth working for.
4. What does your school do to protect and maintain your health?
5. In what ways can you cooperate with your school in protecting and maintaining your health and the health of other students?

ACTIVITIES

1. Using the score card given in your textbook, score yourself in health.
2. Make some definite suggestions for improving your health.
3. If possible, interview your health officer, the head of a hospital, or an official in any other health agency in your community, and report on what he does to improve the health of the community.

UNIT TWO. SUNSHINE AND HEALTH

In one of our large cities the newspapers recently told the pitiful tale of two little girls who had been locked away in a dark room for weeks by a cruel stepmother. When discovered, the children were so weak and underweight they were unable to walk, their bodies were covered with sores, and they were in bad condition mentally. Lack of food, exercise, fresh air, and their filthy quarters

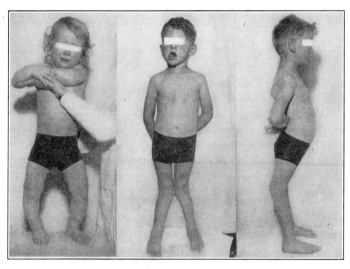

Notice the indications of rickets in these children—bowlegs, flat feet, knock-knees, enlarged joints, and poor posture. Courtesy, Wisconsin Alumni Research Foundation.

had all left their mark. With proper care in healthful surroundings, mentally and emotionally they returned to normal, they gained weight and grew strong, and their skins became clear and free from sores. One indication of this frightful experience will probably be with them always. Some of the joints of the body, such as the knees, will show evidences that they have had rickets.

Rickets is a disease in which the bones of the body do not form properly and are weak because of lack of sunshine or diets deficient in calcium and phosphorus. Calcium and phosphorus are minerals

235

which the body takes from food and uses in building bones, provided vitamin D is present. Our best source of this vitamin is sunshine. When the ultraviolet rays of the sun shine on the skin a substance in the skin called ergosterol is changed to vitamin D.

In addition to being the source of vitamin D, sunshine actually helps to keep the body warm, has a tonic effect on the entire body, improves the functioning of the vital organs, increases the red corpuscles of the blood, and improves nerve action. You can see why even primitive peoples valued the sun to the extent that they often had a sun god which they worshipped.

If you live in a temperate climate, you will get less ultraviolet light during the winter months when the sun is further away because the sunlight must pass through more of the earth's atmosphere, which tends to filter out the ultraviolet rays. Smoke and fog also obstruct these rays, and they will not penetrate ordinary window glass or clothing. However, when the sunshine is very bright there will be much ultraviolet light reflected from the sky, especially from white clouds, and even in the shade there will be ultraviolet rays.

You can readily see that if you are to be in the best of health, it is necessary to get some sunshine each day. For this reason, daily outdoor exercise is very desirable. Clothing that allows the sun to shine directly on the skin is one means of ensuring a supply of vitamin D; hence short sleeves, ankle socks, and sport garments that allow the sun to shine directly on the skin are aids to health, provided that the weather is not inclement. Some people take sun baths on the advice of their doctor as a part of their daily routine.

SUN BATHING

In taking sun baths, it is not good practice to start with too long an exposure to the sun, as this may result in headache, sleeplessness, or sunburn. Being badly burned by the sun is just as serious as being badly burned from any other cause. Such a burn is painful and may be serious, particularly if the skin is broken and an infection sets in. If you spend some time each day in sun bathing, you should gradually lengthen the time of exposure until you can stay out almost indefinitely without any danger from sunburn.

During this period, the outer skin thickens and brown pigment is manufactured which protects you from burning.

However, if you do not have the patience to go through this period of gradual exposure, sunburn preventives may be a help to you. These preparations allow the ultraviolet rays to reach your skin but reduce their intensity, so that you can stay in the sunshine a longer time without being burned. Most sunburn preventives will not protect you indefinitely from sunburn, for if they did, you would not get any benefit from the ultraviolet rays. Eventually your skin will show some redness, which indicates that you have been in the sun long enough.

STUDY-GUIDE QUESTIONS

1. What benefits are derived from ultraviolet rays?
2. Of what value is vitamin D?
3. Describe the symptoms of rickets.
4. Do we have to be in direct sunshine to get the benefit of the ultraviolet rays?
5. Under what conditions are we apt to get little or no ultraviolet light?
6. In taking sun baths, what precautions should we observe?
7. Is there any danger in a severe sunburn?
8. How do lotions which prevent sunburn act? Do you obtain as much benefit from the sun when using these preparations?

UNIT THREE. FRESH AIR AND HEALTH

NEED OF OXYGEN

You are probably familiar with the story of the robber who locks the bank employees in the vault and leaves them to certain death unless help arrives before the oxygen in the vault is exhausted. We must have a constant supply of oxygen if life is to be maintained. When we breathe in air, the red corpuscles of the blood, as they pass through the lungs, pick up the oxygen from the air and carry it to the various tissues of the body. There the oxygen is combined with digested food material. Through this process, which is called oxidation, the body is supplied with energy and warmth.

OXYGEN SUPPLY

If oxygen in a bank vault eventually becomes used up, you may well wonder why, with so many people constantly breathing in oxygen and exhaling carbon dioxide, our supply of oxygen does not become used up. You probably have learned in your science classes that a balance between oxygen and carbon dioxide is maintained by plant and animal life. Plants use carbon dioxide and give off oxygen; whereas animals use the oxygen of the air and give off carbon dioxide. In this way the amount of oxygen in the air is kept practically constant.

PHYSICAL PROPERTIES OF THE AIR

You may have had the experience of spending some time in a poorly ventilated room with a group of other people. Eventually you felt lacking in energy and rather drowsy, and you may even have developed a headache. Perhaps you believed that your discomfort was due to the fact that there was not enough oxygen in the air. However, this is not usually true. Even in poorly ventilated rooms the supply of oxygen seldom gets so low as to be harmful. There is always some air entering around doors and windows, and even through the somewhat porous walls, ceilings, and floors of buildings.

Your feelings of discomfort were generally due to the physical properties of the air, that is, to its temperature, motion, and moisture content. Science has found that the air which surrounds the

Fresh air, sunshine, and exercise promote a zest for living.
Courtesy, O. Roach Studio, Denver, Colorado.

body is just as important to good health as the air we breathe, because it helps keep the body temperature constant. Consequently, we grow uncomfortable in a poorly ventilated room because the physical properties of the air are not in proper balance.

As we breathe cool air into the lungs and exhale warm air, we are aiding the body in getting rid of excess heat and in keeping its temperature constant. The amount of heat that is given off is controlled automatically by the body.

The moisture content of the air is generally spoken of as relative humidity and is expressed in percentages. When we say the relative humidity is 50 per cent, we mean that the air has 50 per cent of the amount of moisture it could hold at that temperature if it were saturated. The relative humidity of outdoor air is usually 30 to 75 per cent. When the temperature and relative humidity are high and there is no breeze, we feel very warm. This reaction is due to the fact that the higher the temperature, the less heat the surrounding air is able to remove from the body. When the relative humidity is high, the air is not able to evaporate so much of our body moisture. Evaporation, as you know, is a cooling process. When the perspiration of the body is not evaporated, we feel hot and sticky. When the temperature is low, a high relative humidity makes us feel cooler. The cool, moist air of a cave reduces the heat of the body more rapidly than does cool, dry air, since evaporation of moisture from the body no longer plays a part. It is evident that moving air has a cooling effect.

INDOOR AIR

Since the temperature, relative humidity, and motion of outdoor air are beyond our control, let us turn our attention to the indoor air in which we live much of the time. Gently moving air with a temperature from 66 to 68° F and a relative humidity of 50 to 60 per cent is considered most healthful.

As the air is heated to higher temperatures, the relative humidity becomes more important. Unless moisture is added to the air by some means, the higher the temperature rises, the drier the air becomes. Hot, dry air has an irritating effect on the membranes of our respiratory tracts. Humidity plays an important part in making us comfortable. We do not feel so warm in an atmosphere of hot, dry air as in air of lower temperature which contains the proper amount of moisture, because hot, dry air increases the evaporation of body moisture, making us feel cool.

Efforts to control the humidity of indoor air by having pans of water on or near radiators are generally ineffective. Modern heating systems are meeting this problem through the use of air-conditioning equipment, which controls the relative humidity of the air.

AIR DURING SLEEP

Have you ever slept in a room with the windows closed? Did you get up the next morning feeling rested, refreshed, and invigorated? Of course, you did not. If you have had such an experience, then you know how beneficial it is to sleep with the windows open. Science tells us that sleeping in the fresh air increases bodily vigor and resistance to disease. Cross-ventilation, that is, windows on two sides of a room, gives us better circulation of air than do windows on only one side.

IMPURE AIR

There is very little danger of contracting disease from bacteria in outdoor air. Bacteria do not multiply under these conditions and generally die when exposed to sunlight. However, indoor air contains bacteria, which are given off when people talk, sneeze, or cough. These bacteria are the means of transmitting disease from one person to another, especially in overcrowded, poorly ventilated places.

Air may also become impure through smoke, ash, and certain gases that are given off. Smoke reduces the beneficial effects of sunshine, since the valuable ultraviolet rays cannot pass through smoke. Smoke, ash, and gases may prove irritating to the lining of the respiratory tract, and no doubt play a harmful role in such diseases as tuberculosis.

Smoke can be made harmless and almost unnoticeable. Some communities have regulations which affect residential and industrial heating plants.

STUDY-GUIDE QUESTIONS

1. What is the function of oxygen in the body?
2. How is oxygen brought into contact with the tissues of the body?
3. How is the balance of oxygen and carbon dioxide maintained by nature?
4. What causes feelings of drowsiness and discomfort when a number of people are housed in a poorly ventilated room?
5. How does the body keep its temperature constant?
6. What is meant by relative humidity?
7. How do we express or measure relative humidity?

8. Why do we feel uncomfortable when the temperature and the humidity are high?
9. Why do we feel more comfortable on a cool, humid day than we do on a hot, humid one?
10. Why do we feel cooler on a windy hot day than on a still hot day?
11. What is considered the most healthful indoor temperature and humidity?
12. Why does it take less fuel to maintain a comfortable temperature in a properly humidified house than in a house where the air is dry?
13. Can moisture be added to the air by putting a pan of water on a radiator?
14. What is the value of sleeping with the windows open?
15. What is meant by cross-ventilation?
16. How can you have cross-ventilation and not sleep in a draft?
17. Why are we less likely to take cold outdoors than inside?
18. What does impure air contain?
19. Why should communities work for smoke-abatement programs?

UNIT FOUR. SLEEP AND HEALTH

When young children become cross and tired, a wise mother puts them to bed. If we could regulate our lives so that adults could have a nap when they are overtired, we should be a much calmer and better-poised group of people.

FUNCTION OF SLEEP

It is through sleep that fatigue is banished and our energy is restored. We know that this is true, because. we generally feel rested and refreshed in the morning regardless of how tired we were when we went to bed. Our bodies work on somewhat the same principle as the furnace which heats your house. Father puts coal in the furnace and provides air through a system of drafts. The result is a brightly burning fire which heats the entire house. With our bodies we take in food and breathe in air. As these are combined, heat is furnished to keep us warm, and energy is provided for our activities. In both cases, however, certain waste products are given off. In the furnace, ashes collect. If these ashes are not removed, eventually the fire will not burn, and the house will become cold. In our bodies, waste products collect in the tissues. During the day, when we are using up a great deal of energy with our activities, these waste products collect faster than we can get rid of them. The accumulation of waste products causes us to feel tired. During sleep, when we are no longer active, our bodies have an opportunity of ridding themselves of these waste products; and, as a result, we awake rested and refreshed.

Then, too, it is during sleep that the nerves are rested to the greatest extent. If we lie down during the day and relax, our bodies have an opportunity to rid themselves of accumulated waste, our muscles are rested, our hearts work more slowly, our breathing becomes less rapid, and our bodies produce less heat. If we remain awake, however, our minds are active. Each thought and impulse that we have involves work on the part of the nerves.

243

Gradually this nerve tissue is worn out. During sleep worn-out nerve tissue is replaced with new, living tissue.

AMOUNT OF SLEEP

The amount of sleep that we require differs with different individuals and with the intensity of our sleep. If we get up in the morning feeling sleepy and dull, we are probably not getting enough sleep. We need sufficient sleep to balance the physical energy that we are using up during the day. If we are getting sufficient sleep we shall get up in the morning feeling rested and ready for our day's work. Since young people are generally more active than older people, and since their bodies must work hard to grow, they require more sleep than adults. The following table* gives the number of hours of sleep required at various ages.

Age	Total Hours of Sleep
6-8 years	12 hours
8-10 years	11½ hours
10-12 years	11 hours
12-16 years	10 hours
16-20 years	8-9 hours

RESULTS OF INSUFFICIENT SLEEP

On school nights Jane always listened to a radio program that was broadcast at eleven o'clock. She maintained that she was getting plenty of sleep because she never felt sleepy during the day. Her mother noticed several things about Jane that made her wonder. She observed that Jane was easily irritated, that she seemed to have a great many colds, that she was impatient and inconsiderate with her younger sisters, and that her grades in school were lower than they had been previously. When her mother talked to Jane, the girl said that her subjects were very boring and that the teachers picked on her. When Jane consistently lost weight, her mother took her to the doctor for a physical check-up. One of his recommendations was an earlier bedtime, for, as he explained to Jane, sleepiness is not the only indication of insufficient sleep.

* E. A. Cockefair and A. M. Cockefair, *Health and Achievement*. Ginn and Company, Boston, 1936.

CONDITIONS CONDUCIVE TO SLEEP

It is normal for healthy people to go to sleep soon after they go to bed. From many advertisements, however, you might be led to believe that a large number of people find it necessary to take one of these advertised products in order that they may sleep. If you have trouble in going to sleep, either you are not in good health or you have formed poor sleeping habits.

A regular bedtime is one of the best ways of making sure that you will go to sleep soon after you get into bed. Going to sleep is a habit, just as waking up at the same time each day may become a habit if practiced regularly. Sometimes people will protest that they cannot go to sleep if they go to bed as early as they should. This difficulty is due to the fact that they have not formed the habit of going to bed at this time every night.

Other conditions which are conducive to sound sleep are a quiet, dark, well-ventilated room, loose sleeping garments, and light, warm covers.

STUDY-GUIDE QUESTIONS

1. What makes us feel tired?
2. Why do we feel rested and refreshed after sleep?
3. How much sleep should you have?
4. Do we all require the same amount of sleep?
5. How can we know whether we are getting enough sleep?
6. What are the results of insufficient sleep?
7. What conditions are conducive to sleep?
8. What do you think about advertisements which advise you to take certain products to induce sleep?
9. What are the causes of insomnia?

UNIT FIVE. EXERCISE AND HEALTH

You will agree that a vigorous, vital-looking person is much more attractive than a scrawny, lifeless one. Exercise helps in improving our general health by promoting normal growth and development, by stimulating the vital processes of the body, and by renewing normal vigor. Hence exercise may be called an aid to beauty.

The fact that exercise promotes the normal growth and development of the body is obvious. You know that a large amount of the body is made up of muscle tissue. You also are familiar with the fact that muscle tissue increases in size and strength through use and that it becomes weak and smaller in size when not used. This is especially evident to you if you have ever had a broken arm. Your broken arm had to be carried in a sling for several weeks, during which time it was completely useless to you. When the break was finally healed, you probably had to learn to use the arm again. You may have started by exercising your fingers and by placing your arm wherever you wanted it. Gradually, as you exercised the arm, the muscles, which had grown weak and flabby through disuse, became strong; and the arm again took its place as a useful member. So it is with the rest of your body. As you exercise, your muscles grow and develop, and you become more skillful in controlling these muscles and in making them work together. Thus, exercise not only helps in developing your body but also in managing it, so that you will have poise and grace.

We have said that exercise stimulates the vital processes of the body. Let us see more specifically how this is true. The processes concerned in the circulation of the blood — breathing, digestion, and elimination — all involve the use of muscle tissue. As these tissues become stronger through exercise, the body is better able to function in these respects.

Muscular activity stimulates the flow of the blood. This in turn benefits the entire body, as it is by means of the blood that all

246

parts receive nourishment, waste products are removed from the tissues, warmth is distributed, and oxygen is carried to the various tissues. As we exercise, the heart beats more rapidly, thus forcing the blood to flow more freely. In this way the heart is able to send more food and oxygen to the muscles for their increased work.

You may have noticed that when you exercise you breathe faster and more deeply. This is due to the fact that your body needs more oxygen and that there is more carbon dioxide to be exhaled as a result of its increased activity. Deeper breathing helps to keep the chest flexible and strengthens the muscles concerned in breathing. When we breathe deeply, all the air sacs of the lungs are used. This helps to keep them in a normal condition.

Exercise makes us feel hungry, because we are better able to assimilate our food when we are active. A good appetite generally means that our food is digested readily and is more fully used by the body.

Since waste products accumulate more quickly when we are active, they also are given off more rapidly. The skin, lungs, kidneys, and intestines are the organs by means of which waste products are eliminated. You are familiar with the red face and moist skin of a person who is exercising vigorously on a warm day. The skin becomes red because of the extra blood supply that is brought to it as a result of increased circulation. The perspiration is a means of getting rid of some of the waste products, as well as an aid in keeping the temperature of the body normal.

Exercise benefits not only the muscle tissue of the body but also the nerves. As the muscles are exercised, the nerves are exercised also. They must receive and send out impulses for every movement we make. Thus, through use, they are able to respond to more delicate impulses, become more stable, and have greater endurance.

TYPE OF EXERCISE

Exercise that is most beneficial is exercise that you enjoy. It benefits both your mind and body. Exercise should be taken not merely for the sake of health but also for the pleasure that you derive from it. For this reason games are more beneficial than formal exercises. A game, such as tennis or golf, or swimming has the advantage of usually being participated in outdoors, where the benefit of fresh air and sunshine is received. You are interested in acquiring skill in the sport rather than in its effect on your

Games are the most beneficial form of exercise.
Courtesy, MacMurray College, Jacksonville, Illinois.

health. This is beneficial mentally, as it takes your attention away from the routine things of every day. Any physical activity which accomplishes this and at the same time results in deeper breathing, stretching, and twisting is beneficial mentally and physically.

HARMFUL EXERCISE

If you are in good health, almost no type of activity will be harmful if it is not too strenuous and is not prolonged beyond the stage of fatigue. Breathlessness and fatigue are two ways that

nature signals when the limit of your endurance has been reached;
however, your will may impel you to continue in your activity
beyond this point. Exercise that seriously taxes the body is not
beneficial.

Vigorous activity should be avoided while you are convalescing
from a disease or a very severe cold. At this time your body is
not in good physical condition, and too strenuous activity may
result in injury to your heart, since exercise puts a heavy burden
on it. The heart may become inefficient and fail to do its work
well through loss of tone. Tone is a state of slight tension which
is characteristic of all healthy muscles. Weak, flabby muscles have
no tone. When a severe strain is placed upon the heart, the muscle
fibers may be stretched beyond the limit of their elasticity. This
results in a dilation of the heart.

STUDY-GUIDE QUESTIONS

1. How is exercise an aid to beauty?
2. How does exercise promote growth?
3. What vital processes of the body are stimulated by exercise?
4. What effect does exercise have on the circulatory system of the body?
5. Why do you breathe more rapidly when you are exercising?
6. Of what benefit is this increase in the rate of breathing?
7. How does exercise affect the appetite?
8. What advantage is a good appetite?
9. What organs help to eliminate waste products?
10. How are your nerves benefited by exercise?
11. Why are games considered more beneficial than formal exercises?
12. When may exercise be harmful?
13. How can you know when you have reached the limit of your endurance?
14. When should vigorous activity be avoided?
15. What is meant by muscle tone?
16. What kind of activity will (*a*) strengthen your back muscles? (*b*) strengthen the muscles of your feet? (*c*) keep your abdomen flat? (*d*) prevent a roll of fat from collecting around your waist?

UNIT SIX. POSTURE AND HEALTH

IMPORTANCE OF CORRECT POSTURE

Take a slumped position; allow the head to fall forward, the shoulders to become round, and the hands to hang limp. In this position, what is your mental reaction? You probably feel that your mind is pretty much a blank, and if you look at yourself in a mirror, your reflection will indicate that your appearance is

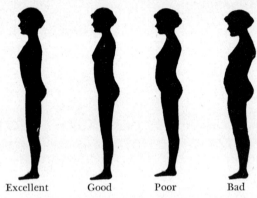

| Excellent | Good | Poor | Bad |

Prevailing postural types (intermediate type girls).
Courtesy, Children's Bureau, United States Department of Labor.

not at its best. Now take a proper position with head erect, waistline in, back flat, feet parallel, and the whole body stretched up tall. What is your mental reaction? Study yourself in the mirror. In which position are you more attractive looking? In which position do you appear alert, vigorous, and successful? Which impression would you prefer to make on strangers?

Certainly, correct posture adds to our attractiveness and inspires confidence and respect, as it implies that we have confidence in and respect for ourselves. Then, too, it promotes poise and grace. Grace is a natural result of all our muscles working together properly. The awkward person is the unskillful one. Have you ever watched a person who is learning to drive a golf ball? His movements are awkward and jerky, and the various parts of his body seem to be working against each other. In contrast, the successful golfer swings his club with ease and grace. His movements are rhythmic, and the various parts of his entire body work together to drive the ball out across the golf course. As you watch this player, you realize that his skill has been acquired through mental and physical effort. So it is with our posture, which will be good only if we are willing to put forth the physical and mental effort that is necessary to make it so.

Correct posture is worth working for, not only because it improves our appearance, but also because it promotes good health. It increases our endurance and makes us tire less readily. It helps in maintaining good health and vigor. When our bodies are erect, the internal organs have plenty of room in which to work properly. When we slump or assume poor posture, our internal organs are crowded, a condition which makes it impossible for them to do their work efficiently. For example, the lungs cannot possibly work so well in supplying oxygen to the blood if they are held in a collapsed state all the time. Poor circulation, indigestion, constipation, painful menstruation, and unwarranted fatigue may result from poor posture.

CORRECT POSTURE

We may be said to have correct posture when the entire body is in such a position that the muscles and the organs can work without friction or interference. The weight of the body should be borne by the skeleton. In correct posture we must constantly resist gravity, which tends to make the head drop forward, the shoulders stoop, and the abdomen protrude. Because of this, our muscles must be sufficiently contracted to hold the body erect.

In correct standing posture, the feet should be slightly apart and parallel to each other. The toes should turn neither in nor out. The weight should be on the outer sides of the feet, and the body should be stretched to its full height. The head should be held erect with the chin in, and the abdomen should be retracted. Correct posture means a poised, balanced body, not a tense, rigid one.

Correct posture is just as important in sitting as in standing. If we slump or lounge in our chair, the body weight rests upon

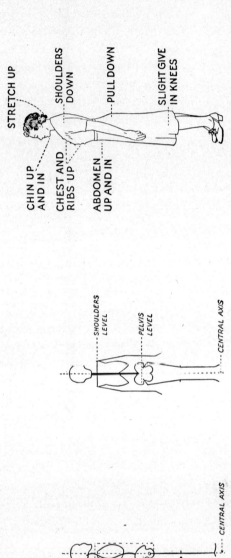

STRETCH UP

CHIN UP AND IN

SHOULDERS DOWN

CHEST AND RIBS UP

PULL DOWN

ABDOMEN UP AND IN

SLIGHT GIVE IN KNEES

FUNDAMENTAL STANDING
(Side view)

A straight line should pass through the ear, shoulder, hip joint, behind the knee joint, in front of the ankle, to the floor.

SHOULDERS LEVEL

PELVIS LEVEL

CENTRAL AXIS

Diagram showing distribution of body weight about an imaginary central axis, as seen from front or back.

CENTRAL AXIS

SPINE

PELVIS

KNEES

TRUNK

Diagram showing distribution of body weight about an imaginary central axis, as seen from the side (arms omitted).

Courtesy, Metropolitan Life Insurance Company.

the shoulder blades and the sacrum. The sacrum, which is the largest bone in the spine, lies between the hip bones. In a slumped position, the back takes the shape of the letter *C*, constricting the chest and thus interfering with the work of the heart, lungs, and digestive tract. Because of this improper placing of the body weight and the hampering of internal organs, nerves are irritated and fatigue is brought on, which results in a sluggish, dull feeling.

In contrast, when we sit in correct position, the weight of the body rests upon the flesh of the hips and thighs. Here there are few nerves to become irritated, and these few are well protected with flesh. Since the body is erect, the organs are free to do their work with the least possible expenditure of energy.

Correct sitting posture means sitting straight and well back in the chair with the back against the back of the chair. The head, chest, and abdomen are in the same position as in standing. In this position the body is alert and able to devote its energy to the task at hand.

CAUSES OF POOR POSTURE

Poor posture may result from several causes. It may be that the muscles which help to hold the body erect are weak, either from lack of exercise or from poor nutrition. High-heeled shoes are another cause. When we wear such shoes, our weight falls forward on the ball of the foot; and the body is thrown out of balance. Habit also plays a part in the way in which we carry our bodies. If we have formed the habit of standing and sitting correctly, we feel awkward when we slouch or lounge in our chairs. A healthy mental attitude is an aid to good posture. Shame and fear are often characterized by a slumped figure with the head hanging forward.

ACQUIRING CORRECT POSTURE

Learning to carry the body correctly requires both physical and mental effort. It is necessary to make correct posture a habit. Establishing any kind of habit involves practice. Thus if you would carry your body correctly, you must practice doing so. Each time you slouch, you are making it easier to slouch again; but each time you stand, sit, or walk correctly, you are making that way of standing, sitting, or walking a part of yourself.

Of course, you must want to acquire good posture. Help yourself to develop a sense of correct posture by noticing the way in which other people carry themselves and by convincing yourself that good posture is worth working for.

If your muscles are weak and flabby from lack of exercise, plan to include some physical activity in each day. As you know, this exercise will be most beneficial if it is in the form of a game or sport that you enjoy.

If your muscles are weak from poor nutrition, look into your food habits. All the practices that make for good health, such as adequate sleep, fresh air, and sunshine, will help to remedy your trouble.

A healthy mental attitude will also assist you in acquiring good posture. Pride in your appearance and respect for yourself will help you to stand, sit, and walk as you should. In turn, others will tend to respect you and have confidence in you.

STUDY-GUIDE QUESTIONS

1. What are the benefits of good posture?
2. What difficulties may begin with poor posture?
3. Describe good posture in standing and sitting.
4. What are the disadvantages of poor sitting posture?
5. Name some causes of poor posture.
6. How can you improve your posture?

ACTIVITIES

1. Select someone in your class who has good posture. Study her standing posture. Ask her to demonstrate good sitting posture.
2. Criticize the posture of any class members who wish their posture analyzed. Show them how their posture can be improved.
3. Ask some class members to demonstrate good posture in various activities, such as walking, climbing stairs, washing dishes, and ironing.

UNIT SEVEN. FOOD AND HEALTH

John and Bobby are schoolmates of the same age, but that appears to be the only point of similarity between them. Johnny is an alert, happy, healthy-looking boy. He is taller and heavier than Bobby, with a well-developed body. He is very active and enthusiastic and is generally in a happy frame of mind. Bobby is thin and scrawny-looking. His skin is sallow. He is irritable, cries easily, and whines and pouts when he doesn't get his own way. Johnny's mother says that he is always hungry, eats a large variety of wholesome foods, and drinks plenty of milk. Bobby's mother says that he is never hungry and will not eat anything but bread, butter, bananas, candy, and soft drinks. Do you think the diets of these two boys can have anything to do with their appearance and their dispositions?

You can see from the illustration on p. 257 that in experimental animals, such as rats, food makes a difference. The rat which was fed an adequate diet is larger and has strong, well-formed bones and a thick, luxuriant coat of fur. Since rats eat both animal and vegetable foods, just as we do, we conclude that diets which affect growth and development in rats affect us in the same way.

DAILY FOOD NEEDS

Contrast the limited diet of Bobby with the wide variety of foods which Johnny eats. Can you see that food undoubtedly has made a difference in these two boys? What kind of food habits have you formed? Do you willingly eat all kinds of food, or do you limit your diet to certain foods and refuse to try others? Make a list of all the foods you ate yesterday. Compare your list with the following list of foods which nutrition experts tell us we need each day:

> 1 quart of milk
> 1 serving of meat or fish (or cheese)
> 1 egg a day or at least 4 a week
> 1 serving of a whole-grain cereal

3 servings of whole-grain bread
3 servings of butter or fortified oleomargarine
1 serving of potato
1 serving of green, leafy vegetable
1 serving of another vegetable
1 serving of fresh fruit (citrus fruit
    several times a week is desirable)
1 serving of another fruit

You can see that we must have a wide variety of foods each day if the needs of our bodies are to be satisfied. You will also notice that the ideal dietary includes several daily servings of fruits and vegetables, a small amount of meat, and no candy. This does not mean that meat and candy have no food value. It merely means that meat is an expensive food and that we do not need it three times a day. One small serving of meat will take care of the needs of our body, provided that other necessary foods are eaten. Candy has some value as food, but it cannot do as much for our bodies as the foods listed. For this reason, and since most of us have a tendency to eat more candy than is good for us, candy is omitted from the list. This does not mean that we should never eat it, but rather that we should never allow it to crowd out more essential foods. Then, too, we want to remember that candy should be eaten at the end of a meal or shortly after a meal, but never when our stomachs are empty. Candy is almost pure sugar and is such a concentrated food that it is irritating to the lining of the stomach. Candy satisfies our hunger before the needs of our body have been taken care of. If we eat it before our meals, our appetites are dulled, and we do not want to eat the foods that we know we need to keep us in good condition.

USES OF FOOD IN THE BODY

Why do we need such a variety of foods each day? Let us first find out what food must do for us, and then see how this ideal dietary fulfills these needs.

We must have food to keep our bodies warm, to furnish energy for our activities, to provide material so that our bodies can grow and repair themselves, to regulate the processes of the body, and to protect us from certain diseases.

Food made the difference
in these twin brothers, 6 months old

This rat ate only meat, potato, bread, and butter. He weighed 89 grams

His bones also show the effect of poor diet

This rat ate plenty of milk and vegetables, besides meat, potato,
bread, and butter. He weighed 194 grams

His bones are strong and well formed

Courtesy, Bureau of Home Economics, United States Department of Agriculture.

FOODS FOR WARMTH AND ENERGY

You are familiar with various kinds of fuel such as coal, gas, oil, and gasoline. You know that, whenever these fuels burn, oxygen must be present, and heat is given off. You also know that your body produces heat constantly. However, you probably have not stopped to think that this heat is produced by fuel, and that in this case the fuel is food. When the food which we eat is digested, it is absorbed into the blood stream by means of the capillaries in the walls of the intestinal tract. This digested food is carried by the blood to all cells of the body. The cells combine the food material with oxygen, which is also brought to the cells by the blood. As a result of this combination, heat and energy are produced.

HOW THE BODY USES FUEL

The heat produced by the union of oxygen and food is used to keep our bodies at 98.6° F, which is our normal temperature. The energy, or power, which is created is used for all the activities of the body. Every movement we make uses up energy. Of course, the more active we are, the more energy we require. For example, we use more fuel in playing tennis than in walking, and more in walking than in sitting. Even when we are asleep, we are using power to keep the internal work of the body going. Such processes as breathing, digestion, and circulation of the blood continue whether we are awake or asleep, and they require energy.

FUEL FOODS

Our best foods for fuel are the fats and carbohydrates. Lard, butter, oleomargarine, cream, and salad oils are some familiar fats. Cheese, fat meat, nuts, and egg yolks also contain fat.

Carbohydrates include foods which contain sugar and starch. Candy, syrups, jelly, honey, fruit, ice cream, and pastries contain large amounts of sugar. Even milk contains some. Typical starchy foods are cereals, bananas, beans, peas, and potatoes.

MEASURE OF ENERGY

In measuring the amount of energy that any food will furnish us, we use the term calorie. A calorie is the amount of heat that is required to raise the temperature of one pint of water 4° F. In other words, a calorie is a measure of heat, just as a foot is a measure of length. A heat measure is used for energy, because the energy used in doing internal work, and most of that used for physical activity, is changed to heat as it leaves the body.

Scientists have worked out the value of given amounts of our foods in terms of calories, so that we are able to estimate the food value of any given day's food. See the table on pp. 420–428.

CALORIES FOR ONE DAY

The number of calories we need per day depends principally upon the extent to which we are active, our age, the size of our body, and the temperature of our environment. The differences due to physical activity have been somewhat explained. You are all familiar with the keen appetite that results from vigorous exercise. This is nature's way of getting an increased amount of fuel to carry on activities. It is easy to understand why a farmer needs more food than a man who sits at an office desk all day.

Our size determines to some extent how much fuel we need. It takes more coal to keep a large house warm than it does to heat a small one. So it is with our bodies. Then, too, tall, thin people have much more surface area than short, fat people of the same weight. The tall, thin person will need more fuel, since he loses more heat through this greater surface area.

The temperature of our environment affects the amount of fuel we need. In cold weather our bodies must produce more heat to keep our temperatures normal.

Young people require more calories per pound of body weight than adults. This is due to the fact that their bodies require energy to grow and to develop. From the following table you can see that, as we grow older, we use fewer calories for each pound of body weight. For example, a child, either boy or girl, two years of age requires 40 calories per pound, whereas a seventeen year-old girl needs only 18 calories per pound. This does not mean, however, that, as we grow older, we use fewer calories per day. Actually, we use more calories per day as long as our bodies are growing and developing.

AVERAGE DAILY ENERGY REQUIREMENT OF CHILDREN PER UNIT OF BODY WEIGHT*

Age in Years		Calories per Pound
under 1		45–43
1–2		45–40
2–5		40–36
6–9		36–32
10–13	girls	32–27
	boys	34–30
14–17	girls	27–18
	boys	30–23

*Mary S. Rose, *Laboratory Handbook for Dietetics*. The Macmillan Company, 1937. Table VI, p. 19.

From this table you can easily estimate the approximate number of calories which you need in one day. If you are seventeen years of age and weigh 105 pounds, your calorific requirement would be 18 calories times 105 pounds, or 1890 calories. If you are either overweight or underweight, your calculation should be made on the basis of the average weight for your age.

OVERWEIGHT AND UNDERWEIGHT

Your weight indicates whether you are eating the amount of food that your body requires each day. When you eat more food than your body uses for its activities, the extra calories are stored in the form of fat. When you eat too little food, the body fat must be used to supply energy for your activities, and you will weigh less than you should. You can find what you should weigh for your height and age by consulting the table on p. 261. Some variation in weight is allowed at each age and height to provide for variations in body build.

Some body fat makes us more attractive by making us less angular. It helps to support the organs of the body, protects us from cold, and acts as a padding to guard us against jars and blows. Individuals who are underweight usually are easily irritated and tire quickly, as they have no reserve supply of fuel on which to rely for extra-vigorous activity. Life insurance records show that to be underweight while you are less than thirty years of age is a real hazard.

HEIGHT-WEIGHT-AGE TABLE FOR GIRLS*

HEIGHT IN INCHES	13 YEARS	14 YEARS	15 YEARS	16 YEARS	17 YEARS	18 YEARS
53	66– 71– 85					
54	68– 73– 88					
55	72– 77– 92	73– 78– 94				
56	75– 81– 97	77– 83–100				
57	78– 84–101	82– 88–106	86– 92–110			
58	82– 88–106	86– 93–113	89– 96–115	94–101–121		
59	86– 92–110	89– 96–115	93–100–120	96–103–124	97–104–125	
60	90– 97–116	94–101–121	98–105–126	100–108–130	102–109–131	103–111–133
61	94–101–121	98–105–126	100–108–130	104–112–134	105–113–135	108–116–139
62	99–106–127	101–109–131	105–113–136	107–115–138	109–117–140	110–118–142
63	102–110–132	104–112–134	108–116–139	109–117–140	111–119–143	112–120–144
64	107–115–138	109–117–140	111–119–143	112–120–144	114–122–146	115–123–148
65	112–120–144	113–121–145	113–122–146	115–123–148	116–125–150	117–126–151
66	115–124–149	115–124–149	116–125–150	119–128–154	120–129–155	121–130–156
67	119–128–154	121–130–156	122–131–157	124–133–160	124–133–160	126–135–162
68	122–131–157	124–133–160	126–125–162	126–136–163	130–138–166	130–138–166
69		126–135–162	127–137–164	130–138–166	130–140–168	132–142–170
70		126–136–163	130–138–166	130–140–168	132–142–170	134–144–173
71		130–138–166	130–140–168	132–142–170	134–144–173	135–145–174

NOTE: The central figure is the average weight. Seven per cent less than this figure and twenty per cent more has been estimated to allow for variations in body build.

*Adapted from the table by B. T. Baldwin and T. D. Wood. Reprinted by permission of the American Public Health Association, New York City.

Reducing diets and the habit of omitting one meal, such as breakfast, are especially dangerous for young people. Dieting for any reason should be carried on only under the supervision of a physician. Self-imposed diets too often reduce essential food elements below the point of safety for the general health of the individual. Tuberculosis takes its greatest toll from girls between fifteen and twenty-five years of age. One form of insurance against this deadly disease is to keep your weight normal for your height and age.

Reducing remedies generally consist of laxatives or drugs. The reducing action of laxatives depends upon their ability to hurry the food material through the alimentary tract before it has time to be digested and used by the body. This is dangerous, because the body does not get all the food elements it needs, and the intestinal tract is apt to become irritated. The reducing action of drugs depends upon their ability to speed up the processes of oxidation in the body. Thyroid extract is often used for this purpose. Because these drugs affect the action of the heart, they should be used only upon the advice of a physician.

USE OF PROTEIN IN THE BODY

Protein is an essential part of all cells. It is used to repair cells that are being worn out by the stress and strain of daily living. During growth it is needed for the building of new cells. Since our bodies are unable to store protein, we must include some foods which are rich in this element in our diet each day.

PROTEIN FOODS

Such foods as nuts, meat, fish, eggs, milk, and cheese contain large amounts of protein which is of good quality; that is, it is able to produce growth and to maintain health. Gelatin, cereals, peas, and navy beans contain protein that is incomplete or of poorer quality. Incomplete proteins are not able to perform both functions of complete protein. For this reason we cannot depend upon them alone for the best results.

AMOUNT OF PROTEIN

Stunted growth, poor muscles, and incorrect posture may result if we eat too little protein each day. On the other hand, if we eat

Some foods rich in protein should be eaten every day.
Courtesy, National Dairy Council.

more protein food than we need, the excess is broken down into simpler products, part of which is excreted through the kidneys and the remainder burned for energy. This not only places an extra burden on the kidneys but also is wasteful. Meat, eggs, and other high-protein foods generally are expensive. If we buy excessive amounts of these foods, we are apt not to have enough money to spend for other important foods that our bodies need. It is much better economy to depend upon less-expensive fats and carbohydrates for fuel and to include only enough protein foods in our daily diets to take care of the needs of building and repair.

Our protein requirement will be taken care of if we include the following foods in our diet each day: one quart of milk, one small serving of meat, one egg or one serving of cheese, one serving of a whole-grain cereal, and three servings of a whole-grain bread.

MINERALS

Minerals are important to the body, because they are necessary for building, repairing, and regulating certain body processes. For example, without minerals we cannot build strong teeth and bones. The minerals in the blood help to give it the power to coagulate, or clot. This prevents us from bleeding to death when we are cut, and is an example of one way in which minerals help to regulate.

Our bodies need about nineteen minerals. If we had to check our intake of this number of minerals each day, we should be able to do little else. We need consider only a few; namely, calcium, phosphorus, iron, copper, and iodine. If our food supplies these minerals, all the others will be furnished.

CALCIUM

Calcium has a number of duties to perform in the body. It helps to build strong teeth and bones. If we do not have enough, our growth is apt to be stunted and our bones to be misshapen. This mineral also helps to regulate the beat of the heart and, as previously mentioned, assists in the coagulation of the blood. It is a part of all tissues and body fluids. Calcium favors the retention of iron and is said to be a coordinator among minerals; that is, it helps to maintain a proper balance of minerals. It also assists the nerves in responding to stimulus. Girls thirteen to fifteen years old need 1.3 grams of calcium each day, and girls sixteen to twenty years old need 1.0 gram per day.

Our best source of calcium is milk. Growing boys and girls should have one quart of milk a day and adults one pint, to satisfy the calcium requirement of the body.

If we do not furnish our bodies with enough calcium each day, this mineral will be taken from our bones for other uses in the body. When this practice is continued, the bones become weak, and there is not enough calcium for proper growth. Poor teeth,

FOODS FURNISHING THE SAME AMOUNT OF *Calcium*

AS ONE QUART OF MILK

1 QT. MILK
4 Glasses

CARROTS 7¼ LBS.

CABBAGE 6¼ LBS.

39 EGGS   28 ORANGES   POTATOES 22 LBS.

Calcium is needed for strong bones and teeth.   Courtesy, National Dairy Council.

bowlegs, knock-knees, and stunted growth may be the results of a diet deficient in calcium.

PHOSPHORUS

Phosphorus is a part of all the cells of the body and is especially important in brain and nerve cells. It also helps to keep the bones and teeth rigid and is an aid to growth. Your body will have sufficient phosphorus if the protein requirement is taken care of. Foods which are good sources of protein are generally good sources of phosphorus. You should have at least 1.25 grams of phosphorus each day.

IRON

Iron is a necessary part of the red cells of the blood. As you know, the blood contains white and red cells. The white cells

fight infection and disease. The red cells pick up the oxygen as it is
breathed into the lungs and carry it to the various parts of the
body. When this oxygen is combined with the digested food material, a waste product, carbon dioxide, is given off. The red cells
pick up the carbon dioxide and bring it back to the lungs, where
it is exhaled. You can see that the red corpuscles of the blood play
an important part in our health. Since many red corpuscles wear
out each day, our body must constantly replace these as well as
provide new ones to take care of growing bodies. People who have
too few red corpuscles are said to be anemic. Anemic people do
not have much energy and are apt to feel tired and irritable. Your
diet should furnish 15 milligrams of iron each day.

COPPER

Since iron is a necessary part of red corpuscles, we must provide some iron in our diets each day. Before our bodies can use
the iron to build red cells, however, there must be copper present.
The copper does not become part of the red corpuscles as iron
does, but merely helps the body to use the iron. Lean meat, oysters,
eggs, whole cereals, leafy vegetables, and dried fruits give us both
iron and copper.

IODINE

Iodine is necessary if the thyroid gland is to function properly.
When our diets are lacking in iodine, we develop goiter.

Iodine may be found in some drinking water, in salt-water fish,
and in vegetables grown in soil which is rich in iodine. In some
sections of the country both soil and water are deficient in this
mineral. In these sections sea foods and iodized table salt will provide iodine.

VITAMINS

Vitamins are substances found in our foods which stimulate
growth, aid in maintaining health, and protect us from certain
diseases. Scientists have discovered and named six vitamins.

VITAMIN A

Vitamin A is necessary for normal growth, reproduction, and a
feeling of vitality. It improves our resistance to disease, particu-

larly diseases of the respiratory tract, helps to keep the tissues of the eye in a healthy condition, and aids in proper tooth formation. Some people experience difficulty in distinguishing objects after dark. This condition is called night blindness and is associated with a deficiency of vitamin A.

Whole milk, cream, butter, cod-liver and halibut-liver oils, egg yolk, and liver are good sources of vitamin A. Green leafy plants, yellow vegetables, and fruits contain carotene, a substance which is changed by the liver to vitamin A. No special precautions need to be taken in the preparation of these foods as far as the vitamin A content is concerned, as this vitamin is not soluble in water and is not destroyed by heat. Vitamin A is, however, destroyed by exposure to air, especially in the presence of light and warmth. If we eat more of this vitamin than we need, the excess can be stored in our bodies and used at a later time. Your diet should furnish 5000 International Units of vitamin A every day.

VITAMIN B$_1$ OR THIAMIN

Vitamin B$_1$ is sometimes called the morale vitamin, for when our diets fail to furnish enough thiamin, we are apt to feel depressed, restless, tired, and irritable. Our appetites generally are not so good as they should be, and we may be troubled with constipation. This vitamin protects us from the disease called beriberi and is necessary for the oxidation of carbohydrates in the body.

Whole grains, yeast, and nuts, especially peanuts, are good sources of vitamin B$_1$. Lean pork and the organ meats are fairly good sources. Fruits, vegetables, milk, and eggs contain small amounts. If we include generous amounts of these foods in our diets each day, and if half of the cereals we eat are whole-grain, we shall have enough of this vitamin, of which we need 1.2 milligrams daily. However, it is well to have some of the fruits and vegetables raw, since vitamin B$_1$ dissolves in water and is partially destroyed by heat.

VITAMIN B$_2$ (G) OR RIBOFLAVIN

Vitamin B$_2$ is necessary to the health of the cells and tissues of the body and to the production of hemoglobin. The daily need is 1.8 milligrams. Without it we should have an unhealthy skin

Riboflavin is found in some animal and vegetable foods.
Courtesy, National Dairy Council.

condition, and our vision would be affected. Yeast, milk in adequate amounts, liver, and kidney are good sources of this vitamin.
Egg yolk, muscle meats, and whole-grain cereals contain some.
Green leafy vegetables and fruits contain small amounts. Since
riboflavin is soluble in water, care should be taken in cooking
foods to conserve this vitamin.

NIACIN OR NICOTINIC ACID

A deficiency of niacin causes pellagra. Symptoms of this disease
are skin lesions, red, swollen tongue, nausea, and vomiting. Mild
symptoms consist of inability to concentrate, depression, and ir-

ritability. Liver is a very good source of this vitamin. Milk, buttermilk, lean meat, canned salmon, peanuts, yeast, wheat germ, green leafy vegetables, peas, and turnips contain niacin. This vitamin is soluble in water; therefore we should be careful not to discard the water in which these foods have been cooked. We need 12 milligrams of this vitamin each day.

VITAMIN B$_6$ OR PYRIDOXINE

Further research is necessary to know all the functions of this vitamin. At present, it seems to be important to the health of muscles and nerves.

Cane molasses, egg yolk, kidney, bran, soybeans, fish, meat, and wheat germ are good sources of pyridoxine. Yeast, liver, and navy beans contain some of this vitamin.

VITAMIN C OR ASCORBIC ACID

Vitamin C is essential to normal growth and to strong, healthy bones, teeth, gums, and blood vessels. It is necessary for the cement-like substance that holds bone, cartilage, and dentine cells together. Without this vitamin the walls of the blood vessels weaken, bones show a tendency to fracture easily, joints are tender, the teeth loosen, the gums become spongy and bleed easily, and wounds do not heal so readily as when we have adequate amounts. If the deficiency is very marked, scurvy develops. In this disease, the teeth loosen and fall out, the joints swell and become very painful, and eventually death results. High school girls should have about 80 milligrams of vitamin C per day.

Citrus fruits, raw or canned tomatoes, raw cabbage, raw onions, fresh strawberries, currants, gooseberries, and raspberries are good sources of vitamin C. Since this vitamin is affected by heat and dissolves in water, you can see why some uncooked foods are an important part of our diet.

VITAMIN D

Vitamin D is needed to protect you against rickets and to ensure strong, healthy bones, jaws, and teeth. Without vitamin D your body is unable to use the calcium and phosphorus in your food. With too little vitamin D you feel restless and irritable and are subject to colds.

You may get vitamin D in two ways. Cod-liver, halibut-liver, and salmon oils are rich in this vitamin. Milk, cream, butter, and egg yolk may contain some. Foods may be irradiated, that is, treated with ultraviolet light, which produces vitamin D in the food. Sunshine is a second source of vitamin D. When sunshine falls directly upon our skin, a substance in the skin called ergosterol is changed to vitamin D by the ultraviolet rays of the sun. However, we must remember that the ultraviolet rays cannot penetrate ordinary window glass or clothing.

VITAMIN E (ALPHA TOCOPHEROL)

The extent to which human beings need this vitamin for growth and health is uncertain. Since many of our common foods, such as grains, green leaves, meat, milk, and most vegetables, are good sources of vitamin E, the average diet is not likely to be deficient in it.

VITAMIN CONCENTRATES

Vitamins are the most widely advertised of the food elements. We have them put before us in concentrated forms in capsules and added to all kinds of products from bread to cold cream. However, from the foregoing discussion you can see that nature has distributed vitamins in our food. True, they frequently occur in small amounts, and no one food contains all of them; however, if each day we have those foods, properly prepared, which scientists list as necessary, we should not suffer from vitamin deficiency.

Vitamin concentrates are expensive. We had better spend our money for food which will furnish vitamins and at the same time supply valuable minerals, proteins, and energy, unless concentrates are advised by a physician.

Concerning products which have vitamins added to them, we should be very skeptical. Many times the form or amount of the vitamin is such as to make any beneficial effects doubtful and certainly would not warrant the extra cost that is usually involved.

SUMMARY OF FOOD NEEDS

You can see that, if the needs of our bodies are to be provided for, we must have some fat and carbohydrate foods to furnish heat and energy, some proteins and minerals to build and repair our bodies, and some minerals and vitamins to regulate and protect us. Since a large proportion of the body is water, we must have some water each day. Scientists say that from six to eight glasses of water a day suffice for body needs.

As you review the daily needs of your body, you can see that each food in the list recommended by nutritionists plays an important part and that it is necessary to have these foods every day. One quart of milk is required to give growing bodies the amount of calcium they need as well as some fat, sugar, protein, and vitamins A, B_1, D, and G. Whole-grain cereals and bread furnish energy at low cost, and at the same time they give us a small amount of protein, phosphorus, iron, and vitamin B_1. Butter is valuable as a source of energy and vitamin A. Meat, eggs, and cheese provide protein, phosphorus, and some iron. Meat is a fairly good source of vitamins. Eggs furnish vitamins A, B_1, D, and G. Vegetables and fruits are good sources of minerals and vitamins, in addition to furnishing some energy.

In addition, the acids and the fibers of fruits and vegetables are helpful in keeping the intestinal tract clean and in overcoming constipation. The acids stimulate the flow of digestive juices and promote peristaltic movement in the intestinal tract. The fibrous material which is found in the skins, as well as in the inside of fruits and vegetables, is called cellulose. Cellulose is not acted upon by the digestive juices. It acts as a broom in the digestive tract, sweeping along and carrying waste materials with it.

DIVISION OF FOOD

Since we cannot eat all the food that we require at one time, we divide the day's food into three meals.

BREAKFAST

Breakfast is usually the smallest meal of the day, but this does not mean that it is unimportant. On a cold winter morning your father would hardly expect the house to become warm unless he added fuel to the fire in the furnace, nor would he try to drive his car to work with an empty gasoline tank. Yet some people think that their bodies can function without fuel. Your body needs food at regular intervals if it is to work with the greatest efficiency, just as a car must have gasoline after it has run a given number of miles. Compare the time between your various meals. You will see that the longest interval is from dinner in the evening to breakfast the next morning. Does it seem sensible to make this interval still longer by omitting breakfast? If you have ever tried to do this, you may have noticed that you felt tired, irritable, and listless during the morning.

Some people say that they are never hungry in the morning. Possibly this is true. If they have not established the habit of eating breakfast, nature will adjust to this custom and will cease sending out the message of hunger. Eating breakfast is a habit, just as going to bed at a given hour is a habit. These same people do not realize how much better they would feel, how much more alert they would be, and how much more efficiently they could attend to the activity at hand if they formed the habit of eating breakfast.

Nutritionists say that one-fourth of the daily calories should be eaten at breakfast. Since you have had little time for exercise before eating, your appetite at breakfast is not so keen as it is for the other meals of the day. Hence breakfast is the smallest meal of the day, is usually composed of simple foods, and is somewhat standardized.

We eat light, medium, or heavy breakfasts, depending upon our energy requirement. A light breakfast consists of fruit, bread or cereal, and a beverage. A medium breakfast includes fruit, cereal or a main dish such as eggs, bread, and a beverage. A heavy breakfast consists of fruit, cereal, a main dish or dishes, bread, and a beverage. If you have ever spent the summer at camp where you were engaged in vigorous physical activity the major part of the day, you probably found a heavy breakfast very welcome. However, you may find that for a typical school day a medium breakfast will fulfill your requirements. The provision of sufficient calories is not the only point to consider in judging the suitability of breakfast. Since your body is still growing and developing, some foods

Do you think this is an adequate breakfast for a high school girl?
Courtesy, Good Housekeeping Institute.

which furnish proteins and minerals should be included in your
breakfast. If your body is to develop normally and to be free
from certain diseases, foods which contain vitamins should be
eaten. If your breakfast is attractive, your appetite will be stimulated, and you will be inclined to eat enough food to take care
of the needs of the morning. Including some warm food in the
meal will aid digestion.

THE NOON MEAL

At noon we may have either lunch or dinner. When the entire family is able to be home at noon, dinner is often served at midday, and supper in the evening. In many families neither father nor the children come home at noon. In this case the various members of the family have lunch at noon, and dinner, the largest meal of the day, is served in the evening.

LUNCH

Our noon meal must furnish enough energy for the activities of the afternoon. If we do not eat sufficient food, we are tired and lacking in energy before the evening meal. However, if we eat a hearty meal and then are not particularly active, but spend the time sitting in a classroom, we probably shall feel drowsy and listless. Scientists tell us that lunch should furnish one-third of the day's calories.

In addition to sufficient calories, our lunch should furnish some proteins, minerals, and vitamins. To stimulate the appetite, lunch should be attractive. It should contain contrasts in flavor, texture, and color. Digestion will be stimulated if some warm food is included. An adequate luncheon for a growing person contains milk, whole-grain bread, butter, a meat substitute, a vegetable, and a dessert.

DINNER

Dinner is the largest meal of the day. We are told that it should consist of five-twelfths of the day's calories. Many of the dishes which we have at luncheon are suitable for dinner, which may be light, medium, or heavy, depending upon the needs of the individual. A light dinner consists of meat or a meat substitute, vegetable, salad, bread and butter, and a dessert. A medium dinner may have an appetizer, such as soup, fruit, or fruit juice, in addition to the light meal. A heavy dinner has an appetizer and an extra vegetable added to a medium meal. What we should have for dinner depends upon what has been included in the other meals of the day, since it is the day as a whole, rather than the individual meal, that is important.

STUDY-GUIDE QUESTIONS

1. What proof can you give that our food influences the way we feel?
2. Make a list of the foods you should have each day.
3. What should be the place of candy in the diet?
4. Why do we eat food?
5. How is food transformed into energy in the body?
6. Does your body use the same amount of energy all the time? Explain.
7. Name the foods which are the best sources of heat and energy.
8. What is meant by the term calorie?
9. Do the same amounts of all foods furnish the same number of calories? Give examples.
10. Do all people use the same amount of energy?
11. Why do we need a normal amount of body fat?
12. What makes people overweight?
13. What are the disadvantages of being overweight?
14. What are the dangers involved in reducing diets? Reducing medicines?
15. What makes people underweight?
16. What are the disadvantages of being underweight?
17. Why do we need protein in our diet?
18. How can we be sure of including enough protein in our daily diet?
19. Name some foods which are good sources of protein.
20. Explain what is meant by complete proteins.
21. What is the effect of insufficient protein on our bodies?
22. Why do we need minerals in our diet?
23. How many minerals do we need? What minerals must we be careful to include in our diets in sufficient amounts? What about the others?
24. Give five uses of calcium in the body.
25. How can we be sure to get enough calcium every day?
26. If we do not get as much calcium in our diets as we need, what ill effects become evident?
27. What does phosphorus do for the body?
28. How can we be sure of getting a sufficient amount of phosphorus in our diet?
29. Why is iron so essential to health?
30. How much iron should you have each day?
31. What is the relation between iron and copper?
32. Name some foods which are rich in iron and copper.
33. Why must we have iodine?
34. Is the soil in your locality rich in iodine?
35. How can we get iodine?
36. What are vitamins?
37. Describe any accounts you have read, heard on the radio, or seen in the movies of the discovery of and experimentation with vitamins.
38. Of what value are vitamin concentrates?

39. Why should we make a practice of eating an adequate breakfast?
40. What determines whether we should eat a light, medium, or heavy breakfast?
41. How should the daily requirement of calories be divided among the meals of the day?
42. Do you usually eat an after-school snack? If so, what kind of food do you ordinarily choose? Is your choice always a good one? What is the test of a good mid-afternoon snack? Is your hunger in mid-afternoon the result of eating an inadequate lunch, is it due to the habit of eating at this time, or is it due to a real need?
43. Criticize the following student lunches, telling what is wrong and suggesting changes:
    Number I. Ham sandwich, cake, milk.
    Number II. Mashed potatoes, cabbage salad, chocolate pie.
    Number III. Fruit salad, buttered spinach, whole-wheat bread, chocolate bar.

ACTIVITIES

1. Make a list of everything you ate yesterday, giving the approximate amounts of each food.
2. Compare the list of foods you actually ate with what you should eat. What foods are lacking? Do you eat so much of some foods that other essential foods are crowded out of your diet? What good food habits do you have? How could your food habits be improved?
3. Estimate the calorific value of the food listed in Activity 1.
4. Estimate the number of calories you need in one day. If you are overweight or underweight, use the average weight for your height and age in making this calculation.
5. How does the number of calories that you require compare with the number that you eat each day? What conclusions can you draw about the amount of food that you habitually eat?
6. How should you modify your diet so that it will furnish the number of calories that you need?
7. Check over your food record to see whether you had enough protein yesterday. How should your diet be changed to meet your protein requirement?
8. Estimate the number of milligrams of iron in the foods listed for Activity 1.
9. Estimate the number of units of each vitamin which yesterday's food furnished.
10. How do these amounts compare with what you should have eaten?
11. How were the calories in your day's food divided? How can you distribute the calories more wisely among the three meals of the day?
12. Revise your day's food as listed in Activity 1, so that your calories will be adequate and will be properly distributed, so that you will get sufficient

amounts of protein, minerals, and vitamins, and so that each meal will be seasonable, attractive, and palatable.

13. From the menu of your school cafeteria plan different lunches at different prices. Does an expensive lunch necessarily mean a good lunch?

14. If you bring peanut butter sandwiches and an apple from home and have ten cents a day to spend in your cafeteria for additional food, what would be a wise choice?

UNIT EIGHT. SOME COMMON HEALTH PROBLEMS

IMPETIGO

Those of you who frequent swimming pools or use showers connected with gymnasiums need to take precautions against certain diseases which are often contracted in these places. Impetigo is a skin disease which may affect any place on the body but often appears on the hands and face. It is highly contagious and spreads very rapidly. It is contracted by using towels, toilet articles, or other articles which have been infected by a person who has the disease, or by direct contact with the sufferer's hands or face. The first sign of the disease is a red spot. In a short time a clear liquid appears just under the skin at this place. This liquid soon becomes yellow pus, which escapes from under the dry, hard scabs that eventually form. Wherever this pus comes in contact with the skin, new sores are started.

Good general health is an aid in preventing this disease and in overcoming it quickly. Absolute cleanliness of the skin, destruction of soiled dressings, and sterilization of personal articles help in controlling it. Scratching should be avoided, as it tends to spread the disease.

RINGWORM

Ringworm, or athlete's foot, is a fungus disease which is acquired by contact with an infected person, his clothing, or other personal articles. Gymnasium floors, swimming pools, and shower baths are common sources of infection, since people often walk barefooted in these places.

The first evidence of the disease is itching. Small blisters appear, or the skin between the toes cracks. Eventually, red, scaly, running sores may spread over the feet.

Absolute cleanliness, washing the feet thoroughly with soap and water, drying the feet carefully, especially between the toes, and changing the stockings frequently are good methods of controlling the disease. Wearing rubber shoes in public showers, swimming pools, and similar places and wearing bedroom slippers rather than going about with bare feet at home help in avoiding this disease.

COLDS

Colds are probably one of our commonest ailments. The average person has two or three a year. In themselves, colds are not serious, but the complications which result may be serious or even fatal. Pneumonia, sinus infection, and mastoid are common complications.

Colds are believed to be due to a virus so tiny that it will pass through a porcelain filter. This virus is found in the nose and throat of a person during the first three or four days of a cold. After that period the virus disappears. During a cold you infect another person by means of the tiny drops of moisture that you give off when sneezing, coughing, talking, or laughing. You can, of course, convey the virus to another through soiled hands, a handkerchief, a drinking glass, or other articles. Since the virus is present only during the first few days of the cold, you can see why you are a menace to others at that time and should take precautions not to infect them.

In treating a cold, rest is of value in that it helps the body to build up resistance. Isolating oneself in bed has one other advantage in that it keeps you from infecting others with the cold. Other helpful measures are hot baths and massage. They stimulate the flow of blood through the muscles and skin, thus aiding in the reduction of congestion in the mucous membrances of the nasal passages. After a hot bath or massage the patient should rest in bed with sufficient covers to prevent taking more cold. Since the application of heat to any infection is beneficial, gargling or irrigating the throat with hot salt water is an aid. Medicated oils, which are dropped into the nose, sometimes give temporary relief, but eventually they may be irritating to the mucous membrane. Most cold remedies which are advertised are a waste of money, as they do not prevent and cannot cure a cold.

In preventing colds, it is obvious that the most effective method is to avoid exposure. This is not always so easy as it sounds, since most people do not consider colds a serious ailment and hence do not isolate themselves. Keeping the body in the best possible condition through rest, proper food, exercise, fresh air, and proper clothing helps to increase our resistance to colds, whereas fatigue, overeating, and constipation lower it. Washing our hands before eating and after handling anything that a cold sufferer has handled, keeping our hands away from nose and mouth, and using an individual drinking glass are all preventive measures.

Persons suffering from colds can help to prevent the spread of their ailment, thus protecting others. Since the first few days are the most infectious, they should give up their usual activities and isolate themselves from others. They should feel obligated to protect others by keeping a distance from them when talking. When coughing or laughing, a handkerchief should be held in front of the mouth and nose. Paper handkerchiefs or tissues should be used, as they can be burned. Washing the hands frequently and avoiding the shaking of hands are preventive measures.

MENSTRUATION

Since menstruation is a function of every normal girl and woman, perhaps an understanding of just what takes place will help us give our bodies more intelligent care. The organs involved in menstruation are the ovaries, Fallopian tubes, uterus, and vagina. There are two ovaries, one on the right and one on the left side of the pelvis. In them an ovum, or egg cell, is produced every twenty-eight days. The Fallopian tubes are, as their name indicates, tube-like structures which are connected with the uterus and serve to carry the ovum to it. The uterus is about the size and shape of a pear and lies in the center of the pelvis. There the fertilized ovum grows and develops into a new individual. The uterus opens into the vagina, a tube-like passage which extends down to the genital region on the outside of the body.

The menstrual cycle actually is a continuous process which goes on for approximately twenty-eight days, not merely the three to five days when you have visible evidence of it. First, the ovum is produced in the ovary. As it ripens, a hormone, or chemical messenger, is produced and released into the blood to notify the uterus that an egg cell is about to be released. The uterus prepares itself to receive the ovum by certain changes in the lining and by bringing more blood into the tiny blood vessels there. The ovum passes into the Fallopian tubes, where it remains for a few days and, if unfertilized, eventually disintegrates. Since the uterus has no fertilized egg to nourish and care for, it stops its preparations. The tiny blood vessels rupture, the lining of the uterus sloughs off, and the menstrual flow is discharged by way of the vagina. The flow continues for three to five days. It is usually greatest on the second day and gradually grows less and less until it stops entirely. Then a new egg begins to ripen, and the cycle is started all over again.

Just as we have many other individual differences, so we have individual differences in the menstrual cycle. There are wide variations in the age at which menstruation begins, in the amount of flow, in the duration of the flow, and in the interval between periods. Probably few women have a cycle of exactly twenty-eight days, and most of us find variations within our own cycle, since shock or emotional strain may cause irregularities.

The menstrual period should not interfere with your regular activities. It is a perfectly normal process, and should in no way disrupt normal living. Activity, provided that it is not unusually strenuous, at this time is actually beneficial, as it stimulates the circulation and helps to overcome congestion in the blood vessels. Keeping the bowels open also helps at this time. When you become constipated, the collected waste material presses on the uterus and may cause you some discomfort.

In a normal, healthy person severe pain at this time is abnormal. A girl who is in good health and has built up a strong, vigorous body is less likely to suffer pain than one who is run-down, anemic, and in poor health. If severe pain is suffered, a competent physician should be consulted.

In caring for yourself, you must realize that the menstrual flow has an odor, and for this reason it is necessary to be especially clean at this time. Changing pads frequently and using a deodorant on them help in overcoming this odor. Daily bathing is more necessary at this time than at any other. Many girls find that they can take a warm tub bath as usual. However, if this interferes with the flow, try a warm shower or sponge bath. You will find, too, that you will be more comfortable and will feel cleaner, if, whenever possible, you sponge the genital region with warm water each time you change the pad. Extremely hot or cold baths should be avoided at this time.

STUDY-GUIDE QUESTIONS

1. Give the prevention, symptoms, and cure for impetigo, ringworm, and colds.
2. Name the organs involved in the menstrual cycle and give the function of each.
3. Explain what happens during the menstrual cycle.
4. Is the menstrual cycle the same with all individuals? What may cause differences in the cycle?
5. What are some causes of painful menstruation? How may this discomfort be prevented or relieved?
6. How can we prevent offensive odor during the menstrual period?

UNIT NINE.   HEALTH – A NATIONAL PROBLEM

Much of our national efficiency and prosperity depends upon the state of our health. Our federal and local health services are evidence that our leaders believe that the health of the nation should be of concern to the government.

It is true that much has been done through research and education to increase our life expectancy and to reduce the death rate from certain diseases. The average age to which people live has been increased from about forty-nine years, which was the life expectancy in 1900, to sixty-two years in 1938. Epidemics of small-pox and typhoid fever, which formerly wiped out whole villages, no longer occur. Conditions, however, are far from ideal. We still have many unnecessary illnesses which are wasteful, not only of money but also of human energy and lives. According to a recent study, only one-half of the people of this country consult a doctor once a year, and only one-fifth visit a dentist. In case of illness some people still consult quacks who have had no scientific training in the care of the sick and who rely on superstitions and humbug in treating people. Many people still doctor themselves with patent medicines, which are often harmful. The danger in using even harmless remedies of this sort is that they are ineffective, and their use tends to delay calling the doctor until the sufferer is beyond aid.

PUBLIC HEALTH SERVICE

We have probably given no thought to the services which our national and local governments provide as aids to good health. A pure water supply, sewage disposal, street cleaning, and garbage and rubbish collections and disposal are all public health measures. The Department of Public Health in your locality enforces quarantine of persons suffering from communicable ailments. It also provides serums and vaccines with which to make people immune to certain diseases. These are services to protect you. Sometimes this department establishes clinics in a community where people can get free medical and dental service as well as information on health matters. Public schools usually have some kind of health examinations for students. In some localities they also give the students treatment, and in others they recommend to parents what should be done to correct deficiencies and to improve the health of their children. Most schools also have some kind of program for educating young people to live so that their health will be improved.

HEALTH SERVICES IN INDUSTRY

Certain occupations are much more dangerous than others. For example, working on a high, steel framework, such as is used to build skyscrapers, presents one kind of hazard, working in a coal mine another, and working with lead or similar poisonous substances still a third.

Some states have laws requiring industries to give their employees all possible physical protection and to pay them if they are injured while working. Many companies have recognized that the health of their workers is an asset to them and have voluntarily taken steps to protect it. Such measures as placing guards on machines, requiring workmen to protect their eyes with goggles from flying particles of steel, maintaining a health department including the services of a doctor and nurse, and making use of educational films and programs on safety are all designed to protect the health of the worker.

INCOME AND HEALTH

Even with all these aids, however, the American people do not enjoy such good health as they should. A study made in Pittsburgh in the years 1928 and 1929, when this country was at the peak of prosperity, indicates that only half the school children have really good health. Recent studies show that there are more deaths and illnesses among people with low incomes than among those with higher incomes. People in low-income groups are sick more frequently and for longer periods of time than people with higher incomes. This is no doubt due to the fact that incomes which are not sufficiently large to maintain a decent standard of living mean poor housing, overcrowding, too little fresh air and sunshine, inadequate food, and lack of proper clothing. If we can raise the standard of living in low-income groups, undoubtedly we shall make great strides in the direction of good health.

INCOME AND MEDICAL CARE

These recent studies give us another bit of interesting information. People in low-income groups have less medical care than those in higher income groups. Of the families whose incomes are under $1200 per year, 47 per cent of the family members have no medical, dental, or eye service during the year. Of families earning from $2000 to $3000 per year, 37 per cent have no such care. When the income is $10,000 or more per year, only 14 per cent lack care. Perhaps these statements seem to contradict the facts presented in the preceding paragraph. However, when we analyze the facts carefully, we realize that the reason people in low-income groups have so little medical care is not that they do not need it but rather that they have no money to pay for it. One solution of this problem, as we have said before, is to make it possible for these people to earn a decent living. Another help is to institute some different plan for health care.

BETTER HEALTH CARE

Some people believe that the only way adequate health service can be made available for everyone is to have all health services organized under the government and supported by taxation. This type of health care has been used in Sweden, where it seems satisfactory. However, the idea is violently opposed by certain groups of people who think the medical service would be controlled by politicians, that there would not be sufficient incentive for doctors to progress in their profession, and that research in medicine would not be pursued as it has been under the present system.

In some localities group-payment plans for medical and hospital services have been organized. This is a system of voluntary health insurance covering a large group of people. Every family in the group pays a stated sum, about $3.00 a month, for which it receives complete medical and hospital service without any further payment. Some plans have been organized which cover only hospital care for a specified number of days each year. This plan

usually costs less per month, but it does not take care of the
doctor's fees. However, it makes it possible for the individual to
specify the doctor he prefers.

In addition to these plans, insurance companies sell various
kinds of health insurance, and some industries have health insurance which workers may voluntarily buy at small cost.

You can readily see that any of these plans, except the tax-
supported one, is impossible for people in the low-income groups.
Their incomes are too small to supply the essentials of life. They
cannot buy adequate food, shelter, or clothing. Even a small pay-
ment for medical care is impossible for them. Some authorities
state that for families with incomes less than $1500 per year,
public health services and free medical care must be provided.

STUDY-GUIDE QUESTIONS

1. Why should the health of the nation be of concern to the government?
2. How has the life span been increased since 1900?
3. What proportion of our population has inadequate medical care?
4. Why shouldn't people use patent medicines?
5. List the public health services which are available in your community.
   How does your list compare with that given in your textbook?
6. Why do most industrial concerns maintain a health service for their
   employees? Name some of the ways in which industry safeguards workers.
7. In what way is the health of our people related to their income? Quote
   figures to prove your statements.
8. Give arguments for and against having health services for all the people
   organized under the government and supported by taxation.

BOOKS FOR FURTHER READING

Borsook, Henry, *Vitamins*. The Viking Press, New York, 1941.
Clark, John A., Frederick L. Fitzpatrick, and Edith L. Smith, *Science on
the March*. Houghton Mifflin Company, Chicago, 1941.
Crisp, Katherine B., *Be Healthy*. J. B. Lippincott Company, Philadelphia,
1939.
Davis, Adelle, *Vitality Through Planned Nutrition*. The Macmillan Com-
pany, New York, 1942.
DeKruif, Paul, *Hunger Fighters*. Harcourt, Brace and Company, New York,
1928.
Krueger, Walter W., *The Fundamentals of Personal Hygiene*, revised. W. B.
Saunders Company, Philadelphia, 1940.

Rose, Mary S., *Feeding the Family,* fourth edition. The Macmillan Company, New York, 1940.

Rose, Mary S., *The Foundations of Nutrition,* third edition. The Macmillan Company, New York, 1938.

Stimson, A. M., *The Communicable Diseases.* United States Public Health Service, Miscellaneous Publication No. 30, Government Printing Office, Washington, D. C., 1939.

Willard, Florence, and Lucy H. Gillet, *Dietetics for High Schools,* revised. The Macmillan Company, New York, 1937.

Williams, Jesse F., *Healthful Living,* third edition. The Macmillan Company, New York, 1941.

Yearbook of Agriculture, *Human Nutrition.* Yearbook Separate No. 1668, Government Printing Office, Washington, D. C.

Good health and good grooming are the basis for beauty.
Courtesy, Procter and Gamble.

SECTION VII
PERSONAL CARE
UNIT ONE. WHY STUDY PERSONAL CARE?

Every girl wants to look attractive. The desire to appear as lovely as a favorite movie star is a perfectly natural one. However, we are not all so favorably endowed by nature as the movie stars, nor can we spend so much time and money on our appearance as they must do, since beauty is an essential qualification for them. Beauty is undoubtedly an asset in any job, since it attracts people to us, but most of us must remember that we are hired principally for the work we are able to do, and not just for decorative purposes. The girl who is so absorbed in her own appearance that she cannot concentrate on her work is not likely to be successful at her job. On the other hand, none of us can afford utterly to disregard our appearance. A sloppy, unkempt exterior repulses us and gives the impression that its owner is careless and sloppy in other things.

" How can I make the most of my appearance? " This is a question of interest to all of us. By applying intelligence to the problem, we should be able to improve our appearance with a reasonable expenditure of time and money. We must realize that good health is the foundation of beauty. A wholesome, vigorous person who is bubbling over with energy and good spirits is far more attractive than a listless, languid, irritable one. All the factors that contribute to good health contribute also to good looks. Proper food, sunshine, fresh air, adequate rest and sleep, exercise, and good posture play their part in making a girl attractive, just as surely as large eyes and a perfectly shaped nose do.

In addition to good health, proper care of ourselves will help to make us more attractive. The horse lover not only sees that the physical needs of his pet, such as food and exercise, are provided, but he also spends much time in grooming the animal. Care is given to keep the horse's coat luxuriant and glossy and his feet and mouth in good condition. We also need to give attention to grooming and should plan time each day for it.

289

UNIT TWO. THE SKIN

The skin is an organ which serves to protect the body and to help in regulating its heat. Since the skin has important work to do in maintaining our health, it should be given intelligent care. It is made up of two principal layers, the epidermis, or outer skin, and the dermis, or true skin.

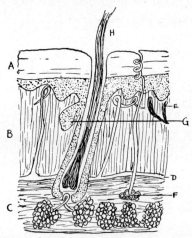

How the skin looks under the microscope. *A*, epidermis or outer layer; *B*, dermis or true skin; *C*, subcutaneous layer; *D*, blood vessel; *E*, nerve ending; *F*, sweat gland; *G*, sebaceous gland; *H*, hair.

The epidermis consists of a horny layer somewhat like the hair and nails. It has no blood vessels or nerve supply of its own. The cells of this layer are constantly being pushed to the surface, and shed or rubbed off. In the epidermis we find the openings of the sweat glands and the sebaceous glands.

In the true skin, or dermis, are located the blood vessels and nerve endings, as well as two sets of glands. The sweat glands help to keep the skin moist as well as aid in regulating the heat of the body through the evaporation of perspiration. These glands assist the work of the kidneys by eliminating waste products in the form of perspiration. The sebaceous glands secrete an oily substance called sebum, which keeps the skin soft and pliable. These glands send their secretion to the surface through the openings of the hair follicles.

Our bodies are constantly perspiring. It is said that we give off from one and one-half pints to two and one-half gallons of perspiration each day. Heat and nervousness increase perspiration. You will recall that, as you grow warmer in playing tennis or any other active game, you perspire freely. Have you ever watched a very exciting movie and suddenly realized that your hands were wet with perspiration? Under ordinary circumstances we are not conscious that our bodies are perspiring, since most of the time the perspiration evaporates as soon as it reaches the surface, leaving a film of solid material on the skin. At the same time the sebaceous glands also deposit materials along the hair shaft. In addition, we are constantly collecting surface dirt, and our skin is shedding dead cells from the epidermis.

BATHING

If the skin is to function as it should, it is necessary to keep it clean. Our greatest aid to cleanliness is the daily bath. The three usual methods of bathing are the sponge bath, the shower, and the tub. The sponge bath is considered the least hygienic, as the same water is used over and over again and it is difficult to keep the sponge or washcloth perfectly clean. In this respect, the shower bath is much superior, since the water is constantly changing. Where prolonged soaking is desirable, as in relieving sore muscles, the tub bath is indispensable.

KINDS OF BATHS

The cold bath acts as a stimulant to the nervous system, increases the activity of the skin, and improves the circulation of the blood, thus benefiting all the organs of the body. A cold bath should never be taken in a cold room, nor when we feel exhausted. It should be taken when we are warm, as upon arising in the morning, or immediately after a hot bath. It may consist of wetting the hands with cold water and rubbing the skin, a cold sponge bath, a cold shower, or a cold plunge. The first two methods, which are less vigorous than the last, are the best procedures to use in the beginning. The cold bath should be taken quickly, ten to thirty seconds being ample, and should be followed by a vigorous rubdown. This type of bath should not be taken unless it makes the skin glow, gives a feeling of exhilaration, and has no depressing effect at any time.

A warm bath with soap should be taken several times a week for the sake of cleanliness. It soothes the nerve tips in the skin, helping us to relax, and stimulates the flow of blood in the skin. For these reasons, such a bath is best taken just before retiring. If it is taken during the day, it should be followed by a cold sponge or shower and a vigorous rubdown, which tend to drive the blood from the surface and conserve body heat.

BODY ODOR AND DEODORANTS

Body odors arise from the secretions given off by the oil and sweat glands which collect on the skin along with dead cells. These secretions are in turn influenced by the state of the individual's health, his emotional condition, and his food and drink. If this waste material is allowed to remain on the skin, an unpleasant odor becomes noticeable. The first step in overcoming body odor is to remove the source of the odor with a cleansing bath.

In addition to bathing, deodorants may be used. These, as well as perfume, should be used in addition to, and not in place of, a bath. There are two types of deodorants on the market. One deodorizes without affecting the flow of perspiration; the other both deodorizes and prevents the flow of perspiration. The first type usually comes in paste or powder form, is harmless, and can be used without injury to clothing fabrics. The second type is usually a liquid or paste which is not harmful to most people if the solution is not too strong and if it is not used to excess. Some deodorants of this type are harmful to fabrics and should be applied only at night. After a deodorant is used, the skin should be rinsed and dried before a garment is put on.

DEPILATORIES

Unwanted hair can be removed in a variety of ways. As far as is now known, there is no salve or lotion that will remove hair permanently and safely. Any such preparation that would be strong enough to destroy the hair permanently would injure the skin. Electrolysis, or the use of the electric needle, is the only way now known of removing hair permanently. This method consists of inserting an electric needle in each hair follicle, thus causing decomposition of the vital portion of the hair. The process is tedious and, unless the operator is skillful, may leave scars.

Chemical depilatories can be recognized by the disagreeable odor they give off when water is added to them. They do not remove hair permanently but merely destroy that which is above the skin's surface. Care should be taken in using them, as they will irritate the skin if it is unusually sensitive or if they are left on too long.

Abrasives, such as pumice or mittens of sandpaper or emery paper, remove hair by rubbing it off. The results are not permanent, and the process takes time and patience.

Some depilatories consist of wax, which is melted, applied to the skin, allowed to harden, and then pulled off. When the wax is removed, the hairs which have become imbedded in it are pulled out. This method has the same effect as pulling hairs out with tweezers. It is not permanent, as the vital strand in the hair follicle is not destroyed.

Removing hair by shaving is probably the least expensive method. Contrary to some opinions, shaving does not increase the rate at which the hair grows, nor does it cause the hair to become bristly. It does require careful manipulation, as any breaks made in the skin by the razor are apt to become sources of infection.

VALUE OF A GOOD COMPLEXION

If you were to ask several people to describe their ideal beauty, someone would describe a tall, slim, dark-haired, brown-eyed girl. Another would mention a small, dainty blonde with blue eyes; still another would picture her as being medium in height, strong and lithe, with red hair and hazel eyes. Everyone's picture would be different, except in one respect. All would imagine this ideal with a clear, lovely skin, for everyone agrees that a beautiful skin is essential to an attractive appearance. A clear skin gives an impression of good health. If the body is not functioning normally, indication is often found in the skin. In the case of a fever, the skin becomes dry and hot and appears flushed. A pale, blotched skin may indicate poor circulation. Pimples and excessive oiliness may accompany faulty elimination and too rich a diet. In addition to indicating your general health, your face reflects your mental and emotional life. Wrinkles etched by discontent and lines caused by a frowning mouth add nothing to the beauty of your skin.

TYPES OF SKINS

The skin, it has been pointed out, is normally kept moist and soft by secretions from the sweat and sebaceous, or oil, glands. When the sebaceous glands are too active and excessive secretion is given off, an oily skin results. In the case of a dry skin the horny substance which should soften to a semisolid and be pushed out of the gland by oncoming material fails to soften, and the skin has too little oil, or else the secretion is dried up by excessive heat or abnormally low humidity in the atmosphere.

CLEANSING THE SKIN

For either a dry or oily skin, most authorities advocate washing once a day with soap and water. Soap is slightly antiseptic and is necessary to remove the surface dirt, perspiration, and oily secretion. It should never be rubbed on the skin; a lather should be made on a face cloth, which is then used to wash face and neck. However, we should keep in mind that we are merely trying to get the oily secretion off the skin's surface, not out of it. If the skin has a tendency to dryness, strong soap, too much soap, prolonged use of hot water, hard water, and overexposure to the sun will tend to make it drier. Rinsing the face in cold water and following the rinse with a brisk massage will help to stimulate the circulation.

Creams may be used, especially on dry skins, as cleansing agents. They also lubricate the skin and help to keep it soft and smooth. Cleansing creams are of two types — cold cream and quick-liquefying cream. Cold cream is a combination of animal and vegetable fats with water. The quick-liquefying creams are made of mineral oils and waxes. They spread easily and melt at body temperature. They are not considered as efficient cleansers as cold cream and are likely to have a drying effect on the skin.

In addition to these two types of creams, there are also vanishing creams and special creams, such as skin foods, on the market. Vanishing creams are often used as a finish to the skin before

In cleansing with cream, do not rub the cream in.
Courtesy, Pond's Extract Company, New York.

make-up is applied. They are essentially a kind of soap, which deposits a thin film on the skin. Skin food and tissue creams are sold to nourish and build up the tissues. As you know, nourishment must come from within by means of the blood stream. As far as it is now known, vitamins, hormones, and the like have no value in the form of cream to be rubbed on the skin. Creams can lubricate and keep the skin soft. Any massage that is used in applying them is beneficial in so far as it stimulates the flow of blood in the skin. Lanolin, a fat taken from the wool of sheep, is considered a valuable constituent in creams, because it is similar to the natural oil of the skin. The value of a cream cannot be gauged by the price, the attractiveness of the package in which it comes, nor the extravagant claims used to advertise it.

In cleansing the face with cream, a generous quantity should be used, so that there will be no need to spread it around, thus rubbing grime and dirt into the skin. For the same reason it is better to pat rather than to rub it on. Using upward strokes, wipe the cream off with a soft cloth or cleansing tissue. A second application will ensure a clean face. The skin should always be cleansed before retiring, either with soap and water or with cleansing cream, to remove powder and other make-up.

USE OF MAKE-UP

In using cosmetics, the effect to be achieved is naturalness. The circus clown paints his face a ghostly white and adds two round spots of red on each cheek to be comical. Cosmetics used with discretion, so that they really enhance the appearance, are an asset, but when used to excess, they result in a ridiculous effect.

Make-up should be put on a clean skin and not daubed over old make-up or the grime of the day. Some authorities recommend the use of a foundation cream. It is claimed that it gives depth to the color of cosmetics, hides imperfections, protects the skin, and makes rouge and powder stay on longer. For this foundation a vanishing cream may be used, or a thin layer of cold cream may be applied and the excess wiped off.

POWDER

Powder is used to conceal blemishes and the shine of the skin. Since concealment is thus the chief function of face powder, we should consider its covering power, which is expressed in terms of weight, such as light, medium, and heavy. Light powders are suitable for dry skins, medium powders for normal or moderately oily skins, and heavy powders for very oily skins.

In selecting the proper shade in face powder, we should remember that powder should not change the natural color of the skin. Powder is used to improve the skin's texture, not to change its color. Select powder which harmonizes with your skin tones.

Face powder should be applied to a clean face and neck with a clean puff or piece of cotton. A powder puff should be considered as personal as a toothbrush. The practice of using a fresh piece of cotton and discarding it after use gives better results than using a soiled powder puff, which tends to rub dirt into the skin. After the face and neck have been thoroughly powdered, use a fresh piece of cotton or a soft complexion brush to dust off extra powder, being sure to remove all excess from around the nose, the eyelashes, and eyebrows.

ROUGE

Rouge is used to add color to the face and to modify its apparent shape. It should always be kept in mind that make-up is best used to highlight our good features and make our poor ones less noticeable. A natural effect, not a highly artificial one, is to be desired. People of good taste prefer a minimum of make-up for daytime and use more of it for evening, when more vivid color is required, since artificial light seems to take color out of our skin rather than to give it color, as sunlight does.

Three types of rouge are available. Dry rouge comes in dry, cake form and is similar to powder in texture. It is easy to apply but does not last a long time. Generally, people with an oily skin find this rouge best. Paste or cream rouge resembles creams in texture. Paste and liquid rouges are more difficult to apply evenly with a natural effect but are more lasting than dry rouge. People with dry skin usually prefer a paste rouge.

In buying rouge, it is best to select a color which most nearly resembles your natural color. One way of determining this is to pinch the skin of the arm and to note the color. Rouges come in clear red or have an orange, blue, or purple cast.

Dry rouge is generally put on after powder, whereas cream rouge is usually applied first, and powder put on over it. The shape of the face determines just where the rouge is to be placed. Since the oval face is considered more or less ideal, the rouge is usually placed on such a face where the color naturally comes. To make a long face look less long, the rouge is placed on the outer

curves of the cheeks and blended with horizontal strokes. To make
a wide face look less wide, the rouge is applied on the inner curve
of the cheeks with vertical strokes. Rouge should be kept high
on the cheekbones, above the level of the nostrils, as lower application tends to make the face look heavy. The edges of the rouge
should always be blended with the finger tip to soften them and
to give a more natural effect.

LIPSTICK

Lipstick is similar to paste rouge, except that more wax has
been added to make it stiffer and more lasting. Lipstick calls attention to the mouth and teeth. People whose teeth are not especially
attractive should use lipstick very conservatively. The color should
harmonize with the color inside the lower lip and should blend
with that of the rouge.

In applying lipstick, the apparent shape of the mouth can be
modified. If the mouth is large, accent the center of the lips and
do not extend the color to the corners of the mouth. To make a
small mouth seem larger, carry the color to the corners. Thin lips
can be made to seem thicker by blending the color over the edges
of the lips.

The lips should be perfectly dry before lipstick is applied.
Begin in the center of the upper lip and work toward the outside.
Blend the lipstick with the finger or a brush. Repeat on the lower
lip. Blend the color in toward the mouth to a point just beyond
where the lips meet, so that there will be no sharp line where the
color stops. Remove excess lipstick by placing a piece of cleansing
tissue between the lips and pressing on it.

EYE MAKE-UP

Many of you probably do not use any kind of make-up in connection with your eyes. Anything of the sort is certainly in poor
taste and out of place for school, business, or street wear. An excess
of make-up around the eyes is apt to give an impression of cheap
artificiality; therefore care should be taken if the eyes are made
up.

Generally speaking, the eyebrows should follow the natural
line of growth. Plucking the brows until they are just a fine line

is likely to make the face look weak. On the other hand, heavy, shaggy brows that meet above the nose give a severe, unkempt look to the face. Hairs which are obviously out of line with the natural arch should be plucked.

Eyebrow pencils are sometimes used to make very light brows darker in color. These pencils may be purchased in brown or black. Brown is generally considered to give the more natural effect. In applying the pencil, use short hair-like strokes, and color only the hairs.

Eye shadow is said to give depth and sparkle to the eyes. It is available in the form of a creamy paste in a wide range of colors. The color that harmonizes with the natural shadow at the inner corner of the eye is the best. Eye shadow is used only on the upper lid. Start with a very small amount in the inner corner and work out, using the little finger to shade it toward the eyebrow. Dusting over eye shadow with powder will give a more natural effect.

If mascara is used to darken the lashes, is should be brushed on, working from the roots of the lashes to the tips and curling the lashes back as you work. After the lashes are dry, they should be brushed gently to keep them from sticking together.

Most liquid colorings are somewhat like hair dyes in composition, and, according to the Food and Drug Administration and the American Medical Association, are not safe to use around the eyes. Products advertised to make the eyelashes grow long and thick are worthless for this purpose. Many of these products are greasy substances which make the lashes stand out but which have no power to stimulate their growth. Eyelashes grow to a given length, then drop out, and are replaced by new ones.

SKIN DIFFICULTIES

Pimples, blackheads, and acne are common skin difficulties, especially during the adolescent years. Let us recall that the skin contains two sets of glands — sweat glands, which excrete perspiration, and sebaceous glands, which excrete an oily substance called sebum. You may have been told that blackheads are caused by dirt collecting in the skin. This is not necessarily true. Normally, as the sebum accumulates in the sebaceous glands, it softens as it nears the skin's surface and is poured onto the skin through the opening of the hair follicle as an oily substance. When the sebum does not soften as it nears the surface but remains rather hard, however, you can see that it would have a difficult time in leaving the hair follicle. In this case it remains in the skin, and, through chemical changes which take place at the end exposed to the surface, it darkens and appears as a blackhead.

If the gland continues to secrete and at the same time the sebum is unable to make its way out of the hair follicle, the skin swells and stretches. Bacteria which live in the gland but normally are harmless become active, and a pimple results. A pimple really is an infected blackhead.

These skin difficulties occur most commonly during the years of adolescence, which is a time when many changes are taking place in the body. All glands, including the sebaceous glands, are in a state of activity. The degree to which you will suffer from skin difficulties depends upon the rate at which this change takes place. A chronic condition of this sort is called acne.

All conditions which promote good health will, of course, help to keep the skin in good condition. Excessive use of sweets tends to create favorable conditions for the growth of the bacteria that live in the sebum, hence people who are troubled with acne are generally advised to eliminate sweets from their diet, to eat plenty of fruits and vegetables, and to drink from six to eight glasses of water each day. Using a minimum of cosmetics and washing the face each night with soap and warm water before retiring are aids to a good skin. Even with careful cleansing, close attention to the diet, and the regular elimination of body wastes, acne sometimes persists. In these cases a skin specialist should be consulted. Home remedies and beauty lotions are of little help, since the trouble comes from within. The use of X-ray by a specialist has sometimes been found helpful.

STUDY-GUIDE QUESTIONS

1. What is the purpose of the skin?
2. Describe the structure of the skin.
3. What is the function of the sebaceous glands and the sweat glands?
4. How much perspiration is given off by the body in one day?
5. Name the three usual methods of bathing. Give the advantages of each.

6. When should you take a cold bath? Why? How can a girl determine whether a cold bath is beneficial or harmful for her?
7. What is the purpose of a warm bath? How often should it be taken?
8. What is the source of body odor?
9. How may unwanted hair be removed? Discuss each method.
10. Why are some skins dry and others oily?
11. How should each type of skin be cleansed?
12. Name the kinds of face creams on the market.
13. Generally, what do we expect face creams to do for our skin?
14. What is the difference between a cold cream and a quick-liquefying cream? What is the purpose of each?
15. Give directions for cleansing the face with cream.
16. Why do we use face powder?
17. Explain the meaning of the terms light, medium, and heavy powder.
18. Give directions for applying face powder.
19. Why do we use rouge?
20. What are the three types of rouge? When should each be used?
21. How can one decide the best color of rouge and lipstick to use?
22. How can rouge be applied to make a face look less long? Less wide?
23. Would you apply rouge before or after powder?
24. How can lipstick be applied to decrease the apparent size of the mouth? To make a small mouth look larger?
25. Give the directions outlined in your textbook for applying lipstick. Do you agree with them? Why?
26. When do people use eye make-up? What is it supposed to do for the eyes?
27. Explain how blackheads are formed; how a pimple develops.
28. What is acne? What can be done to cure acne?

ACTIVITIES

1. Select a member of your class to demonstrate the various methods of removing hair.
2. Select a member of your class to demonstrate cleansing the face with cream.
3. Examine several of the various types of cream on the market. Try some on your skin, noticing the texture of each, and the rate at which it liquefies and is absorbed.
4. Examine samples of light, medium, and heavy powders, as well as powders of different colors. Try these various powders on selected class members with different types of skin and skin tones. Criticize the effect in each case.
5. Select a class member and make up one-half of her face to make it appear longer and the other half to make it appear wider. Which effect is best for her?
6. Demonstrate, using a class member as a subject, the application of lipstick to achieve different effects.

UNIT THREE. THE HAIR

In both poetry and prose a woman's hair has been described as her crowning glory. However, it can be her crowning glory only if it is kept immaculately clean and if it is becomingly arranged.

STRUCTURE OF THE HAIR

A hair is a filament which grows from a depression, or hair follicle, in the skin. The hair follicle is lined with a layer of outer skin and contains one or more sebaceous glands. The oily secretion from these glands keeps the hair soft and prevents it from

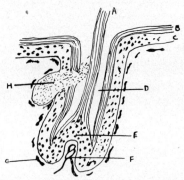

How the hair looks under the microscope. *A*, hair; *B*, outer layer of epidermis; *C* and *E*, layer of living cells of epidermis; *D*, follicle; *F*, projection of the dermis out of which the hair grows; *G*, blood vessels; *H*, sebaceous gland.

breaking. It is by means of the nerves and blood vessels, which lie in the true skin below the outer layer, that the hair is nourished. As each hair grows old, it falls out and is replaced by a new hair within the follicle, provided that the part which has the power of producing a new hair remains in the follicle. Physical well-being, maintained by following the laws of health, is the first essential for a healthy head of hair.

CARE OF THE HAIR

Since brushing and massage stimulate the circulation of the blood in the scalp, they are an aid to keeping the hair in good condition. Brushing should be a part of the daily grooming program. Your brush and comb should be used only by you and should be kept scrupulously clean. Frequent washing in warm, soapy water or in warm water to which a few drops of ammonia

Your hair should be washed as often as necessary. Courtesy, Procter and Gamble.

have been added is necessary to keep your brush and comb clean. Brushing the hair daily helps to keep it clean as well as to stimulate the flow of blood in the scalp. The motion should be upward, lifting the hair from the scalp. Separate the hair and brush it from underneath as well as from on top. Massage the scalp with the finger tips, using rotating and lifting movements.

Your hair should be washed whenever it is dirty. Oily hair, which tends to hold the dirt, requires more frequent washing than dry hair. In summer it may be necessary to wash your hair more often than in winter, because of perspiration. For washing the hair, it is best to use a mild, liquid soap, as it is difficult to rinse out cake soap that has been rubbed on the hair. Liquid soap may be made by shaving cake soap into hot water and stirring it until it is dissolved. Before starting a shampoo, collect the necessary articles, such as clean towels, liquid soap, comb, brush, and a bath spray. Although the bath spray is not necessary, it will be a great help in rinsing your hair. Be sure to have plenty of warm water available. First loosen any dandruff on your scalp by going over your head with a comb, preferably a fine-tooth comb. Brush your hair thoroughly, and wet it with warm water. Pour on enough liquid soap to make a good lather. Using the finger tips, work the soap into the scalp with a circular motion. Rinse thoroughly, using warm water. Repeat the soaping and washing to be sure that the hair is perfectly clean. Rinse the hair thoroughly until no trace of soap remains. Wrap your head in a towel and pat up the excess moisture. Rub and brush your hair until it is dry. It is generally considered better to dry the hair in this way rather than by artificial heat, which has a tendency to make the scalp too dry and the hair brittle.

A hot-oil shampoo is used for dry hair and dandruff and to overcome the drying effects of a permanent wave. This shampoo consists of massaging warm lanolin or olive oil into the scalp and then steaming the scalp by applying towels which have been wrung out of hot water. As soon as one towel becomes cool, it should be removed and another applied until about six applications have been made. A regular shampoo should follow.

DANDRUFF

The skin is constantly shedding dead cells, which the hair tends to hold to the scalp. In addition, excessive oil dries, leaving a flaky substance. This condition, known as dandruff, is aggravated by poor general health and neglect of your scalp and hair. Daily brushing and frequent washing to keep the scalp clean and stimulated are the best remedies known today.

PERMANENT WAVING

Permanent waving consists of winding the hair tightly around a rod, softening it with a solution, and heating it. Since hair can be stretched, this process makes curly that part of the hair which was treated. However, not all permanent waves are equally successful. The skill of the operator, the condition of the hair, the

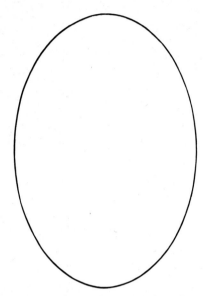

quality of the materials used, and the care given afterwards are all factors in its success. The time of heating must be carefully regulated, the solution used must suit the type of hair, and the wave must be properly cared for after it is given. The use of oil to offset

Lucky is the girl who has this oval type of face. Almost any type of hair-do will become her. Her most becoming hair-dos, however, will be those which follow the oval outline and thus accentuate its perfection, as does the hair-do shown here. Courtesy, Procter and Gamble.

the drying effect of a permanent wave is generally recommended. Also, daily brushing will help distribute the natural oil and will stimulate the circulation of blood in the scalp. As you know, a permanent wave makes the hair curly, but it is still necessary to have the wave " set " in your hair; otherwise the effect is likely to be frizzy and fuzzy.

You may have heard it said that singeing and cutting make the hair grow. When you know that the only living part of the hair is in the follicle under the skin and that the part which is exposed contains no blood vessels or nerves, you can see that such a belief is without reason.

ARRANGING THE HAIR

In deciding on the best way to arrange the hair, it should be kept in mind that most of us have a limited amount of time to spend on our personal appearance. It is better to arrange the hair

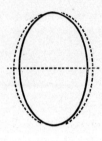

Long, narrow face (elongated oval) — This face needs a soft, loose hair-do, wider right across the center, to widen the elongated oval. Note how the hair-do at right achieves this, with a soft *low* wave on top, and fluffed out at the sides. A too-long bob is bad for this face, because it *adds length* to it. So is any stiff, close hair-do, because it accentuates the length of the too-long oval.

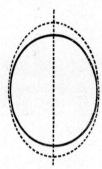

Broad, round face (widened oval) — What this face needs is lengthening, and so the most becoming hair-dos will be those which add height to the top of the head and are long below the face but held in on the sides. Note how the hair-do at the right achieves this. The tricky little braid, made of yarn, adds height. A pompadour would do the same.

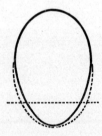

Wide forehead, narrow chin (oval narrowed and pointed at bottom)—Here it is obvious that the most becoming hair-do will be one which fills in the narrowed line at the bottom and thus helps complete the oval. The hair-do at right accomplishes this very well.

The right hair-do for different types of faces. Courtesy, Procter and Gamble.

simply, so that a neat, trim effect is achieved, rather than in an elaborate manner that is so time-consuming that we either do not have time to do it well or some other items in our personal grooming schedule must be neglected. If our hairdress is to be becoming, we must consider the shape of the face and the indi-

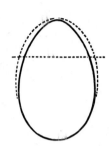

Narrow forehead, wide jaws (oval narrowed at top and widened at bottom) — With this face, the problem is exactly the opposite of that of the face with the wide forehead and narrow chin. The hair-do at right (the new, short "feather bob") lends itself very well to a widening arrangement at the top, with the bottom hair combed back and away from the face (to narrow it). Long hair could be arranged to follow the same contour principle. Keep in mind that the problem is to achieve a hair-do which will *help to complete the oval shape.*

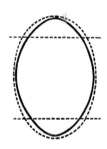

Narrow forehead, narrow chin, wide across middle (sometimes called diamond-shape, because the oval is pointed top and bottom) —Here it is clear that the problem is to arrange the hair so that it will fill out the face both top and bottom, where the oval begins to taper into points, and to avoid width across the middle. Note how the hair-do at right meets the problem. The braids, brought up from the sides, widen the top of the head, fluffy ends widen the bottom.

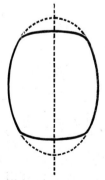

Broad, square face (oval flattened both top and bottom)—With this kind of face, the hair-do must add both height and length to the face and avoid any extra width anywhere along the side of the face. In other words, hair close at the sides, high on top, and shoulder-length at bottom but held well back is desirable. Pompadours, with or without bows, always add height.

The right hair-do for different types of faces. Courtesy, Procter and Gamble.

vidual features, such as the size of the nose and ears. As you know, the ideal face is oval in shape. Since most faces are variations of the oval, let us consider some principles that can guide us in dressing the hair becomingly for these various-shaped faces.

In arranging the hair for a person with a long, thin face, the purpose is to make the face appear wider and less long. If the hair is worn flat on the top of the head and somewhat fluffed at the sides, without allowing it to come over onto the cheeks, the face will look shorter. Dressing the hair high on top of the head should be avoided, as it will tend to make the face look longer.

If your face is round, your hair should be so arranged that it does not accent the roundness of your face but, rather, makes the face seem less round. Hair arranged high on top of the head will give length to the face, A soft wave, which may even be brought slightly to the sides of the face, will tend to make the face seem narrower. Extreme fluffiness or a bush effect, which adds width, should be avoided. A severe, sophisticated hairdress is usually unbecoming, as a round-faced person often has small, dainty features.

In profile view the hairdress should aid in giving the head a well-shaped appearance. A prominent nose is accented by hair slicked back tightly from the forehead but is minimized by a soft arrangement of the hair at the top of the head. An extremely high forehead can be made less conspicuous by bangs or by an irregular hairline which breaks its height. Similarly, a long neck looks less long if the hair is worn low on the back of the neck in a soft arrangement rather than clipped extremely short.

STUDY-GUIDE QUESTIONS

1. When can a woman's hair be rightly called her crowning glory?
2. Define a hair; a hair follicle.
3. How is the hair nourished?
4. What is the first requirement for a healthy head of hair?
5. Why are brushing and massaging beneficial to your hair? Give directions for each procedure.
6. Name the steps to be followed when washing your hair.
7. When is a hot-oil shampoo desirable? Give directions for giving a hot-oil shampoo.
8. What is dandruff? What causes it? How may it be cured?
9. What happens to the hair when it is given a permanent wave? What can be done to offset the drying effect of a permanent wave?

10. Is the hair benefited by singeing and cutting?
11. On the assumption that the most beautiful face is oval, what should a person with a long, thin face do to make her face appear oval? A person with a round face?

ACTIVITY

Select class members with different shaped faces, and arrange their hair so that it emphasizes the shape of the face. Then rearrange the hair so that it modifies the shape of the face.

UNIT FOUR.   THE HANDS AND NAILS

If your hands are to look their best, they must be well cared for. The skin should be soft and smooth and the nails well manicured.

CARE OF THE HANDS

Chapped hands are caused by the loss of natural oil in the skin as a result of using strong soap and not drying the hands thoroughly, especially in cold weather. Preventive measures consist of protecting the hands by wearing gloves while working, using a dish mop when washing dishes, and drying the hands thoroughly.

To keep the hands and nails clean, scrubbing with a hand brush is desirable. Stains can be removed by such simple household remedies as lemon juice or peroxide of hydrogen. Hand lotions are advertised as aids in overcoming chapped skin. Those containing large amounts of glycerin actually may have a drying effect upon the skin, since glycerin tends to absorb moisture. Lanolin or warm olive oil rubbed thoroughly into the skin is more effective. The lotion can be applied before retiring, and a pair of cotton gloves put on to prevent getting the bedclothes greasy.

CARE OF THE NAILS

In caring for your nails, the following equipment is necessary: a file, emery boards, orangewood stick, small scissors, bowl, nail brush, cotton, polish remover, nail polish, olive oil or cold cream, a towel, and cleansing tissues. If you use liquid polish, begin your weekly manicure by removing the old polish. Next, file the nails to the desired shape, smoothing them with an emery board. In filing, work from the corner of the nail toward the center of it, rather than see-sawing back and forth on the nail. Proper filing helps to prevent hangnails. The shape of the nails depends upon the shape of the fingers. Extremely long and pointed nails are not practical. After you have filed your nails, soak your finger tips in warm, soapy water for a few minutes. Then scrub your nails with a brush and dry them thoroughly. Wrap a bit of cotton around the end of your orangewood stick, dip it into a little warm olive oil or cold cream, and gently push back the cuticle around the nail. Remove any excess cream or oil with cleansing tissue. Trim any hangnails with scissors, but avoid cutting the cuticle if possible.

Clean under the nails with the pointed end of the orangewood stick. Never use a sharp instrument to clean the nails, as this practice is likely to roughen the skin under the nail and make it catch and hold dirt more readily. If stains remain under the nails, use lemon juice or peroxide to bleach them. Nail white, in the form of a pencil or paste, may be used if desired. Nail white does not actually whiten the nail but merely deposits some material under it which makes the tip look white.

The nails may be polished by using dry or paste polish and buffing them or by using liquid polish. If the first method is followed, apply some powder or paste to the buffer and rub the buffer lightly across the nails in one direction only.

Liquid polishes come in a wide range of colors as well as colorless. Liquid polish chips easily. If conspicuous colors are used, considerable time must be given to removing the polish frequently and replacing it. If you cannot spare the time, it is best to use colorless or natural shades. Then, too, highly colored polishes must be carefully selected, so that they blend well with the color of clothes and of other cosmetics used. Before applying liquid polish, it is best to buff the nails with a dry polish to make them perfectly smooth. This preparation makes the liquid polish last longer. Be sure that no powder remains on the nails. Taking care that the brush is not too full of polish, begin at the top of the moon and apply the liquid polish in long strokes to the tip of the nail. It is a matter of personal choice whether you cover the white portion at the tip of the nail with polish. Remove excess polish along the edges of the nails with cleansing tissue.

DAILY CARE

Daily care of your nails consists of keeping them smooth with an emery board, scrubbing them with a brush, cleaning under them with a dull instrument such as an orangewood stick, and pushing back the cuticle with your finger covered with a towel. If your cuticle seems very dry, massage warm olive oil or cold

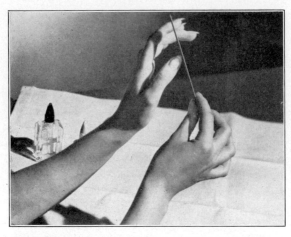

Check your filing system.   Courtesy, Cutex Corporation.

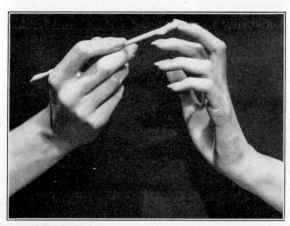

Apply bleach with a cotton-tipped orangewood stick to remove stains under the nails.
Courtesy, Cutex Corporation.

To keep the cuticle pliable and soft, give the nails an oil bath once a week.
Courtesy, Cutex Corporation.

Apply liquid polish with long strokes.   Courtesy, Cutex Corporation.

cream into it several times a week, pushing the cuticle back from
the nail. Care should be taken to do this gently. A sharp instrument should never be used on the cuticle. As you know, the only
living part of the nail is at its base under the skin. Any injury
to this part will show up in the nail and must gradually grow out
with it.

STUDY-GUIDE QUESTIONS

1. Describe well cared for hands.
2. What causes hands to chap?
3. How can you prevent your hands from chapping?
4. What effect does glycerin have on the hands?
5. What oils are helpful in keeping the hands soft?
6. List the equipment needed in caring for your nails.
7. Outline step by step the procedure to follow in a weekly manicure.
8. What kinds of nail polishes are on the market? What are the advantages
   of each?
9. Give directions for applying the different kinds of nail polishes.
10. What should be done daily to keep the nails in good condition?

ACTIVITY

Select a class member to demonstrate the correct way to give a manicure.

UNIT FIVE. THE EYES

Our eyes are not only an asset from the standpoint of appearance and the enjoyment of living but also are essential in earning a living. Since they cannot be replaced in case our sight is lost, it behooves us to take the best possible care of them. Defective eyesight affects our general health, is likely to make us irritable, decreases our efficiency at our jobs, and may be a cause of accidents.

STRUCTURE AND STRUCTURAL DEFECTS OF THE EYE

The eye is a delicate organ which may be said to operate somewhat like a camera. In looking at far or near objects, it is necessary for the eyes to focus images by flattening or rounding the lens by means of the muscles of the eye.

Astigmatism, nearsightedness, and farsightedness are all defects of vision due to imperfections in the construction and mechanism of the eye. These defects can be corrected only by wearing glasses that have been prescribed by a competent physician. Eyestrain may be due to weak eye muscles and may result in headaches, nervousness, painful vision, or watery, inflamed eyes.

CARING FOR THE EYES

In caring for the eyes and conserving the vision, it is necessary to obtain medical advice if the vision is not clear, if you are easily fatigued, if you have frequent headaches, or if you are nervous without cause. Your general health influences to some extent the functioning of the eye. If the entire body is in fine physical condition through the use of proper foods, sufficient exercise, and rest, the eyes benefit thereby, just as do all the other organs of the body.

Eyes become tired, and unnecessary strain is put upon them by poor light. Good light is steady, uniform, and adequate without glare. For floor, table, and desk lamps the Cleveland Sight Saving Council recommends the following rule for adequate light: In a single-socket lamp use a 100-watt bulb; in a double-socket lamp use two 60-watt bulbs; and in a triple-socket lamp use three 40-watt bulbs.

In any kind of close work, such as reading or sewing, there will be less strain on your eyes if you assume an erect posture and if the source of light is from the left. The whole room should be well lighted with extra light upon your work. When the room is fairly dark with light concentrated in a circle on your work or

Proper light for study.   Courtesy, Sight-Saving Council, Cleveland, Ohio.

book, undue strain is placed upon the eye muscles in looking from the light spot to the dark place. Besides securing adequate light, there are other things we can do to save our eyes. When we are doing close work, we should rest the eyes occasionally by looking far away. Reading in bed is a poor practice, as the book is usually not held in the correct position and the light is often inadequate. Glasses with tinted lenses may relieve the eyes of the sun's glare in the summer as well as protect them from dust and wind. Illness makes the eyes tire more readily, a fact which should be kept in mind during convalescence.

EYEWASHES

Much advertising suggests that eyewashes should be used regularly. However, your eye is equipped to take care of itself without the aid of man-made washes. Nature washes away the dirt and dust which are constantly collecting on the eye by means of tears, which are released over the eyeball with the blinking of the lids. If your eyes are irritated by an unusual amount of dust, a saturated boracic acid solution will help to relieve the irritation.

If a particle of dirt or a foreign substance gets into the eye, it is best to close the eyes for a few minutes, being careful not to move the eyeball. Usually this causes tears to collect, which will wash out the particle. Be sure not to rub the eye, since doing so serves to lodge the particle more firmly. If it is necessary to have someone remove a foreign body, be sure that everything used is absolutely clean. Your eye is already irritated and can easily be infected. The person who is going to work on your eye should scrub his hands thoroughly with soap and water, and any cloth that is used should be perfectly clean. Sometimes putting a few drops of boracic acid solution in the eye will help wash the particle away.

STUDY-GUIDE QUESTIONS

1. What effects might you expect from defective eyesight? From eyestrain?
2. When is light said to be good?
3. What kind of bulb does the Cleveland Sight Saving Council recommend for (a) a single-socket lamp? (b) a double-socket lamp? (c) a triple-socket lamp?
4. Describe correct lighting conditions for close work, such as reading.
5. What other measures, besides being careful to have adequate light, can we take to save our eyes?
6. Of what value are eyewashes?
7. How would you remove a foreign substance from the eye?

UNIT SIX.   THE EAR

THE STRUCTURE OF THE EAR

Sound waves produced by vibrations in the air set up vibrations in the inner ear. These are conveyed to the brain by nerve cells, thus enabling us to recognize various tones. Deafness may result from a change in any part of the ear. An injury may impair the auditory nerve, the drum may thicken and become less sensitive,

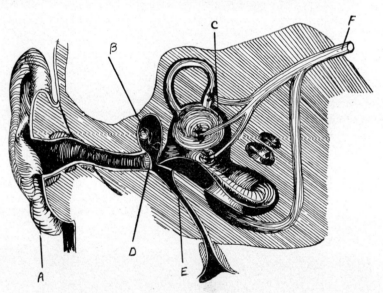

Structure of the ear. *A*, outer ear; *B*, middle ear; *C*, inner ear; *D*, drum; *E*, Eustachian tube; *F*, auditory nerve.

the bones of the middle ear may become stiff, or the liquid of the inner ear may thicken. Diseases of the throat, nose, and tonsils often result in impaired hearing, due to the fact that infection from these parts may reach the ear by way of the Eustachian tube, which is a passage connecting the ear and the upper part of the throat at the back of the nose.

CARE OF THE EARS

Earache, any discharge from the ears, or defects in hearing should be considered danger signals, and a good doctor should be consulted at once.

Avoid injury to the ears by refraining from digging into them with a toothpick, hairpin, or similar object. The wax in the ear canal is secreted by the lining of the passage and is very bitter, a circumstance which prevents insects from penetrating into the ear. If the ear canal becomes stopped by excess wax, the wax should be removed by a physician. In washing the ears, do not go any further into them than the finger can reach. In blowing the nose, there is danger of forcing germs back along the Eustachian tube into the ear. When it is necessary to blow the nose, blow one nostril at a time, leaving the other one entirely open and holding your handkerchief loosely over both. The ears should be protected from cold water in diving and swimming.

Good hearing, like good eyesight, is an asset which will benefit from fine physical condition and the practice of wise health habits.

STUDY-GUIDE QUESTIONS

1. Explain how the structure of the ear enables you to hear sounds.
2. What causes deafness?
3. Name some danger signals of possible serious ear trouble.
4. To avoid ear infection, how should the nose be blown?
5. What can you do to avoid injury to your ears?

UNIT SEVEN. THE TEETH

Teeth that are well cared for contribute to your beauty by maintaining the shape of your face and by adding to the attractiveness of your smile. Anyone who is familiar with the sunken face and empty smile of a toothless person will not question the statement that good teeth are an asset. The degree to which they are an asset is determined by how regular they are in shape, how healthy they are, and how clean they are kept. Good teeth are also an aid to health, as they make it possible for us to masticate our food thoroughly, which, in turn, aids digestion. Unhealthy teeth are often the cause of rheumatism, arthritis, and heart trouble.

THE STRUCTURE OF THE TEETH

The part of your tooth that you can see is called the enamel. This enamel, which is the hardest material of the body, is made up principally of calcium phosphate. Beneath this layer of enamel is a layer of dentine, which forms the major portion of the tooth. The composition of dentine is similar to that of bone. In the root the dentine is covered with cement, which is really bone. The dentine contains many minute canals which extend into the next layer and which contain a fluid called lymph.

The pulp, the central portion of the tooth, is made up of connective tissue which contains nerves and blood vessels. The root of the tooth, which extends below the gum and is surrounded by it, fits into the jawbone. Thus we see that a tooth has a continuous stream of blood flowing through it, carrying food materials to it and removing waste products.

ESSENTIALS OF HEALTHY TEETH

In order that we may have healthy teeth, we must have an adequate diet, vigorous circulation of the blood, and regular habits in caring for the teeth. For healthy teeth we need foods which supply vitamins and necessary minerals. Calcium, phosphorus, and vitamins C and D are probably the most important. Experiments have shown that when the diet has been inadequate, the teeth can be improved by better eating habits. In general, a

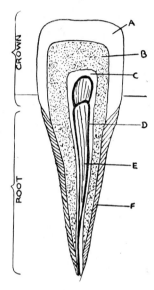

Structure of a tooth. *A*, enamel; *B*, dentine; *C*, pulp, which consists of connective tissue containing blood vessels, *D*, and nerve, *E*; *F*, cement.

diet which is adequate in other respects and which contains generous amounts of milk, orange juice, fresh fruits, and fresh vegetables, as well as vitamin D, as supplied by the sun or by cod-liver oil, is considered sufficient for the health of the teeth.

CLEANING THE TEETH

The circulation can be stimulated by sufficient exercise of the entire body. The flow of the blood through the teeth and gums can be increased by eating coarse foods that require chewing and grinding. These foods also stimulate the flow of saliva and so help to keep the teeth clean. Proper brushing of the teeth will help to keep the circulation vigorous.

In brushing the teeth, use a small brush, so that the back teeth and the inside surfaces may be cleansed easily and thoroughly. If the bristles are short and stiff with the tufts placed fairly far apart, the brush will be more effective. Cold water is better than warm, as it does not soften the bristles. Most tooth pastes and powders are very little help in cleaning the teeth; they merely make the process more pleasant. If they contain gritty substances that wear away the enamel, they are actually harmful. A safe and effective dentifrice is bicarbonate of soda.

To use the toothbrush correctly, place the bristles on the teeth, and, applying enough pressure to force the bristles between the teeth, move the brush with a slightly vibratory motion which will massage the gums and tend to make them firm. The inside, outside, and grinding surfaces of the teeth should be cleaned after each meal and before retiring, if possible. The surfaces between the teeth should be cleaned with dental floss. The brush should be rinsed out and placed where it will dry thoroughly. Using several brushes alternately overcomes the problem of trying to clean your teeth with a wet, soggy brush. After cleaning your teeth, rinse your mouth thoroughly to remove any food particles.

MOUTHWASHES

The well-advertised halitosis is often caused by decayed teeth or by decaying particles of food which accumulate around the teeth; however, it may also be due to diseased tonsils, indigestion, or constipation. Obviously, the solution of this difficulty is to remove the cause of the trouble rather than to use a mouthwash, which gives relief for a very short time. Most mouthwashes have very slight antiseptic properties, and their chief value is the feeling of cleanliness which results from their use. A healthy mouth has no need of a mouthwash, and one that is unhealthy needs much more effective treatment.

DISEASES OF THE TEETH

What is the cause of tooth decay, and how can it be prevented? There are various theories as to the cause of caries, or decay. Some authorities believe that diet is a principal factor. If the diet fails to provide the necessary materials, the teeth suffer. Other authorities believe that deposits formed from the saliva contain bacteria. These bacteria cause the fermentation of carbohydrate foods, which results in the formation of acids. These acids act on the defects in the enamel of the teeth and start decay. Preventive measures consist of eating a well-balanced diet, which promotes normal saliva, and keeping the mouth clean, thus preventing salivary deposits from accumulating. Whichever theory of decay you accept, experiments have shown that deficient diet affects the health of your teeth as well as your general health and that tooth decay takes place more rapidly in a dirty mouth than in a clean one.

Pyorrhea is a disease which affects the teeth. The gums usually become inflamed, bleed easily, and recede from the teeth, which eventually become loose. Abscesses are formed around the roots of the teeth. A deficient diet, injury or irritation of the gums, and an imperfect closing of the teeth are causative factors in this disease. Tartar should not be allowed to collect on the teeth, as it tends to press against the gums and to irritate them. As the deposits increase in size, they tend to loosen the gums from the teeth, and pus pockets are formed. Proper brushing of the teeth helps to keep the gums healthy. Plenty of green vegetables, fruits, and milk in the diet and regular visits to the dentist aid in the prevention of pyorrhea.

It scarcely seems necessary to mention that regular dental inspection and care do much to preserve the teeth. Surely everyone recognizes the value of seeing a dentist at least twice a year.

STUDY-GUIDE QUESTIONS

1. How may teeth contribute to beauty?
2. Describe the structure of a tooth.
3. What are the essentials of healthy teeth?
4. Describe the best type of toothbrush.
5. Describe the correct way to clean the teeth.
6. Of what value are most tooth pastes?
7. What causes halitosis?
8. How effective are mouthwashes in overcoming halitosis?
9. What causes tooth decay?
10. How may we prevent decay in teeth?
11. What is pyorrhea?
12. How may it be prevented?

UNIT EIGHT. THE FEET

Most foot troubles do not usually appear until middle age; they are generally the result of neglect or abuse. As people grow older, the foot loses some of its flexibility, and troubles begin to develop. Properly fitted shoes and hose, cleanliness, exercise, and care will help you to avoid these troubles later on. Foot structure and properly fitted shoes and stockings are discussed in Section V; therefore there is no need for discussion at this point.

Since the feet perspire just as does any other part of our body, and often more excessively than some parts, it is necessary to wash them every day. Because feet are encased in leather during the day, they do not have a chance to move around as our hands do and therefore need extra stimulation. This can be provided by scrubbing the feet with a brush. After washing, they should be well dried, especially between the toes, and powdered. Toenails should be cut straight across and should not be tapered. When nails are cut diagonally at the corners, they often become ingrown. Take care not to cut the flesh, as such an injury may become infected.

CORNS AND CALLUSES

Calluses usually are found where there is a great amount of pressure. Nature attempts to protect the foot by developing many layers of skin, which we call a callus.

Since corns are the result of ill-fitting shoes, their prevention is obvious. If you see a little hard place appearing on your toe, put a piece of adhesive tape over it and leave the tape in place for several days. This will relieve the pressure on the toe and will soften the hard skin so that it will come off when the adhesive is removed. If you have any serious foot difficulties, consult a competent chiropodist.

STUDY-GUIDE QUESTIONS

1. To what are most foot troubles due? When do most foot troubles appear?
2. How can foot troubles be prevented?
3. Give directions for correct bathing of the feet.
4. Why do your feet need extra stimulation during bathing?
5. What causes ingrown toenails?
6. How can ingrown nails be prevented?

BOOKS FOR FURTHER READING

American Medical Association, *Cosmetics and Allied Preparations.* Bureau of Investigation of the *Journal of the American Medical Association,* 1937.

Chilson, Francis, *Modern Cosmetics.* The Drug and Cosmetic Industry, New York, 1938.

Diehl, Harold S., *Textbook of Healthful Living,* second edition. McGraw-Hill Book Company, New York, 1939.

Goodman, Herman, *Principles of Professional Beauty Culture.* McGraw-Hill Book Company, New York, 1938.

Hawes, Elizabeth, *Good Grooming.* Little, Brown and Company, Boston, 1942.

Household Finance Corporation, Better Buymanship Bulletin, " Cosmetics," revised. Household Finance Corporation, Chicago, 1939.

Phillips, M. C., *Skin Deep.* The Garden City Publishing Company, New York, 1934.

Rockwood, Reuben, and Irene Ruddock, *Modern Cosmetology.* Prentice-Hall, New York, 1940.

Verrill, A. Hyatt, *Perfumes and Spices.* L. C. Page and Company, 1940.

Play is good for the body and spirit.   Courtesy, Western College, Oxford, Ohio.

SECTION VIII
LEISURE-TIME ACTIVITIES

UNIT ONE. LEISURE

WAYS OF SPENDING LEISURE

How do young people use their leisure time? Perhaps a survey of a large high school after dismissal time will shed some light on this question. On the athletic field we find a group of boys practicing baseball. As we watch them, we feel that their practice is not so much a matter of fun as of work; however, this activity is not part of their school curriculum. They receive no grade for it and are not required to engage in it, but have chosen to spend their free time in this way. In addition to the pleasure that these boys are getting from this game and the skill they are acquiring, they are developing strong, healthy bodies and are learning self-control, concentration, and cooperation. In addition to this group, we see boys and girls playing tennis and badminton, and the archery range and the swimming pool are occupied by busy, happy groups.

Inside the building we find a group of girls in the chemistry laboratory, making up some cosmetics " for the fun of it." In the art rooms we find students modelling in clay, painting, drawing, and working in metal " just because they want to." One girl is weaving, and several are knitting in the handicraft room. Next door, girls are making costumes for a school play that is to be given in the near future. We find other girls in the foods laboratories, preparing refreshments for a party. In another part of the building boys and girls are assembling copy for the school paper. The students interested in photography have taken pictures and developed them, others have sold advertising space, and another group has written stories or poetry or reported interesting school happenings. The auditorium stage is occupied with a group which is rehearsing a coming play, and nearby a stagecraft group is preparing scenery, while the students interested in electricity work with lighting effects. Across the hall we find a debating team in action. The library is a busy spot, with a large number of students using books and magazines for recreational reading and for furthering their knowledge along different lines of interest. In the school greenhouse and garden boys and girls are working because they enjoy it. As we observe all these students, we cannot help noticing how much pleasure they seem to be getting from their chosen activity and how wholeheartedly they have thrown themselves into whatever they are doing.

As we leave the building, we see some girls sitting on the steps talking. Their conversation seems to consist for the most part of groaning over the amount of homework they have to do or wondering what to do with themselves. We cannot help thinking that the busiest people are surely the happiest ones. Again, as we pass the corner drugstore, we see still another group inside sipping " cokes " and smoking. Yes, there are many ways of spending leisure time, but certainly not all of them are equally profitable.

LEISURE AND WORK

Leisure is that time in which we are free to do the things which we choose to do. Most people must spend the greater part of their waking hours earning a living or preparing to do so. At the present time, you spend the major portion of your day at school, as you are compelled to do by state law and your parents' will. During your school day you are required to do many different things as a part of your work, but any activity in which you choose to engage after school is considered a leisure-time activity. For example, if you are taking arts and crafts in school and, as a part of the course, you are required to make a piece of pottery, that project is part of your work. But if you choose to make a pottery bowl after school just because you enjoy working in clay, then you can call clay modelling one of your leisure-time pursuits.

DETERMINING FACTORS IN USE OF LEISURE

As you think over the various activities in which young people engage during their leisure time, you can see that many of the things you are learning in school furnish a basis for activities that not only occupy your leisure time now but also will continue to do so in the years to come. The way in which you use your leisure will be determined by several considerations. Obviously, a man who has done hard physical labor all day, such as ploughing, will probably not want to play a game of baseball when his day's work is over; whereas a girl who sits at a desk all day will feel a need for active physical exercise, such as tennis or swimming, in her leisure time.

Then, too, many of us may be interested in some types of activities which we are not able to pursue, because we do not have the opportunity to do so. A person who lives in Florida may be tremendously interested in skiing, but certainly does not have the opportunity of following up this interest, at least not in his own community. Limitations are placed upon us not only by climate but also by lack of proper equipment and often by cost.

The individual's attitude and intelligence have much to do with his choice of activities. If you are the type of person who is always perfectly contented to sit and watch someone else do things, you will probably always be a " watcher." Your leisure time will be spent passively sitting on the sidelines. But if you are the type of person who likes to *do* things and likes the challenge of doing things that are new and unknown, you will be constantly turning up new interests, developing your abilities to their fullest, and, indeed, living richly.

IMPORTANCE OF LEISURE

You are probably wondering what is the purpose of all this fuss about leisure. At the present time you may truthfully feel that you are happy. Before long, however, your high school days will be over, your friends will be scattered, and you will be entering upon a new phase of your life. If you go on to college, you will find a setup somewhat like that of your high school. There will be many extracurricular activities and many planned social occasions to occupy your leisure time.

If you go to work, your problem is quite different. You no longer have planned activities, and your associates at work may not have anything in common with you for leisure-time pursuits. Perhaps your work will be more or less routine, with little opportunity for development of your talents or your personality. You will undoubtedly feel the need of release from this routine in constructive, challenging types of leisure activities that will renew and refresh both your mind and body and will prevent you from becoming a dull, drab, uninteresting person.

NEED FOR SATISFYING LEISURE

In years gone by, leisure was no problem, for most people had no leisure time. The business of earning a living took all the individual's waking hours. There was no labor-saving machinery. Factory and farm operations were all done by hand, as was the work of the home. As a result, it took many long hours and much physical work to accomplish what can be done in a very short time today with very little output of energy. In those days most workmen were skilled craftsmen with great pride in their skill. They carried on the making of their product from beginning to end and thus felt a certain pride and satisfaction in their workmanship and in their finished product. For example, a shoemaker contracted personally with his customer for shoes, measured him for them, and made them entirely himself. Today a shoemaker has no contact whatever with the ultimate wearer of the shoes, and he does only one small job in their making. This particular job he repeats many, many times a day in a routine sort of way that requires very little thought and no initiative or creative ability. His working day, instead of being twelve or fourteen hours long, is probably no more than eight, leaving him several hours free to do as he chooses. During this time he needs activities which will give him release from the monotony of his work, renew and refresh his mind and spirit, and cultivate those latent abilities for which his work provides no outlet.

PLANNING FOR LEISURE

If we are to enjoy our leisure to the fullest and are to have some time each day to do as we choose, we must plan our lives so that essential, routine activities, such as dressing, grooming, and household duties, take as little time as possible. You probably have dawdled over a bath or a manicure when there was no particular incentive for doing these things quickly and efficiently; and, on the other hand, you probably have also done these things well in a minimum of time when an unexpected date or invitation turned up. Having a regular time to do these chores and setting a limit on the amount of time to be spent in doing them will help to increase our leisure hours.

Secondly, if our leisure is to be truly satisfying, we must plan for it. Everyone needs some time that isn't scheduled for activities to spend in just loafing. But too much time spent this way results in boredom and leaves a dissatisfied feeling. You have probably experienced such times during school vacations when your friends were away and everyone seemed to have something to do except you. You felt neglected and unhappy and thought the day would never end. When evening finally came, you realized that the day had been wasted. After all, happiness is not handed to most of us ready-made. We must seek it. The possibilities and materials from which it can be fashioned are all around us, but we must be alert to these possibilities and must plan our use of time.

From the following example you will see what planning can do. When Elizabeth graduated from high school, she wondered what she would do with the long summer months before she went away to college. In talking with some of her friends who had returned from the college she had chosen, she learned that girls who could type had opportunities for earning money at school. Therefore Elizabeth decided to increase her skill by taking an advanced typing course in summer school. This course occupied her mornings. Since she was an apt typist, through the recommendation of her teacher she got enough typing jobs to pay for her summer course. To this work she devoted two hours each afternoon. This schedule still left her enough time to attend to her regular household tasks, take care of her clothes, and get her fall wardrobe ready, as well as go to many picnics, swimming parties, and other social affairs. The extra typing not only paid for her summer course but also gave her valuable experience. When she went to college in the fall, she was given a part-time job in the school office because of this skill. Elizabeth had planned wisely and spent her time well. She decided upon an activity, set aside a definite time for it, and allowed nothing to interfere with her plans. When fall came, she felt that her summer days had been full, happy ones, and she had the satisfaction that comes from achieving an objective.

SATISFACTION FROM LEISURE

Many people feel that the only way to get fun from leisure is to seek it directly, as, for example, going to a movie. As you know from our observation of the leisure-time activities of young people around school, this is a false idea. The pleasure we get from leisure-time activities is usually in proportion to the effort and the preparation we put into doing them. The fun we have in passively watching most movies is soon forgotten. In fact, it is only a short time until we can hardly recall anything at all about the picture. But the memories of family celebrations at Christmas stay with us for a long time. True, much planning and preparation must be made for these festive occasions, but what fun we have when the relatives are all gathered together, the table is loaded with good things to eat, and everyone is in a holiday mood!

Leisure that is really satisfying must have an interest that lasts over a period of time. A father went to a puppet show with his very young son. He was so intrigued by the interest and joy that the audience of youngsters showed in the puppets that he began to read about them. Soon he himself became so interested that he decided to try making some puppets, which he used in a simple show given in his basement for the neighborhood children. The response of the children was so enthusiastic that he was inspired to do other shows, each one becoming more artistic and skillful. Soon near-by schools and churches asked him to give benefit performances. His fame grew until he finally gave up his regular job and now travels from coast to coast with a hobby that has become his business. Not all leisure-time activities grow into money-making schemes, but many have done so, and unless they have the power to challenge our intelligence and to hold our interest over a period of time, they are not worthy of our efforts.

Then, too, our leisure-time activities should be as different from the things which we are required to do as possible. You have all heard the expression a busman's holiday, meaning a holiday which merely repeats whatever a person has been doing in his work. For example, a conductor takes a streetcar ride, or a postman takes a walk in the city; such a way of spending free time indicates that these people have given no thought or made no plans for their holiday and hence drop into their usual routine. Their lives follow the same routine daily with no change to refresh and to renew their bodies and minds, and their various abilities remain latent and undiscovered.

Making a dress may be a refreshing change from studying all day.
Courtesy, Bradford Junior College, Bradford, Massachusetts.

Leisure which is satisfying should be physically and mentally beneficial. Games which teach people to cheat and be dishonest are scarcely worth while. Activities which afford such stimulation to the emotions as gambling are generally harmful, whereas activities which help to develop strong, healthy bodies, teach self-control, and teach cooperation with a group and concentration on an objective are both physically and mentally helpful.

STUDY-GUIDE QUESTIONS

1. What is leisure?
2. Why would a dress which you made in your clothing class at school be considered work, but one which you made at home be considered a leisure-time activity?
3. What factors determine the way in which people use leisure time?
4. Why is the wise use of your leisure time more of a problem after you leave school?
5. Explain why past generations had no leisure-time problems. Why was the worker of former generations able to get his satisfactions from his work?
6. What should well-spent leisure do for the worker of today?
7. How can our leisure time be increased?
8. What is the value of loafing?
9. Why is it necessary to plan our leisure time?
10. Would you consider Elizabeth's summer well spent? Why?
11. What qualities should satisfying leisure-time activities have?

ACTIVITIES

1. Make a survey of the way in which the students in your school spend their after-school time. Evaluate these activities.
2. Write a short account of a leisure-time activity which gave you satisfaction and one which did not. Analyze and explain why the first was satisfying and the second was not.

UNIT TWO. RECREATION

Recreation activities are those which we choose to carry on during our leisure time and which, if wisely chosen, relax and refresh us. There are several different types of recreation suited to different individuals and serving different purposes.

Physical recreation includes all kinds of sports and outdoor activities at which we may be a participant or a spectator. The spectator may secure refreshment and a change of thought, but the participant is the one that receives the greatest benefit. Through all kinds of sports and outdoor activities he not only develops a strong, healthy body but also learns concentration, good sportsmanship, self-control, and persistence.

Social recreation consists of such group activities as are carried on in clubs, community centers, and public forums. Boys and girls meet together, which gives them social experience, helps to develop social competence, and aids in overcoming feelings of inferiority.

Creative recreation is necessary for mental health. The product of one's own hands or mind brings a satisfaction that probably nothing else can supply. It also provides an escape from the monotony of the routine job and gives one confidence in his own abilities. This type of recreation includes many different activities, such as painting, singing, acting, and wood carving.

The home should be a center for the worth-while use of leisure. The types of recreation carried on there will to some extent direct young people in the use of leisure, especially during their early years, and, as time goes on, will help to make parents and children more companionable. A wide variety of interests may be followed in the home, such as gardening, photography, and various games. In one family each child learned to play a musical instrument, and in a fairly short time this family was able to have a small orchestra of their own from which they all derived much pleasure.

COMMERCIAL RECREATION

By commercial recreation is meant the type of amusement which is operated or provided for profit and is supported by fees paid either directly or indirectly by the patron — for example, movies, radio, dance halls, amusement parks, bowling alleys, skating rinks, pulp magazines, and professional athletics. As you will notice, some of these amusements call for little participation on your part. In some of them you are the spectator, and you are given no opportunity for initiative or creativeness. As recreation, they may give relaxation and a means of escape from the monotony of everyday living, but in many cases they are useless or even harmful. Some people habitually and automatically go to the movies several nights a week, thus producing a monotony in their leisure rather than an escape from sameness. Since all these various commercial agencies are competing for your leisure time, you must discriminate carefully as to which you will patronize if you want to obtain real recreational value for your money.

MOVIES

Since movies are one of the most popular forms of recreation among young people, they deserve special consideration. They probably influence us much more than we realize. Many times their influence is evident in the clothes, hairdress, and manners of confirmed movie-goers. If this influence is so pronounced in external things, it undoubtedly plays an important part also in our thoughts, ideals, and habits. It is true that through the movies we are able to secure quickly a great deal of information, which, if accurate, is of value. Unfortunately, the information so gained is not always accurate, although the movie-goer usually does not realize this. Movies portraying noble deeds may inspire us to be better persons. Pictures showing other countries and customs may give us a desire to travel and to increase our understanding of other nationalities. On the other hand, many pictures influence us in undesirable ways, and often these influences are the stronger ones. A picture may so glorify a criminal that we think of him as a courageous person rather than as a violator of the law, and hence it weakens our respect for law and order and makes us more tolerant of crime. Romantic pictures may give a distorted idea of love and sex, and young people are apt to get an exaggerated idea of their place in the lives of normal people. Choosing a life partner is a serious problem which young people have to face, but romance as usually portrayed by the movies does not give a very sound basis for making such a choice. The scenes of luxury which are often shown are apt to make us dissatisfied with our lot in life and to place undue emphasis on material things. Young people particularly need to broaden their interests and develop their personalities, so that their lives may be rich and interesting. The movies do very little for them along this line. They might better learn to choose more carefully the movies which they attend and to spend the time and money which many use for poor movies on recreation which will give them greater dividends in wider interests and personality development.

JUDGING MOVIES

How can you know which movies are worth while? Many people select a movie because of the actors in it, the cost of the production, advertisements they have seen, the title of the picture, or someone else's recommendation. None of these methods is a sound basis for selecting a picture. Your daily newspaper generally publishes reviews of pictures when they are shown in your locality for the first time. Of course, the moving-picture theaters advertise in these papers, a fact which reviewers undoubtedly take into consideration in criticizing pictures. Many reviewers, however, point out fairly the merit or lack of merit in a picture, and the review gives some idea of what the picture is about and so helps you in deciding whether a particular picture is worth while. Certain magazines, such as *Time, Liberty,* and *Parents' Magazine,* rate current pictures, and some of them indicate whether the picture is suitable for children and young people as well as adults. Worthwhile movies can do many things for us. They can stimulate us to read and learn, they can move us to think about social, religious, and political problems, they can give us patterns for the finest and most intelligent kind of living, they can help us to discover what goals are worth striving for, and they can show us that certain consequences inevitably follow certain modes of conduct. On the other hand, some pictures do no more than take us away from our cares and worries into the land of forgetfulness for a few hours. In selecting our movie fare, we should be sure to keep a balance of comedy, mystery, tragedy, and problem pictures for the sake of mental health, just as we try to eat a balanced diet for the sake of physical well-being. In judging a picture, you may consider whether it presents real situations, whether the plot is logical and the ending realistic, and whether it broadens your under-standing of life and people and makes you better able to face and solve your problems. If good pictures are well attended, others of good quality will be produced, as the box office is the greatest influence in determining what kinds of pictures are made. Probably all pictures contain both good and bad influences. If, as we see a movie, we accept only the parts which we feel are true to the best in life, the bad features will have less effect on us.

RADIO

It has been estimated that in the average home the radio is on for five hours each day. The radio is present on all occasions. We find it not only in our homes but also in our cars, on trains, and on boats. There are also small portable radios which resemble luggage and can be easily picked up and taken on outings, to picnics, and, in fact, anywhere. Through the radio we are able to keep up with world events or to indulge our taste for symphony, grand opera, or the drama. We are able to hear various sides of a question, presented through forums, speeches, or interviews. By a twist of the dial we can have music for dancing, a concert by a great artist, or a professional ball game. Radio has made all this accessible to people in rural districts, to invalids, to the blind, and to men working on boats or in out-of-the-way places.

For the very reason that radio offers such a wide variety of entertainment, we must choose our programs carefully. Much that is on the radio is planned for very immature minds and is therefore trivial. If we always listen to jazz, how can we ever learn to know and to appreciate better music? We need to cultivate and educate our taste for radio programs just as we do for the movies or for reading. A well-balanced radio diet should have cultural and educational programs in the majority. Many good programs of this type are put on by museums, libraries, universities, and various clubs. These organizations have no product to sell, and their programs are generally worth while and uninterrupted by excessive advertising that is not only distasteful but often also ridiculous. Intelligent listening is a matter of selecting the program that we feel is worth our time, rather than turning on the radio and accepting whatever happens to be on the air.

If a group of your friends can meet for the purpose of listening to some particularly worth-while program along a line of common interest, you will all enjoy the program more, and you will have an opportunity to discuss it while it is still fresh. You may be interested to know that there are about fifteen thousand organized radio listening groups in this country.

STUDY-GUIDE QUESTIONS

1. What do we mean by recreation?
2. What is the purpose of recreation?
3. What are the different types of recreation? Give examples of each type and explain its value.
4. What is the underlying motive of commercial recreation?
5. Name some forms of recreation that are commercialized.
6. What are the disadvantages of commercial recreation?
7. How do the movies influence us?
8. In what way can the movies be a good influence?
9. In what undesirable ways do the movies influence us?
10. How can we determine whether a movie is worth seeing?
11. What are some indications of a good movie?
12. In what ways is the radio an asset?
13. Why is it a poor practice to turn the radio on and let it continue on the same station for several hours?

ACTIVITIES

1. Collect reviews of the same movie from several different sources. If possible, see the movie, then reread the collected reviews, and write a paragraph stating which review you think is most dependable and why.
2. From a recent movie that you have seen, list the good and bad influences, giving reasons for your opinions.
3. If possible, have some class members responsible for posting reviews of the movies being shown at your local theaters each week.
4. Make a list of the programs to which the members of your class listen regularly. Listen to any of these programs with which you are unfamiliar and evaluate them.
5. Write a paragraph about a radio program that you think is particularly worth while, and explain why you think this program is a good one.

UNIT THREE. YOUR LEISURE AND RECREATION

As you think over the ways in which you spend your leisure time, perhaps you will decide that much of your free time is frittered away. Many boys and girls do whatever happens to come up. They have no special plan for using their free time, but depend on the inspiration of the moment. Everyone, as we have learned, needs some time in which to relax. Time in which we merely loaf gives us an opportunity to free our minds from care and worry and to get a proper perspective. Too much time spent this way, however, makes us feel bored and dull. Very often a change of activity is what we need. An absorbing interest or hobby will relieve the nervous tensions that have been set up by regular work and will rest and refresh even more than a period of loafing. At the same time pleasure, self-confidence, and a sense of achievement, as well as increased knowledge and a broader viewpoint are derived from having a hobby.

TYPES OF HOBBIES

In choosing a hobby there are three general types that you will want to consider. First, there is the type that is concerned chiefly with mental processes. This statement would seem to imply that in any other type the mind does not function. We know that this is not true, for in any type of activity the mind must direct the body and there are certain techniques which require thought. But in the mental type of hobby the mind plays the most conspicuous part, as in such games as checkers and chess and in puzzles, dramatics, debating, reading, and stamp collecting.

If you are a person who likes muscular activity, the physical type of recreation will appeal to you. All kinds of sports come in this group, for example, hiking, swimming, skating, dancing, riding, croquet, tennis, and badminton.

If you like to think out problems and then execute them, a third type, which is really a combination of the mental and the physical, will be your choice. All kinds of crafts, such as wood-working, metalworking, and pottery making, fall into this group. The playing of musical instruments, working out scientific experi-ments, designing and making clothes, refinishing furniture, redec-orating your room, photography, raising and painting gourds, and gardening are also of this type.

An hour in the country will refresh your mind and body.
Courtesy, Ohio Northern University, Ada, Ohio.

CHOOSING A HOBBY

In choosing a hobby, you should be sure to select an activity that appeals very strongly to you. Unless you can become absorbed in your chosen hobby and enjoy it very much, it loses its recrea-tional qualities for you. Then, too, unless you are very fond of the particular activity, you will tire of it before you have had a chance to explore its possibilities and thereby broaden your own interests.

Your hobby should be distinctly different from your work. Anyone who engages in strenuous physical labor all day will probably not find a physical hobby the most satisfying. He will do better to choose a mental type. On the other hand, a girl who sits at a desk all day may find such a hobby as gardening very satisfying. It will give her an opportunity to be outdoors during her leisure hours. Working with the soil and plants is usually soothing and relaxing to people who have been under a nervous strain all day, and there is much to learn about planning and caring for gardens, as well as a satisfaction in creating beauty.

Your hobby should also be one that can be carried on with some success in the time that you have for it. You may have time for a small flower garden, but taking care of a large vegetable garden in addition may make you feel like a slave. It is better to start on a small scale and to grow with your hobby.

Your hobby must also be suited to your age and ability. If you have chosen some activity which takes a particular skill or technique that you cannot master, your results will be discouraging, and you will miss the sense of achievement which comes with success.

Then, too, your pocketbook must be considered in choosing leisure-time activities. Some hobbies require expensive equipment which you cannot afford. Many of you would like to travel as a hobby, but if you have neither time nor money for it, you will have to be satisfied with the armchair variety. However, there are many hobbies which require no outlay of money and which can be lots of fun. Sleight of hand or reading palms will make you popular with your friends and will give you much pleasure. Hiking requires no equipment aside from proper shoes, and it will give you an opportunity for outdoor exercise as well as a chance to study nature along the way.

Whatever you choose to do in your leisure time must fit in with your kind of life. You must first decide what kind of person you want to be, and then choose games, books, friends, music, and movies for your leisure time that will give you experiences which will make you that kind of person, for our personalities are the result of our accumulated experiences.

STUDY-GUIDE QUESTIONS

1. What is a hobby?
2. What should a hobby do for you?
3. What are the different types of hobbies? Give an example of each.
4. What factors would you consider in choosing a hobby?

ACTIVITIES

1. Make a list of hobbies that you think girls in your community could cultivate.
2. Describe a hobby that you or one of your friends has cultivated. Tell how you or she became interested in it and what benefits and pleasures have been derived from it.

UNIT FOUR. ENTERTAINING AS A HOBBY

Entertaining your friends may be considered a worth-while way of using leisure time. Informal gatherings in your home not only give pleasure to your friends but also provide one way of widening your circle of acquaintances and acquiring social experience and poise, as well as giving pleasure to other members of your family. If these occasions are to give the greatest possible pleasure, it is best to do some planning ahead of time. Successful parties usually do not just happen. They are the result of time, thought, and labor which the hostess has expended.

PRELIMINARY PLANNING

In planning a party the first thing to do is to consult your mother as to the date and type of party. By so doing you can make sure that the time of your party will not interfere with any previously made plans of the family and that your mother and father will be at home when you entertain so that they and your friends can become acquainted. The modern American girl is not attended by a chaperon every place she goes, but, on the other hand, she does not defy convention. It is not advisable for young groups to have dances and parties in their homes or take week-end trips without having some older people present in case an emergency arises or as insurance against unfriendly remarks. Furthermore, you will no doubt need and expect some help from your mother, and it will not only be to your advantage but will also be an act of courtesy to talk things over with her. She will be able to give you many practical suggestions from her own experiences.

During the conference with your mother, you will probably decide upon the kind of party you are going to give. A wide variety of parties is possible. You may have an early morning nature hike terminating in a breakfast cooked outdoors, a swimming party which ends with a picnic supper, such outdoor games as badminton, croquet, and quoits with supper cooked over the fireplace in the backyard, a coasting, skating, or skiing party with

344

a hot supper in your own recreation room or around the kitchen table, with everyone helping. You may have a group which gather together to hear and discuss a radio program, to listen to the records of a composer and discuss his life and works, or to read and discuss an author and one of his recent books. There is an endless variety of things that we can do and enjoy in groups.

Reading an interesting book is a valuable leisure-time activity for a congenial group. Courtesy, Wilson College, Chambersburg, Pennsylvania.

The size of the group and the people who comprise it will be determined by the kind of party you decide upon. At an outdoor party which requires very little equipment you can entertain more people. An indoor party is of necessity limited by the size of your home. Then, too, you will want to invite the people who you know will enjoy the kind of entertainment you have planned, as well as people who will enjoy being together.

At the same time you are discussing the date and kind of party with your mother, it will be well to discuss the food which you will serve. If you are having an outdoor breakfast after a hike, your menu should follow the usual breakfast pattern and should contain substantial foods. Chilled fruit or fruit juice makes an appetizing beginning. Scrambled eggs and bacon are usually popular and are quickly cooked over an outdoor fire. Most young people like sweet rolls, and milk makes a satisfying beverage.

If some foods for a picnic supper are previously prepared and some are cooked over the open fire, there will be a maximum of pleasure from the meal without too much work for any one person. Some popular dishes for such an occasion are hamburgers or grilled frankfurters wrapped in bacon, potato salad or potato chips, sliced tomatoes, rolls, and watermelon for dessert.

After a skating or coasting party hot food is very desirable. Eating bowls of hot chile con carne with crackers and pumpkin pie with cocoa would probably be a good way of warming up after several hours in the cold and snow.

For afternoon or evening refreshments one of the following menus might be served: fruit salad, assorted sandwiches, iced chocolate, nuts, and candies; individual ice cream molds, cake, cocoa, nuts, and candies; or individual strawberry shortcakes, fruit punch, nuts, and candies.

PREVIOUS PREPARATIONS FOR THE PARTY

When you and your mother have decided upon the date, the guests, the kind of party, and the food to be served, you are ready to go into action. The following list indicates some of the things which you can do before the day of the party:

Telephone the invitations.
Collect the necessary equipment for games and other entertainment.
If you are using card tables, be sure that you have the right number and check on the necessary number of chairs.
Get out needed silver and polish it.
Get out needed china and wash it.
If paper dishes, napkins, and the like are to be used, purchase them.
If there is to be an outdoor fire, assemble the materials for it.
Make a list of food supplies to be purchased.
If there are to be prizes, purchase them.
Decide on house decorations.

The day before the party you will probably plan to help your mother in cleaning and straightening the house and in shopping for food supplies. The morning of the party you can do any necessary picking up around the house, arrange garden flowers in bouquets, put guest towels in the bathroom, tie up prizes, if any, and help prepare the food.

DUTIES OF THE HOSTESS

As the hostess it is your duty to make your guests feel welcome by greeting them at the door. You should see that they are properly introduced to each other, that they are made as comfortable as possible, and that the conversation is kept going. You should bring out the best qualities in each of your guests without paying undue attention to any one of them.

DUTIES OF THE GUEST

At the same time your guests have certain obligations to you, their hostess. They should show consideration for your property as well as your feelings. They should never show annoyance and should be able to listen sympathetically as well as to carry their share of the conversation. Showing enthusiasm for the entertainment provided regardless of their real feelings and expressing appreciation to the hostess for the entertainment are other responsibilities of the courteous guest.

STUDY-GUIDE QUESTIONS

1. What benefits can you derive from entertaining at home?
2. Why is it advisable to consult your mother when planning a party?
3. Why should your parents be at home when you entertain?
4. What determines the size of your party?
5. What factors would you have in mind in deciding on your guest list?
6. What things can you do several days before a party?
7. What things should you do the day before the party?
8. What things should you do the day of the party?
9. What are the duties of a successful hostess?
10. What are the obligations of a guest?

ACTIVITIES

1. List the different kinds of parties you have given or attended.
2. Plan a party for your home room to be given at school.

3. Plan an informal evening party for a group of boys and girls of your age to be given in your home.

4. Organize your class into committees. Have each committee plan and give a party for the rest of the class.

In planning parties you will find such books as the following helpful:

Party Fun by H. S. Fisher, Associated Authors, Chicago, 1938.

Games For Young People by A. Froh and M. King, The Wartburg Press, Columbus, Ohio, 1943.

The Year Round Party Book by W. P. Young and H. J. Gardner, J. B Lippincott Company, Philadelphia, 1936.

UNIT FIVE.   COMMUNITY RECREATION

Your community recognizes the value of the wise use of leisure time to such an extent that it actually spends money to help you use your leisure to advantage. Leisure time that is constructively spent not only enriches the lives of individuals but also advances

Your community provides many opportunities for recreational leisure.
Courtesy, Stratford College, Danville, Virginia.

civilization, whereas destructive activities retard progress. When individuals spend their leisure time planning crimes, our social structure is weakened. Hence communities realize that they can advance and improve only as individuals within the community improve, since the achievements of society are the sum of the achievements of individuals.

Our communities, therefore, have parks with various kinds of recreational facilities, such as tennis courts, swimming pools, and baseball grounds. Community centers afford meeting places for clubs, discussion groups, and public forums, as well as for indoor sports and games. Libraries and museums make it possible for people to widen their interests and increase their knowledge and appreciation at no cost. Playgrounds are maintained in the interest of health and safety. Symphony orchestras are supported to bring good music within the budgets of the middle class. State and national parks are set aside, where natural wonders are made accessible to all. Clubs, churches, and individuals support such organizations as the Boy Scouts and the Girl Scouts, the Campfire Girls, the Y.M.C.A., and the Y.W.C.A. Some localities have highly organized and extensive recreational facilities, whereas others have not felt a need for them or have been slow to appropriate money to help people in their play. Most progressive communities feel that worth-while recreation is just as essential to the physical and mental health of their people as is a system of public education.

YOUR OBLIGATION

Are you aware what facilities are available in your community? Usually the use of community facilities costs little or nothing, as they are supported through taxes. It does, however, impose one obligation upon us. Since these facilities are not our personal property, we are obligated to treat them in such a way that the next user will find them in good condition. For example, pencil-marking books that are your personal property is legitimate, since you paid for them, and marking passages which are especially meaningful to you is often helpful; but to mark library books this way is inconsiderate and selfish. It gives the book a worn appearance which encourages misuse on the part of others, and the passages which you liked especially may make no appeal to other readers.

The same principle applies to public picnic grounds. Since other people will use them, we should feel obliged to leave them in good condition by cleaning up all paper and refuse and by putting out fires that we have made.

STUDY-GUIDE QUESTIONS

1. Why is wholesome recreation important to society?
2. How is community recreation financed?
3. What are your obligations in using community recreational facilities?

ACTIVITIES

1. Make a list of recreational facilities in your community that are free.
2. List additional facilities and prove that they would be valuable to the community.

BOOKS FOR FURTHER READING

Collins, A. F., *How to Ride Your Hobby.* D. Appleton-Century Company, 1935.

Greenbie, S., *Leisure for Living.* G. W. Stewart, New York, 1940.

Hambidge, G., *Time to Live.* Whittlesey House, McGraw-Hill Book Company, New York, 1933.

Lamphand, R., *Hobbies for Everybody.* Harper Brothers, New York, 1934.

Neumeyer, M. H., and E. S. Neumeyer, *Leisure and Recreation.* A. S. Barnes and Company, New York, 1936.

Overstreet, H. A., *A Guide to Civilized Leisure.* W. W. Norton, New York, 1934.

Pack, A. N., *The Challenge of Leisure.* The Macmillan Company, New York, 1934.

Pangburn, W. W., *Adventures in Recreation.* A. S. Barnes and Company, New York, 1936.

Tunis, J. R., *Sport for the Fun of It.* A. S. Barnes and Company, New York, 1940.

Wrenn, C. G., and D. L. Harley, *Time on Their Hands.* American Council on Education, Washington, D. C., 1941.

Social poise comes from knowing the rules.
Courtesy, MacMurray College, Jacksonville, Illinois.

SECTION IX

THE SOCIAL LIFE OF THE HIGH SCHOOL GIRL

UNIT ONE. THE FOUNDATION AND VALUE
OF GOOD MANNERS

After finishing the ninth grade in the village school near her farm home, Jo Ann Wilson went to live with her aunt, Mrs. Johns, who lived in a city in the Middle West.

Although Jo Ann was pleased with the opportunities afforded by the large high school which she would attend, she felt somewhat uneasy about adjusting to life in the school and in her aunt's home. During the last few days before going to her aunt's, Jo Ann found herself comparing her present home with that of her aunt — the free and easy way of her parents and the noise and confusion caused by her younger brothers and sisters, with the quiet orderliness of her aunt's childless household. She wondered too whether her aunt would think less of her if she didn't do and say the correct thing on all occasions. As she thought about the matter seriously, she realized that there were many social customs she wasn't quite sure about and decided that she would ask her aunt to give her a few lessons in etiquette.

However, when Jo Ann arrived at her aunt's lovely home, she was so interested in getting settled in her new surroundings that she forgot all about her plan for finding out how to act and what to say until she was being introduced to the dean of girls at her new school. She heard her aunt say, " Miss Manning, this is my niece, Jo Ann Wilson, who is entering your school this fall." Then Jo Ann thought, " What should I do? Should I shake hands with Miss Manning? What should I say?"

Before Jo Ann had time to decide these points, Miss Manning was extending her hand to her and saying, " How do you do, Jo Ann? I hope you will enjoy the school year with us." And then her aunt and Miss Manning were making plans for one of the other pupils to meet Jo Ann at the school the next morning to show her through the building.

When Jo Ann and Mrs. Johns were talking over their plans that evening, Jo Ann again thought of her resolution and said, " Aunt Mary, I am a little worried about how I am going to get along in such a large school." Mrs. Johns looked surprised, and Jo Ann continued, " Well, it isn't about my studies, for I like to study, and I have always been able to succeed in my work, but I am afraid I won't always know what I should say and do. Life here seems so much more formal than it is at home. For example, at school this morning when you introduced me to Miss Manning, I really didn't know whether I should extend my hand to her or wait for her to offer her hand."

" Well, Jo Ann, I think I know something about the way you feel, and I want to help you all I can. However, before I talk about your specific problems of responding to an introduction, I should like to talk a little to you about the foundations of good manners — those factors upon which we build our rules of etiquette or social behavior.

FOUNDATIONS OF GOOD MANNERS

" Have you ever wondered why the majority of the people whom you know and meet respect one another's rights and obey the laws of social conduct? The reason is that they have found that life is more comfortable, more pleasant, and easier when they obey the rules of fair play and justice. Generally the rules or laws of social conduct that have been retained through the years and are practiced by people of fine feeling and a sense of fair play have been formulated out of respect for the rights of others and a desire not to hurt them.

" So, I would say to you, Jo Ann, that regardless of how well you know the rules and however proficient you may be in putting them into practice, unless you are sincere and kind-hearted and have a sense of fair play, you will not be really well mannered. You must be considerate of other people's prejudices, their little peculiarities, their individual likes and dislikes. As far as you know these things about your friends, you will, if you are really desirous of being well mannered, respect them and avoid saying anything to hurt their feelings."

" Would you say then, Aunt Mary, that a sincere, kind-hearted person with a sense of justice need not bother to learn the rules of etiquette, that he may just follow his own good judgment?"

Consideration for others is the basis of good manners.
Courtesy, Mary Baldwin College, Staunton, Virginia.

" You have asked a very good question, Jo Ann, considering the things I have said to you. I didn't really mean to lead you to conclude that the rules of etiquette are useless. On the other hand, I consider them very valuable, but they are of little worth without the inner qualities of character which we have mentioned.

" Maybe I can best illustrate this point with an incident from my own experience. Some years ago I knew a person who was very skilled in the technique of social usage, but he lacked kindliness. On brief acquaintance you were charmed by his perfect manners; he always stood when a woman came into the room, on the street he lifted his hat, he was immaculate in dress and had perfect table manners. But, if you spent as much as an hour in his company, you would hear him say something to hurt

someone's feelings. Once he said to an old woman who prided
herself on keeping youthful, ' My, how I dislike seeing old ladies
aping young girls. Why can't they grow old gracefully?' On
another occasion he said to a young, beautiful girl who had just
gotten her first permanent, ' Why on earth did you have your hair
done in that ridiculous style?'

" I need not tell you that in spite of this young man's perfect
manners, he was not popular. He had built his habits of social
usage on a poor foundation.

VALUE OF GOOD MANNERS

" Now, Jo Ann, I believe I am ready to answer more directly
your last question about the advisability of learning the rules of
etiquette. Yes, I think one should know as much as he is able to
find out about the code of conduct which is acceptable to people of
fine feeling. Furthermore, he should be so adept in practicing the
code that he acts as though from instinct, rather than from conscious following of rules.

" Nothing adds so much to one's poise and feeling of social
security as knowing the accepted form of behavior for any given
occasion. Young people have, no doubt, spent more time worrying
about what to wear, how to act on a date, how to eat fastidiously
in public, how to respond to an introduction, or how to meet
similiar problems of social usage than they have about how to
succeed in their studies at school. If a person is going to be able
to enjoy social contacts, he must feel at ease; that is, he must meet
each occasion with the calm of self-assurance which comes with
confidence in himself to cope with a situation.

" There is no doubt that the people who are gracious and at
ease in company are the ones who are invited the second time.
They are the people who make social contacts most satisfying and
enjoyable for others as well as for themselves. In other words, a
knowledge of good manners and skill in practicing them tend
to make a person popular with his friends and acquaintances."

" Aunt Mary, you have convinced me that it is desirable to
know and be able to put into practice the rules of etiquette. How
do you think I can most efficiently acquire the information and
skill it takes to do so?"

" Jo Ann, you have a good start toward the goal you have set for yourself. The desire to learn is always the first step on the road to acquiring any knowledge. For the rest, I shall be glad to give you the benefit of my experience. From time to time we can discuss your problems as we have done this afternoon. Then, if you observe the actions of others, I believe you will be able to learn a number of things. Please feel free to ask me questions whenever anything troubles you.

" In the meantime, you will do well to follow your own instinct to be honest and to consider the feelings of others. Avoid pretense and falseness. It is better to break a rule of etiquette than to hurt someone's feelings.

" As I remember, you asked a question which prompted this discussion, one which we have not answered, concerning introductions. Would you like to consider the matter of introductions tomorrow morning before you go to school? You may be meeting some new people at that time."

" Yes, indeed I should — that is, if you can spare the time."

" We can arrange for it. I have some knitting which I should finish shortly and which I can do while we talk tomorrow morning."

" Thank you so much, Aunt Mary. I appreciate your helping me in this matter."

STUDY-GUIDE QUESTIONS

1. Name the characters mentioned in Unit One and tell all you can about each.
2. Why have certain social behaviors come to be regarded as correct and others incorrect?
3. What should be the basis for all laws of social conduct?
4. Why is it desirable for even a sincere, kind-hearted person to learn the rules of etiquette?
5. What is the " first step on the road to acquiring any knowledge " mentioned in your textbook?
6. When one is not familiar with the rules governing a social situation, how should he be guided in his reactions?
7. Describe a situation in which you or some other person in the group did not know the rules of social conduct which govern the situation.

UNIT TWO. INTRODUCTIONS

" Since our talk yesterday, Jo Ann, I have been thinking that it would be nice for you to keep notes on the points of etiquette that are new to you so that you may refer to them from time to time. You know that we don't always remember everything we hear, even though we are interested in it."

" Yes, I think that would be a good thing to do. I have a notebook that would do very well. If you will excuse me a minute, I will get it."

" Now we are ready. Yesterday, Jo Ann, you mentioned the matter of responding to an introduction. Should we start with that phase of the problem or begin with the introduction itself?"

" Probably it would be better to start at the beginning. I also have a question about introductions. I have been wondering why, when you introduced me to the principal of the school, you said, " Mr. Beach, this is my niece, Jo Ann Wilson," and to the dean of girls you said, " Miss Manning, this is my niece, Jo Ann Wilson." Is the form of introduction the same when you are introducing two women as it is when men and women are being introduced? What difference is there in the introductions between young people and older people?"

" You are right in questioning the fact that I used the same form when introducing you to both Mr. Beach and to Miss Manning. Usually men and boys are introduced to women and girls on social occasions. When men and boys come to our home, I shall introduce them to you, except in the case of an older man of distinction. For example, I would introduce Mr. Green from your uncle's office and Jim Parker, a high school boy, to you. In making the introductions I might say, ' My niece, Jo Ann Wilson, Mr. Green,' and ' My niece, Jo Ann Wilson, Jim Parker.' An equally correct form of introduction would be, ' Mr. Green, I should like to introduce you to my niece, Jo Ann Wilson.'

" In business relationships women, as well as men, are introduced or presented to their superiors. Your relationship to the principal of your school comes under business. In a social situation, I would introduce the principal of a school other than your own to you.

" If I were introducing you to an older woman, I should say, ' Mrs. Older, this is my niece, Jo Ann Wilson,' or ' Jo Ann, I should like to introduce you to Mrs. Older.' To Mrs. Older I should say, ' My niece.' On formal occasions use, ' May I present.'

" When introducing two girls of the same or approximately the same age, it does not make any difference which name is mentioned first. Either may be introduced to the other. For example, I might say, ' Betty Jones, this is my niece, Jo Ann Wilson,' or, in the case of Evelyn Smith, of whom you have heard so much and who knows you equally well through me, I should simply say, ' Evelyn, this is Jo Ann.' The same rules apply to introductions between men and boys.

" Before we go further with our discussion of introductions, I should like to have you formulate rules covering the examples which I have given. Probably it would be easier for you to consider the last ones first. I see you have the rules written in your notebook."

" Yes, I have three here."

GENERAL RULES FOR INTRODUCTIONS

1. In social situations men and boys are usually introduced to women and girls. In business relationships women as well as men are introduced or presented to their superiors. In social situations a women or girl is introduced to a man of distinction.

2. Young people are introduced to older persons of the same sex.

3. In making introductions, the name of the person to whom deference is shown should be mentioned first, except when the term " introduce to " is used.

" Jo Ann, you have done well so far. Taking into consideration our discussion, how do you think a woman should be introduced to the President of the United States?"

" I don't know exactly, but I do know from my reading that women are presented to a royal personage and to a high official of the church. I should like to know just how I might some day be presented to the President."

" I hope you may have that privilege. The person who makes the introduction would say, ' Mr. President, I have the honor to present Miss Wilson.'

" At long last, Jo Ann, we are about to come to your original question that started all this discussion — how to respond to an introduction. Do you recall what Mr. Beach and Miss Manning said when you were introduced to them?"

" Yes, Aunt Mary. Mr. Beach said ' How do you do, Jo Ann? We shall be glad to have you in our school.' Miss Manning said, ' How do you do, Jo Ann? I hope that you enjoy the school year with us.' It hadn't occurred to me before that both of them said, ' How do you do?' Was that a coincidence, or must one always say, ' How do you do?' "

" Again you have guessed correctly. ' How do you do?' is the accepted response to an introduction. Both people being introduced may say, ' How do you do?' or one may smile and bow as you did when you were introduced to the principal and the dean of girls."

" Why, did I do that? I didn't realize that I did."

" Yes, you smiled and bowed your head slightly. I felt proud of you. Usually when a man is introduced to a woman, the woman says, ' How do you do?' and the man smiles and bows."

" But, Aunt Mary, shouldn't you repeat the name of the person to whom you are being introduced? I noticed that Uncle James did that yesterday when someone was introduced to him."

" Men usually repeat the names of people when they are introduced to them, especially if they meet in business. However, it is not necessary to do so, though it helps you to remember the name of the person whom you have met."

" Aunt Mary, do people always shake hands when they are introduced? Both Miss Manning and Mr. Beach extended their hands to me, and I noticed that Uncle James shook hands with the man to whom he was introduced."

" Men always shake hands when they are introduced; women usually do not. However, if they are near one another, they may do so. The younger woman waits for the older woman to extend her hand. You will recall that Miss Manning extended her hand to you.

" It is the woman's privilege to extend her hand to a man when he is introduced to her if she cares to; however, she does not refuse to shake hands if he offers his hand to her. Usually women do not shake hands with men when they are introduced to them."

Men always shake hands when introduced.
Courtesy, Heidelberg College, Tiffin, Ohio.

" While we are discussing hand shaking, Aunt Mary, please explain to me how one is to know when to offer to shake hands with people on other occasions than introductions."

" A hostess or host usually offers her or his hand to guests who are invited for a special occasion or who come to call infrequently. One does not usually shake hands with people who run in every day or so. Have you noticed that the hand is offered with the palm up?

" At a dinner or luncheon party the guests usually shake hands with one another and with the hostess when they take their leave.

" Some people shake hands more often than others. Hand shaking is a friendly custom which is practiced more often in some communities than in others. Older people shake hands more frequently than young people."

STUDY-GUIDE QUESTIONS

1. Give the correct form of introduction and the response used when introducing the following people:

   a. Alice Smith and John Brown, both high-school pupils. What would you say if they had both graduated and were working?

   b. Alice Smith, a new secretary, to her boss, Mr. Brown.

   c. Alice Smith and Mrs. George, a friend of her mother's.

   d. Alice Smith and Mrs. Betts, a friend the same age as Alice.

   e. John Brown and Mrs. George, a friend of John's father.

   f. The President of the United States and Mrs. Smith.

   g. Your classmate, Betty Roberts, and the principal of your school.

   h. Your mother and the principal of your school at a formal occasion.

   i. Mrs. George Smith and Miss Betty Jones at a formal occasion.

   j. Mrs. George Smith and Mrs. John Brown at a formal occasion.

2. What should Alice Smith say when John Brown is introduced to her? What should John say?

3. Under what conditions do people shake hands when being introduced?

4. On what other occasions do people shake hands?

UNIT THREE.   INVITING GUESTS TO DINNER

On Friday afternoon of Jo Ann's first week in her new home, Mrs. Johns told her that she would like to invite some old friends, Mr. and Mrs. Fowler and their daughter, Betty, who was the same age as Jo Ann, to dinner some time soon. Jo Ann's response to this was, " Why, Aunt Mary, grand! Do you mean it?" Then her face fell, and she became very quiet.

" What can be the trouble, Jo Ann?"

" Well, Aunt Mary, it would be nice, but won't it be a great deal of work for you? Mother said I must be careful not to cause you too much extra work and trouble."

" Yes, it would be quite a lot of work for one person, but I thought maybe you would help me with it."

" Of course, I would love to, but I am afraid I shall be poor help. I know so little about giving dinners."

" This will be an opportunity for you to learn. I am sure you will enjoy the dinner as much as I will. We will keep it simple."

" Indeed I will try. When do we start planning? What do we do first?"

" My idea was that we might plan the party this evening while we have plenty of time. Your uncle will be working all evening, so we shall be alone. How would you like to have the party two weeks from tomorrow? That would give us time to make our plans and preparations as well as to invite our guests before they make other plans."

INVITATIONS, ACCEPTANCES, AND REGRETS

" I should like very much to have such a party on a Saturday. The week-ends are the times when I am a little afraid of being homesick.

" I am curious, Aunt Mary, to know how you will invite the guests. Would it be good form to ask them over the telephone, or should you write a note? Then too I should like to know what is the right thing to say when extending an invitation. One of the girls at home called me one day and asked me what I was doing the next day. Then, when I answered, ' Nothing,' she wanted to know whether I would like to come over for a visit with a couple of her friends whom I find boring. There wasn't anything else for me to do but to go after I had told her I had no other plans. I felt that she should have invited me and explained what the occasion was instead of asking me what I was doing."

" Your friend made the mistake that many thoughtless people do. One should never lead up to an invitation by saying, ' What are you doing?' or ' Are you going to be busy?' for the reason that you gave — the would-be guest may be embarrassed. One should extend an invitation immediately, stating the time and giving the guest-to-be some idea of the nature of the occasion.

" When I call Mrs. Fowler, I shall probably say, ' Martha, this is Mary Johns. I should like to have you, John, and Betty come to dinner Saturday at seven. Please be sure to bring Betty, as I am anxious for her to meet my niece, Jo Ann Wilson, who is staying with me this winter and attending high school. I shall invite two of our own neighborhood girls in after dinner to play games with Jo Ann and Betty.'

" You will notice that I called Mrs. Fowler ' Martha ' and myself ' Mary.' If I were calling someone whom I do not know intimately or making a business call I should say, ' Mrs. Brown, this is Mrs. Johns.'

" It would be equally good form to write a note inviting the guests to dinner. Such an invitation might read as follows:

Dear Martha,

Will you, John, and Betty come for dinner at seven o'clock on Saturday, the twenty-seventh? I am anxious for Betty to meet my niece, Jo Ann Wilson, who has come to spend the winter with me and to attend our high school.

We shall invite two girls in our neighborhood to come in after dinner to play ping pong with Jo Ann and Betty. Perhaps the rest of us will play bridge, but bring your knitting for the interim when the men are talking shop.

We shall look forward to seeing you. We enjoy you all so much.

Sincerely yours,
Mary Johns

September the sixteenth

" Usually one replies to an invitation in the same way as the invitation is extended. If it is given over the telephone, the recipient either accepts or regrets at the time it is given. If the invitation is relayed through another person, the acceptance or regret is telephoned as soon as possible. When the invitation is written, one usually answers it in the same way.

" Mrs. Fowler might respond on the telephone by saying, ' Thank you so much. We should love to come.' Or, ' I am so sorry, but we are invited to Mrs. Powell's for dinner that night. Thank you for thinking of us.' A written acceptance might read,

Dear Mary,

John, Betty, and I will be pleased to have dinner with you on Saturday, the twenty-seventh, at seven o'clock.

Betty is thrilled at the thought of meeting Jo Ann. John says that with the prospect of bridge with you and James there will be very little shop talk. I know them too well, though. I am bringing my knitting.

Thank you so much for thinking of us.

Sincerely yours,
MARTHA JONES FOWLER

September the eighteenth

STUDY-GUIDE QUESTIONS

1. What should Alice Smith say when telephoning to invite Mary Jones to a party? How would Mary accept the invitation? How refuse it?
2. What should John Brown say when asking Alice Smith for a date? How would Alice accept? How refuse?
3. What rules should be followed when extending invitations?

ACTIVITY

Write an invitation to a friend for a dinner at your home. Then write an acceptance which your friend might send.

UNIT FOUR. TABLE MANNERS

A few days after Mrs. Johns and Jo Ann decided to have the Fowlers to dinner, Jo Ann said to her aunt, "Aunt Mary, do you think we might have a discussion or two on table manners before the Fowlers come to dinner?" The following are copies of Jo Ann's notes on these discussions.

APPEARANCE

Every person who eats with others is obliged to be neat and clean. Even when alone with one's family this obligation holds. When dining out, dress should be suitable for the occasion. At an informal dinner people usually wear afternoon dresses. A girl may wear a dressy blouse and skirt or any dress which she considers suitable to wear to church.

ENTERING THE DINING ROOM AND BEING SEATED

At an informal dinner party the hostess leads the way to the dining room. The gentlemen step back and the women follow the hostess, who takes her place at the end of the table nearest the kitchen if she is to serve or facing the kitchen if someone else does the serving.

If the party is large, place cards may be used, but for the usual home dinner the hostess stands at her place and tells each guest where to sit. The woman guest of honor is placed at the host's right and the man guest of honor at the hostess's right. Members of families and people who see a great deal of one another are usually separated. When there are equal numbers of women and men, they are placed alternately around the table.

The chairs should be placed so that the front edge of the seat is in line with the edge of the table. A guest should be able to seat himself without moving the chair. If such is not the case, however, he should seat himself as quietly as possible. The chair may be drawn under the table by taking hold of the sides of the seat near the front, raising oneself slightly, and noiselessly drawing the chair forward. A gentleman always assists the lady near him, usually the one on his right, by pulling the chair out slightly for her to get in place and then pushing it gently under her. One seats himself from the side of the chair that is most convenient.

During dinner everyone should sit at a comfortable eating distance from the table. He should not touch the table; neither should he be so far away that he cannot eat in an upright position. A good posture not only adds to one's appearance but also aids digestion. The hands should be kept in the lap when not eating. Do not toy with the silver or make pleats in the table linen. When leaning forward, pivot from the hips. Do not drop your shoulders and rest your arms on the table. Avoid circling your plate with your left arm and using the table for a pivot for the right arm in carrying food to your mouth. Both feet should be flat on the floor and close together, with the left foot slightly behind the right.

BEHAVIOR AT THE TABLE

Many families say grace before eating. In some homes it is said before the guests are seated; in others, just after they are seated. When you are a guest, watch the hostess and follow her lead. Do not start a long story until you find out what the custom of the family is.

The conversation at the table should always be cheerful and agreeable to all present. Avoid discussing personal affairs that have no interest for the group. At a small table the conversation is general, whereas at a school banquet or other large functions you will confine your conversation to the people near you.

At a home dinner you do not begin eating until all at the table have been served, but at a large table, such as those at a school banquet, you wait only for the people near you to be served. When there is a hostess, you wait for her to begin eating before you start.

When you are asked whether you prefer dark or light meat or a similar question involving a choice of foods, you should express a preference if you have one.

THE NAPKIN

The napkin is placed either to the left of the fork or on the service plate. When you are comfortably seated and the hostess has picked up her napkin, take yours up by the open corners and draw it across your lap. If it is a large napkin, you will not need to unfold it more than half way. If it is small, you will find it more practical to open it to full size.

The napkin is to be used to protect your clothing and to wipe your mouth when necessary. Wipe your lips before taking a drink of water so as not to leave a soiled spot on the glass, after drinking milk or cocoa to remove any of the liquid from your lips, and at any other time during the meal that you feel the need to do so. Be careful, however, not to form the nervous habit of wiping your lips every few minutes.

At the end of the meal a guest who is staying for another meal notices the hostess to see what she does with her napkin and then follows her example. A dinner guest partially folds his napkin and places it on the table to the left of his place. Guests always wait for the hostess to put her napkin on the table, which she does just before getting up. Napkins are folded under the table on the lap, not up above the table.

THE FLAT SILVER

The dishes and silver found before each diner at the beginning of the meal are called a cover. The flat silver is arranged as follows: forks to the left of the dinner plate, knives to the right of it, and spoons to the right of knives. These pieces of silver are placed in the order that they are to be used, beginning at the outside of the cover. If a butter spreader is used, it is placed on the bread and butter plate. The exception is the oyster fork, which is placed at the extreme right of the spoons or on the oyster service plate.

In setting the table for a formal dinner no more than three knives or three forks are placed on the table at one time. The silver for dessert and coffee is placed when needed. For an informal dinner served without a maid or with one maid, all the flat silver for the entire meal is usually placed on the table at the beginning of the meal to save unnecessary steps.

Since the salad is usually on the table when the meal is announced and since it is eaten with the meat course, the salad fork, to give balance, is generally placed to the left of the dinner fork, which is next to the plate and on the left of it. However, it is also correct to place the salad fork next to the plate and the dinner fork to the left of it.

THE FORK

When food is to be cut, the fork is held in the left hand between the thumb and the second finger with the index finger extended down the back of the handle and the other fingers curled around the handle, which is concealed in the palm of the hand. The food thus cut may be carried to the mouth with the fork held in the left hand, tines down. Instead, you may cut off two or three pieces of food, transfer the fork to your right hand, and convey the food to your mouth, either with the tines down for meat or the tines up for vegetables. Foods that are soft, tender, or crisp are cut with the fork and are carried to the mouth with the fork shovel-fashion, tines up. When the fork is used in the right hand, it is held pencil-wise with the side of the handle resting between the base of the thumb and the first finger.

You must be careful not to use your individual fork to take food from any serving dish. It should be used to take butter from your bread-and-butter plate to vegetables on your plate. It is also used to eat relishes and jellies served with meat and placed on the dinner plate.

When you are not using the fork, rest it on your plate, tines up.

THE KNIFE

The knife is used to cut food and sometimes to spread butter, jams, preserves, and sandwich mixtures. It is held in the right hand in exactly the same way as the fork is held in the left hand. When the knife is not being used, it is placed across the edge of the plate on the upper right-hand side with the handle toward the right.

When you have finished eating with the knife and fork, place them close together near the center of the plate with the handles extending slightly over the rim in the lower right-hand corner.

THE SPOON

The spoon is used to stir and to convey certain foods to the mouth. The spoon is held in the right hand like the fork. When

Position of knife and fork in cutting.

Position of knife and fork at the end of a course.

eating soup, dip the spoon away from you and sip the soup from the side of the spoon. When eating cereal, dip the spoon toward you and eat from the end of the spoon. The spoon should never be left in the cup when you are drinking tea or coffee. It should rest in the saucer when not being used to stir in the sugar or to test the beverage for temperature. When eating food from a sherbet dish, such as ice cream or a fruit cocktail, place the spoon on the plate under the sherbet dish when not using it.

THE BUTTER SPREADER

The butter spreader found on the bread-and-butter plate is used to spread butter and any spreads such as jam and marmalades, that are to be eaten with bread and butter and placed on the bread-and-butter plate.

THE SECOND HELPING

If you are asked to pass your plate for a second helping of any food, place your knife and fork to one side of the center of the plate with the handles on the rim. If the serving dishes are on the table, you may ask for a second helping if you wish. When the hostess offers a second helping to a guest, she should say, " May I serve you some potatoes?" or whatever other food she is offering. Instead she may say, " Will you please help yourself to some potatoes?" but not " some *more* potatoes."

EATING EVERYTHING

It is considered polite to take some of everything that is offered to you and to eat at least part of it, unless it would make you ill to do so. If you participate in the conversation, probably no one will notice if you do not eat everything that you have on your plate. You are not expected necessarily to eat all the food on your plate, neither are you expected to leave anything. It is polite to eat everything that is served to you if you can do so. A hostess is pleased when the guests enjoy their food. You may praise anything that you find especially to your liking. However, you should remember that too many compliments bespeak insincerity.

FINGER FOODS

Foods that are difficult to handle with a fork and that do not soil the hand when touched are usually taken from the service dish with the fingers and held while being eaten. Such foods are olives, small cucumber pickles, celery, green onions, strips of carrots, radishes, potato chips, rolls, bread, dry cake, cookies, crackers, small sandwiches, candy, lump sugar if tongs are not available, crisp, dry bacon, corn on the cob, and fresh fruits with the skin on or in bunches or on stems or caps.

BAKED POTATOES

Baked potatoes are taken from the serving dish with the fingers and placed on the plate. They may be broken in two pieces with the hands and eaten from the shells with a fork, which is used to mix butter and seasoning into the potato as it is eaten. If you like to eat the skin of the potato, you may cut the potato with your knife, a few pieces at a time, and then transfer the fork to your right hand and butter the pieces with your fork as you eat them.

ARTICHOKE

The artichoke, another finger food, is eaten by taking a leaf with the finger, dipping it in the sauce provided, and eating the soft end. The tough end of the leaf is not eaten but is left on the plate. When all the leaves have been removed, the outer covering and the ends of the stalk are removed and the inner tender part is eaten.

THE FINGER BOWL

Finger bowls may be used at the end of a meal or whenever fruits are served that soil the fingers. They are not generally found in informal houses, but are frequently brought to you when you dine out. If a finger bowl is brought after you have eaten fruit for breakfast, use it before you eat the next course. Dip the tips of your fingers, one hand at a time, in the bowl and wipe them on your napkin held in your lap. You may dampen your lips with your fingers and dry them with your napkin, but do not dip your napkin into the finger bowl and use it to clean your hands and face. If such extensive cleaning is necessary, wait until after the meal and go to the dressing room. The finger bowl is usually placed on a matching small glass plate, which may have a doily on it.

You may sometime have placed in front of you the finger bowl on the dessert plate along with the silver for this course. If so, place the finger bowl and doily, if there is one, on the tablecloth to the left of your plate. Under these formal circumstances the dessert is placed on the plate by the butler.

STUDY-GUIDE QUESTIONS

1. What would you wear to an informal dinner at the home of a friend? To a dinner at school? To a dinner in a hotel?
2. At an informal dinner party given at home, who leads the way to the dining room?
3. In what order are guests at a dinner party seated?
4. How should a gentleman assist a lady to be seated at the table?
5. How do you seat yourself at the table?
6. Describe the proper eating posture.
7. What should be done with the hands during a meal when not eating? What motions should be avoided when eating?
8. Why should you wait for a signal from the hostess before seating yourself at the table?
9. Make some general rules to govern conversation at the table.
10. Is it necessary to wait to begin eating until everyone at the table is served?
11. Where should the napkin be placed when setting the table for an informal dinner? A formal dinner? How should a dinner napkin be folded? When should you wipe your lips with a napkin? What should you do with the napkin when you have finished eating?
12. What rules of table setting apply to the cover for a formal dinner, but not to that of an informal dinner?
13. How do you hold a fork for cutting? For conveying food to the mouth? Be able to demonstrate.
14. For what is the knife used? How is it held in the hand? Where should it be placed when not in use? What disposition is made of the knife and fork when you have finished eating?
15. For what is the spoon used? Give directions for using the spoon when eating cereal; soup. What should be done with the spoon when you are drinking tea? When eating sherbet?
16. Where is the butter spreader placed when setting the table? For what is it used?
17. What should you do with the knife and fork when you pass your plate for a second helping?
18. What should you say when asking a guest to have a second helping of food?

19. Under what circumstances are you allowed to refuse food offered to you?
20. When is it polite to compliment the food you are eating?
21. What is meant by finger foods? Name some.
22. Should you take baked potatoes from the serving dish with your fingers or with a fork? How should baked potatoes be eaten?
23. Tell how you eat an artichoke when it is served to you.
24. Give directions for the use of the finger bowl.

ACTIVITY

Make a sketch of a cover for the informal dinner, the menu of which is given in Unit V.

UNIT FIVE. DINNER GIVING

On the Monday after the discussion of invitations, acceptances, and regrets, Mrs. Johns extended the invitation for dinner to Mrs. Fowler, who accepted it.

Mrs. Johns then planned the following menu:

Tomato Juice — Crackers
Roast Leg of Lamb — Mint Jelly
Browned Potatoes — Buttered Peas
Tossed Green Salad — French Dressing
Whole-wheat Rolls — Butter
Ice Cream with Chocolate Sauce — Cookies
Milk — Coffee

In planning the above menu, Mrs. Johns kept in mind certain principles of menu making. These rules are stated below and are followed by statements explaining how she applied them to her dinner menu.

1. A menu to be served without a maid should be made up of dishes which do not need too much last-minute preparation.

The tomato juice could be seasoned and the ingredients for the salad and the salad dressing prepared sometime during the morning. The rolls and ice cream could be bought or made ahead of time. The roasting of the meat could be so timed that the lamb would be ready to serve at the dinner hour. By serving the tomato juice in the living room, the hostess could have the roast and vegetables placed on the table before the diners were invited into the dining room.

2. A menu should contain foods contrasting in texture and flavors.

Tomato juice is liquid; lamb and potatoes, solid; ice cream, semisolid; lettuce, crackers, and rolls, crisp. Tomato juice is tart, mint jelly gives flavor to the lamb, and peas balance the bland flavor of potatoes.

375

3. A menu should be balanced as to hot and cold dishes.

The tomato juice, salad, and ice cream would be cold, and the meat, vegetables and rolls, hot.

4. In a small dinner party, the tastes of guests should be catered to if the hostess is fortunate enough to know their likes and dislikes.

Mrs. Johns knew that Mr. Fowler liked lamb especially well, that Mrs. Fowler's favorite salad was a green tossed one, and that Betty and Jo Ann liked ice cream with chocolate sauce.

5. When planning the meals for her family, a housewife should be careful to see that each member has all the foods required for an adequate diet (see Section VI on health) .

For this reason Mrs. Johns considered in planning the menu not only the food which her family eat in one day but that which they eat over a period of a week. All she could do for her guests was to give them a wholesome, balanced meal and hope that it would fit in with their other meals.

SETTING THE TABLE

Jo Ann helped Mrs. Johns set the table Saturday afternoon. After lengthening the table to accommodate six people, they spread a silence cloth over the asbestos pad and then a white linen damask tablecloth, laundered with only one crease through the center. This cloth lay perfectly flat and hung over the edge of the table eighteen inches on the sides and at the ends. Mrs. Johns liked the effect of the white linen as a background for her silver and glass; however, any other tablecloth or luncheon set would have been equally suitable for an informal dinner. She might have used a colored cloth of linen or rayon or one of lace.

Since most of the meal was to be served at the table, Mrs. Johns decided to set two plates on each side and one at each end of the table. This plan of table setting allows space for the serving dishes.

If the dinner were to be served from the side and the table was long and narrow, all the diners might be seated along the sides, leaving the ends vacant. With this seating arrangement, the decorations are put at the ends of the table, and the food may be presented to the guests in serving dishes or the dinner plates may be served in the kitchen and placed before the guests.

The dishes, napkin, and serving silver set for each person at the beginning of the meal are called a cover. The covers should be placed an equal distance apart. Jo Ann determined the location of the covers by placing the dinner plates first.

An attractive dinner table.   Courtesy, Towle Silversmith.

To the right of the plate she placed the silver to be used in the right hand, the dinner knife and two teaspoons. The knife was placed next to the plate with the cutting edge toward it and the teaspoons next to the knife with the bowls up. At the tip of the knife she placed the water goblet.

To the left of the plate she placed the silver to be used in the left hand, the salad fork and the dinner fork. The dinner fork was placed next to the plate and the salad fork next to the dinner fork. The bread-and-butter plate was placed just above the forks, and the salad plate was placed to the left of this plate and slightly nearer the edge of the table. Across the upper edge of the bread-

and-butter plate the butter spreader was placed, parallel to the edge of the table, with its cutting edge toward the center of the plate and the handle toward the right. The napkin was placed to the left of the forks with the open corner toward the plate.

This informal cover shows that the salad may be placed at the right when a hot beverage is not served with the main course. Courtesy, Good Housekeeping Institute.

Jo Ann was careful to keep the articles of the cover close together, but she did not allow them to touch. Each cover should appear as a unit. The silver was kept in a straight line parallel to the edge of the table and about one inch from it. Between every two covers a salt cellar and a pepper shaker were placed.

After the covers were laid, Mrs. Johns arranged a low dish of flowers from her garden in the center of the table with four tall candles placed in the form of a rectangle just outside the flowers.

The carving knife was placed to the right of the space above the host's cover where the meat platter would be placed, and the carving fork to the left of this space. The serving spoon for the potatoes was placed to the right of the carving knife.

Since Jo Ann was going to sit on Mr. Johns's left and help with the serving, the serving spoon for the peas was placed to the right of her cover. The spoon to be used for the mint jelly was placed on the table above and to the left of Jo Ann's plate.

The serving table which stands just inside the dining room door leading to the kitchen always plays an important part in Mrs. Johns's dinners. On it was placed some extra silver, a small tray with a doily on it, a medium-sized plate with a folded napkin on it, a stack of dessert plates, and the coffee service, consisting of a silver tray with cups and saucers, sugar, and creamer. Later the water pitcher, filled three-quarters full of iced water, and a dish of butter would be placed here.

When the table was completely set, the dinner plates were collected and placed in the kitchen to heat. They would be brought back into the dining room when the food was placed on the table and stacked on a small table placed at the right of the host.

SERVING THE DINNER

Mrs. Johns and Jo Ann had everything ready when the guests arrived at five minutes before seven. Mrs. Johns received the guests and introduced Jo Ann. After they had chatted a few minutes, Jo Ann excused herself, went to the kitchen, and returned with a tray on which were six small glasses of tomato juice, a small plate of crackers, and six very small napkins. She presented the tray to Mrs. Fowler, who took a napkin, then a small glass of the juice and a cracker. After serving Mrs. Fowler, Jo Ann continued around the room, serving each person in turn as they were seated. She placed the tray on the coffee table in the living room and helped herself to the appetizer.

When the glasses had been emptied, Jo Ann picked up the tray, collected the glasses and the napkins, and took them to the kitchen. Mrs. Johns excused herself also at this time.

While Mrs. Johns placed the roast and accompanying dishes on the table, Jo Ann filled the water glasses, placed glasses of milk for Betty and herself, put the butter on the bread-and-butter plates, and placed the salad on the table.

When everything was in place, Mrs. Johns stepped to the

living room door and said, " Will you come to dinner now, please?"

The men dropped back and allowed Mrs. Fowler to precede them into the dining room. Mrs. Johns seated Mrs. Fowler on Mr. Johns's right, Mr. Fowler on her right, and Betty on her left. Jo Ann sat on Mr. Johns's left so that she might assist him in serving the dinner. In seating her guests, Mrs. Johns followed the general rule of seating the woman guest of honor to the right of the host and the man guest of honor to the right of the hostess.

After the diners were seated and grace had been said, Mr. Johns carved the roast, carving enough meat for all the diners. He then served one plate with meat and potatoes and passed it to Jo Ann, who added the peas and passed the plate to her left. The first plate went around the table to Mrs. Fowler and the last plate to the host.

The gravy and rolls had been placed near Mrs. Fowler. Mrs. Johns asked her to help herself and pass them to Betty. They were passed from one to another around the table, ending with Mr. Johns, who placed them on the small table to his right. Jo Ann picked up the jelly dish, put the serving spoon in it and handed it to Mr. Johns, who passed it to Mrs. Fowler. She helped herself and passed it to her right.

When everyone had finished eating, Jo Ann cleared the table for dessert. She placed her napkin partly folded on the table to the left of her place. She first removed serving dishes and then the soiled dishes and silver of each cover, taking one complete cover at a time. She placed the dishes from one cover on the serving table while she cleared another, and then took the dishes from two covers to the kitchen.

In clearing each cover, Jo Ann removed the dinner plate with her left hand from the left of the diner, transferred it to her right hand, and then picked up the salad plate with her left hand and placed it on the dinner plate. Next she picked up the bread-and-butter plate and placed it on top of the salad plate. She was careful to stack the dishes so that they would not slip out of place. As she stacked the small plates on the larger one, she placed the butter knife and salad fork next to the meat knife and fork.

Next Jo Ann took the small tray with the doily on it and collected the salt cellars and pepper shakers and any unused silver from the table. Returning the tray and its contents to the serving table, she took the plate with the napkin and removed any crumbs from the table, using the napkin to brush them onto the plate. Then she refilled the water glasses, being careful not to move them. She carried a folded napkin, which she touched to the lip of the pitcher after each pouring to keep the water from dripping on the diners.

Jo Ann then took the coffee service from the serving table and placed it before her aunt. She brought the coffee from the kitchen and placed it on the tray. Next she brought the dish of chocolate sauce and placed it with the serving spoon beside the bowl on the table between Mrs. Fowler and Betty, and the plate of cookies near the sauce bowl.

While Jo Ann was serving ice cream, Mrs. Johns poured the coffee, asking each person whether he would have cream and sugar. She served Mrs. Fowler first, then asked Mr. Fowler to pass a cup to Mr. Johns. It is not good form to serve a person and then ask him to pass the next serving to someone on the other side of him. Next she served Mr. Fowler and, lastly, herself.

In the kitchen Jo Ann dished the ice cream into sherbet dishes, placed the six dishes on a tray, and brought them to the serving table. She placed a filled sherbet glass on a dessert plate and served it to Mrs. Fowler with her left hand from the left. She continued in this manner to the right around the table, ending with her uncle.

Mrs. Johns asked Mrs. Fowler to help herself to the sauce and the cookies and to pass them to Betty.

You will realize that, when a dinner is served such as the one described here, it takes more time than when a maid is available. When it is done in this manner, the hostess proceeds leisurely, and the guests should do all they can to make the dinner a festive occasion. Even though they are busy people who ordinarily eat hurriedly, they must adjust themselves to the occasion and help to keep the conversation going, especially when the host or hostess is busy with serving.

382

DINNER GIVING

STUDY-GUIDE QUESTIONS

1. State five rules to be followed when planning a menu. Show how these rules apply to the menu given in this unit.
2. What kinds of table coverings are suitable for a home dinner?
3. How does a hostess announce dinner to her guests?
4. Before a host begins serving, does he carve enough meat to serve one plate or enough to serve all the plates?
5. In what order are the dishes removed from the table at the end of the meat course?
6. Describe the procedure for clearing a cover.
7. How and when does the person serving a dinner remove the crumbs from the table?
8. What must you remember to do when filling water glasses at the dinner table?
9. From which side does the person doing the serving place and remove the dishes?

ACTIVITIES

1. Make a drawing of the Johns' table as it appeared with the meat course on the table ready to be served. Label your drawing.
2. Set a table for the menu given in your textbook.
3. Select members of your class to be guests, host, hostess, and waitress. Serve a mock meal, using the menu given in your textbook.

UNIT SIX.   THE FIRST DATE

During Jo Ann's sophomore year in high school she entertained different groups of boys and girls for an evening and was in turn entertained in the homes of some of her fellow pupils, but she did not go out alone with boys. In the early fall of her junior year when George Wilcox, a neighbor's son, asked her for a date, she was just a little uneasy about the way she should conduct herself.

Jo Ann had found her aunt understanding and sympathetic. It was natural that she should go to her with this problem, as she had previously done with other things that bothered her. She stated her problem thus, " Aunt Mary, George has asked me for a date on Saturday night. I suppose we will go to a movie. Again I need help. I have read the section on friendship in my home economics textbook, but it does not deal with such questions as these: What should a girl say when a boy asks her for a date? If George's father will not let him have the car, should we stay at home or is it all right for a couple to go on the street car to the movies? Who goes down the aisle first at a movie? If a girl wants to go to the ladies' room after the show is over, how does she excuse herself? If the boy suggests having something to eat, should the girl accept even though she knows he doesn't have very much money? If a boy and girl do stop in the corner drugstore or a restaurant for something to eat, who does the ordering? How does a girl decide what to order?"

Jo Ann wrote the following notes in her notebook as Mrs. Johns answered her numerous questions.

ACCEPTING AND REFUSING AN INVITATION

A boy usually asks for a date with a girl in some such way as, " Will you go to the movies with me Saturday night?" or " The basketball game promises to be a fast one Friday night. Will you go with me to see it?"   To such a question a girl may reply, " Thank you, I would love to," or, if she has a previous engagement, " I'm sorry that I can't this time. John asked me yesterday.

Some other time maybe." When the boy says " Good-bye," she may say, " Thank you for asking me." If for some good reason a girl does not want to go with the boy who asks her, she may say, " Thank you, I am going to be busy."

TRANSPORTATION

The girl who can have a good time going places by streetcar as well as by automobile will have more opportunities to go out than the one whom the boys feel they can't ask unless they can get the family car. Of course, a boy will not ask a girl to go on the streetcar when they are going to a formal dance. People are conspicuous in long dresses and fancy shoes on a public conveyance, but there is no reason why a boy and girl can't go on the streetcar to any informal type of entertainment.

CALLING FOR THE GIRL

When a boy has a date with a girl, he calls at her door for her. If he comes in an automobile, he does not drive up and honk the horn as a signal for her to come out. Boys usually like to have the girl, rather than some other member of the family, receive them. Most parents make it a rule to meet the boys who take out their daughters. It is polite to ask your escort to come in for a while before starting on a date.

ENTERING AND LEAVING A STREETCAR OR AN AUTOMOBILE

The girl enters a streetcar first, but the boy gets off first and may, if there is not a crowd, turn and offer his hand to his companion. On entering an automobile in a quiet street, the boy opens the door and, when the girl is comfortably seated, closes it and then goes around the car and gets in on the other side. In traffic the boy may say to his companion, " Do you mind if I get in first? The traffic is so heavy." Or the thoughtful girl says, " You had better get in from this side. This is such a busy street." Getting out of a car, the boy will, in a quiet street, get out first, open the door for the girl, and extend his hand to help her. In case the traffic is heavy, the girl may open the door and get out first.

When getting into the back seat of a car, it is more convenient for the first person who enters to sit on the left side of the car. In case a boy and girl are sitting in the back seat, it is convenient for the boy to be on the right side when they alight.

AT THE MOVIES

When a couple arrives at the theater, the boy says, " Excuse me," and steps to the window to buy the tickets. The girl may step into the lobby or stand beside her date and chat with him while he waits his turn at the window. The boy hands the tickets to the doorman, preceding the girl through the door. When the usher takes the tickets, the boy steps back and the girl follows the usher to the seats. If there is no usher, the boy leads the way, stepping back to allow the girl to enter the row first. If there are two couples, they go down the aisle in the order in which they expect to sit, first a girl, then her escort, and then the other girl followed by her escort.

If it is necessary to pass in front of others to reach your seat, face the screen and say, " Excuse me, please." If people who are seated stand to allow you to pass, you may say, " Thank you " or " I am sorry." When it is necessary for others to pass in front of you, make room for them. If necessary, rise to your feet.

Refrain from talking to your companions while the picture is being shown. It is needless to say that well-mannered people do not show affection in movies or in any other public place.

Girls often like to repair their make-up after the show. In that case, say, " Excuse me, please. I will meet you here in a few minutes."

HAVING AN AFTER-MOVIE SNACK

If you go to a restaurant where there is a head waiter or a hostess, he or she will seat you. The girl precedes the boy and is seated by the head waiter, if there is one. A hostess usually indicates the table and places menus at the places, but she does not seat the guests. In this case or in a less formal place, such as the corner drugstore, the boy seats his companion. He selects the most desirable place at the table for her and sits either opposite her or to her left.

If two couples are eating together, the girls usually sit opposite each other and each boy to the left of his partner.

The boy gives the order to the waitress after consulting the girl. Usually the boy says, " What would you like? The chocolate soda sounds good to me," or " Would you like a sandwich or some ice cream? I'm hungry. I'd like a club sandwich," or something similar. You may take your cue as to price from your escort's choice. If he just asks you, " What would you like?" choose something moderate in cost and be guided the next time by his choice. At all times express your real choice, and do not seem too much concerned about the cost of the food. It is not complimentary to your host to assume that he cannot afford whatever you desire. The boy should check over the bill before paying it.

GOING HOME

It is the girl's privilege to say, " I think we should go now. The folks expect me home at eleven thirty." Of course, it isn't fair to the management for one group to occupy the tables in a public eating place for an overlong time, especially if others are waiting. When a girl suggests going, her partner should agree immediately. If he wants to take the girl out again, he must see that she gets home at the appointed hour.

If the couple are driving, it is the girl's place to make a move to get out of the car when they arrive at her home. The boy accompanies her to the door, helps her with her latchkey, and thanks her for an enjoyable evening. The girl should express her appreciation for the entertainment. She may say, " The picture was wonderful. And wasn't that soda delicious?"

EATING AT HOME

Instead of stopping at the corner drugstore for something to eat, the girl may arrange with her mother ahead of time that she will bring her escort home for refreshments. Boys and girls have fun in helping prepare the food and even in cleaning up afterward. Incidentally, this is one way the girl can assume some responsibility for their good times together.

GOING DUTCH

When a boy asks a girl for a date, he expects to pay the bill. If boys and girls happen to meet at the soda fountain, each pays his or her own check. A girl can best pay back dates by entertaining in her own home.

DATING AT HOME

Resourceful, intelligent girls and boys spend some of their evenings together at home. There are many interesting things that people can do together. One group of three girls and two boys who were interested in dramatics met one evening a week to read new plays together. They produced a play or two each season, using the recreation room of one of the group. One boy and girl got a great deal of pleasure from collecting stones. They cut, polished, and mounted them. Another boy and girl enjoyed photography. They spent a great deal of time taking, developing, and mounting pictures. They worked together and with other people interested in the same type of thing. Common interests of this type often furnish more pleasure than paid entertainment does and are a sound basis for a lasting friendship.

STUDY-GUIDE QUESTIONS

1. What would be polite for a boy to say when asking a girl for a date? How should the girl accept the invitation? How should she refuse the invitation?
2. Should a boy ask a girl for a movie date when depending upon the streetcar for transportation?
3. When a boy comes in an automobile to take a girl out, is it all right for him to signal for her to come out by honking the horn?
4. Is it considered good form for the girl herself to open the door for her date when he calls at her home?
5. Who enters a streetcar first, the boy or the girl? Which one gets off first?
6. On which side of the car does a girl in the back seat of an automobile sit?
7. How should a boy help a girl enter an automobile? Alight from one?
8. What does the girl do while her date buys the tickets for a movie?
9. Who enters the theater first, the boy or the girl?
10. Who goes first down the aisle? When there are two or more couples, in what order do they go down the aisle?
11. How do you pass in front of people who are seated? What should you say when passing?
12. Is it all right for your date to sit with his arm around you and to kiss you occasionally during the movie?
13. If you would like to repair your make-up after the show, how should you excuse yourself to your escort?

14. When a girl and a boy enter a restaurant, who decides where they will sit? Who seats the girl?

15. When eating in a restaurant, should the boy sit on the girl's right or left or opposite her? If two couples are eating at the same table, in what order are they seated?

16. When a girl and a boy are eating in a restaurant, who gives the order to the waitress?

17. How can a girl decide what to choose when a boy invites her to have an after-movie snack?

18. After the after-movie snack, whose place is it to suggest going home?

19. When a couple who are driving reach home, whose place is it to make a move to get out of the car?

20. How should a girl express her appreciation for an evening's entertainment?

21. How can a girl share in the responsibility for the good times she and her date may have together?

22. Name some things that intelligent girls and boys may do together at home. Of what particular value are such types of entertainment?

UNIT SEVEN. THE SENIOR PROM

At the end of Jo Ann's junior year Jim Martin, a senior, invited her to the senior prom. Although she had gone to many informal school dances, she had never attended a formal dance before. Of course, she was excited about the event and, as usual, somewhat concerned over doing the correct thing.

Jim asked her three weeks ahead of the time set for the dance, so that she had plenty of time to get a dress in order for the occasion and to find out the customary routine for a school prom. A few days before the dance Jim talked to Jo Ann about the time he would call for her and suggested that she get her aunt's approval for their staying until the end of the dance, which was scheduled from nine to twelve o'clock.

The day before the dance Jim called Mrs. Johns to ask what color dress Jo Ann would wear, so that he could order a corsage in a harmonious color. He selected one to be worn on the shoulder and had it sent to the Johns home the afternoon of the dance. Mrs. Johns put the corsage in the refrigerator to keep it fresh.

When they arrived at the school, Jim offered to drive up to the door and let Jo Ann out, but since he was able to find a parking place on the street near the school, Jo Ann suggested that they go in together.

She was grateful to Jim for his understanding of girls when he suggested in an offhand way, " Miss Manning and the committee have spent some time arranging room 30 for a dressing room. When you feel a need for a little repair work, you'll find it quite nice."

Jo Ann replied, " I think I'll take a look in now." She was anxious to look her best, because Jim had warned her there was to be a receiving line.

The receiving line consisted of the chaperons, the chairman of the dance committee, and the president of the senior class. They stood just inside the door of the gymnasium, which had been decorated for the occasion. Jim introduced Jo Ann to Betty Grahm,

the student chairman of the dance committee, who headed the
receiving line. Betty turned to Miss Manning, who stood next to
her, and said, " Miss Manning, Jo Ann Wilson and Jim Martin."
Jo Ann and Jim were introduced in turn down the line.

A long-anticipated occasion, the Senior Prom.
Courtesy, Stephens College, Columbia, Missouri.

Several of Jim's friends and the girls they had brought agreed
upon a spot not too far from a punch bowl to which they would
come when they wanted to sit out a dance or to rest between
dances. Other boys and girls joined them from time to time.

Jim danced with Jo Ann the first and the last dances, the supper
dance, and several between. He saw that she always had a partner.
Although she realized that the dances had been arranged in many
instances, she enjoyed the attention she received. When the boys
asked her, " May I have this dance?" she replied, " Thank you,
yes," or " I should be delighted."

Jo Ann was careful to maintain good posture while dancing. She did not dance cheek to cheek. She had made an effort to learn to dance well, for she realized that good dancers are popular dancers.

Supper was served buffet style in the cafeteria at eleven thirty.

Before going home, Jo Ann and Jim thanked the members of the dance committee for all their work and the chaperons for giving them a good time.

STUDY-GUIDE QUESTIONS

1. Why should a boy ask a girl several weeks ahead of time for a date for a formal dance?
2. Does a boy always send a corsage to the girl he is taking to a formal dance?
3. How many times should a boy dance with the girl he takes to the prom?
4. Why should a boy and girl always speak to the dance committee and the chaperons before going home from a prom?

BOOKS FOR FURTHER READING

Allen, Betty, and Mitchell P. Briggs, *If You Please*. J. B. Lippincott Company, Philadelphia, 1942.

Allen, Lucy G., *Table Service*. Little, Brown, and Company, Boston, 1938.

Boykin, Eleanor, *This Way, Please*. The Macmillan Company, New York, 1940.

Goodrich, Lawrence B., *Living with Others*. The American Book Company, Cincinnati, 1939.

Lounsberry, Elizabeth, *Let's Set the Table*. Funk and Wagnalls Company, New York, 1938.

McLean, Beth Bailey, *The Table Graces*. The Manual Arts Press, Peoria, 1941.

Moffitt, M'Ledge, *When We Meet Socially*. Prentice-Hall, New York, 1939.

Post, Emily, *Etiquette*. Funk and Wagnalls Company, New York, 1940.

Sprackling, Helen, *Setting Your Table, Its Art, Etiquette, and Science*. M. Barrows and Company, New York, 1941.

Stratton, Dorothy C., and Helen B. Schleman, *Your Best Foot Forward*. Whittlesey House, McGraw-Hill Book Company, New York, 1940.

Wilson, Margery, *The New Etiquette*. Frederick A. Stokes Company, New York, 1940.

The advice of your counselor will help you in planning for the future. Photograph by Russell R. Benson. Courtesy, News Bureau, Denison University, Granville, Ohio.

SECTION X
PLANNING FOR THE FUTURE
UNIT ONE. GOING TO WORK

VALUE OF WORK EXPERIENCE

One afternoon in October during Jo Ann's sophomore year at school, she surprised Mrs. Johns with the remark, " Aunt Mary, what would you think of my getting a part-time job? I have been wondering if it wouldn't be possible for me to earn some money to help buy my clothes and pay for other expenses. During the summer when I was at home, I was more conscious than ever before of how hard mother and father both work. I should like to be able to have some of the many things I want and think I need without feeling that they are making too great a sacrifice in order that I may have them."

" That may not be a bad idea, Jo Ann, but why have you just mentioned the subject today if you have had it on your mind for so long a time?"

" Probably I haven't told all the story. Today at school we had a speaker in assembly who said that it is a valuable experience for young people to work at different things. He felt that any job which we might be able to get now would afford experience that would be invaluable to us in launching ourselves on our chosen careers or, in more everyday language, in getting and holding a job when we graduate. He also pointed out that by working at a variety of things we should be better able to know the type of work we enjoy and are best fitted for. You know, I am anxious to get a permanent job as a stenographer after I graduate. However, I realize that I am not prepared now to take an office job. What do you think I might be able to do?"

SOME PART-TIME JOBS FOR HIGH SCHOOL GIRLS

" It might be a good idea to make a list of the things that you can do."

393

Jo Ann drew up the following list: child care, housework, clerk-ing, acting as waitress, assisting in the school library, serving at the counter in the school cafeteria. After Jo Ann had studied the list for some minutes, she said, " I think that child-care jobs are the most plentiful, with housework and serving next in popularity. With the work in child care which I have had in my home eco-nomics class at school and the experience I have had at home, I believe that I can take care of children. Then, with the work I have done helping you serve dinners, I might be able to qualify for the serving jobs and probably the housework jobs, if one is supposed merely to help with the meals and not actually plan and cook them. I have often thought I should like to do some clerking. Do you think I might get a job?"

" Yes, I think you might do very well any of the jobs which you have named. Most of the jobs of caring for children come in the evening when parents want someone to stay with their children while they are away. The children usually go to bed early, so you would be able to do your school work while they sleep. Then, occasionally, you might help with serving dinners and washing the dishes afterwards on Fridays or Saturdays.

" Since you help me considerably with the housework, I believe it would not be wise for you to plan on taking a job for more than a couple of nights a week. Of course, you may be able to get a clerking job next summer; that is, if there is one available. You will be old enough then to take such a job, or you might get work as a waitress in one of the local restaurants.

" You have asked what you should do to get a job. I think it might be well for you to keep some notes on our discussion here, as you have done before. There are some specific immediate things that you may do to get work, but before we take them up, I should like to discuss with you some fundamental principles to keep in mind when working for other people."

The following statements are taken from Jo Ann's notebook.

SOME THINGS TO BE KEPT IN MIND BY WOULD-BE EMPLOYEES

A beginner should recognize the fact that the employer is giving him valuable training and that he isn't worth a raise until he has learned the job and is able to make a real contribution to the employer.

A beginner should welcome every opportunity to learn all he can about the job.

Any job that is worthy of your time should have your interest and respect. If you do not have both for the job, do not take it.

Be willing to do anything that needs to be done. Any honest work is honorable.

Do all work cheerfully and graciously. Even though you may think some things should be done differently, follow the instructions of your employer. If you are not given directions for doing a piece of work, use your own judgment and knowledge in getting it done. Ask questions if you need to.

Be loyal to the people for whom you are working. Guard all business secrets if working for an organization, and treat the personal affairs of a family just as you do your own family affairs. Do not repeat family secrets.

Believe in the concern for which you are working. Be loyal to it as you are to your school.

Always maintain a businesslike relationship with your employer. Look to your home and church for your social life. Do not depend entirely upon your business associates for your friendships.

Keep your own self-respect at all times. Do not allow yourself to lose your temper at any time. When you lose your emotional control, you are unable to think clearly.

When dealing with patrons or customers of a business organization, be tactful, patient, and courteous.

Have your friends and acquaintances telephone you at home and make their calls on you at home.

Keep yourself neat and clean and suitably dressed. If you make it a habit to take a bath every day, you will not annoy others with a body odor.

Plan your day, if possible, to include some time for exercise outdoors.

Look to your diet; remember the importance of an adequate diet to good health.

Always get to work on time. Do not take more than the allotted time for lunch.

Do more than is expected of you. Do whatever you see that needs to be done and that you are capable of handling. Be alert to things that need to be done and also for ways of improving the methods of doing things.

STUDY-GUIDE QUESTIONS

1. Compare the available part-time jobs in your community with those on Jo Ann's list.
2. Arrange in the order of their importance the fundamental principles to be kept in mind when working for other people. Can you think of any other principles which should be added to these?

UNIT TWO. WORKING IN THE HOMES OF OTHERS

" To get back to your question, Jo Ann, of how to go about finding a job, the first thing to do is to make contacts with prospective employers. Often some member of your family or a friend may know someone who has a job such as you are looking for. When you are graduated and ready to take an office job, probably your uncle will be able to give you a few leads.

" When the school maintains an employment bureau such as yours does, you should register with the teacher who directs its activities and fill in an enrollment card for her file. If you did not have an employment office at school, there are state and federal employment agencies, as well as private agencies, that help people to find jobs. You must be eighteen years old before these agencies will enroll you. Another means of contacting prospective employers is to watch the ads in the local newspaper.

" Large concerns that employ a number of people have either a personnel manager or an employment manager who takes care of hiring. Personnel managers are usually pleased to interview prospective employees whether they are in immediate need of someone or not. When they interview a person, they have him fill in a card for the firm's files; then, when the need arises, they have a record of interested people for the job.

" Before you visit the employment bureau find out, if you can, the name of the person who has charge, so that you may call her by name. When you go to the office, introduce yourself and state your business in a straightforward, businesslike way. For example, Jo Ann, you might say, ' Mrs. James, I am Jo Ann Wilson, an 11B pupil from Miss Brown's home room. I should like to have a job taking care of children or serving meals.'

" After such an introduction Mrs. James may ask you some questions and then request that you fill in a personal card which she may refer to when answering calls for jobs. You should be prepared to give the date and place of your birth, your height and weight, and the names of teachers who know something of your qualifications for the job. Be sure that you know these things and that you are able to spell the names of the subjects which you are taking, your references, and the church which you attend. You must be careful to fill in all the blanks and to write so that your penmanship can be easily read.

" If there is a question as to the amount of pay you are willing to accept, ask Mrs. James what you should put down, for, since you haven't worked before, you would not know what you should ask. In all probability there is a fixed price in your school for various types of work.

" Answer honestly and directly any questions that Mrs. James finds it necessary to ask you. Keep in mind the fact that it is through Mrs. James's recommendation that you will be given an opportunity for a job. The impression you make on her will be a determining factor in whether or not you will be recommended for a job."

TAKING CARE OF CHILDREN

Evidently Jo Ann made a very good impression on Mrs. James, for she was called the following week to Mrs. Whiteside's to stay with her three-year-old daughter, Alice.

Jo Ann was pleased with the prospect of her first job and was very eager to do well. She got out her notebook, read over the statements under " Some Things to Be Kept in Mind by Would-be Employees," and decided that some of them could be applied to her present job.

Since she had taken a bath in the morning, she didn't think it necessary to take another before going to work, but she did wash her face and hands and put on a fresh wash dress. She wanted to be sure that she didn't take any germs to the child for whom she was responsible, and, too, that she could do anything necessary without soiling a good dress. She started from home in time to arrive five minutes before the appointed hour.

When Jo Ann arrived, she introduced herself to Mrs. Whiteside, saying, " I am Jo Ann Wilson. Mrs. James from the high school sent me to take care of your daughter."

Mrs. Whiteside's small daughter was having her supper, and

Jo Ann was instructed to stay with her until she had finished eating and then to allow her to play with her toys until she wanted to go to bed.

Jo Ann was surprised that Mrs. Whiteside didn't tell her to put Alice to bed at a definite time, but she remembered that her aunt had told her to follow instructions. She also remembered from her home economics course at school that children should play quietly before going to bed; therefore she did not initiate any stimulating play but encouraged the child to amuse herself quietly.

When Jo Ann was pretending to read, hoping that her little charge was getting sleepy, one of her friends telephoned to her and wanted to come over. She remembered that in her enthusiasm over her first job, she had told the friend where she was going. She was sorry that she had done so, for she remembered also that her aunt had said that she must not visit and talk over the telephone while at work. You see, Jo Ann rightly felt that she wanted to build up the proper habits of work, no matter how small the job. Therefore she said to her friend, " Betty, I'm sorry but I can't have you come here. Mrs. Whiteside doesn't expect me to have company while I am here. Won't you plan to come over to my aunt's tomorrow after school?"

When Alice showed signs of tiring, Jo Ann helped put the toys away and suggested that she might tell her a story while she helped her get ready for bed. As Jo Ann repeated over and over one of Alice's favorite rhymes, her voice became softer and softer, until the little girl closed her eyes.

At last Alice was sleeping peacefully. Jo Ann picked up Alice's doll that had fallen to the floor, put the chairs in place, opened the window, and left the room. As she went by the breakfast room, she realized that she had been so intent on taking Alice out of the high chair and getting her interested in the toys that she had forgotten to clear away the dishes. She put things in order and took the dishes into the kitchen to wash them.

As she was preparing to wash Alice's dishes, she saw that Mrs. Whiteside had stacked the dinner dishes but had evidently not had time to wash them. Jo Ann remembered again one of the principles that her aunt had told her: " Do more than is expected of you." Accordingly, she washed the dishes and left them in order on the table.

Do you wonder that not only did Mrs. Whiteside call on Jo Ann whenever she needed someone to stay with Alice, but also Mrs. Whiteside's friends asked her to stay with their children?

SERVING MEALS

Mrs. Whiteside liked Jo Ann's attitude toward work so much that she asked her to come and help her one evening when she was having company to dinner.

In getting ready for this new job, Jo Ann washed her hands and face, arranged her hair in a neat style with a net over it, used just enough make-up to give her a natural, healthy look, and put on a fresh white dress. She arrived at Mrs. Whiteside's ten minutes ahead of the scheduled time.

With the experience Jo Ann had had in helping Mrs. Johns, it was very easy for her to follow Mrs. Whiteside's directions for serving. The meal was served in the same way as the one at Mrs. Johns's, which was described in Section IX of this book. Jo Ann did not sit at the table. She was quiet and poised in manner, working efficiently without hurrying.

After the dinner was over, Jo Ann stacked the dishes, washed them, and put them in the cupboards. She worked quietly and left the kitchen in perfect order.

STUDY-GUIDE QUESTIONS

1. What things should you know when you go to enroll at an employment bureau?
2. What principles of work did Jo Ann follow when she took care of Mrs. Whiteside's child? Do you think Jo Ann was wise to wash the dishes?
3. If you were called upon to help someone serve a dinner, would you make the same preparations as Jo Ann did? If not, what would you do?

UNIT THREE.   LEARNING TO SELL

About a month before the end of the school year Jo Ann again visited Mrs. James in the employment office at school. This time she told Mrs. James that she was anxious to get a clerking job for the summer. Since she had included this kind of work when she filled in her enrollment card in the fall, she did not need to fill in another card. Mrs. James asked Jo Ann a few questions which she answered truthfully and courteously.

In a few days Mrs. James asked Jo Ann to get in touch with Mr. Bennett, manager of a local store, who had asked her to recommend two or three girls for a salesmanship job in the notion department. Jo Ann called at the store that afternoon and asked to see Mr. Bennett's secretary. From the girl who directed her to Mr. Bennett's office she found out that the secretary's name was Miss Parker. When she arrived at the office, she said, " Miss Parker? I am Jo Ann Wilson, a pupil at Lakeland High School. Mrs. James from the high school told me that Mr. Bennett is looking for a salesgirl for the notion department. I should like to be considered for the job. Can you tell me when I might be able to see Mr. Bennett?" Jo Ann was told to call Saturday morning between ten and eleven.

PREPARING FOR AN INTERVIEW

After talking to her uncle about what a girl might do to prepare for an interview with a prospective employer, Jo Ann made preparations for this very important event.

She looked over the unit on clothes for work in her home economics textbook and decided on the clothes to wear and the kind of make-up to use. Mr. Johns had told her that appearance is a very important factor in any interview

Next she wrote on a piece of paper the data which she would need if she were asked to fill in an application blank. Her list included the place and date of her birth, her present address, her aunt's telephone number, the subjects she had taken at school, the complete names of three teachers at school who knew her qualifications for the job, the name of her minister and his address, and the names and addresses of three of the women for whom she had worked. Jo Ann had previously obtained permission from the people whose names she gave as references.

Mr. Johns advised her to be able to tell Mr. Bennett, if he asked her, why she felt that she could do the job for which she was applying. Since she didn't have experience, she realized that she would have to rely on other qualities. Although she thought that her appearance was in her favor, she couldn't tell Mr. Bennett that, and, furthermore, he would be the judge in such a matter. She was eager to work and to do the job as he would want it done. She was sure that she would be able to follow directions and that she could meet the public. She was tactful, courteous, and patient. She was able to control her temper and had a manner that inspired confidence. As she thought these things over, she decided that she couldn't tell all of them to Mr. Bennett, but she could tell him that she usually got along well with people, that she was eager to work, and that she was eager to do the job the way he wanted it done.

The next day she went back to see Mrs. James to find out what salary she should expect. Mr. Johns had told her that she should have an idea of the amount usually paid for the kind of work she hoped to do.

On Saturday morning Jo Ann dressed carefully for her first interview for a job. She arrived a few minutes before ten o'clock and again introduced herself to Miss Parker, saying, " I am Jo Ann Wilson. I have an appointment to see Mr. Bennett this morning." Miss Parker asked her to be seated and told Mr. Bennett she was there.

THE INTERVIEW

After Jo Ann had waited for about twenty minutes, Miss Parker told her that Mr. Bennett would see her.

Mr. Bennett was seated on the other side of the room behind a large desk. When Jo Ann entered, he seemed absorbed in some material on his desk. She took a few steps forward and then stopped. Mr. Bennett looked up and said, " Good morning, Miss

Wilson, have a chair, please." Jo Ann answered, " Good morning, Mr. Bennett," and continuing across the floor in her habitual good posture, seated herself in the chair indicated. When Jo Ann reached the chair with one foot a step ahead of the other, she turned on the balls of her feet and lowered herself onto the chair by bending her knees. She kept both her feet on the floor with one slightly in front of the other. She placed her purse on her lap with one hand holding it lightly and the other relaxed beside the purse.

Jo Ann paused a few minutes for Mr. Bennett to open the interview, but, when he seemed to be waiting for her to do so, she said, " I came to see you about the job of salesgirl in the notion department. Mrs. James, who has charge of the employment bureau at Lakeland High School, sent me."

Mr. Bennett then took charge of the interview and asked Jo Ann what her qualifications for the job were, why she thought she could do it, and why she wanted the job. He also asked some personal questions about where she lived, what she did in her leisure time, and what she expected to do in the future. Jo Ann answered all these questions honestly, briefly, and courteously. She tried to give the impression that she could do the job without seeming overconfident. When he gave her an opportunity, she asked him what the duties of the job were, whether she would be expected to wear a certain type or color of dress, and also what the job paid.

At the end of the interview Mr. Bennett asked Jo Ann to stop at Miss Parker's desk for an application form to fill in. When he said this, she said, " I shall be glad to do so," and, realizing that the interview was over, she stood up and continued, " Thank you for the interview. Should I call back in a few days to find out who the lucky person is or will you let me know?" She was told that the decision would probably be made within the next week and that she would be notified.

THE JOB OF CLERKING

Jo Ann was delighted when she received in the mail a few days later notice that she had been chosen for the job of clerking in the notion department during the summer months.

She had found out in the interview with Mr. Bennett that she might wear a white dress, a black one with white collar and cuffs, or a black skirt and white blouse. Her shoes were to be white or black, and she was requested to use a minimum amount of make-up.

On the morning when she reported for work, she was asked to report to Mr. Bennett's office, where she found several other young people who were also new employees of the firm. Mr. Bennett explained to the group that he had asked them to come so that he might explain some of the policies of the store to them. Jo Ann, as was her custom, took notes as he talked. The following notes are taken from her book.

You must remember that the public is very exacting and demanding. Give prompt, efficient service.

You represent the business firm which employs you. Be sure to interpret the firm correctly to the public.

Remember at all times that your job is to serve. You must treat your customers in such a way that they will have confidence in you.

You must be polite, alert, cheerful, tactful, patient, and intelligent.

When a customer approaches your counter and you are busy showing merchandise to another customer, you should look up, smile, and say, " I shall be able to serve you in a few minutes." You must not neglect your present customer; neither should you carry on a prolonged conversation with her after you have closed the sale.

Listen carefully to a customer's request for merchandise and bring her what she asks for if you have it. If not, tell her you do not have the particular color, style, or brand that she has specified, but that you will be happy to show her what you do have that is similar. Do not bring her white gloves if she asks for black ones.

Poorly dressed or illiterate customers must be treated with the same deference and consideration as well-dressed ones.

Take time to inform yourself about the merchandise which you sell. You will find that this knowledge pays well in both sales and satisfaction.

Try to remember your customers' names. When you have made

out a sales check for a customer, call her by name when you return her change. Cultivate the habit of connecting a person's name with some personal characteristic, such as the color of his hair or the shape of his face.

A sales person should never argue with a customer; neither should a customer be allowed to leave the store dissatisfied. If you are unable to take care of the matter under consideration so that your customer will be satisfied, refer it to the person above you in the department. Someone with more experience may be able to pour oil on the troubled waters.

When you receive money from a customer, mention the amount. Say, " Twenty-five cents out of one dollar." Be sure that the customer hears you; look at him and speak distinctly. This will serve as a precaution and will prevent the customer from saying when you return the change, " Why, I handed you five dollars." When you return the change to a customer, count it out by first mentioning the amount of the sale and then adding on to it until you have counted the full amount received: " Twenty-five cents, fifty, seventy-five, one dollar." Finish all sales with " Thank you, call again, please."

When speaking on the telephone, remember that you are representing the firm and that the customer must judge from your voice alone. Try to express pleasure, cordiality, and sincerity. Speak clearly and slowly. If you answer the telephone, say, " Jones and Company, Miss Wilson speaking." Give very close attention to a request given on the telephone. If possible, avoid asking the customer to repeat. If you are unable to take care of the business without securing information, ask the customer for his telephone number and tell him you will call him back in a few minutes.

Do not be afraid to say, " I am sorry " when you have made a mistake. When a customer comes in with a grievance, be sympathetic and show a genuine interest in helping her.

Be as polite to your coworkers as you are to the customers.

You should not be a member of an organization which you do not respect and to which you do not feel loyalty. Never speak in public of difficulties encountered in your daily job.

Observe the hours for beginning, quitting, and eating lunch set by the management of the store.

STUDY-GUIDE QUESTIONS

1. What preparation did Jo Ann make for her interview with Mr. Bennett? Can you think of anything more that she should have done or anything that she should have omitted?
2. Practice the method which Jo Ann used in seating herself in Mr. Bennett's office. Be able to demonstrate it before the class.
3. List the things which Jo Ann did when she went for her interview with Mr. Bennett. Which ones do you consider the most important?
4. What does a customer expect of the store and sales person where she shops?
5. How should a sales person greet a customer?
6. Pick out six important rules which a sales person should observe when serving the public.
7. If you, as sales person, sold a bill of goods amounting to $4.23 and were given a 10-dollar bill in payment, tell what you would say when you received the money and when you returned the change.
8. Suppose that you were employed by the May Company. What would you say when answering the telephone?

UNIT FOUR. BEING A WAITRESS

During Jo Ann's junior year at school the Whitesides had financial reverses, and Mrs. Whiteside opened a tearoom in her home. When selecting waitresses, she remembered how well Jo Ann served meals at home and therefore asked her to help in the new tearoom.

Tearoom work is one way of earning money while you are still in school.
Courtesy, MacMurray College, Jacksonville, Illinois.

When Mrs. Whiteside met with the girls who were to be waitresses, she explained the things she hoped to do and what their part was to be in the scheme. After her talk she gave the following mimeographed list of rules to each girl, suggesting that she not only study them before coming back to work but also that she reread them from time to time.

HOW TO BECOME A SUCCESSFUL WAITRESS

Think of yourself as a hostess who is eager to make her guests comfortable and happy. When people are hungry, they are likely to be low in spirit and physically tired. A cheerful, calm, well-poised, neatly groomed and dressed waitress is a great help in creating a restful, quiet atmosphere for eating. Form the habit of getting sufficient rest at night so that you will be able to get up in time to make suitable preparation for the day. See that your body is clean and free from odors, your shoes are clean, your uniform is freshly laundered, your hair is neatly dressed with a net over it, and your make-up is natural, not overdone.

A good hostess never allows her guests to become conscious of the machinery of the household; neither does a good waitress allow her patrons to sense any of the irritations which she may feel concerning her work or personal affairs. Patrons expect efficient service and are not interested in the technicalities of it. Do not make it necessary to apologize for cold coffee, soiled linens, warm drinking water, and the like. Keep your table in order with clean linens. See that hot foods are served hot and cold ones cold. Keep the condiment containers clean, filled, and in working order.

Besides keeping your tables in order and serving food, you will be expected to do other routine work. You may be asked to assemble salads, cut butter, keep the dining room in order, or act as hostess.

Remember that when handling foods you must be clean and sanitary at all times. Be sure to wash your hands before going on duty, after using your handkerchief, when leaving the toilet, and whenever they may become soiled from food. Never place your fingers on tops of plates with food on them or in the top of water glasses. When silver falls to the floor, place it with other soiled silver; do not return it to the table. Use a special cloth, not a soiled napkin, for wiping tops of tables. When setting your tables and removing the soiled dishes, follow the suggestions on pp. 376–381 for such service at home.

In order that you may give your patrons quick, personal service, familiarize yourself with the menu each day. You should know about how long it takes for the preparation of the various dishes offered and be able to make suggestions to the person who doesn't know what he wants. You should keep a watchful eye on your patrons at all times. If one of them is not eating the food he has ordered, suggest that you would be glad to bring something else. See that the water glasses are kept filled and that the usual accompaniments are served with certain foods. For example, serve tartare sauce with fillet of sole, cream and sugar with coffee, and crackers with soup. Whenever you see a patron turn and look in your direction, go to him immediately to see what you can do for him.

Use your head to save your heels. Never go to the kitchen with empty hands if there are soiled dishes to be taken.

Work quietly and efficiently without hurrying. Never run to and from the kitchen.

Present the check to the patron when he has finished eating; do not wait to be asked for it.

On the days when you are asked to act as hostess, you will wear a street dress instead of a uniform. You will stand near the door, greet the patrons, calling them by name if you know them, and then seat them. When there are possible choices of places, you might say, " Where would you like to sit?" If they do not have a choice, keep in mind the comfort of your patrons. Seat groups with children to the side of the room, older or crippled people near the entrance, men or women alone at the side, and young couples to the back and side, and try to place the more attractive groups in different parts of the room.

STUDY-GUIDE QUESTIONS

1. Why is it desirable that a waitress be neat in appearance and dignified? Describe the appearance of your ideal waitress.
2. What is meant by the technicalities of good service?
3. Name some of the things which a waitress may be asked to do in addition to keeping her tables in order and serving food.
4. What are some habits of cleanliness which a waitress should practice?
5. Why should a waitress familiarize herself with the daily menu?
6. What may a waitress do to help make her patrons comfortable?
7. What are the duties of the hostess?

UNIT FIVE. BEING A TYPIST

APPLYING FOR A JOB BY LETTER

In May, before Jo Ann was graduated, she took the advice of Mr. Johns in following up as many leads as possible. She again called on Mrs. James in the employment bureau at school, wrote letters to three friends of her uncle, and visited the local state employment agency.

She decided to enclose in each letter a record sheet on which she listed her personal qualifications, such as her age, height, weight, state of health, religion, courses taken at high school with the average grade made in each, high school activities and leisure-time interests, work experience, and the names of people who were able and willing to vouch concerning her qualifications for the positions she was seeking.

She was very careful in composing the letters which she sent. She followed meticulously the instructions for letter writing which she had received in her typewriting classes. She spaced the letters in the center of the page with an equal margin on each side and typed them so that her potential employers could see a sample of her work. She remembered that her commercial textbooks had stressed the fact that one should always sign letters in longhand. The reason why the names of executives are typewritten under their signatures is that so many of their signatures could not otherwise be understood. She kept her letters businesslike and as brief as possible, but she included all the necessary information. Mentioning how she had heard of the position and the type of work in which she was interested, she asked that she might have an interview. She made all the letters which she sent as much alike as was practical. It was a great convenience to have all the data concerning her qualifications assembled on a separate sheet of paper that she could enclose with her letters and not have to include them in the body of each letter.

Here is a copy of the letter that led to a position for Jo Ann and a copy of the personal record sheet she worked out for herself.

1538 Elbur Avenue
Lakeland, Ohio
May 24, 1945

Mr. Paul M. Masters, Vice-President
Sigler & Brown Company
1616 Broadway Avenue
Cleveland, Ohio

Dear Mr. Masters:

My uncle, Mr. Albert Johns, has suggested that I write to you concerning the position of typist in your general office. I should like very much to call and talk with you concerning my qualifications for the position so that I may be registered with you in case of a future opening in this line of work.

In June I shall be graduated from Lakeland High School, where I have taken the stenographic curriculum. Enclosed you will find my record sheet, on which I have outlined my training and listed some references.

If you are interested in me as a candidate for the position, I can come for an interview at your convenience.

Very truly yours,
Jo Ann Wilson

PERSONAL RECORD SHEET
Jo Ann Wilson
1538 Elbur Avenue, Lakeland, Ohio
LA 0313

Social Security Number — 252480

Personal Qualifications

Age — 18 years   Health — Excellent
Height — 5 feet 4 inches   Religion — Protestant
Weight — 123 pounds

High School Record

COURSES	CREDIT HOURS	AVERAGE MARK
English	25	A
Physical Education	5	B
Swimming	5	A
Modern History	10	B
American History and Civics	10	B

Clothing	10	B
Personal Regimen	10	A
Handicrafts	5	A
Glee Club	4	A
Bookkeeping	10	B
Typewriting	20	A
Shorthand	20	A
Office Practice	5	A

High School Activities
   Friendship Club — secretary one semester, president one semester
   Commercial Club — president two semesters

Leisure-Time Interests
   Singing   Tennis   Dancing
   Swimming   Knitting

Experience
   Taking care of children, two evenings a week for the past two years
   Clerking in notion department, Jones and Bennett Company, for 3
      months
   Assistant clerk in the main office at school, one period a week for one
      semester

References (by permission)
   Mr. John W. Bennett, Manager
   Jones and Bennett Company
   13960 Detroit Avenue
   Lakeland, Ohio

   Mrs. Benton H. Whiteside
   1240 Waterbury Avenue
   Lakeland, Ohio

   Miss Carolyn Burns, Teacher of Shorthand and Typewriting
   Lakeland High School
   Lakeland, Ohio

   Miss Grace Weber, Teacher of Office Practice
   Lakeland High School
   Lakeland, Ohio

   Miss Mary Cook, Home-room teacher
   Lakeland High School
   Lakeland, Ohio

The Reverend George Goodman
Pastor, Lakeland Christian Church
Lakeland, Ohio

After following up her letter of application to Mr. Masters with an interview, Jo Ann was chosen for the job of typist in his office. She had found the advice which her uncle gave her for making application for a position so valuable that she went to him for advice on how to make a success of a job after getting it. As usual she took her notebook and jotted down points as he talked to her. She took advantage of this opportunity to use her shorthand. When Mr. Johns finished, she had several pages of neatly written symbols.

Later Jo Ann read through the notes from Mr. Johns's talk and compared them with those which she had taken in a discussion with Mrs. Johns at the beginning of her junior year. She had headed these notes "Some Things to Be Kept in Mind by Would-be Employees." She was surprised to find a great similarity between the two sets of notes. The following items are the ones from Mr. Johns's talk that were new to her.

QUALITIES OF A BUSINESS WOMAN

A successful business woman is neatly dressed in simple, smart clothes and is immaculately groomed. She is impersonal and businesslike without losing her womanly traits of kindliness and thoughtfulness of others. She is courteous at all times and is accurate, orderly, and quick in her work. She cooperates with and is loyal to her coworkers and superiors. She is honest and honorable in all her dealings.

OFFICE ETIQUETTE

It is the privilege of executives to speak first to the people who work for them; however, people who work together day after day usually speak simultaneously. When an office girl sees her employer outside the office, she may wait for him to speak first.

In an office people say, "Miss Jones" and "Mr. Smith," not "Sallie" and "Tom," regardless of how well they know each other. When answering a question, say, " Yes, Miss Jones," " No, Mr. Smith."

Men in business do not rise when women employees come into the room, although they do rise when women outside the firm come into the office.

Neat dress and immaculate grooming are essential to success in business.
Courtesy, MacMurray College, Jacksonville, Illinois.

In business, men and women alike are introduced to their superior officers. For example, a new typist would be introduced to the office manager thus, " Mr. Office Manager, this is Miss Wilson." The office manager may or may not offer to shake hands.

PREPARING FOR A PROMOTION

Keep in mind your objective in the business world. If you want to be a secretary some day, prepare yourself for the position through study and reading.

Make yourself invaluable in your present position. Keep up with the business you are in, grow with it. Read professional magazines.

Keep yourself physically and mentally fit through proper obedience to the laws of health and through a full personal life.

STUDY-GUIDE QUESTIONS

1. What facts should be included in a personal record sheet?
2. What qualities should a letter of application have?
3. Select from among your acquaintances a successful business woman. List her personality qualities. How do they compare with those found in Jo Ann's notebook?
4. How does the etiquette in a business office differ from social etiquette? Give specific examples.
5. What things should a business person do to prepare herself for promotion?

ACTIVITIES

1. Make out a personal record sheet for yourself.
2. Write a letter of application to a local firm for a job of your own choosing.
3. If you have ever earned money, tell what you consider your most valuable work experience.

UNIT SIX. GOING TO COLLEGE

SHOULD I GO TO COLLEGE?

When a high school girl begins to consider whether she is going to college, she will do well to ask herself the following questions: Can my parents afford to send me to college? If not, am I a good enough student and independent enough to work my way through? Am I interested in the type of work I would do at college? Is college training necessary or desirable for the work which I expect to do in life?

People go to college for many reasons. If you were to ask a group of college students why they are in college, they would probably give the following reasons: " It is a family tradition. I grew up with the idea of going to college." " My parents want me to have the advantages in life that they missed." " Because my friends go to college." " Because I want to live in a sorority house." " So that I may study to be a teacher." " That I may train my mind." " That I may learn how to get along with people." " So that I may have the opportunity to develop into a well-rounded person with sufficient knowledge to be a successful wife and an intelligent member of society." " To find a life companion."

If a person is serious in her intentions, has sufficient means at her command, and chooses the right college, she will no doubt profit from college life.

CHOOSING A COLLEGE

There are many colleges in our country. We have private colleges, state colleges, junior colleges, graduate colleges, coeducational colleges, colleges for men, colleges for women, vocational colleges, colleges which emphasize religious training, secular colleges, academic colleges, small colleges located in small towns, and large universities, consisting of a number of schools, located in large cities.

When deciding which college to attend, consider first your reason for going to college. If you want to become a physician,

416

for example, select a college with a good pre-medical course. If you want to be a journalist, select a college which is well known for its school of journalism. If you are interested in studying music, select a school which has a well-known music department. Anybody who knows what he wants from his college training and selects the right school should benefit from going to college.

College is a good foundation for democratic living. Photograph by Russell R. Benson. Courtesy, News Bureau, Denison University, Granville, Ohio.

When you have decided on the type of college you would like to attend, either your home-room teacher or a librarian should be able to suggest several colleges for your consideration. It is wise to write to each of these recommended institutions for one of its catalogues, which will give you a complete description of the school, the entrance requirements, the courses required for graduation, the scholastic training and experience of the faculty, the extracurricular activities, and the school calendar — in fact, almost everything you would like to know about the college. After you have studied your catalogues, it will be helpful to visit the different schools before making a final decision. In this way, you can see the buildings and can interview the head of the division or department of the school in which you are interested. He will be able to give you a good idea of what you may expect to accomplish as a student in that particular institution. Private schools usually send out field representatives to interview prospective students.

Since the administrative staff and the faculty determine, to a large extent, the policies and ideals that govern a college, find out what you can about these people. A forceful president of high ideals and sound character exerts a good influence on the lives of the students under his supervision.

PREPARING FOR COLLEGE

The sooner you can decide where you are going to college, the better able you will be to prepare yourself for your new responsibilities. If your chosen college requires two years of a foreign language, one year of mathematics, three years of English, and two years of science, you can easily see that you will have to begin early in your high school career to work on these requirements.

Then too, a college-preparatory pupil should acquire economical and effective methods of study, some facility in using reference materials, and some skill in expressing himself in writing. You will be able to improve yourself in these matters by conscientiously preparing your daily assignments.

STUDY-GUIDE QUESTIONS

1. For what reasons do people go to college?
2. What factors should you consider when choosing a college?
3. How can a high school pupil make preparation for college life?

ACTIVITIES

1. Give a specific example of each of the types of colleges listed in your textbook.
2. Secure a catalogue of a college in which you are interested. If you are

unable to borrow one, write to the registrar of the school for one. Study the catalogue, and fill in the following outline:

A. Entrance requirements
B. Experience and training of the teachers in the department in which you are interested
C. Probable cost of one year's work.
D. Courses required for graduation
E. Extracurricular activities in which you would be interested

3. If possible, interview an alumnus of your chosen college or someone else who knows the college to find out the policies and ideals that govern it. You might ask such questions as the following:
Is there a dean of women and a dean of men who supervise the social life of the student body?
Are the students required to live up to a desirable set of rules governing their social life?
Are there enough wholesome social activities planned to provide sufficient recreation for the student body?
Do the students who do not belong to sororities and fraternities have reason to feel left out of the life of the institution?
4. Find out, either from a list of the alumni of your chosen school, which may be found in a library, or from a former student of the school, something about what the graduates of the school are doing. If the record of the alumni includes a goodly number of successful people, you can reasonably conclude that their college training was sound.

BOOKS FOR FURTHER READING

Greenleaf, Walter J., "Working Your Way through College, and Other Means of Providing for College Expenses." Vocational Division Bulletin No. 210, Occupational Information and Guidance Series No. 4, Government Printing Office, Washington, 1941. (20 cents)
Hopkins, Mary Alden, *Profits from Courtesy, Handbook of Business Etiquette.* Doubleday, Doran, and Company, Garden City, New York, 1937.
MacGibbon, Elizabeth Gregg, *Fitting Yourself for Business.* McGraw-Hill Book Company, New York, 1941.
MacGibbon, Elizabeth Gregg, *Manners in Business.* The Macmillan Company, New York, 1936.
McCann, Max, *Planning for College and How to Make the Most of It While There.* Frederick A. Stokes Company, New York, 1937.
Mills, Phoebe, *Hints to Business Maidens.* Mendor Publishing Company, Boston, 1939.
Post, Emily, *Etiquette.* Funk and Wagnalls Company, New York, 1940.

APPENDIX

NUTRITIONAL VALUES OF COMMON FOODS*†

FOOD	SIZE OF PORTION — Average Serving	VALUES — Calories	VALUES — Proteins, Grams	MINERALS — Calcium, Grams	MINERALS — Phosphorus, Grams	MINERALS — Iron, Mg.	MINERALS — Copper, Mg.	Vit. A, I. U.	VITAMINS — Vit. B₁ (Thiamin), Mg.	VITAMINS — Vit. B₂ (Riboflavin), Mg.	VITAMINS — Niacin, Mg.	VITAMINS — Vit. C (Ascorbic Acid), Mg.
FRUITS												
Apples, fresh, fall	1, 2½" diam.	60	0.4	0.010	0.015	0.520	0.130	90	0.051	0.038	0.65	8
Apricots, fresh	2, 1½" diam.	15	0.3	0.006	0.012	0.150	0.07	3245	0.018	0.062	---	1
Dried	10 halves	105	2.4	0.032	0.060	3.37	0.19	5250	0.05	0.01	---	1
Banana	1, 7"x1½"	120	1.6	0.010	0.037	0.750	0.262	375	0.056	0.750	0.780	10
Blackberry, fresh	½ cup	30	0.8	0.010	0.020	0.60	0.10	11.40	0.120	---	---	2
Standard, canned	⅔ cup	105	1.1	---	---	---	---	---	---	---	---	0.3
Blueberries, fresh	⅔ cup	50	0.6	0.025	0.020	0.41	0.11	52	0.04	0.01	---	5
Cantaloupe	¼, 5" diam.	25	0.6	0.017	0.015	0.51	0.06	200	0.02	0.03	---	0.14
Cherries, fresh	½ cup	60	0.8	0.014	0.023	0.375	0.105	75	0.03	---	---	6
Cranberries	½ cup	20	0.2	0.006	0.005	0.23	0.450	10	0	0	0.065	5
Cranberry sauce	⅓ cup	185	0.2	---	---	---	---	20	0	0	---	4
Dates, dried	2 lg.	40	0.2	0.009	0.006	0.659	0.049	22.1	0.009	0.0039	0.28	0
Figs, fresh	1 lg.	25	0.3	0.024	0.016	0.355	0.027	3.33	0.04	0.03	---	0.76
Grapefruit	½, 4" diam.	25	0.6	0.021	0.020	0.27	0.03	0	0.23	Trace	---	45
Grapes, Concord	24	70	1.4	0.004	0.016	0.34	0.08	29	0.03	0.0072	---	1.79
Honeydew melon	¾ cup, diced	65	1.4	---	---	---	---	---	0.10	---	---	16.80
Lemon juice	1 tablespoon	6	0	0.003	0.001	0.03	0	0	0.009	0	0.012	7.95
Orange, whole	1 medium	50	0.8	0.026	0.020	0.51	0.13	220	0.11	0.014	---	56.0
Juice	½ cup	65	0.7	0.022	0.015	0.34	0.10	240	0.12	0.01	0.264	54.0
Peaches	2, 2" diam.	60	0.8	0.015	0.031	0.54	0.012	75	0.06	0.06	1.425	13.50
Pears, Bartlett	1, 3" long	60	0.6	0.012	0.021	0.98	0	0	0.45	---	0.21	0.20
Pineapple	1 cup, diced	65	0.6	0.012	0.025	0.48	0.105	34.47	0.09	0.029	---	15.51

Food	Measure											
Plums	2, 2½" long	20	0.4	0.010	0.016	0.39	0.08	17.75	0.06	0.022	0.28	2.2
Prunes	2 medium	30	0.5	0.008	0.015	0.41	---	14.45	0.01	0.035	---	0
Raisins, seedless, dried	⅓ cup	165	1.0	---	---	2.48	0.12	30.60	0.090	0.720	---	0
Raspberries, red	⅔ cup	35	0.8	0.036	0.039	0.74	0.098	---	---	---	---	---
Rhubarb, cooked without sugar	⅔ cup	15	0.4	0.072	0.015	0.28	0.09	31	0.006	---	---	6
Strawberries, fresh	¾ cup	35	1.0	0.041	0.028	0.66	0.02	73.05	0.019	Trace	---	38.2
Tangerines	2, 2" diam.	35	0.9	0.041	0.017	0.61	0.09	245.6	0.084	0.021	---	26.31
Watermelon	1 cup, diced	75	0.9	0.019	0.031	0.552	0.168	181.2	0.084	0.084	---	16.66
VEGETABLES												
Asparagus, cooked	6, 3¼" stalks	15	1.8	0.022	0.072	0.75	0.17	500	0.178	0.102	---	10
Beans, green, string	⅔ cup	25	1.3	0.065	0.066	1.23	0.13	1600	0.084	0.144	0.84	20
Lima, cooked	½ cup	170	11.2	0.020	0.093	2.70	---	625	0.19	0.316	3.08	18.75
Navy, dried	½ cup	270	16.9	0.118	0.362	6.19	0.517	0	0.29	0.188	---	0
Soy, green, cooked	½ cup	185	18.0	0.121	0.341	2.68	---	125	0.656	0.325	0.750	50
Beet greens	1 cup	30	2.0	0.094	0.040	3.55	0.09	Excel†	---	0.625	---	18
Beets, fresh, cooked	½ cup	35	2.3	0.030	0.036	0.70	0.14	100	0.054	0.095	0.64	4
Broccoli, cooked	½ cup	15	3.0	0.122	0.059	3.30	0.13	6880	0.052	0.402	---	30
Brussels sprouts, cooked	½ cup	15	2.4	0.027	0.045	0.63	0.08	400	0.171	---	---	32
Cabbage, red, raw	½ cup	15	1.1	0.032	0.019	0.34	0.054	870	0.048	0.046	---	16
White, raw	½ cup	20	1.2	0.038	0.022	0.42	0.042	50	0.09	0.086	0.238	60
Carrots, raw	½ cup grated	20	0.6	0.037	0.030	0.48	0.064	2488	0.08	0.072	1.176	3
Cauliflower, cooked	⅔ cup	15	1.6	0.023	0.033	0.48	0.06	49	0.113	0.185	---	25
Celery, raw	2, 7" stalks	4	0.4	0.027	0.019	0.24	0.004	10	0.014	0.017	---	6
Chard, Swiss, cooked	⅔ cup	25	2.4	0.087	0.040	4.02	0.11	16700	0.45	0.097	---	20
Collards, cooked	½ cup	40	3.5	0.202	0.074	1.68	---	4080	0.123	0.255	---	23

* Compiled by Sarah Merritt Wenger, Director of Education, Wisconsin Alumni Research Foundation.
This information is derived from sources which we believe to be reliable. It is obvious, however, that some of the information may be, or may appear to be, in error, for there are differences in the samples of various foods. Moreover, the nutritional authorities themselves differ in some of their views and findings.
Following are sources used:
Milton A. Bridges and Marjorie R. Mattice. *Food and Beverage Analyses.* Lea and Febiger, Philadelphia, 1942.
Clara Mae Taylor. *Food Values in Shares and Weights.* Macmillan Company, New York, 1942.
H. A. Waisman and C. A. Elvehjem. *The Vitamin Content of Meat.* 1941.
L. J. Tepley, F. M. Strong, and C. A. Elvehjem. "The Distribution of Nicotinic Acid in Foods." *The Journal of Nutrition,* Vol. 23, No. 4, April, 1942, pp. 417-423.
Joseph Coffin. "The Lack of Vitamin D in Common Foods." *Journal of the American Dietetic Association,* Vol. XI, No. 2, July, 1935, pp. 119-127.
McCollum, Orent-Keiles, and Day. *Newer Knowledge of Nutrition.* 1939.
† A blank space or series of dashes in a column indicates that information was not available. A zero (0) means absence or negligible amounts.

NUTRITIONAL VALUES OF COMMON FOODS (Continued)

FOOD	SIZE OF PORTION Average Serving	VALUES Calories	VALUES Proteins, Grams	MINERALS Calcium, Grams	MINERALS Phosphorus, Grams	MINERALS Iron, Mg.	MINERALS Copper, Mg.	Vit. A, I.U.	VITAMINS Vit. B_1 (Thiamin), Mg.	VITAMINS Vit. B_2 (Riboflavin), Mg.	VITAMINS Niacin, Mg.	VITAMINS Vit. C (Ascorbic Acid), Mg.
Corn, yellow, cooked	1 ear, 8"	100	3.1	0.006	0.103	0.51	0.08	500	0.135	0.06	---	5
Cucumber, raw	2½x2"	10	0.6	0.012	0.019	0.26	0.04	26	0.06	0.056	0.24	6
Dandelion greens	½ cup	30	1.2	0.031	0.022	3.02	0.07	8925	0.065	---	---	5
Eggplant	2 slices	65	3.0	0.027	0.057	1.52	0.25	1075	0.15	0.315	---	25
Endive	¼ of sm. head	3	0.2	0.016	0.005	0.18	0.135	2250	0.014	0.035	---	2
Escarole, green leaves only	⅓ heart	5	0.6	0.002	0.001	0.77	---	1000	0.042	0.125	---	4
Kale, cooked	½ cup	25	1.8	0.197	0.072	2.54	---	18150	0.09	0.45	---	34
Lentils, cooked	½ cup	205	12.0	0.032	0.131	2.60	0.27	0	0.161	0.068	---	0
Lettuce	2 large leaves	6	0.6	0.002	0.021	0.88	0.03	220	0.050	0.097	---	8
Mustard greens, raw	½ cup	15	1.2	0.033	0.033	2.27	0.06	---	0.067	---	---	66
Mushrooms, boiled	½ cup	2	0	0.022	0.045	5.60	---	0	0.150	---	---	---
Okra, cooked	½ cup, 5 pods	15	1.0	0.072	0.062	0.63	0.12	480	0.134	0.482	---	10
Onions, white, medium	1, 2" diameter	20	0.8	0.017	0.022	0.22	0.04	0	0.015	0.045	0.05	40
Parsley	1 teaspoon	0	Trace	---	---	0.19	0.002	300	---	---	---	1
Parsnips, boiled	½ cup	40	1.0	0.029	0.025	0.36	0.08	---	0.119	---	---	11
Peas, black-eyed, dried	½ cup	350	21.4	---	---	---	---	50	0.9	0.3	---	---
Green, cooked	½ cup	35	3.5	0.009	0.058	0.85	0.10	840	0.371	0.161	---	8
Pepper, green	3" piece	5	0.2	0.002	0.005	0.10	0.02	1250	0.017	0.009	---	30
Potatoes, white, baked	1 medium	175	4.6	0.015	0.079	1.58	0.3	36	0.15	0.088	1.77	9
Sweet, baked	1 medium	150	2.1	0.021	0.044	0.62	0.15	3035	0.15	0.09	1.29	9
Pumpkin, canned	½ cup	40	1.0	0.038	0.017	0.18	---	3125	0.056	0.056	---	4
Radishes	6 medium	11	0.7	0.015	0.015	0.68	0.08	Trace	0.037	0.015	---	8
Rutabagas, cooked	¾ cup	40	1.3	0.088	0.067	1.28	---	15	0.078	0.092	---	25
Sauerkraut	⅔ cup	20	1.1	0.056	0.010	3.28	0.10	26	0.025	---	---	5

Food	Measure										
Spinach, cooked	½ cup	13	2.0	0.005	0.093	4.00	0.26	20000	0.08	0.45	0.72	17
Squash, summer, white, cooked	⅔ cup	15	0.5	0.018	0.016	0.35	0.08	300	0.032	0.081	---	2
Winter, boiled	⅔ cup	25	1.0	0.019	0.028	0.05	0.04	3000	0.048	0.081	---	6
Tomatoes, fresh, ripe	1 small	25	1.1	0.015	0.032	0.55	0.07	1063	0.108	0.058	0.725	28
Canned	½ cup	25	1.6	0.009	0.033	1.56	0.12	1105	0.065	---	---	30
Turnip greens, cooked	½ cup	20	2.0	0.098	0.045	3.08	0.09	18200	0.13	0.32	---	18
Boiled	½ cup	30	1.1	0.069	0.023	0.43	0.046	13	0.46	0.076	---	16
Watercress	½ cup	3	0.6	0.031	0.011	1.44	0.008	380	0.025	0.045	---	11
Yams, fresh	1, 5½"x1½"	110	2.6	0.010	0.051	9.25	---	---	---	---	0.837	---

CEREALS

Food	Measure										
Barley, whole-grain	½ cup	115	3.7	0.0153	0.120	1.42	---	---	---	---	---	---
Biscuits, baking powder	1 biscuit	70	2.0	0.0124	---	0.10	---	40	0.01	0.021	---	0
Bran, prepared	1 tablespoon	9	0.5	0.0036	0.036	0.381	0.035	4.04	0.014	---	1.02	0
Bread, corn (1 egg)	1-4½" square	275	6.6	0.051	0.102	0.9	---	1350	0.214	0.250	---	0
Rye	1 slice	65	2.3	0.006	0.037	0.60	0.07	---	0.035	0.008	---	---
White with milk	1 slice	65	2.4	0.011	---	0.21	---	---	0.016	0.016	0.23	---
White with water	1 slice	55	1.6	0.005	---	0.18	---	---	---	---	0.136	---
White enriched	1 slice	60	1.7	0.011	---	0.40	---	---	0.056	0.16	0.341	---
White enriched and fort. vit. D	1 slice	60	1.7	0.011	---	0.40	---	---	0.056	0.16	0.347	---
Whole-wheat 50%	1 slice	65	2.3	0.008	---	0.33	---	---	0.039	0.017	---	---
Whole-wheat 100%	1 slice	75	2.6	0.017	---	0.86	---	---	0.093	0.029	0.864	---
Corn meal, yellow	1 tablespoon	55	1.2	0.0024	0.022	0.19	0.08	17.55	0.003	0.0017	0.150	---
Crackers, soda	3 crackers	45	1.0	0.002	0.010	0.15	---	---	---	---	---	---
Graham with vitamin D	3-2" square	45	1.0	0.002	0.020	0.019	---	0	---	---	---	---
Farina, dark, cooked	2 tablespoons	70	2.2	0.004	0.040	0.37	---	---	0.016	0.005	0.196	---
White, enriched with vitamin D	3 tablespoons	100	3.3	0.005	0.026	0.37	---	---	0.018	---	---	---
White flour	¾ cup	365	13.7	0.016	0.106	1.30	0.17	---	0.080	0.04	0.80	---
With added vitamin D	¾ cup	365	13.7	0.016	0.106	1.30	0.17	---	0.080	0.04	0.80	---
Enriched	¾ cup	365	13.7	0.110	0.106	1.321	0.17	---	0.365	0.04	1.321	---
Whole wheat flour	¾ cup	365	11.4	0.031	0.238	5.00	---	---	0.50	0.15	---	---
Hominy, cooked	1 scant cup	130	4.0	0.004	0.040	0.20	---	---	---	---	---	---

Nutritional Values of Common Foods (*Continued*)

Food	Size of Portion — Average Serving	Values		Minerals				Vitamins				
		Cal-ories	Pro-teins, Grams	Cal-cium, Grams	Phos-phorus, Grams	Iron, Mg.	Cop-per, Mg.	Vit. A, I.U.	Vit. B$_1$ (Thia-min), Mg.	Vit. B$_2$ (Ribo-flavin), Mg.	Nia-cin, Mg.	Vit. C (Ascor-bic Acid), Mg.
Macaroni, cooked	1 cup	220	7.2	0.0096	0.060	0.6	0.624	---	---	---	2.94	---
Noodles, egg, cooked	½ cup	225	7.1	0.0021	---	0.12	---	---	0.011	---	---	---
Oats, rolled, vitamin D fortified, cooked	¾ cup	109	5.0	0.016	0.126	1.36	0.209	---	0.16	0.07	0.65	---
Pablum, dried	2 tablespoons	20	0.7	0.156	0.124	6.00	0.26	---	---	---	---	---
Rice, brown, steamed	1 tablespoon	70	1.3	0.003	---	0.10	---	3.40	0.012	0.006	1.38	---
Puffed, added vitamins D and B$_1$	1 cup	60	0.9	0.0015	0.015	0.16	0.109	---	0.256	0.057	---	---
White, steamed	1 tablespoon	75	1.3	0.040	0.004	0.04	---	130	0.0016	---	0.18	---
Rolls, Parkerhouse	1 roll	155	4.5	0.0325	---	0.39	---	130	0.035	0.080	---	---
Spaghetti	¾ cup	365	12.1	0.004	0.025	0.21	---	---	---	---	---	---
Wheat, puffed, added vitamins D and B$_1$	1 cup	55	2.3	0.006	0.063	0.615	0.105	---	0.230	0.011	---	---
Shredded and added vitamin D	1 biscuit	86	2.6	0.011	0.086	0.85	---	---	0.074	---	---	---
Flakes enriched vitamin D	⅔ cup	115	3.7	0.012	0.374	4.50	0.16	---	0.120	---	---	---
Wheat germ	1 teaspoon	35	2.4	0.0063	0.094	0.90	---	---	0.240	0.056	---	---
Zwieback	1 piece	30	0.7	0.007	---	0.10	---	---	---	---	---	---
Meats, Fish												
Bacon, broiled	4 pc. 7" long	115	7.2	0.002	0.43	0.6	0.10	4	0.018	0.018	---	---
Beef, dried (chipped)	⅛ lb.	105	15.8	0.010	0.184	3.72	---	---	0.055	---	---	---
Roasted	¼ lb.	185	31.6	0.007	0.272	5.28	0.19	57	0.138	0.250	11.73	---
Steak	¼ lb.	350	29.0	0.010	0.348	5.98	---	57	0.138	0.258	8.83	---
Chicken	½ lb.	255	49.6	0.025	0.621	4.83	---	---	0.253	0.35	10.92	---
Fish, halibut steak	½ lb.	290	42.8	0.018	0.460	2.16	0.52	---	0.168	0.370	---	---
Oysters	½ cup	55	6.8	0.057	0.165	3.46	3.38	246	0.276	0.505	---	3.58

Salmon, pink, canned	½ cup	116	16	0.049	0.213	0.96	0.03	235	0.027	0.169	9.77	---
Shrimp	8 medium	60	12.5	0.062	0.114	1.74	0.28	---	0.052	0.101	---	0.507
Trout, brook	¼ lb.	130	24.3	0.021	0.234	0.89	0.409	160	---	---	---	---
Tuna	½ cup	155	22.9	0.021	---	1.08	---	---	---	---	---	---
White, steamed	¼ lb.	245	21.2	0.127	0.302	0.48	0.218	---	---	---	---	---
Ham, baked or boiled	¼ lb.	175	30.4	0.013	0.250	1.95	---	---	0.138	0.230	6.90	---
Heart, beef	¼ lb.	125	19.4	0.010	0.217	5.52	0	---	0.690	---	4.9	---
Kidney, veal	¼ lb.	135	19.3	0.103	0.196	5.6	---	863	0.51	2.24	---	---
Lamb chops, broiled	¼ lb.	225	35.6	0.013	0.232	1.84	0.48	---	0.287	0.230	---	---
Lamb, leg roast	¼ lb.	210	35.2	0.013	0.243	1.95	---	---	0.172	0.30	9.75	---
Liver, calves, fried	¼ lb.	305	33.3	0.010	0.662	0.25	---	8050	0.241	1.84	25.87	---
Beef, fresh	¼ lb.	155	23.4	0.013	0.253	0.09	2.47	10350	0.258	2.07	31.62	43
Pork, fresh	¼ lb.	155	24.6	---	---	---	---	13800	0.345	2.07	31.62	30
Mutton, roast	¼ lb.	430	18.4	0.004	0.278	4.95	---	---	---	0.230	5.11	---
Pork chop, broiled	¼ lb.	215	32.9	0.011	0.205	1.49	---	---	0.690	0.230	9.775	---
Pork roast, lean	¼ lb.	325	27.1	0.008	0.236	2.99	0.10	---	0.690	0.205	---	0
Sausage, bologna	6 slices, 2"	180	14.0	0.002	0.045	2.10	0	24.4	0.312	0.205	---	0.37
Frankfurter	7"x¾"	310	23.5	0.013	0.259	3.00	---	46	0.58	---	---	6
Liverwurst	2 slices, 2 oz.	195	10.0	0.022	---	11.4	---	5280	0.456	1.692	---	---
Turkey, roast, dark meat	¼ lb.	205	31.3	0.026	0.486	---	---	---	0.230	0.392	---	---
Light meat	¼ lb.	175	36.5	0.023	0.428	---	---	---	0.092	0.092	---	---
Dairy Products												
Cream, light (20% fat)	1 cup	495	6.9	---	---	---	---	2944	0.0828	---	---	4.6
Medium (30% fat)	1 cup	680	5.9	---	---	---	---	---	---	---	---	---
Whipping (32% fat)	1 cup	725	5.6	0.223	0.173	0.495	0.3375	4960	0.068	0.152	---	4
Whipped (32% fat)	1 tablespoon	30	0.3	---	---	---	---	225	0.004	0.015	---	0
Skim milk	1 cup	90	8.9	0.292	0.230	0.6	0	5	0.108‡	0.435	---	4§
Dried	2 tablespoons	50	5.3	0.177	0.132	Trace	0	---	---	---	0.133	---
Whole Milk	1 cup	170	7.9	0.288	0.223	0.576	0.048	470	0.129‡	0.531	2.448	5§
Irradiated	1 quart	680	31.6	1.152	0.892	2.296	0.192	1880	0.515‡	2.124	9.792	20§

‡ Pasteurized — 15% less. § Pasteurized — 30% less.

425

Nutritional Values of Common Foods (Continued)

Food	Size of Portion — Average Serving	Values — Calories	Values — Proteins, Grams	Minerals — Calcium, Grams	Minerals — Phosphorus, Grams	Minerals — Iron, Mg.	Minerals — Copper, Mg.	Vitamins — Vit. A, I.U.	Vitamins — Vit. B1 (Thiamin), Mg.	Vitamins — Vit. B2 (Riboflavin), Mg.	Vitamins — Niacin, Mg.	Vitamins — Vit. C (Ascorbic Acid), Mg.
Fortified with vitamin D	1 quart	680	31.6	1.152	0.892	2.296	0.192	1880	0.516‡	2.124	9.792	20§
Whole dried milk	2 tablespoons	75	4.5	0.123	0.093	Trace	0	250	0.050	0.256	----	0
Whole skim milk, dried vitamin D	2 tablespoons	60	4.4	0.15	0.021	----	----	315	0.054	----	----	----
Evaporated milk (reconstituted milk)	1 cup	165	7.5	0.326	0.264	0.576	0	480	0.083	0.420	2.16	2
Evaporated irradiated milk	1 cup	165	7.5	0.326	0.264	0.576	0	480	0.083	0.420	2.16	2
Goat milk	1 cup	170	9.6	0.307	0.247	0	0	240	----	0.096	----	----
Human milk	1 ounce	20	0.4	0.006	0.006	0.045	0	----	----	0.010	0.072	----
Buttermilk	1 cup	88	9.0	0.263	----	0.75	----	423	0.080	0.374	0	4
Butter	1 tablespoon	80	0.1	0.002	0.001	0.02	0.003	----	0	0	0	0
Cheese, American cheddar	1½" cube	120	7.8	0.232	0.175	0.325	0.012	690	0.010	0.121	----	0
Brick, American	1½" cube	70	4.0	----	----	----	----	----	----	----	----	----
Cottage cheese (skim milk)	¼ cup	50	11.6	0.041	0.131	0.056	0.039	35.7	0.009	0.150	----	----
Cream	2½ tablespoons	120	3.0	0.108	----	0.150	----	630	----	0.005	----	----
Swiss	1 slice	130	8.3	0.325	0.243	0.360	0.039	591	----	0.156	----	----
Eggs, whole	1 average	75	6.7	0.034	0.112	1.16	0.115	600	0.063	0.167	0.031	----
White	1 average	20	4.3	0.005	0.004	0.035	0.105	Trace	Trace	0.077	0.026	----
Yolk	1 average	55	2.4	0.195	0.088	1.14	0.06	595	0.060	0.09	0.005	----
Ice cream (50% overrun)	1 sm. scoop	110	2.0	0.075	0.060	0.08	----	32	0.011	0.06	----	0.03
Malted milk, chocolate	1, 10 oz. glass	460	19.0	0.492	----	1.20	----	670	0.222	0.783	----	5
Sherbet	2 ounces	85	1.2	0.052	----	0.014	----	180	0.039	0.077	----	11
BEVERAGES												
Coffee	1 cup	9	0.5	0.0075	0.007	0	0	----	----	----	----	----
Tea, black	1 teaspoon	1	0.4	----	----	----	----	----	----	----	----	----

Food	Amount											
Cocoa beverage with milk	1 cup	180	7.0	0.225	0.295	0.55	0.382	385	0.096	0.386	—	2
Cocomalt	1 ounce	115	4.0	0.150	0.160	5.0	—	800	0.225	1.80	—	—
Hemo	1 ounce	112	2.3	0.564	0.690	11.0	—	3000	0.750	1.5	1.65	—
Ovaltine	½ ounce	58	2.0	0.085	0.085	3.5	0.25	500	0.171	0.83	—	—
DESSERTS												
Brownies	1½" square	100	1.3	0.007	—	0.20	—	135	0.012	0.009	—	—
Cake, angel	1 slice	140	4.2	0.0028	—	—	—	—	—	0.0550	—	—
Chocolate, no icing	1 piece	170	3.0	0.022	—	3.60	—	130	0.036	0.072	—	0
Fruit, light	1 slice	240	2.6	0.013	—	0.70	—	300	0.03	0.09	—	1
Plain white	1 piece	165	3.0	0.012	—	0.55	—	115	0.048	0.036	—	0
Cookies, oatmeal, plain	1 cookie	100	—	0.0258	0.003	0.797	0.193	0	0	0	—	0
Molasses	1 cookie	40	0.6	0.002	—	0.05	0.02	100	0.006	0.009	—	—
Sugar	1 cookie	50	0.7	0.063	0.065	0.25	0.49	212	0.024	0.120	—	—
Custard, egg, baked	---	55	2.6	0.0094	0.024	0.729	0.042	100	0.030	0.063	—	—
Doughnuts	1 3" diameter	200	3.0	0.0216	0.048	0.756	—	—	—	—	—	—
Gelatin dessert	½ cup	130	2.0	—	0.000	—	—	65	0.018	0.027	—	0
Gingerbread	1 square	205	2.5	0.002	—	—	—	—	—	—	—	—
Pie crust only	3½" wedge	75	1.1	—	—	—	—	—	—	—	—	—
MISCELLANEOUS												
Candy, caramels	1 medium	45	0.2	—	—	—	—	—	—	—	—	—
Fudge	2" square	185	0.9	0.0216	—	0.18	—	117	—	0.0234	—	—
Gumdrops	8 small, 1 large	32	—	—	—	—	—	—	—	—	—	—
Lollipops	212	212	—	—	—	—	—	—	0.010	—	—	—
Chocolate, unsweetened	½ ounce	90	1.7	0.0128	0.063	0.42	0.41	—	0	0	—	—
Gingerale	1 cup	150	—	—	—	0.80	0.05	0	—	0	—	—
Honey, clover	1 tablespoon	80	—	0.001	0.004	0.07	0.007	—	—	—	—	—
Jams and jellies	1 teaspoon	30	—	0.0015	—	0.015	0.003	—	—	—	—	—
Lard	1 tablespoon	140	0	0.0001	0.001	—	—	—	—	—	—	—
Marshmallows	5	105	2.0	—	0	—	—	—	—	—	—	—
Mayonnaise	1 tablespoon	150	0.3	0.0014	0.003	0.05	—	50.0	0.0056	0.0114	—	—

Nutritional Values of Common Foods (Continued)

Food	Size of Portion — Average Serving	Values — Calories	Values — Proteins, Grams	Minerals — Calcium, Grams	Minerals — Phosphorus, Grams	Minerals — Iron, Mg.	Minerals — Copper, Mg.	Vitamins — Vit. A, I.U.	Vitamins — Vit. B1 (Thiamin), Mg.	Vitamins — Vit. B2 (Riboflavin), Mg.	Vitamins — Niacin, Mg.	Vitamins — Vit. C (Ascorbic Acid), Mg.
Molasses, medium	1 tablespoon	60	----	0.0006	0.0	1.975	0.048	----	----	----	----	----
Oil, corn	1 tablespoon	130	0	----	----	----	----	----	----	----	----	----
Cottonseed	1 tablespoon	100	0	----	----	----	----	----	----	----	----	----
Olive	1 tablespoon	130	0	----	----	0.112	0.0098	----	----	----	----	----
Oleomargarine (added vitamin A)	1 tablespoon	115	0.1	----	----	----	----	555	----	----	----	----
Olives, ripe	3	25	0.2	0.0147	0.001	0.056	0.04	17.50	0.0025	0	0	----
Green	3	25	0.2	0.015	0.002	0.12	0.06	35	0.002	0.074	0	0
Peanut butter	1 tablespoon	95	4.4	0.0108	0.049	0.027	----	----	0.094	0.060	2.79	----
Peanuts, shelled	30	360	16.9	0.0426	0.239	1.38	0.576	----	0.033	0.21	----	----
Pecans, shelled	6 whole	185	2.4	0.0222	0.083	0.064	0.340	35.0	0.050	0.075	----	----
Pickles, sweet	2 small	30	0.1	0.0054	0.011	0.766	0.152	----	----	----	----	----
Popcorn, popped	1 cup	60	1.6	0.003	----	0.032	----	----	----	----	----	----
Potato chips	1⅓ cup	175	2.0	0.012	----	1.0	----	----	----	0.064	----	----
Salad dressing, boiled	1 tablespoon	35	0.9	0.003	----	0.10	----	150	0.012	0.036	----	----
Soda pop	1 bottle	66	----	----	----	----	----	----	----	----	----	----
Sorghum	1 tablespoon	50	----	----	----	----	----	----	----	----	----	----
Sugar, brown cane	1 tablespoon	35	----	0.008	----	0.23	----	----	----	----	----	----
White cane (gran.)	1 tablespoon	50	----	----	----	----	----	----	----	----	----	----
Syrup, corn	½ cup	490	0.4	0.0032	0.049	0.140	----	----	----	----	----	----
Maple	1 tablespoon	50	----	0.0191	0.002	0.54	----	----	----	----	----	----
Walnuts, English	6 whole	195	4.4	0.0311	0.125	0.749	0.35	45	0.158	----	----	----
White sauce, medium	2 tablespoons	60	1.0	0.034	----	0.10	----	183	0.012	0.063	----	----
Yeast, compressed	1½" square	15	1.4	0.0028	0.067	----	----	2660	0.385	0.128	----	----
Fortified with vitamin D	2 cakes	28	4.2	0.048	1.122	Trace	----	4000	1.000	0.300	2.5	----

INDEX

Acceptance, for dinner, 365; for a date, 383–384

Accessories, clothing, 186–188

Acne, 299–300

Activities, participation in school, 44–45; leisure-time, 327–351

Adjusting to family life, 46–57; through family philosophy, 49–50; through developing confidence in self, 50–51; through achieving a feeling of security, 51; through learning to work and play together, 51–53; through achieving maturity, 53–55; through gaining independence, 56–57

Adjusting to school life, 39–45; through realization of the purpose of education, 39–42; through wise choice of curriculum, 42; through understanding the learning process, 43–44; through participation in school activities, 44–45

Adolescence, 34

Advancement, proportion of income for, 152

Anger, controlling, 123–125; temper tantrums, 124

Artichoke, how to eat, 372

Attitudes, definition of, 17; healthful, 17; poise, 17; persistence, 17; cooperation, 18; sympathetic understanding, 19; unhealthful, 20; regression, 20; suspicion, 21; blame, 21; jealousy, 22; to control, 23; rationalization, 23; fear, 24; illness, 24; daydreaming, 25; inferiority complex, 25; toward sex, 120–121

Automobile, how to enter and leave, 384–385

Baked potatoes, how to eat, 372

Basic needs, 6

Bathing, 291

Baths, kinds of, 291–292

Blackheads, 299–300

Blame, 21

Body odor, 292

Breakfast, importance of, 271–272; habit of eating, 272; types of, 272; qualities of an adequate, 272–273

Budget, definition of, 142; advantages of, 142; divisions of, 148–153; standard, 153; making, 155–156; need of records for, 157–158; of an individual, 159–161; girl's, setting up goals for, 159–160

Butter spreader, use of, 371

Buying clothes, problems in, 190–191; wise buying, 191–192; aids in, 192–195; judging textiles, 195–200; judging the fit of a garment, 200–201; judging quality in coats, 202; judging quality in ready-made dresses, 202–203; judging quality in undergarments, 203–204; gloves, 204–205; stockings, 207–210

Calcium, function of in body, 264; source of, 264; results of insufficient, 264–265

Calories, definition of, 259; for one day, 259; table of number required per pound of body weight, 260; relation to overweight and underweight, 260–262; table of in common foods, 420–428

Care of clothing, need for, 213; equipment for, 213–214; daily, 215; weekly, 221; seasonal, 226–227

Center of interest in dress, 168–169

Childhood, early, 33; later, 34

Children, understanding and caring for, 99–137; value of study of, 99–100; different reactions of, 101–103; aids to the health of, 104–105; adjustments of to everyday living, 116–129; and play, 131–137; the job of caring for, 398–400

Citizenship, 40–41

School, adjusting to, 39–45
Security, achieving feeling of, 51
Self, forgetting, 13; development of, 32–37
Self-confidence, acquiring, 50
Senior prom, 389–391
Setting the table, 376–379
Sex, developing wholesome attitude toward, 120–121
Shelter, proportion of income used for, 148
Shoes, suitability of, 186–187; care of, 216
Skin, 290–301; structure of, 290–291; types of, 294; cleansing of, 294–295; difficulties, 299–300
Sleep, and children, 110–111; and health, 243–245; function of, 243–244; amount of, 244; results of insufficient, 244; conditions conducive to, 245
Smoking, 77–78
Spoon, use of, 369–371
Stages of life, 32–37; early childhood, 33; later childhood, 34; adolescence and maturity, 34
Stains, removing, 221–223
Stockings, suitability of different kinds of, 187–188; buying, 207–210; care of, 217–218
Streetcar, how to enter and leave, 384–385
Subjective restraint, 30
Substitution, 29
Suitability of clothing, 180–181; for home, 181–182; for school, 183; for street and church, 183; for sports, 183–184; for parties, 184; for work, 184–186; in accessories, 186-188

Sunshine and health, 235–237
Suspicion, 21
Sweaters, washing, 224–225
Sympathetic understanding, 19

Table, setting of, 376–379
Table manners, 366–373
Task, importance of, 15
Teeth, 320–323; hygiene of, 320; structure of, 320; cleaning of, 321–322; diseases of, 322–323
Textiles, used for clothing, 195; yarns used in making, 195; natural characteristics of various, 196; weaves used in making, 197–199; finishes used in, 199–200
Transportation and dating, 384
Typist, working as, 410–415

Undergarments, buying, 203–204; washing, 219–221

Values, sense of, 12
Vitamins, function of, 266; vitamin A, 266–267; vitamin B_1 or thiamin, 267; vitamin B_2 or riboflavin, 267–268; niacin, 268–269; vitamin B_6 or pyridoxine, 269; vitamin C or ascorbic acid, 269; vitamin D, 236, 269–270; vitamin E, 270; concentrates of, 270

Waitress, working as, 407–409
Weaves, kinds of, 179–199
Wholesome personality, how to maintain, 11–15
Work experiences, value of, 393